Yellow Brick Roads

Shared and Guided Paths
to Independent Reading 4–12

Janet Allen

Stenhouse Publishers
Portland, Maine

Stenhouse Publishers, 477 Congress Street, Portland, Maine 04101
www.stenhouse.com

Credits
Pages 5, 39, 115, 127, and 202: Bill Watterson, *Homicidal Psycho Jungle Cat: A Calvin and Hobbes Collection*. Copyright © 1994 by Bill Watterson. Published by Scholastic by arrangement with Andrews and McMeel. Reprinted by permission.
Page 52: "O Romeo, O, Like, Wow" by Mike Harden. Published November 8, 1989, in *The Columbus Dispatch*. Reprinted by permission.
Page 56: "Winner" by Sara Holbrook, from *The Dog Ate My Homework*. Copyright © 1996. Reprinted by permission of the author.
Page 64: "A Mouthful" from *Uncovered!: Weird, Weird Stories* by Paul Jennings. Copyright © 1998. Reprinted by permission of Penguin Books Australia.
Page 77: "Naked" by Sara Holbrook, from *Chicks Up Front*. Copyright © 1998. Published by Cleveland State University Press. Reprinted by permission of the author.
Pages 83 and 263: "The Day of the Hunter" by Edward M. Holmes. Copyright © 1976. Reprinted by permission of the author.
Page 134: "Ballad of Birmingham" by Dudley Randall, from *The Black Poets*. Copyright © 1971. Published by Bantam. Reprinted by permission of the author.
Page 135: "The Sunday School Bombing 9/27/63" from *Bridges and Borders: Diversity in America*. Copyright © 1994. Reprinted by permission of Time Life Syndication.
Page 142: "Fry's Readability Graph: Clarification, Validity, and Extension to Level 17" by E. Fry. Copyright © 1977. From *Journal of Reading* 21, 3: 249. Reprinted by permission.
Page 151: "Invisible" by Jane Medina, from *My Name Is Jorge on Both Sides of the River*. Copyright © 1996. Reprinted by permission.
Page 154: "The Trouble with My House" by David Harrison, from *The Boy Who Counted Stars: Poems*. Copyright © 1994. Reprinted by permission of Boyds Mills Press.
Page 167: "Destination Tule Lake Relocation Center, May 20, 1942" by James Masao Mitsui. Copyright © 1986. Reprinted by permission of the author.
Page 167: "Holding Center, Tanforan Race Track, Spring 1942" by James Masao Mitsui. Copyright © 1986. Reprinted by permission of the author.
Page 234: List from D. W. Moore, T. W. Bean, D. Birdyshaw, and J. Rycik. *Adolescent Literacy: A Position Statement*. Newark, DE: International Reading Association. Copyright © 1999 by the International Reading Association. All rights reserved.

Library of Congress Cataloging-in-Publication Data
Allen, Janet, 1950-
    Yellow brick roads : shared and guided paths to independent reading 4–12 / Janet Allen
    p.   cm.
    Includes bibliographical references
    ISBN 1-57110-319-8
    1. Reading (Elementary) 2. Reading (Middle) 3. Reading (Secondary) I. Title.
    LB1573.A445 2000   00-055614
    428.4—dc21

Cover design by Dick Hannus, Hannus Design Associates

Manufactured in the United States of America on acid-free paper
16 15 14 13 12 11 10   20 19 18 17 16 15 14

To those who help me find my paths—in literacy and life...
Troy, Anne, Rick, Gail, Kelly, Mary, Chuck

Contents

Acknowledgments   vii

1. Looking for the Wizard   1

2. Places for Wonderful Ideas: Establishing Environments
   That Support Reading Diversity   9

3. What Gets in the Way of Reading Success?   31

4. Life Is Short—Eat Dessert First! The Value of
   Read-Aloud Beyond the Primary Years   43

5. Shared Reading as the Heart of Reading Instruction   58

6. Guided Reading: "On the Run" Strategies Toward Independence   80

7. Creating (and Living with) Independent Readers   98

8. Organizing for Choice: Supporting Diversity in Reading,
   Writing, and Learning   114

9. "Am I the Only One Who Can't Make a K-W-L Work?"
   Literacy Paths to Content Knowledge   127

10. Help for the Most "Tangled" Readers   149

11. Reading the Way to Writing   178

12. Full Circle: Assessing, Evaluating, and Starting Again   199

13. Living the Professional Life   229

Appendix A: *Resources*   237

Appendix B: *Literature Supporting Content Literacy*   239

Appendix C: *Web Sites Supporting Lesson Plans and Classroom Instruction*   242

Appendix D: *Books on Tape*   249

Appendix E: *Short Story Collections Supporting Read-Aloud, Shared, Guided, and Independent Reading*   252

Appendix F: *Poetry Collections*   255

Appendix G: *"The Day of the Hunter" by Edward M. Holmes*   263

Appendix H: *Forms*   265

Literature References   291

Professional References   299

Index   305

Acknowledgments

I am always amazed at how many people it takes to write a book. The students and teachers with whom I work make the theory come to life in their reading classrooms. I am grateful for all they teach me as we teach and learn together. I am especially thankful for those teachers and students who have shared their learning samples for this book:

Ann Bailey, Marshall Middle School, Long Beach, California
Tara Bensinger, Trussville Middle School, Birmingham, Alabama
Becky Bone, Hunter's Creek Middle School, Orlando, Florida
Lana Clark, Vanguard High School, Ocala, Florida
Lee Corey, Oak Ridge High School, Orlando, Florida
Mary Giard, The Center, Auburn, Maine
Kyle Gonzalez, Boone High School, Orlando, Florida
Julie Joynt, Titusville High School, Titusville, Florida
Lynnette Kaiser, Stonewall Jackson Middle School, Orlando, Florida
Holly Lang, St. Cloud High School, St. Cloud, Florida
Heather Magner, Long Beach Preparatory Academy, Long Beach, California
Stacy North, Roosevelt Middle School, San Diego, California
Jill Perry, Pasco County, Florida
Nancy Roberts, Sarasota Middle School, Sarasota, Florida
Kelly Stevenson, Immokalee High School, Immokalee, Florida

There is never a day that I am not thankful I found my way to Stenhouse Publishers (well, there may be a few days near the end of a book when I'm not so thankful). The professionalism and friendship offered by Philippa Stratton always make my book better than I would have imagined. She is the editor every writer deserves. Brenda Power's insights and daisy-plucking helped me find the path that was sometimes lost in the text. Tom Seavey's wry sense of humor helped keep me on task in anticipation of the real clam chowder. Martha Drury's production expertise turns all our work into something that is both appealing and useful to teachers.

Anne Cobb once again stayed through the process of writing this book from beginning to end. She took on each of the research and production tasks with a good spirit. She maintained her sense of humor while inventing a wonderful "WTF" style for the citations. Her hopefulness is a blessing. Dee Beasley joined us at the end of the book and made the process of researching and citing texts manageable. It was an honor to work with these two women who both believe in meaningful work.

Looking for the Wizard

*"Then you must go to the City of Emeralds. Perhaps Oz will
help you."*
"Where is this City?" asked Dorothy.
*"It is exactly in the center of the country, and is ruled by Oz, the Great
Wizard I told you of."*
"Is he a good man?" inquired the girl, anxiously.
*"He is a good Wizard. Whether he is a man or not I cannot tell, for I
have never seen him."*

L. Frank Baum, The Wonderful Wizard of Oz

I well remember beginning my teaching career and wishing for a wizard who
would show me how to teach. My city (not to be confused with the City of
Emeralds) was at the northeastern edge of the country, where we had no man-
dated direction from our state department of education and no school- or
department-mandated curriculum. In fact, just prior to our first day of school, I
was told there were no textbooks for students in the classes I was teaching.
Without the support of textbooks and curriculum resources, each day of teaching made me feel more like a failure. Like Dorothy, I had ended up in a place
inhabited by people I didn't recognize from my past experiences as a student and
intern teacher. Unlike Dorothy, I had no idea where to begin looking for a wizard
who could help me learn how to teach struggling and reluctant secondary school
readers. Most days I couldn't even have found the yellow brick road if it had
been there! So I began counting the days until I could resign. Each day as I
crossed off another day on the wall calendar in my room, students would come
and ask me what the calendar was for. My response changed only by the number
of days remaining in my contract: "In fifty-five days you'll know what this calendar is for."

Twenty years (and thirty-six hundred days) later I finally left that classroom
and moved to central Florida. Shortly after moving, I made my first school visit

to an inner-city school and once again I felt like a displaced Dorothy, in a community I only vaguely recognized from television and movie screens. As I walked past the security guards at the school entrance, I paused to summon my courage and to wonder in what ways these classrooms would be different from those in my background. I made my way to the English class I was to observe; my intern found me a seat in the back; and I began taking field notes to document my initial impressions. I knew that my intern would not be teaching this period. When her supervising teacher had heard I was coming, he had suggested I observe the class while he taught so I could see "just what these kids are really like." He assured me it would change my expectations for the intern's performance, and she had seemed visibly relieved by his plan. I wasn't introduced to the students and initially no one seemed to notice I was there.

During the first ten minutes of my observation, students made their way into the room in a leisurely manner. They chatted, pushed, laughed, made witty comments, and generally enjoyed each other's company. After several minutes, the teacher said, "Take your black books and turn to page 371. Read the introduction on those pages and write down what is important." The students groaned, made a production of getting the texts, glanced at me, and slumped back in their seats. The animated voices and moments of joy had vanished. Minutes passed like hours until finally the teacher stood next to an overhead projector, placed a handwritten overhead transparency on the projector, and proceeded to read what he considered the important points in the introduction that the students had "read." The students sat copying from the barely readable transparency, seemingly having blocked out the person standing by the machine. Occasionally, students stopped the sound of his voice with questions such as, "What's the fifth word on the third line?" The task ended and the students brought up the issue of vocabulary.

"Why do we have to know these stupid words anyway?"

"I told you. They're going to be on your SATs."

"Well, I can't do them analogies. Those words don't make no sense to me."

"You have to know them and we're going to have a test on them this Friday." Unanswered questions, unquestioned answers.

The vocabulary debate continued until the bell rang. Students slammed their books closed, jammed papers into book bags, and meandered from the room as the teacher was saying, "Don't forget the vocabulary test and your research paper topics." No one acknowledged his words, either through looks or response. English IV was over for another day.

Just as I was about to stand and leave, a young man walked up to my desk, leaned down so his eyes were level with mine, looked into my eyes, and said, "I don't know who you are, but it's time for a change." He walked away and although his words were more pleading than threatening, still I felt assaulted. I felt part of a system that perpetuated the curriculum I had seen played out before me that afternoon, and I felt guilty. I wanted to run after him and say, "Wait. My classroom wasn't like this." Instead, I smiled inanely as he walked away from me. I drove back to the university with his words ringing in my ears. "It's time for a change." Unfortunately, students' pleas for change are often the ones that get the least attention. The pleas for change that usually grab our attention (and time) are those from politicians, state boards, business leaders, and the media.

The cry for change is not new in education. In fact, I recently found a special issue of *Life* magazine in an antique store with a cover declaring "U.S. Schools: They Face a Crisis" (1950). The articles could have come from any newspaper in the country this year. "Obviously, something should be done," said one. "But nobody agrees exactly what this something is" (11). The cry for change may be the same, but the stakes certainly seem higher these days. When these widespread, and often opposing, views of desired changes are combined with attempts to "fix" everything at once, the result is a maelstrom not unlike Dorothy's tornado.

How Many of Us Feel Like Dorothy?

If you remember the beginning of the *Wizard of Oz* movie, Dorothy was leading a relatively happy life. She may have been looking for a little adventure, but she was surrounded by people she cared about and who cared about her, and she believed she had found her place in the world. Alas, Miss Gulch soon arrived with her threats. Dorothy felt unjustly accused by her attack and began running. Our educational Miss Gulches have kept us running for many years. Often not knowing where we're going and not quite sure what we're looking for, we spend our days in a frenzy of activity, trying to meet mandates that change by the minute and attempting to get kids ready for high-stakes tests.

In Eleanor Duckworth's book *Teacher to Teacher,* she talks about why teachers get worn out from the demands of teaching: "They are too often dealt with as functionaries—meant to carry out some hierarchy's directives" (1). In the last twenty-five years, teachers and students have experienced many such directives. We have been Hunterized and computerized. We've struggled to define the difference between authentic and alternative assessment and then been told to abandon both to get ready for *the* test. We've learned independently, collaboratively, and cooperatively in whole groups, small groups, and with buddies. We've been whole languaged and fonicated. We've been taught to behaviorally objectify the curriculum while being encouraged to see our classrooms as having no walls. We have been told to create classrooms with attention to multiple intelligences, brain-based learning, cultural awareness, character education, technology as a tool, inquiry-based essential questions, and developmental/gender issues. And, just to keep things interesting, every few years someone gives the battle cry to get back to the basics, except no one seems to agree on what those basics are or how we should all get back to them. I think that, like Dorothy, we've ended up in a place that most of us don't recognize, not sure how we got there.

Making Sense of the Journey

So, what can we learn from Dorothy's journey along the "yellow brick road"? For me, a place to begin is acknowledging that—for Dorothy and for us—there is no wizard who can solve the problems. We will have to get off the road and create our own paths to literacy. And we don't have to make the entire journey to discover that truth.

When we are working with students who have reading problems, a critical aspect of overcoming those problems is getting students to believe they are capable of making choices and taking action that would help solve the problems. If students attribute their lack of literacy success to something outside their control, such as genetics, family background, poor teaching, frequent moves, learning disabilities, or social status, it is difficult to get them to take action that would change their patterns of failure. On the other hand, if students believe that their reading difficulties have occurred because they didn't understand the tasks, didn't use effective reading strategies, practiced passive learning, or were assigned to unsupportive learning environments, they could make a decision to change.

Teaching is the same way. If we attribute success or failure to a program, a text, a well-known speaker, an administrator, community support, or the kinds of students who enter our classrooms, we attribute success or failure to things that are mostly out of our control. Over time, that can lead to what Seligman (1975) calls "learned helplessness." If, however, we acknowledge that all those factors can make teaching easier or more difficult but that ultimately we are in charge of making choices that will affect students' learning, we then take on the responsibilities and rewards of professionalism. We learn how to choose and create effective resources and methods for the students we have, not those we wish we had. We learn to use our time to have the most lasting effect on students' learning. We develop strategies for ongoing assessment that help us identify learning problems, and we learn how to make appropriate interventions to change the outcomes. We also learn to become cautious consumers because we understand the limitations of any product. We don't look for wizards; we refine the strengths we have in order to create our own magic.

Obstacles and Rest Stops Along the Path

You may remember that although Dorothy landed in a place that seemed perfect, it wasn't perfect for her. Dorothy was in Oz only a few minutes before she dis-

covered that even "perfect" places have people and events that get in the way of success. If we're aware of those roadblocks, sometimes we can figure out ways around them.

Some of the most challenging people to work with are those who think they have no need to change their methods if only everyone around them would get better at their jobs. As a high school teacher, I often heard that things would be so much better if the middle schools would get their acts together. When I started working in Orange County's systemwide middle school literacy project that Kyle Gonzalez and I wrote about in *There's Room for Me Here,* we frequently met teachers who refused to learn new teaching methods because they were just waiting for the elementary schools to figure out how to teach reading the *right* way. I think lots of people thrive on the kind of change Calvin advocates.

As a teacher and department chairperson, it was a painful lesson for me to discover that I couldn't change others around me. All I could do was provide resources and hope that our classroom success would be infectious. When we began the literacy project in Orlando, I advised the literacy teachers to focus on their own classrooms and students, and not try to force the literacy project methods and materials on those around them. In just a matter of months, teachers who had been skeptical were coming to the literacy project teachers asking for advice because they had seen positive results.

Finding your own path is difficult, and there will be those who make it more difficult by telling you there is no reason to do all that work. They believe that if they wait long enough the necessity for change will go away, and in the meantime your excitement over "new" methods or materials makes them look bad. Many new teachers have left teaching early in their careers because of the negativism of "mentors" in their new profession. If you haven't had the opportunity to read Codell's *Educating Esme: Diary of a Teacher's First Year,* it is well worth your time. It is a sobering reminder of the way we can influence the newest members of our profession. Early in the book, Codell describes the excitement she felt as she designed her Fairy Tale Festival proposal. She first had to form a committee because proposals require committees. The committee finally convened, only to explain "that it was not realistic to do, as I would surely have known had I been teaching awhile" (9). Dorothy encountered many who tried to get in her way; fortunately, she didn't have to encounter those negative forces alone.

Early in Dorothy's travels, she met three who would travel with her: the tin man, the cowardly lion, and the scarecrow. Each joined Dorothy's journey because he realized something was missing from his life. The tin man needed a heart; the cowardly lion needed courage; and the scarecrow needed a brain. Do you teach with anyone in need of those critical components?

There have certainly been times in my career when I would have been quick to characterize some educators as heartless, spineless, or stupid. With time and experience, I have come to realize that we aren't all going to be in the same professional place at the same time. In retrospect, I can well remember times when I lacked heart, courage, or brains for the task. If you have been in education for a time, you know that those who travel with us can make the trip miserable or energetic and rewarding. They can also bring their strengths to compensate when ours fail. Sandra Leighton taught across the hall from me in my early years of teaching. Each day as I crossed off days on the calendar before I could resign, Sandra came in to tell me that she had noticed something about my teaching that told her I was going to be a great teacher. She helped me find my teaching heart before I was lost. When I tended toward complacency, Gail Gibson and Connie Piper spent hours of their lives saying, "Have you read this book? Do you think we should try to figure out how to rethink this problem? Don't you think you should write about that?" They gave me brains when my brain got tired. Glenna Smith and John Moran spent many days before retirement saying, "You can't argue with fools. Think of the kids. Choose a battle you can win for them." They gave me courage and purpose when mine failed. I believe that finding those who want to create their own paths by doing the difficult work of identifying effective methods of learning together is a critical piece of the journey.

In Your Own Backyard

When Dorothy and her friends followed the yellow brick road and finally made it to the Wizard, he pointed them back to themselves. He told them they didn't need him after all; they had what they needed all along in their own backyards. So, what do effective teachers have in their own backyards that supports wizard-less paths to lifelong literacy? In our literacy projects, I look for common characteristics of effective teachers of language and literacy. While each teacher brings some unique teaching methods and materials, I have found several observable characteristics these teachers share:

- They know how to differentiate curriculum so all students are challenged and supported.
- They know how to identify students who are falling through the cracks.
- They know how to plan for individual, needs-based small groups, and whole-group instruction.
- They know how to create classrooms where choices are supported.
- They know how to help students make academic, personal, text, and world connections.
- They have both current and historical knowledge of literacy research and practice.
- They are effective observers and listeners, which leads them to solid "kid-watching" decisions.
- They employ practices consistent with their stated beliefs.
- They use academic freedom and decision making as opportunities for professional growth.
- They are critical thinkers, which makes them good judges of fads du jour.
- They know how to mentor and coach.
- They understand the difference between assessment and evaluation, and use both to influence instruction.
- They know how to create environments and conditions that support literacy.
- They have both a personal and a practical knowledge of reading and writing processes. They are readers and writers.
- They know how to use time and resources effectively.
- They can explain their beliefs and practices to others.

Neil Postman and Charles Weingartner published *Teaching as a Subversive Activity* over thirty years ago. I believe the introduction to their chapter "What's Worth Knowing?" is even more significant for our consideration today than it was in 1969:

> Suppose all the syllabi and curricula and textbooks in the schools disappeared. Suppose all of the standardized tests—city-wide, state-wide, and national—were lost. In other words, suppose that the most common material impeding innovation in the schools simply did not exist. Then suppose that you decided to turn this "catastrophe" into an opportunity to increase the relevance of the schools. What would you do?

What *is* really worth knowing? Implicit in that question is the parallel question, What is really worth teaching? The chapters in this book detail the approaches and strategies other literacy teachers and I have found worth knowing and teaching in order to help learners find competence and confidence in their own paths to lifelong literacy. Some of these approaches may seem a bit messy to you because they require that teachers make daily decisions

Difficult Lessons

I remember clearly the day Shawn walked into our classroom. First days are never easy, and in those chaotic first minutes of class changes, it would have been easy for the kids to blend together. Shawn didn't blend. He lumbered into the room, fell into the first seat in the first row, and put his head on his desk. It wasn't just his crew cut, plaid shirt, and Dickies amidst the sea of long hair, T-shirts, and jeans—Shawn had a "don't come near me" presence. As other students came into the room, they seemed to give him lots of space, choosing to walk down other rows rather than chance an encounter with him. Knowing that there are often intense histories among high school students, I decided to give our classroom community a chance to form before trying to figure out what was going on between Shawn and the other members of the class.

As the days passed, I became more and more concerned about Shawn. When I gave students a beginning-of-the-year survey, Shawn's copy stayed on his desk, unmarked, until he walked out of the room at the bell. Although the situation was uncomfortable, there were thirty other students clamoring for my attention, and so it was a week into the school year before I realized that I still had not heard him speak one word. His anger was so palpable that even I was almost afraid to go near him and without thinking had started to leave him lots of space as I walked around the room talking with other students.

As with most explosive events, the day started normally enough. As I walked around the room assigning students to groups, I decided that I would force the issue with Shawn. After all, it had been more than a week since the beginning of school; surely that was enough time to get comfortable in a new situation. Purposefully, I walked over to Shawn's desk, stood near him, and announced, "Shawn, why don't you work with that group in the corner." No movement. No acknowledgment that he had heard me. I pressed on.

"Shawn, did you hear me?" Again, no response. I reached out to touch his shoulder when one of the other boys in class jumped up from his seat and grabbed my arm.

"Don't touch him, Mrs. Allen!" With Peter's yell, Shawn got up from his seat and walked out of the room. The noisy class became totally silent. It felt as if we were all holding our breath. "Don't ever touch him, Mrs. Allen," Peter said. "He'll kill you."

I had no frame of reference for Peter's comment. Those acts of violence might have been occurring in urban schools, but in our small city in northern New England, students definitely did not kill teachers. I gave him and the rest of the class a puzzled "You've got to be kidding me" look, and the Shawn stories erupted.

"He threw a kid out of the window in junior high."

"He been locked up for years."

"He beat up a whole gang of seventh graders."

Finally, I managed to settle the class and get back to our task. I would just manage to put the incident out of my mind for a few minutes and then a student would say, "Where do you suppose Shawn went?" and I would panic that he was wandering the halls, angry and unsupervised.

Just when I had decided to leave my class to their own devices and look for the principal, a custodian came in with Shawn shuffling behind him. "Does he belong to you?" I hesitated only a second before nodding. Shawn came back into the room, fell into the same seat, and class continued as if the drama had never occurred.

At the end of the day, I went to the assistant principal and told him my story. "You'd better see the guidance counselor." So, I trudged to our guidance office. After several minutes of passing the buck, one of the counselors finally acknowledged that Shawn's presence in school had been a trial situation. The students had gleaned a few kernels of truth from Shawn's background; he had been in a group home for two years and this year was to be a trial at putting him back into public school.

"Why wasn't I told? Do other teachers know?"

The counselor's shrug said it all before he even began talking. "I guess we probably should have told his teachers." Another shrug—conference ended.

Shrugs and Silence

The days turned to weeks and then months, and still Shawn sat. When I handed out work, Shawn never picked his papers up from his desk. At the end of the class, he stumbled from the room, papers still stacked on his desk. When I read aloud to the class, students moved their chairs to be near me. Not Shawn. There were no explosions of laughter from Shawn's desk, no sign that he had even heard us as we made up limericks that were not quite appropriate for this eleventh-grade English class.

Every couple of weeks, usually after being inspired by a teacher book such as those written by Torey Hayden or Mary MacCracken, I would go back to the guidance counselor and demand that something be done for/about Shawn. "Is he causing any problems in there?"

Now I was the one reduced to shrugging, "Well, no..."

"Let's just leave it for a while then and see what happens."

"But he isn't doing any work!"

"Yeah, well, he also isn't causing any problems."

Exasperated, I would return to class and continue teaching just as if a seventeen-year-old boy weren't sitting in the first seat, first row, never uttering a word. I continued to talk to him as I did the others, but he never responded, and eventually I think I got used to his lack of response. My initial anger and frustration gave way to an uneasy compromise, and days would go by before it would once again strike me as totally ludicrous that neither I nor anyone else was doing anything for this student. Unlike Susan Ohanian's Pete, who did nothing but play Scrabble for six months (*Who's in Charge?*), Shawn did absolutely nothing.

Amazingly, the same students who noticed minute changes in hairstyle or shoe color seemed not to notice that Shawn existed. There was this large young man sitting in the room every day, and students simply worked around him. If his desk happened to be in the way of some activity students were performing, someone would say, "Shawn, move your desk." Receiving no response, they too would shrug, and simply set up their performance in another part of the room. In fact, the back of the room eventually became the front of the room as students simply avoided the obstacle Shawn had become to them.

When grades were due, I asked the counselor what I was supposed to do about Shawn's grade. "Why don't we just wait and see what happens next quarter? Give him an incomplete for now."

"Incomplete," I shrieked. "He hasn't done anything. He hasn't said one word."

"Well, then, his work is certainly incomplete, isn't it?" More shrugs— another conference ended.

Environments of Possibilities and Hope

Winter descended. We made it through early December with our shared reading of *Lovey* (MacCracken) and planning a trip to a local school for mentally challenged children and adults. We made gifts, created workbooks, wrote Christmas poetry, and practiced songs we would sing. Still Shawn sat mute. On the day we trudged through the snow with our Christmas party in our hands, Shawn ambled along behind the group. He stood for two hours with his hat and coat on while we sang, played games, and talked with the clients at the school. When we left, he followed us back to our classroom and sat until the next bell rang.

January seemed endless, snowmobiles and basketball games the only reprieve from days of gray sameness outside the classroom windows. While students and teachers looked forward to the annual basketball tournament, I was counting the minutes until my trip to Florida during February break. The students, many of whom had never been three hours south to Bangor, were filled with questions about my upcoming trip.

"How long does it take to get there?"

"Where will you stay?"

"Does the sun shine all the time?"

We were reading *The Lottery Rose* (Hunt) together, and the Florida setting of the novel was another stimulus for students looking at maps and brochures to find tourist attractions. They read about alligators and armadillos. They researched hurricanes and snakes. They even gave me a new name: Mrs. Allengator. Students made lists of things they wanted me to bring them from Florida, and I pretended that once away from the snow I would forget about them.

After a vacation that ended all too quickly, I returned to our classroom with oranges and boxes of slides of my trip. On a snowy Friday afternoon, we settled down in the back of the room to watch the slides and talk about places far away from where we lived. We set up the projector and screen, turned out the lights, and forgot the howling winds outside our classroom.

"See those alligators. They look like they're all asleep and then the trainer throws something in to them and, *snap,* their jaws grab it. He told us that once something is in their mouths, their jaws lock until the food is digested."

"Even people?"

"I guess. Look at those flowers. Remember the flowers Georgie mentioned in *The Lottery Rose*? No wonder he loved flowers, huh? Can you imagine seeing those every day?"

"Yeah, but what do they do for fun? How do they celebrate Christmas with no snow?"

As we moved though the slides of Gatorland, I realized we were about to come to slides my husband had taken of me as I stood feeding a huge bear. Embarrassed at showing slides where I was the subject, I decided to go past those with a quick commentary, "And there's Mrs. Allen feeding the bear."

"Which one's the bear?" a deep voice questioned from the front of the room.

There was absolute silence in the room. Finally, the silence gave way to nervous giggles, "Shaaawn . . . you'll hurt Mrs. Allen's feelings." Students looked from me, to Shawn, and then back to me again.

I knew my response was critical. "Obviously, Shawn, the bear is the one without the pantsuit." With a great flourish, I clicked the remote to bring up the next slide. I smiled at Shawn and he grinned back at me, and I think we both knew that there was no turning back now.

For Shawn with his dry sense of humor, the opportunity to tease me the way the other students did on a daily basis was just too inviting. And while I was a bit tentative after his initial talk, the students acted as if Shawn had been talking every day since August. As we continued our slide show, the boys' running commentary now included Shawn. It was a turning point—for Shawn, the class, and me.

Conditions That Invite Learning

Do I believe slides of a teacher clad in a polyester pantsuit and feeding a bear are the answer to reaching students who refuse to learn? Perhaps not, although it

seemed to work better than anything else I tried. I use Shawn's story here to illustrate the path I took in beginning to understand what happened that day.
Individual turning points in learning are often cumulative. The event that seems to
cause the change is often as improbable as the bear-feeding slide, so we can
assume that something or many somethings have led to the point of a change in a
student's interest in learning. As I reflect on those weeks of Shawn's silence and his
eventual movement into our class work, there are several things that were instructive for me. I can see now that there were certain environmental, academic, and
emotional conditions in place in our classroom that allowed for both Shawn's
silence and his eventual talk. I also realize that Shawn's silence did not mean he
wasn't participating in the events of the class. Shawn's response to what was happening in the class was just a different response than I had expected. These understandings related to conditions for learning were critical in my development as a
teacher because of their applicability to all my teaching and learning.

    When I first encountered Cambourne's conditions for learning in *The Whole
Story* in 1988, Shawn immediately came to mind. While the conditions
Cambourne highlights (expectation, responsibility, immersion, demonstration,
approximation, use, response, and engagement) are necessary for all students,
they are particularly significant in the lives of students who are at some stage of
active or passive not-learning. In *"I Won't Learn from You,"* Kohl notes that
many children make active decisions to not-learn in school: "Learning how to
not-learn is an intellectual and social challenge; sometimes you have to work
very hard at it. It consists of an active, often ingenious, willful rejection of even
the most compassionate and well-designed teaching. It subverts attempts at
remediation as much as it rejects learning in the first place" (10–11). It is not difficult for students to resist learning when it consists of a steady diet of lecture,
rote learning, note taking, and regurgitation of factual information. However,
when the conditions for learning are right and students spend their days with
engaging texts, generating and pursuing questions that are intriguing to them
and getting feedback that helps them understand there is something larger than
the lives they know, it becomes more difficult for them to continue in their
unwillingness to learn. Those conditions for learning become the foundation for
environments that support reading diversity.

Expectation

When I worked with secondary students who had been placed in my class
because they had reading problems, I began the year by telling them that while
they might have had reading problems in the past, I knew that every one of them
could become great readers and writers. I also told them I had learned how to
help them become great readers and writers. When I said those words, I didn't
necessarily know exactly what I planned to do each day of the school year, but I

did know that it was important for me to set up that expectation of success on the first day of school. This kind of class expectation, what Cambourne calls "global expectations," is extremely important for the motivation and self-esteem of any class, but especially for intervention classes. The students and the teacher have a shared goal at this point: creating lifelong readers and writers. Everyone knows where we're going, and over time everyone believes the entire class can get there. It wasn't until my last three years of teaching that it occurred to me that I should write reading goals that would break the goal of "lifelong reading" into concrete goals. In order to do this, I asked myself what attitudes, understandings, and behaviors I wanted to note in my students after our time together.

I want students who…

- Enjoy reading
- Are critical readers (understanding that writing comes from a perspective and has a purpose)
- See reading as knowledge and therefore read a variety of texts
- Recognize and employ different purposes for reading
- See texts as models for their own writing styles and genres
- See reading as a risk-free way to test their theories about themselves and the world
- See reading as a way to learn about themselves and the world
- Read for conversations with unknown others
- See the supportive relationship between reading and the other language arts (listening, speaking, writing, thinking, and viewing)
- See reading as therapy
- See reading as part of their lives so they develop the habit of reading
- See reading as a way to support healthy choices
- Read between and beyond the lines to see authors' purposes and intentions

We posted these goals in each of our journals and on the classroom wall, and I asked students to let me know when the work we were doing together wasn't meeting any of the goals. Believe me, they were eager to let me know when we weren't meeting the goal of reading enjoyment! And although it was an aggravation at times, I learned a lot by noting the things they told me that got in the way of that reading enjoyment.

A significant aspect of expectation for me was changing the expectations students had in terms of curriculum and classroom activities. With time, I came to realize there were some classroom practices I needed to eliminate and some that I needed to institute or modify so that neither the students nor I would give off negative expectations. The first thing that had to go was round-robin reading. This activity set students up to expect that reading wouldn't make sense, because in this situation reading didn't make sense. The person reading was so focused on pronouncing the words correctly that there was no comprehension occurring.

The person next in line for reading was usually in such a panic about reading aloud that her time was spent practicing the next passage rather than following along with the passage being read. In all situations, we want to build confidence in readers that we expect the text to make sense and we expect readers to make sense of the text. Round-robin usually derailed both. I think Jason well summarized the problems he saw with round-robin reading: "People don't realize how boring a reading-writing class can be when you have a teacher that lets the other kids read out loud. Sometimes you can't hear them and other times they read so fast you can't understand a word they're saying. Teachers don't let kids take the necessary time to do things right. There's no time to spend time individually with their kids." We should expect students to work at meaning making, and they should be able to expect that we will be there to support that work at the individual student level.

I had to make a conscious effort to reinforce my statement that all reading has value. For struggling readers, the texts they could read independently and that they needed in order to develop reading fluency were seen as "baby books" until I started using those same texts to build background knowledge, as writing prompts, and as books I entered in my reading log as books I had read. My reading and recording of all books—novels, poetry, picture books, informational texts—made all texts legitimate for the students.

One of the hardest practices for me to let go was the use of prepared questions that would follow the reading. I had long been the queen of study guides at our school and had come to believe that all major works of literature needed study guides so that students could really get to the heart of the text. One day when a teacher from southern Maine was observing our class, Gene asked her, "Do you use textbooks and textbook questions?" When she said she did, his reply was filled with pride. "Our teacher doesn't believe in that." My smile as I overheard the exchange was short-lived when I heard one student say to another, "What difference does it make? We just have questions on paper instead of in a book now." I realized that those study guides were still giving the subtle (or perhaps not so subtle) expectation that someone else decides what the important questions are before, during, and after reading. While I often said to my students that good readers constantly ask questions of themselves, the author, and the text, I was constantly establishing and reinforcing the expectation that students could and should sit passively and wait for someone else's questions.

I also had to establish the expectation that assessment and evaluation were shared responsibilities. I had to give students concrete support (see Chapter 12) to help them begin the process of thinking about what their next literacy steps would be. Most students didn't know what reading success looked like. Even those who knew what it looked like ("fast reading, no mistakes") didn't know how to get there. They didn't know how to establish reading goals or how to break those goals into incremental, achievable steps.

Sharing responsibility involved my learning a different language to use when talking with students. As the quarter came to an end and students asked, "What are you giving me for a grade?" I had to learn to say, "What have you learned? How have you changed? We'll have to look at that together. I can't make that decision alone." The environment where individual assessment of accomplishment is valued has to be established and reestablished each day in order for students to take that valuable skill into other learning situations. My students and I learned together to establish reasonable goals both at the class and the individual levels so we could see where we had been and where we should move next. This expectation of constant progress and gradually increased levels of proficiency was something my students told me they had never experienced. Students said, "English is English. You do the same boring things every year." Expectations for progress, not just getting work done, should be a foundation in our classrooms.

Responsibility

For some teachers, the notion of giving students responsibility for establishing and making good learning choices is tantamount to chaos. I admit that some days it was just that in our classroom. Somehow we have come to believe that students would choose to be bored or apathetic. When I tell teachers that my students had the responsibility for making their own learning choices at least two days a week, they often look at me as if I had attempted to establish a public school version of A. S. Neill's Summerhill. Actually, it was rare that students did not quickly decide what they would engage in during those days of ILE (independent literacy exploration) once they knew what their choices were and they could trust that I would let them choose (see Chapter 8). As a high school teacher with students in class less than an hour each day, I found it more workable to allow entire periods for them to decide on curriculum rather than a short bit of time each day. In my block class (ninety minutes five days per week), student-choice curriculum occurred for two forty-five minute periods each week. Ten to fifteen minutes per day was not enough time for them to get engaged in sustained meaningful activities. As soon as students learned what my expectations were for the time and what the parameters were for their choices, they chose work that was engaging and significant.

Kohl talks about the importance of these kinds of choices in *"I Won't Learn from You"*:

Teaching well means encouraging the widest diversity and greatest depth of learning possible, and always being open to adding a dimension or theme to what one is doing . . . providing students with opportunities to have encounters with learning that might transform their lives. This means freeing youngsters from the traps of a set curriculum, letting them on occasion wander aimlessly across subject matter, craft, art, technology. (64)

As part of the ongoing teacher research I did in my classroom, I asked my students, "Why do I ask you to take responsibility for choosing your own reading (or literacy exploration) two days each week?" While their responses were at times puzzling, they did help me see the value in opportunities for students to learn to make responsible choices:

- Because you know, maybe, we don't want to read the books or do the things you choose for us
- To have fun
- Because some days we're happy
- To give us a day or two where we're not busy all the time
- Don't know
- We'll be bored with something you pick for us
- If we pick it, we're more interested
- So we can feel like you trust us
- So we can't blame you/get mad at you if we're bored
- Because when you choose, something might come up and we'd do something else instead

Students may have had a variety of understandings of my rationale for this time, but they clearly were in favor of the increased interest level that accompanied that freedom.

In order to create a structure supporting student choice, I had to learn to use language and practices that would force students into increased responsibility and independence. While visiting Mary Giard's first-grade classroom over an extended period of time, I never once heard her answer a student's question. She would say, "Is there anyone here who could help with that?" or "Where do you think we could find an answer for your question?" After observing her classroom, I realized that I spent an inordinate amount of time in my high school classroom answering questions. In fact, my students seldom utilized any way to find answers other than asking me. While this was not an easy practice for the students or me to change, I think this is one of the most significant ways we can help students become independent rather than dependent learners. After years of expecting teachers to give the answers, students were not all that thrilled with my saying, "Where could we find an answer to that?" They thought they had come to a place where they could find an answer! I once heard a teacher say her rule was "three before me"; students knew they had to check three other sources of information before coming to the teacher.

In addition to asking students to take responsibility for their individual learning, I also began asking them to help make curricular choices for whole-group learning. While not shifting my responsibility entirely, I did ask them to choose from several possibilities in terms of whole-class novels and activities. If I planned to be absent from school, I also asked students to choose the work they would do with the substitute. In addition to choosing their work for the day (in advance), they also chose how progress and problems would be tracked. Amazingly, they sometimes chose to take tests, and they always chose not to have the substitute continue reading our shared novel. With students taking on this responsibility, substitute teacher problems (at least those related to planning) were almost nonexistent.

Each of these changes in our classroom alone would have made a difference in students' perceptions of their responsibility for learning, but all together they had an incredible impact on the students' development as lifelong learners. On one of my first days in Mary Giard's first-grade classroom, she asked students, "Whose responsibility is it for you to learn to read?" and they chorused, "All of ours!" I was shocked. My students would have yelled, "Yours!" Teaching responsibility for choices is an incremental, necessary step on a pathway of continued learning. Tim's poem "Motivate" and his reflection on why he wrote the poem always remind me of the importance of forcing students to take on the tough choices related to learning:

Motivate
I sit in the classroom with nothing to do,
I don't want to read,
Then you say, "It's all up to *you.*"
I think to myself, "She must be crazy;
I can read and write,
But I'm too damn lazy."
Then it happens—and I take a
    book off the shelf.
If I fail this class,
I'm failing myself.

I wrote this poem to say that I work better on my own motivation. Now, I can't stand to have someone else telling me what and how and when all the time. I like to know I did work because I chose to, not because the whole class had to. I think this class has shown me that work is good but not for anybody but me.

I think Tim would agree with Margaret Meek's words to teachers in *Learning to Read*: "But no exercise, however well ordered, will have the effect of a genuine reading task that encourages the reader to learn what he wants to know as a result of his own initiative" (207). Lifelong readers are adept at making their own reading choices.

Immersion

Our expectations for reading success and students' abilities to demonstrate that success in reading are directly tied to the ways we immerse them in oral and written language. Cambourne states, "Immersion is more than a simple teaching 'activity' or 'strategy.' It is an underlying pervasive or 'overarching superordinate' condition which becomes part of one's teaching consciousness" (47). Classrooms where reading diversity is celebrated have at their foundation immersion in rich language that is used for a variety of purposes and audiences. Each day I tried to choose sources of rich language to immerse students in language that represented diverse perspectives:

- Newspapers
- Novels representing a range of reading and interest levels
- Passages from texts demonstrating effective writing (rich description, engaging dialogue, dialect, effective leads)
- Magazines
- Nonfiction that answers and invites interesting questions
- Books on tape (fiction and nonfiction)
- Poetry anthologies
- Language play (Mad Libs, alphabet books, riddles, Richard Lederer's *Anguished English*)
- Student writing
- Picture books
- Interesting advertisements
- Writing that elicits emotional responses
- Video clips that build world knowledge
- Persuasive speeches
- Art and music
- Stories that connect to students' lives
- Rich talk (students and invited others)
- Interactive computer software

I found this immersion in language helped my students in many ways. They quickly began to imitate, both orally and in writing, the language they heard often. I know many teachers use sentences or complete pieces of student writing for mini-lessons (Atwell 1987). I realized the significance of the language models I was putting before the students when our class was looking at our Stupendous Sentences and Fabulous Phrases one week. It was the first time I had used a phrase from Trent's writing; I was really taken with the language he had used in his description of the place where he went to be alone: "Our yard has everybody's old junk cars all over the place, so sometimes I go and hide in the old Ford that sits all by itself under the canopy of trees." When I showed this line to the students on the overhead, I said, "Can't you just picture these trees making a canopy over that old car?" We talked about what canopies are used for—over beds and entrances—and what great language Trent was using so that we could picture the canopy protecting the old Ford. We went on to other sentences and phrases, or at least most of us did. Every piece of Trent's writing for the next several weeks seemed to have a need for the word *canopy*. It finally took my sharing a piece of my writing where I had overused the word *change* for Trent to move on to other Fabulous Phrases in his writing.

The range of language immersion also influenced students' reading selections. When I shared "Tuning" from the beginning of Paulsen's *The Winter Room* as an example of rich language, many students went on to read several other Paulsen novels. A letter read from Bissel's *Letters I Never Wrote, Conversations I Never Had* led to a quest for collections of letters and many discussions about what we might say in a letter. Many students then began writing letters to people who had made a difference in their lives as well as people who weren't making a difference and who should have been. A ninth-grade student, Dan, used this reading model as a way to let his middle school principal know the things that needed improvement at his school:

> Dear Mr. Principal . . .
> In middle school the lockers are too small, the food is not very good. The lunch is too short. Some of the teachers are boring. The physical equipment is top of the line. To improve, get bigger lockers and better teachers. Good By.
>   Your friend, Dan

Students often came in before school, during my planning period, and after school to sort books by popular authors (Paulsen, Voigt, Blume) or genres (suspense, adventure) into individual crates. Our walls were covered with language they collected after I shared with them my journal that had interesting quotes, signs, graffiti, and conversations. Students were so immersed in language in our classroom that Warren (who frequently napped) complained one day, "It's impossible to sleep in here. Your head falls back and you open your eyes and there are all these words staring at you from the ceiling."

This constant talk about academics and life also had an effect I had never considered until I asked a colleague, Barbara Frick, to facilitate a year-end discussion with students so I could hear their perspectives on what mattered to them in our classroom. The transcript that follows (Allen 1995, 112) illustrates the importance of immersing students in language as an environmental condition for risk taking.

STAN: This class is more sociable than others.
FRICK: You talk more?

STAN: Yeah, we talk a lot about what we're doing and not just in here either. I mean, now I know most of these people. I know a lot about them—not just in this area, but personally. You just get to know each other.

JENNIFER: In my other classes, I don't even know people's names.

FRICK: That's a real problem.

ANNE: And if you're reading out loud, it's easier to read with people you know than others—people who believe in you.

Immersion in language has an effect on students' writing, on their reading, and on their thinking and talk. In Rachel's piece about how she had changed as a learner, she wrote, "Sometimes I say words to my friends and they'll be looking at me weird and I stop and think, 'Where did that word come from?' Then, I'll remember hearing it in a book you read to us or something."

The great news is that the resources for creating immersion in rich oral and print language environments are everywhere. English as a Second Language (ESL) students at Immokalee High School in Immokalee, Florida, were even encouraged to collect language as they watched television on Super Bowl Sunday (see Figure 2.1).* These teachers understand that language immersion, both in and out of the classroom, is critical for reading success.

Demonstrations

Demonstrations of Literacy The immersion described here leads students to diverse opportunities for showing us they are learning. Cambourne defines demonstrations as "artifacts and/or actions from which we can learn" (47). Each of us is bombarded with demonstrations during our daily lives. While the demonstrations may vary from formal to informal, conscious to unconscious, as active learners we are constantly picking up demonstrations of language and learning from these "artifacts and actions." The demonstrations that occur in our classrooms are often a significant, but unplanned, part of the curriculum.

Emerson has said, "Who you are speaks so loudly I can't hear what you're saying." I am convinced that while we are often quick to blame society, parenting, and former schooling for adolescents' lack of interest in reading and writing, some of the blame must be carried by those of us in whose classes these learners sit. It is a sobering thought for me to recognize that everything I do on a daily basis is a demonstration of my attitudes toward reading, writing, and learning. So, how can we consistently give honest demonstrations of interest, excitement, and even passion for books?

First, I would advocate beginning each class by reading a short piece from something you have read that has hooked you because of its mystery, humor, or

---

*The graphic organizers, or forms, shown in the figures are provided in Appendix H as blanks for reproduction.

Figure 2.1

H.1 Things We Can Read From, A–Z

A-B	C-D	E-F
beating the team blocker brothers a person talking	coke coaches coin toss chest pads Dads cousin cars	football fight big field football shoe fans

G-H	I-J	K-L
hot girls having fun helmet hurt people hot dogs grandmother grandfather	jersey injure someone	look at the team kill the teams leg pads light

M-N	O-P	Q-R
nasty girls moms noises	pop someone popcorn penalty paramedics	referee quarterback running back running shoes roar

S-T	U-V	WXYZ
tackle soak seller side line safety shoulder pads sister		watch the player wave wide receiver yards

emotion. For example, read the first paragraph of Paulsen's *The Car* and watch students rush for the book: "He was alone. His name was Terry Anders. He was fourteen years old, living in Cleveland, Ohio, and his parents had left him" (5). You'll find the same response when you read the beginning of the last chapter of a gut-wrenching book such as Craig's *The Moon Is Broken*: "Two weeks after she came home, I saw that my Annie was dying" (245).

I also try to demonstrate for my students that my reading depends on my mood and purpose by sharing a variety of texts with them. One day I read aloud an article in the newspaper that so angered me I wrote a letter to the editor. I read aloud from professional books on education and asked my students if they agreed or disagreed with people like the Goodmans, Romano, and Kirby, Liner, and Vinz as they talked about ways to help students become more literate. Some days I read to them from my latest beach reading, and other days I read Hugh Prather's *Notes to Myself*. Each of these demonstrations helped students in their choices for reading and writing.

I also spent some time talking with students about the times that reading made a difference in my life. My students knew that I turned to books when I needed something to help me find my way. I shared with them how moved I had been when I first read Robert Newton Peck's *A Day No Pigs Would Die* (1972) while I was still grieving over my father's death. I read Judith Viorst's *How Did I Get to Be 40 and Other Atrocities* (1973) as we talked about "getting old." I talked with them about books that reminded me of vacations I had taken and books that I couldn't wait to share with friends.

One of the interesting things I found as I shared texts with students is that the same event can be described in several writing styles and types of media. A few years ago in central Florida a holiday parade was canceled, in part because of conflict that had arisen from the Ku Klux Klan's wanting to march in the parade. After weeks of debate, the city council canceled the parade. My students and I explored how differently that event would have been described depending on the person telling the story: a member of the city council who has spent many hours in debate; a member of the KKK who felt his civil rights had been denied; a girl who had spent weeks practicing to march in the parade; the parents who had taken children to the annual parade each year; or a lawyer for the American Civil Liberties Union. There may be no need to record every shared text, but when writing of such diverse perspectives and styles is explored, students may want to note in their academic journals the sample types and text characteristics as a way of making the reading-writing connection.

Demonstrations of Language at Work As literacy teachers, we spend hours each week demonstrating how language works: reading aloud, sharing pieces of writing, and talking with students about books and writing. One of the most valuable tools I found in my classroom for demonstrating how language works is language experience activity (LEA). Van Allen (1966) highlights the theory that underscores the advantages of LEA as follows: "What I think about, I can talk about; what I can say, I can write or someone can write for me; what I can write, I can read; and I can read what other people write for me to read." As students dictate, the teacher acts as scribe and guide, documenting the words students use to express themselves. Rather than using the chart paper commonly used for LEA, I used the technology we had available at our high school. With an LCD panel hooked to both a computer and an overhead projector, we could write in an LEA format that all the students could see on the overhead screen. Some teachers have their LCD panels attached to the television monitor in the room for the same purpose. While this extremely important activity is often used in primary literacy instruction, I think it has been overlooked as a way of demonstrating the way language works when learning with adolescents.

As we worked together in this way to do group summaries, reflections, text responses, and creative writing projects, students could see how language worked as I word-processed the language they used. Sometimes we would print hard copies of what we had written together so that all students could put copies in their academic journals as reference for their own writing. I found that using LEA with my secondary students was extremely effective for teaching or reinforcing sentence structures, spelling, grammar and usage, topic development, organization, and word choices. In fact, the text shown in Figure 2.2 is an example of the first time the ninth-grade students in Literacy Workshop seemed

Figure 2.2

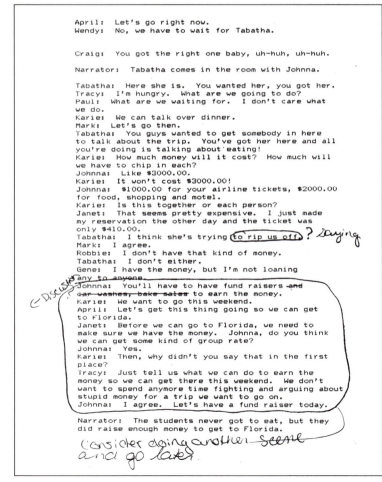

to comprehend that revision literally means reseeing. This text is one page of Karie's copy of a play we wrote using the LEA approach. After we had finished two acts of the play, I made arrangements for the students to watch as the Play Production class prepared their student-written plays for production. Following those observations, I asked the Play Production teacher to confer with students about changes that would make their dialogue and action more effective. Karie's handwritten notes indicate changes she brought to our class discussion. Her comment, "You mean this is what people do every time they write?" highlighted this first experience the group had had with revision. Using LEA we were able to see our text and resee based on feedback.

With LEA in the primary years the teacher's role is mainly that of transcriptionist so that students can see their words in print. That role continues with intermediate and secondary students but can be expanded to include a more interactive approach. The teacher begins with students' words and clarifies meaning, supporting details, word choices, mechanics, and spelling. The goal is that students would begin to do the same: question words, argue about language and sentence structure, discuss appropriate punctuation, and make guesses about spelling patterns. As teachers guide this process, students begin to see the many options writers have for communicating their ideas.

Student Work as Demonstrations of Learning Student work can not only serve as a model of effective writing for class discussion but also give students concrete models for their own future writing. For example, when my ninth-grade students were struggling to move beyond summary to personal connection in their independent reading, I used excerpts from Brandi's response to Salinger's *Catcher in the Rye* as a way for these students to generate some characteristics of personal response:

> This was definitely a wonderful book; a bit tragic, but I can honestly say I enjoyed it. I'm still a bit puzzled about what he's seemingly trying to save people from. There were also a few male insights I picked up on which I hadn't understood before and a few which were confirmed. It's funny how easily a person of the male persuasion can tell a person of the female persuasion he loves her, if she is appealing to look at. What a crock! (I hope you don't mind the informality of this paper but I can't express my innermost thought formally.)
>
> What else did I notice about the book? The main character in the book was very complicated, but very simple, if you know what I mean. His ways of thinking were very mature at some points, but some of his actions were a bit immature. I guess maybe he seemed mature in some ways because he had experienced the death of a person he was close to and I'm sure that had something to do with it. Usually if a person loses someone they are closely bonded to, reality seems to slap you in the face harder and sooner.

I actually found myself envious of Holden sometimes for his ability to see through "crap." Sometimes, however, I found myself wanting to just yell at him to accept people for being "fake." I mean some people just are fake. There is nothing you can do about it. About the only thing you can do is hope that others can see through their fakeness.

I half feel bad for my boyfriend at times, now that I've read this book. Now that I know a little bit about what and how men think of women, it's a little unfortunate for him. I know that men can be suckers for a pretty face sometimes. Oh, I think I'm getting off track.

I was angry at Holden's parents because they kept sending him to those stinking schools that he didn't want to go to. I mean it's kind of obvious when your kid flunks out of four different schools that he doesn't want to be in school; or, at least that type of school.

And just exactly what did Holden want to save all those kids from? Themselves? An inevitable destiny of being surrounded by "fakes"? Peanut butter and jelly sandwiches for the rest of their lives? I just don't know, but maybe it has to do with them losing their real sense of who they are. Maybe he doesn't want them to end up like himself—cynical toward most people.

When we finished reading Brandi's response, I asked students to tell me what they noticed about this response. I didn't have to use any responses of theirs for contrast because they already knew what their responses were like. Students came up with the following list:

- She talks to you (or somebody).
- She wrote about what the book made her think about even after she finished the book.
- She said things that would show you she read the book (talked about parents, the school, and his attitude).
- She told you how she felt about the book.
- She asked questions.
- She wrote about things in her own life that were like this guy's.

Students then recorded this list in their academic journals (see Chapter 10) as a reminder for their own responses. Giving students the opportunity to see how other students respond to class assignments or personal learning helps them expand their own repertoire for demonstrating learning.

Approximation, Use, and Response

In our classroom I found these three conditions for learning were inextricably connected. My secondary students had experienced the truth of Cambourne's observation, "Approximation is one of the conditions of natural learning which teachers find easiest to understand but most difficult to implement" (66). They had spent years in classrooms where mechanical correctness and "GIRFT (get it right the first time) logic" (70) had been a priority. They came to my class unwilling to take risks and therefore put as little energy as possible into reading and writing. They had learned that the fewer words they put down on paper, the less opportunity there was for them to make mistakes. Many students responded to survey questions or writing prompts in those first weeks of school with yes, no, or maybe (sometimes all three in the same response). I knew that if I wanted them to develop fluency in reading and writing, an environment had to be established where risk taking was valued.

One of the things that made students begin to take more literacy risks was that I stopped using only written responses to reading. When students were limited to written responses, the responses were shallow, summarizing, and without passion. Tammy's written response to our shared reading of *The Lottery Rose* (Hunt) was totally void of personal connection (see Figure 2.3). This was a book

Figure 2.3

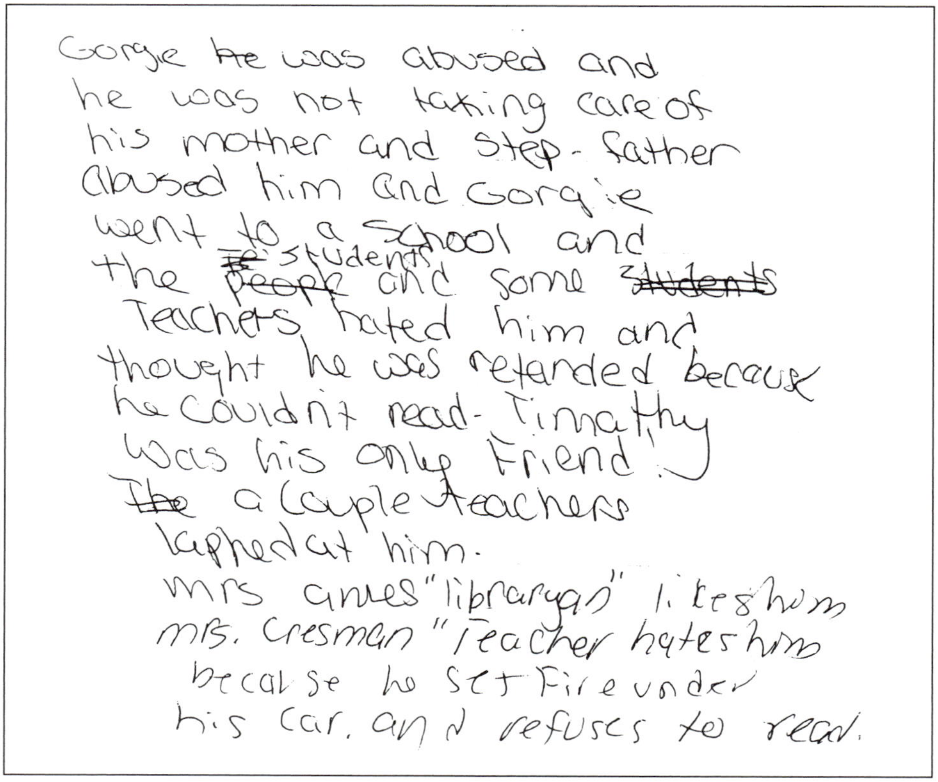
Gorgie he was abused and
he was not taking care of
his mother and step-father
abused him and Gorgie
went to a school and
the people students and some students
Teachers hated him and
thought he was retarded becaus
he couldn't read. Timathy
was his only Friend.
The a couple teachers
laphed at him.
mrs anles "libraryan" likes him
mrs. Cresman "Teacher hates him
becalse he set Fire under
his car. and refuses to read.

she loved so much that she went to a bookstore on her own and bought it so she could have her own copy, and yet her writing did not reveal this love.

But when I used a tape recorder and interviewed Tammy about her independent reading of *The Boyfriend* (Stine), she talked and laughed and questioned her way through the text until there were seven typewritten pages. Just one of those seven pages demonstrates the quality of Tammy's real ability to respond to her reading:

JANET: What did you like about it?

TAMMY: At first it was weird, like when she said she was coming back. There must be a part II to it, because at the end she says, "I'm coming back," or something like that, so there must be a part II to it. Here it is, right here. "Shep, I have to talk to you," she said. "I'm back from the grave." So, there must be a part II, where she dies and comes back or something.

JANET: What has happened between Shep and Joanna?

TAMMY: She cut his hand and he got mad at her because she tried to pretend that it was his fault that there was blood on the floor so she cut his hand with a knife and he got mad and left.

JANET: What do you think she is trying to do with Shep here in this passage?

TAMMY: She's trying to get back at him, because he tried to get back, well, 'cuz Dex tried to get back at her so now she's going to try to get back at him.

JANET: So, Shep has kind of dumped her, huh?

TAMMY: Yuh, because he was mad at her so he didn't want anything to do with her anymore. So, she's trying to get back at him because she really liked him.

JANET: Do you think she's trying to get back at him in the end or she's trying to get him back? [The latter is the obvious interpretation. Tammy has really put a strange twist to the end of this book.]

TAMMY: She's trying to get back at him.

JANET: She's mad at him for dumping her? That's unusual, I think, don't you?

TAMMY: I don't know.

JANET: Would you do that? What if you were Joanna and your boyfriend dumped you———

TAMMY (*interrupting*): I would try to get back at him. I'd get real mad at him and I'd say everything and if he went out with a girl, I'd tell her all these things to make them break up.

Tammy was clearly fluent and filled with personal response when talking about her reading but was unwilling to take too many risks by putting it to paper. After my praise of her oral summary and our strategizing ways for her to get some of those great ideas down on paper when asked, she began to take more chances. Once she realized she could always tape-record her responses instead of writing them, she read and responded to eleven novels in the month of September. When I saw the success with Tammy, I bought cassettes for each student, labeled them, and encouraged students to do some of their responses orally and compare them to the written ones they did.

All students need to use language in a variety of ways for both their own and others' purposes on a daily basis. Students need to read, write, and speak in the presence of those who can give them honest and consistent responses as to how they are doing at being persuasive, thoughtful, and engaging. I believe it is the opportunity to use language in this way, without fear of mistakes, that gives students the opportunity to approximate insightful and articulate language. As students feel free to take risks with language, teachers are given more windows of opportunity to see where students' next learning steps are. When students stay at a very safe level of language use, it is almost impossible to know what kind of response to give. The transcription of Tammy's interview response allowed me an excellent opportunity to work through word choices, appropriate language choices, reading between the lines, and organization of thoughts in a way that made sense to her. With so much "writing," I had the opportunity to help Tammy begin to revise keeping the needs of the reader or listener in mind. She was then able to begin making the transition to writing in the shadow of a reader.

Whether you have taught for one year or twenty, you know that there are students who seem to reject the opportunity to learn regardless of learning conditions in place in your classrooms. I think Cambourne would agree that while the conditions for learning that he has described must be in place for learning to occur, this is to no avail unless learners are engaged in learning. Chapter 3 explores engagement in relation to the things that get in the way of success in reading, because it is that very engagement that often stops students before they ever get to the point of challenging themselves as learners.

Environments that support wonderful ideas have at their core the belief that all children can learn if appropriate conditions, resources, and support are available. When these are in place, we create opportunities for success, set challenges for unexpected choices, provide stimulating resources, help students discover their learning voices, and teach them how to ask for help. Environments for wonderful ideas are places where students can unlearn a sense of failure and replace it with a sense of wonder and possibility.

3

What Gets in the Way of Reading Success?

I realized, standing in front of Nettie right then, that when I read I am
like a bat soaring and swooping through the night, skimming across the
treetops to find my way through the densest forest in the darkest night.
I listen to the shining needlepoints of sound in every book I read. I am
no bookworm. I am the bookbat.

KATHRYN LASKY, MEMOIRS OF A BOOKBAT

As teachers we all hope for classrooms filled with students who are "bookbats." These are the kind of readers who don't think we're crazy when we
arrive on Monday morning raving about the great book we read over the
weekend. They are voracious, self-motivated, addicted, and self-sustaining.
While that is our dream and our goal, we often find our classrooms filled with
students like Derek, whose experience of reading is the very opposite of Harper
Jessup's "bookbat" relationship with reading.

When I have to read, I punch a hole. To me books are dumb. I like to
read about agriculture and I'd rather read than write. When I read, I
don't read, I only pretend to. I would read more if everything I read was
only a sentence or two.

I recently saw a poster reading "We put the fun in dysfunctional," and reluctant readers can certainly do that. Students who come to us as reluctant readers
may be challenging, but they also can bring an incredible amount of joy into our
teaching. Part of the challenge and the joy occur as we try to fit puzzle pieces
together for students who have had years of academic failure. Marie Clay calls
these readers "tangled readers," and they are indeed tangled if they have had to
spend years trying to survive without a reading foundation in an academic system built on literacy. Students who struggle to find success and students who

appear to have abandoned the struggle each have a unique set of experiences that has brought them to this point in their lives.

In *Reluctant Readers,* Jobe and Dayton-Sakari characterize readers' stances toward reading with four different descriptive labels: I Can't, I Don't Know How, I'd Rather, and I Don't Care. They describe each of these groups and the instructional strategies that might work for each group. For my purposes, I want to use their categories to talk about the unique qualities each reluctant reader brings and the ways in which we must adapt our teaching to meet the needs of those students. I also want to use these categories as a reminder that not all reluctant readers are struggling readers, and not all struggling readers are reluctant.

"I Can't" Readers

In my years in the classroom I encountered hundreds of students I would characterize as "I Can't" readers. In fact, I would probably call them "I Can't Right Now" readers. Jobe and Dayton-Sakari say these readers "come in two versions: those that act out and those that hide out" (17). When it was time for reading in our classroom, these students had a long list of reasons why they couldn't read right then. They were quick to tell me they didn't have any reading problems; they just couldn't read right that minute. When we started our Literacy Workshop classes for the most struggling readers, these students always told me their membership in the class was a mistake. Their reasons for not reading will probably sound familiar to you: Reading gives me a headache. I think I might need glasses; I'm having my eyes checked soon. I need to go to the bathroom. My neck/back hurts. I'm too tired to read. Reading always makes me sleepy.

At the end of our first month of Literacy Workshop, the principal asked if I had developed any great theories about reading instruction. I told him I had. In fact, I said, I could save the district lots of money being spent on testing if my theory could get accepted. After baiting him a bit more, I told him I thought there was a direct correlation between struggling readers and urinary problems: "Every time I ask these students to read, someone has to go to the bathroom. I think we should get rid of the reading test and just put all the eighth graders in a room together and ask them to read. Those who ask to go to the bathroom probably need an intervention program." We laughed over the idea, but I'm convinced there are behavioral signs that are good indicators of reading reluctance or struggles: inability to choose books for independent reading; frequent requests for bathroom or office breaks; sleeping during reading; winding and rewinding of tapes if using recorded books; and class disruption or digressions at the beginning of reading times.

With "I Can't" readers, it is difficult to tell if they are choosing not to read or if they truly don't know how to read. In order to figure that out, I had to get them reading. I found that "I Can't" readers need lots of support in getting started and staying with reading. They often need to choose from among three to four book titles I've selected for them based on their stated interests prior to independent reading time rather than from the shelves with hundreds of books. Sometimes they need shorter works—*Stone Fox* (Gardner), *Drive-By* (Ewing), *The Wild Kid* (Mazer)—so they can feel the immediate success of completing a book. If a longer novel is chosen, success in finishing short chapters such as those in Sachar's *Holes* often will keep them reading. I used to keep a box of short stories, high-interest news articles, and short nonfiction on a shelf behind my desk just for these students. I would acknowledge their eye/back/sleep difficulties and say, "I've got something here that is short/really interesting/has lots of pictures/large print. Why don't you just try and get through this today, and then you can choose a novel tomorrow when you're feeling better."

"I Don't Know How" Readers

Many struggling and reluctant readers do not know that reading is supposed to *make sense*. Older readers may have become dependent on someone's telling them what the text means. They may have learned to pay scant attention to reading because they see no value for it in their lives. Or, in content area classrooms, they may have discovered that textbooks could not be read in the same way as narratives and therefore developed coping habits rather than reading habits.

During my last year of teaching I was listening to one of my students read. I had put Robbie on my check-in list because I had noted a significant change in the number of pages he was reading each day. When he read Hinton's *The Outsiders,* he seemed to experience few problems. When he started reading Paulsen's *Hatchet,* I noted he was reading only two or three pages a day. As I sat beside Robbie listening to his halting reading of *Hatchet,* I was shocked. Each time he came to a word he didn't know, he substituted a "letter person" for each letter of the unknown word. (In "letter people," each letter of the alphabet has a character name: T = Tall Teeth; A = Miss Achoo, R = Ripping Rubber Bands.) Having never heard of "letter people," I could not imagine what Robbie was doing. I thought he was on drugs or something. I asked him to go back and reread the sentence, and he read it the same way. I looked at him and said, "What are you doing? Does this make any sense to you?"

He said, "It's not supposed to make sense, Mrs. Allen. It's sounding out."

I told him that I didn't know all the intricate parts of sounding out but that I did know reading was supposed to make sense. Robbie was not unique; his view of reading only exemplified the missing or inaccurate pieces many older students bring to us. Even some students who are enrolled in college preparatory classes really do not know that reading is supposed to make sense, or they would not be so quick to tell us, "I read all of chapter three but I didn't get a thing out of it."

For many students, the broad problem is their belief that reading is a passive activity. They don't engage, as fluent readers do, in an active reading process: activating background knowledge, predicting, confirming or rejecting predictions, inferring, questioning, monitoring, clarifying, strategizing, rereading, making connections, synthesizing, analyzing, and criticizing. With so little reading process work on their parts, no wonder they have so much energy left at the end of the school day!

Many struggling readers come to us not knowing the importance of *questioning*. A critical difference between struggling and fluent readers is their ability to question before, during, and after reading a text. Struggling readers often believe that good readers are better at answering questions. Sometimes they are. More critical to reading, however, is their ability to question themselves, the author, and the text during the reading experience. Fluent readers question themselves by putting themselves into the text and asking what they would do in that situation or context. They question the author by wondering why the work was titled that way or why the story ended the way it did. They question the text by asking the purpose of things like bold and italic type, extra white space, charts and graphs. This questioning leads them to higher levels of fluency as they transfer the newly gained insights to further reading.

Struggling readers may also not know how to *monitor* their reading. Even if they know that reading should make sense, they often "read" several pages or an entire chapter even after they are totally lost or distracted. Reading is usually tedious enough for them that if they actually stopped every time it did not make sense, they would feel they were never making any progress.

Another difficulty for many struggling readers is in the area of *fix-up strategies*. They often have only one way to try to make sense out of a failed or confused reading and that is rereading the same way they read it the first time. They haven't learned that if you do what you've always done, you'll get what you have always gotten. In this case, readers reread and are still left confused.

Finally, many "I Don't Know How" readers do not know how to *communicate learning* or demonstrate personal response, text connections, or new understandings from their reading. In the absence of teacher questions or textbook assignments, these struggling readers have a difficult time showing a personal connection or demonstrating learning after reading. In Caine and Caine's *Making Connections,* the authors highlight a reason for learners' dependence on teacher- or text-constructed ways of demonstrating learning. "An essential problem is that almost all our testing and evaluation is geared toward recognizing surface knowledge" (8). Adolescents have had so much experience with someone else telling them how to demonstrate they learned something in school, they struggle when asked to show learning in the absence of a template. This is one of the reasons "I Don't Know How" readers will often make an attempt when given worksheets, sentence completions, fill in the blanks, or sentence starters but will leave the page blank when asked to respond, summarize, create, analyze, or apply what they have read. The good news is that once students become adept at choosing how they will show they have learned something from their reading, they are shocked they ever needed such support. Andrea, one of the students in my Directed Studies class, said, "For a few years I was in English classes that did everything together—they read the same books, watched the same movies, and everyone even took the same tests!"

"I Don't Know How" readers need more direct instructional time than other reluctant readers. They often need the support of a tape so they can be successful reading the books of their choice. Even with a recording, these students need extra support in terms of reading strategies and ways to document and communicate their learning. They were the ones who benefited the most from the structure of our academic journals. Two sections of our journals were Things I'm Learning How to Do and Things I Know How to Do. As students used academic journals to document the steps we used to summarize, compare and contrast, characterize, predict, and solve problems, they created a reference that helped them transfer the strategies to new texts.

"I'd Rather" Readers

Students I would characterize as "I'd Rather" readers would always rather do something else other than reading. Typically, these students come to us having been fairly successful in school. On standardized reading tests, they score somewhere near grade level. They are, however, reluctant to read for sustained periods of time. Instead, they offer to do art-related projects, writing, computer searches, video analyses, and communication tasks such as interviews. They don't tend to get labeled as struggling readers and in fact they aren't. They are, however, reluctant readers.

Our mentoring role with these students differs significantly from the role we take with "I Don't Know How" readers. One of the ways I could usually draw these students into sustained reading was with nonfiction, especially nonfiction that would lead them into a project. Informational texts such as Macauley's *The New Way Things Work,* Platt's *Stephen Bietsy's Incredible Cross Sections,* Hinojosa's *Crews: Gang Members Talk to Maria Hinojosa,* Steiger's *Mysteries of Animal Intelligence,* Hyman's *Crazy Laws,* Macaulay's *Motel of the Mysteries,* Voorhees's *Why Does Popcorn Pop?,* and Quinlan's *The Case of the Mummified Pigs* are the type of books these students tend to read and reread. I also found they enjoyed novels and short stories if these involved projects, games, or informational quests such as Cleary's *Dear Mr. Henshaw,* Scieszka's Time Warp Trio books, Paulsen's *Hatchet,* Raskin's *The Westing Game,* or Fleischman's *Whirligig.* These were sometimes the most difficult students if they couldn't find the right book. If, however, the right book was found, they could become totally absorbed to the point of ignoring all other classroom activities. For this reason, I stocked an entire bookcase with informational books and novels that seemed informational in the reading.

"I Don't Care" Readers

"I Don't Care" readers were often the most difficult students in our classroom. They presented themselves with well-shored-up walls that were tough to overcome, especially in whole-class reading activities. Their body language and words reminded me each day that they were there only because someone was forcing them to come to school. Sometimes they were there because of court orders, and other times they were students who had suffered so much academic failure that they had lost any energy to attempt success. Rather than admitting they didn't know or risking failure, they often just stated they didn't care. They said they didn't care about school or grades, about which classes they got or who taught those classes. They refused to take standardized tests in spite of pizza offers, and they refused to be lured with reading contests or prizes. These were not the students who complained that the work was boring but then finally got involved anyway. They sat in class absolutely refusing to take part in any class activity. In fact, it was unusual for me to have more than one or two students at this extreme in any single class. But when teaching five classes I might have five or six of them a day, enough to make me question desperately whether there were any way to change these behaviors.

During my last three years of teaching, I started conducting interviews with each of my students. It was while I was interviewing students I would have characterized as "I Don't Care" readers that I made an interesting discovery. My assumption with these students had usually been that they were struggling readers who had given up on school. As I interviewed them, however, I found that many of them were actually avid readers. They just weren't school readers. In fact, a large number of them were science fiction/fantasy readers. When I asked Derek why he didn't at least read during independent reading when he could choose his own books, he said, "I'm not going to bring my book to school like some stupid schoolkid and tell you or anyone else how many pages I've read. How would you like to do that? Besides, I'm not reading for you or for the school. I'm reading for me. The stuff we read in school is a waste of time. After all, it's not like if we know who killed King Hamlet, we'll know how to solve the federal deficit." He had been listening; he just was not participating.

So, how do we work with "I Don't Care" readers? I don't know and I don't think anyone else does either. I do know that no one plan will work for all the students in this extreme category. I can relate what worked with Derek and what might work with other students with similar characteristics, but it didn't work with all such students. Derek and I met every Friday afternoon for fifteen minutes and planned his "curriculum" for the following week. His curriculum included reading of his choice that would exceed the amount of reading that I would have assigned my other students. He also had to show me he was learning something from the reading, and he had to complete a piece of writing each week. Since all students were being asked to learn to use computers at the time, Derek had to demonstrate that he was using the computer. Finally, Derek had to write a reflection each week related to what he was learning and where he thought he should go next for new challenges. Initially, I worried because I hadn't asked him to keep any kind of vocabulary list. One day, another student asked him why he wasn't doing what everyone else was doing. Derek replied, "I've had a dispensation from the popette." No need for a vocabulary list for him.

You might ask if it's right for one student to have that much control over his learning. I asked the same thing on many days. Who knows what the personal and academic background is that makes one student out of thirty decide he will not participate in school while others embrace it or pretend to? In *"I Won't Learn from You"* Kohl contends not-learning "tends to take place when someone has to deal with unavoidable challenges to her or his personal and family loyalties, integrity, and identity. In such situations there are forced choices and no apparent middle ground. To agree to learn from a stranger who does not respect your integrity causes a major loss of self. The only alternative is to not-learn and reject the stranger's world" (6). I never plumbed those depths with Derek. I do know that with students like Derek, if they don't have some control over their learning, they cannot be forced into compliance. Although I was still establishing the outer parameters of Derek's school-related learning, Derek was in control of making his own choices within those parameters. Years later I read Kohn's *Punished by Rewards* and recognized the value of the weekly negotiation Derek and I did together. "The emphasis here is on shared responsibility for deciding what gets learned and how the learning takes place. That negotiation can become a lesson in itself—an opportunity to make arguments, solve problems, anticipate consequences, and take other people's needs into account—as well as a powerful contribution to motivation" (224). I'm not sure what I taught Derek—perhaps that some adults are willing to negotiate—but I know that he taught me a great deal about the importance of choice with all students.

What Can Get in the Way of Reading Success for All Students?

Fortunately, not all our students come to us with the stances toward reading described at the beginning of this chapter. Many come to our classrooms each day who are willing, even eager, to learn. In spite of their presence, good nature (on some days), literate backgrounds, and supportive environments, there are things that can get in the way of reading success even for these students. I'm always disturbed when I talk with my friends' children who have been avid readers and who have stopped reading in high school. From interviews with them, with students in middle and high schools where I now work, and with students in my high school classroom, I have discovered there are patterns of habits and activities that can get in the way of reading pleasure and competence for any student:

- Lack of interest or motivation
- Insufficient or inappropriate resources
- Standards and testing
- Absence of appropriate support
- Inability to break the language code
- Insufficient background knowledge
- Lack of independent reading strategies
- Insufficient reading experience
- Inappropriate teacher interventions

Since these students tend to make up a larger percentage of our classes, perhaps their lessons to us are even more instructive. I write about only three of these patterns in this chapter: lack of interest or motivation; insufficient or inappropriate resources; and standards and testing. The remaining reading blockers are addressed in detail, with strategies for overcoming the problems, in subsequent chapters: Chapter 5 (shared reading); Chapter 6 (guided reading); Chapter 9 (content reading); and Chapter 10 (tangled readers).

Lack of Interest or Motivation

Many students I interviewed were vocal in their dislike of and lack of interest in the curriculum as it exists in many middle and secondary classrooms. Many comments echoed Chanelle's words: "We spend all this time studying stuff and you just have to wonder, like, what difference does it make? There's all this important stuff going on and we sit in school talking about iambic crap and I want to yell at the teacher, Who cares? So what?" In English class, students cited three major issues that created this lack of interest: literature that is boring and outdated ("nothing to do with real life"); doing the same stuff year after year ("parts of speech, five-paragraph essays"); and having to memorize lists of literary terms, names, dates, and so on.

Lack of interest, however, was not the only influence causing a lack of motivation. For many students, the cumulative effect of years of academic failure had reduced their motivation to "I just do enough to get by—you know, so I don't have to take the class again." In a school district that sponsors yearly writing

contests, many students told me that weeks of class time were spent getting writing ready for the contest when "everybody already knows who will win—the same people win every year."

This sense of futility can be deep-rooted in terms of students' sense of helplessness related to success or improvement. I was sitting with a tenth-grade student in our school discussing the importance of his taking steps to become a better reader. He finally erupted, saying, "Hey, nobody in my family is a good reader. I figure if God wanted me to be a good reader, he would have made me one." I smiled at him and said, "God sent me. Let's get started." Students need to have a sense of hope—a belief that there is a way to improve and that each step will take them into reading that is more exciting and challenging than what they could have read before.

Insufficient or Inappropriate Resources

I recently found an enlightening quote by Nathaniel Hawthorne: "It is odd enough that my own individual taste is for quite another class of works than those which I myself am able to write. If I were to meet with such books as mine by another writer, I don't believe I should be able to get through them." Interesting. Hawthorne didn't enjoy reading his own writing, yet we insist that all high school students need the experience. Many students have never discovered the magic of books, so we are attempting to build the study of literature on a nonexistent foundation. In order to get to the point where the study of literature can be interesting and exciting, readers must first have had the strong personal experience of discovering the magic of books, which seems available just to the individual. It isn't that the works of Hawthorne and other classic writers aren't significant and interesting; it's just that they likely wouldn't capture the interest of most young readers. Alice Hoffman says that books may well be the only true magic. Readers have to discover that magic long before they are ready or willing to analyze it.

In *It's Never Too Late* (Allen 1995), I described how I discovered the power of reading aloud with students when I found two young adult novels: *Bless the Beasts and Children* (Swarthout) and *Mr. and Mrs. Bo Jo Jones* (Head). Despite the incredible success of those two books in our classroom, I felt guilty that I wasn't using "real" literature—literature with a capital *L*. So I asked myself which one work of classic literature I thought everyone should have read, and I decided it was *Death of a Salesman* (Miller). The text was chosen, and I thought the twelfth-grade students in my makeup English class would enjoy the play more than other students. After all, those young men had failed ninth-, tenth-, or eleventh-grade English and therefore were older and closer to looking at the relationship between work and life. I borrowed a record player, records, and copies of the play. I created the quintessential study guide: questions at the end of every act and scene, vocabulary words for students to look up, pages of "match the quote to the character," and background information related to Arthur Miller and the play. I lured the students into reading the play by telling them they might want to ask their parents if they approved of their reading this play because of the sex and swearing. "Oh, all right, Mrs. Allen. If we're going to read this, let's just get started." So, we did.

As we moved through each scene and act of the play, I became convinced that the students were really enjoying the play. They could answer all the questions and complete the study guide. As we moved closer to Willy Loman's suicide, I began to worry about something else. I feared that this class of eighteen-to-twenty-year-old young men would cry at Loman's death and would blame me for embarrassing them in front of their friends. As the recording reached a crescendo of music when Loman crashed into the concrete abutment, I looked up expecting to see the guys dissolved in a sea of sympathetic tears. Just as I looked up, I made eye contact with Warren. He slammed his book shut and said, "Thank God he's finally dead."

I was devastated. "What are you talking about? This is a great work of American literature—Willy Loman is a classic figure in literature."

"This is the worst thing we have ever read," he said. "I thought this thing would never end." I wanted to remind him that the only things the class had ever read were *Mr. and Mrs. Bo Jo Jones* and *Bless the Beasts and Children*, but I didn't.

"Give me back those books," I said. "You're too insensitive and too immature to read these great works of literature." They gladly returned the books, and we went back to reading literature they enjoyed. I left the experience convinced that these students just weren't ready for literature with a capital *L*; they left the experience distrusting my judgment for the next book we read together.

The following year, however, I knew I had students who were more mature and more sensitive than the prior year's students. I lured another group into reading the play in the same way. I ran off copies of my study guide with additional pages because I had learned how to make word search games over the summer. Now all the vocabulary words, characters, and even the final test were embedded in word search games. As we approached Loman's death, I had the same fears and the students had the same response: "Why in the hell didn't Arthur Miller kill him in the first act?" I gathered the books and left the experience feeling deflated again.

For eight long years I copied my study guide and read the play with students. Each year I was convinced that these students were more mature and sensitive than those of previous years. Each year brought essentially the same response. Finally, in the eighth year of teaching *Death of a Salesman,* I asked the students, "Why don't you feel sorry for Willy Loman?"

"We're supposed to feel sorry for him? I never knew that. Why would we feel sorry for him?"

"Of course you're supposed to feel sorry for him. He's a tragic hero. He has flaws in his character that make him unhappy and lead to his downfall."

"Mrs. Allen, nobody would feel sorry for him. There's nothing wrong with his life. He's a whiner."

I was shocked. In those eight years it had never occurred to me to ask students why they had responded as they did. "What do you mean?"

"There's nothing wrong with his life. He has a place to live. His sons think he's crazy but they still come back to see him."

"He gave his wife's pantyhose away and she still stays with him!"

"He yells and screams all the time and gets away with it."

"He treats his friend, Charley, like crap and still Charley bails him out every month when he needs money." I stood listening to the chorus of reasons why Willy should have been happier with his life. Finally, one of the boys in the class made it even clearer.

"Somebody should write a play about my life. I've been living in a silo since last fall [northern Maine] when my father threw me out. If somebody wrote about my life and kids had to read the story, they'd feel sorry for me."

A young woman in the class nodded in agreement. "Yeah. Someone should write a play about my life. I've got two kids and my mom keeps them during the day while I go to school. At night, I go home and play with them, feed them and stuff, and my mom goes to work. I do my homework until she gets home, talk to her for a while and then go to bed. I get up at five every day and come to school so I can help in the school cafeteria. Someone should write about my life and make kids read it—they'd feel sorry and make different choices. No one is ever going to feel sorry for Willy Loman."

They were right. For these students who were living with the results of poor caregiving, poor choices, inadequate resources, and a lack of reading experience, I was trying to start in the wrong place. It wasn't that *Death of a Salesman* was bad literature; it was just a bad choice for these students at this time in their lives. As with everything, timing is critical in the literary experiences we share with students.

Standards and Testing

A friend of mine sent me a quote from *Commentary,* September 29, 1993, stating that the testing movement had taken on a *Field of Dreams* quality: "Just build a test and they will learn it." In terms of general goals, I have yet to find printed standards with which I would not agree. And it isn't that I don't believe having standards can help each of us make our teaching productive for all learners. What does cause me many moments of angst is listening to teachers plan their classes and instruction to "make kids get higher test scores." This focus on scores rather than standards is getting in the way of reading success for many students. Teachers are moving back to literature and content reading that is safe. They have been asked to examine their use of time so that each reading selection can be used to teach strategies for the test. I was working in a school district in Florida, and teachers kept referring to FCAT (our state-mandated test) strategies. I finally asked them to list these strategies for me, and they listed things such as predicting, summarizing, inferring, understanding cause and effect, and problem solving. I pointed out to them that these have always been used by fluent readers to make sense of texts. They were taken aback. "You mean these aren't just things we're supposed to teach in order to get kids ready for the test?" I could have walked away from that experience concluding, "At least they are now teaching the strategies," but they weren't. They weren't teaching the students that these strategies could help them when they encountered new or difficult texts; they weren't teaching the strategies as processes transferable to all reading. They were teaching them as test-taking strategies, not reading strategies. In that process, they were leaving out critical conditions of reading: engagement, immersion in diverse texts, and opportunities and time for choice.

Redefining Success in Reading

There are many who would try to define success in reading for us—those who see success as a number, especially a higher number than the community down the street, and those who tell us that it is knowledge of authors, texts, time periods, and characters. There are even those who believe the focus on reading should be found only in reading classes or in intervention programs for the most struggling readers. My definition for reading success mirrors the spirit of Mooney's words: "True readers and writers are 'self-winding' and choose to read and write well beyond the care and guidance of the school system" (1991, 1). Our classroom goals are beyond testing: we want students who can read, who will choose to read, and who will know strategies for overcoming rather than avoiding difficult reading tasks. Knowing what gets in the way of those goals makes a critical difference in the daily instructional choices we make in *all* our classrooms.

4

Life Is Short—Eat Dessert First! The Value of Read-Aloud Beyond the Primary Years

Reading aloud improves listening skills, builds vocabulary, aids reading comprehension, and has a positive impact on students' attitudes toward reading. It is the easiest component to incorporate into any language program at any grade level. Reading aloud is cost effective, requires little preparation, and results in few discipline problems.
REGIE ROUTMAN, INVITATIONS: CHANGING AS TEACHERS AND LEARNERS K–12

know many of us share fond memories of having been read aloud to: someone we loved reading us great stories filled with people who seemed more real than life, evoking places and events we might never have imagined. In each of my adult moves I've discarded clothing and furniture, dishes, knickknacks, and even friends but have always managed to keep my 1945 set of *The Home University Bookshelf: Famous Stories and Verse* from which I was read to every day during my childhood. I seldom meet adults who tell me that what inspired their love of reading was a textbook but often meet people who tell me of a special teacher or parent or grandparent or aunt who read aloud to them. They have tattered copies of E. B. White's *Charlotte's Web* and Piper's *The Little Engine That Could* that were somehow salvaged after multiple readings.

Two years ago when my great-nieces, Madelyn and Melissa, were in Florida visiting me, we had an *Alice and Greta* marathon. The night they arrived from northern Maine, I read the story to them, and I read it at least twenty times during the next few days. Our daily reading time always began or ended with Simmons's *Alice and Greta* until I vowed I would give the book away. Fourteen months later, they were back in Florida again. We were at the beach, playing in the water on a sandbar several feet from the shore. After a while, we came out of the water to read and eat lunch. When we went back into the water, Madelyn said, "Look, Aunt Janet, the sandbar is bigger." Not willing to let a teachable moment pass, I immediately moved into questioning mode.

"Do you think so?"

"Well, it looks bigger."

"What do you think would cause it to look that way?" Madelyn looked puzzled. I continued. "Do you think it could have something to do with the tide?"

"I don't know. What's a tide?" I was thinking about how to explain the tide to a six-year-old when she said, "Oh, I know. 'Come now moon, turn the tide. Take this castle for a ride.'" I just stared, amazed at such a clear example of the power of *Alice and Greta,* read aloud over a year ago.

"So, what do you think the tide is?"

Her reply was worth a course in the power of literature. "Well, I think it's hooked to the moon somehow, and it can make the water go way up on the beach or way out in the ocean. And when the water goes way in, it would cover the sandbar, but when it goes way out, the sandbar would be uncovered so it would look bigger." I breathed a sigh of relief that *Alice and Greta* had saved me from having to explain tides. Later, when Anne asked how she had made that wonderful connection, Madelyn said, "I don't know. My head—it's a book."

We know the value of read-aloud with young children, but some of us may not be comfortable presenting read-alouds to intermediate or secondary school students. Reading aloud is like any other instructional approach in that practice improves fluency, timing, and expression. When I am on the road speaking, I often spend time in my hotel room reading aloud the pieces I plan to use the next day. Some people may appear to be natural oral readers, but everyone who reads fluently has practiced to get to that point. Believing in the importance of this approach makes each read-aloud easier than the last.

Given the body of research supporting the importance of read-aloud for modeling fluency, building background knowledge, and developing language acquisition, we should remind ourselves that those same benefits occur when we extend read-aloud beyond the early years. You may have to convince your students of the importance of this practice, but after several engaging read-alouds they will be sold on the idea. You may even have to convince your colleagues that you aren't wasting time. I had spent lots of time convincing my high school students that read-aloud was an important aspect of our reading program because it let us learn about new books and authors quickly. All that work was ruined for several weeks after a substitute teacher told students he certainly wasn't going to read to them because they were old enough to read to themselves. In Katherine Paterson's *Jip, His Story,* when Jip is assigned a reading of *Uncle Tom,* we see a clear picture of the value of hearing someone read to us so our minds are free to explore meaning:

> But for all her preacher airs, the writer trapped him. Indeed, he was so impatient to know how the lowly of the tale would manage that he did hardly any of the reading himself. He made Put read. He wanted to get the tune of the words in his head. Listening was so much better than pounding out the sounds for himself, for he lost the sense of the story in the struggle to read it. (112)

All students, regardless of age, deserve the opportunity to see the story without struggling with the text. Five to ten minutes spent in this way each day has a significant influence on students' literacy and learning lives.

Read-Aloud Is Risk-Free

Reading aloud to my students each day in our classroom was one of the most important times we shared. This time was significant both in terms of community building and literacy learning. The authors of *Becoming a Nation of Readers* (Anderson et al.) state: "The single most important activity for building the knowledge required for eventual success in reading is reading aloud to children" (23). While the context of this passage relates to parents reading to their young children, I do not believe that value is restricted by age. Students at the Long Beach Prep Academy in California would agree. Students who have received failing grades in the eighth grade are required to spend a year at the Prep Academy before entering high school. When several students returned to visit teachers this year after moving on to high school, Heather Magner interviewed them about what they had done at the academy that had made the biggest difference in their reading. "Starting every day by reading books to us—especially picture books," they said.

Any middle or secondary teacher who builds time into the daily schedule for read-aloud can attest to the fact that no one is too old to enjoy read-aloud time. For students who have had difficulty reading, this time can be one of the few when language and literacy can be enjoyed with no risk. The students at Long Beach Prep had experienced the safety of read-aloud, and those positive experiences transferred to the other reading instruction that occurred in their classrooms. Mooney sees this as a time when "they do not have to concentrate on, or take responsibility for, the mechanics of gaining meaning from the printed word. ... [They] are able to experience the satisfactions and delights of the product of reading—meaning" (1990, 10). For students who struggle with word-by-word reading, experiencing the whole story can finally give them a sense of the wonder and magic of a book. Rachel, one of my high school students, said that she loved read-aloud time because it set her mind free to see the story. I think storyteller/writer Joseph Bruchac would agree. He says, "You begin to sing a song and when they know it, they begin to sing it with you." Read-aloud provides the time for children to begin to hear the song: the rhythm of language, the beauty of well-chosen words, and a voice that makes marks on a page come alive.

Read-Aloud Builds Mental Models

While there is a great deal of research supporting the importance of the mental model building stage in early childhood development, I have come to believe that even our older students must go back and capture it in order to develop as self-motivated readers. The time when someone else reads to us is magical, at least in part, *because* the act of decoding is done by someone else. This allows readers to carry out the cognitive task of forming pictures in their heads as they listen to the words. Creating such mental models (Bransford, Sherwood, Hasselbring) is a necessary step in order for readers to move from assisted to independent reading.

I was visiting a literacy classroom at Roosevelt Middle School in San Diego, where the teacher, Stacy North, was giving a delightful reading of Scieszka's *The True Story of the Three Little Pigs!* At the point where Mr. Wolf defends his eating of the pigs by saying that it would be a shame to leave "a perfectly good ham dinner lying there in the straw," one girl looked up at the teacher incredulously and said, "Pigs have ham in them?" Perhaps this young woman is visualizing ham dinners stacked end-to-end in pigs, but at least she now knows that pigs have ham in them.

Teachers across the country have seen the same creation of mental models as they read to their students. When students hear Park's *My Freedom Trip: A Child's Escape from North Korea,* they leave that read-aloud with some knowledge of the causes of the Korean war, the struggle for survival, and the aftermath. That mental model becomes the frame for any other study or textbook reading students do related to the Korean war or for other war-related reading such as Tsuchiya's *Faithful Elephants,* a picture book that tells the story of three elephants in Tokyo who are starved to death during World War II.

Similarly, a read-aloud in science from Arnold's *Disgusting Digestion* could build mental models for communicable diseases. What student could resist this tempting lead about Typhoid Mary? "Mary Mallon was a killer and her lethal weapon was ice cream." A math read-aloud such as the folktale adapted by Barry, *The Rajah's Rice: A Mathematical Folktale from India,* helps students develop an understanding of the magnitude of powers of two (doubling). These read-alouds do not take much time but assist all readers by providing perspectives in addition to or in place of the textbook. There are hundreds of sources for such high-quality read-alouds in content areas. Appendix B lists content-related resources for read-alouds in critical thinking, math, science, and social studies.

Read-aloud time should not be seen as something added on "if we have time" but as instructional time that meets a number of literacy and learning goals. For struggling readers, read-aloud time provides the opportunity to give their full attention to enjoyment of language and the visual images that language creates for them while someone else does the decoding; for both struggling and fluent readers, their worlds grow larger with each new word, character, situation, or event. Noted author Robertson Davies in his book *A Voice from the Attic,* supports the value of reading aloud. "Our emphasis on the eyes as the high road to the intellect is a new thing, and we all use our ears readily when we are asked to do so. Even when we do not desire it (as with advertising jingles), what enters our consciousness through the ear is likely to stick" (16). With each new thing that sticks from a read-aloud, the reader's world expands.

Read-Aloud Sets the Stage for Learning to Read and Reading to Learn

Enjoyment of reading is certainly a significant missing piece of the puzzle for students who have not discovered the joy of reading. Jim Trelease, author of *The Read-Aloud Handbook,* notes, "Before a child can have an interest in reading, he must first have an awareness of it. The child who is unaware of the riches of literature certainly can have no desire for them" (9). This awareness level is critical not only for those students who are at risk in terms of literacy. All students benefit from the rich language, exposure to new authors and texts, and a common sense of world knowledge that is built during read-aloud.

In *Extensive Reading in the Second Language Classroom,* Day and Bamford cite the importance of such exposure in relation to comprehension. "Crucial to comprehension is the knowledge that the reader brings to the text. The construction of meaning depends on the reader's knowledge of the language, the structure of texts, a knowledge of the subject of the reading, and a broad-based background or world knowledge" (14). Read-aloud is an ideal way to help students build an awareness of critical reading components: reading motivation, word knowledge, syntax, story grammar, genre knowledge, authors' intentions, readers' choices, and understanding. In response to those who question the importance of read-aloud, I created the list shown here as my justification for the instructional practice of reading aloud on a daily basis.

Read-aloud

- Exposes students to a wide variety of literature in an enjoyable way
- Builds content area background knowledge as well as general world knowledge

- Helps students develop interests for later self-selection of reading material
- Provides opportunities for assessing story development and characterization
- Facilitates students' abilities to compare and contrast by providing opportunities to look at commonalities among themes, texts, authors, characters, and conflicts
- Fine-tunes students' observational/listening skills
- Creates an atmosphere for developing good discussion skills
- Develops higher-level thinking skills
- Offers opportunity to assess students' growth as listeners and thinkers
- Allows students to anticipate or predict
- Models effective reading behaviors
- Offers time for students to practice cloze in a risk-free setting
- Provides opportunity to assess reading strategies students already possess
- Creates a way to assess interest/attention span and allows for increase over time
- Provides opportunities to share a love of books with readers
- Helps students develop a cohesive school program by connecting books to their academic and personal lives
- Provides concrete models of writing for students as apprentice writers
- Helps create a community of learners
- Provides an opportunity to model respect for a range of reading and response

While most of us probably don't need an excuse to read aloud, I think this list gives us sufficient support if we need it. In fact, if you have been reading aloud with your students, I would guess you could add to this list. For me, the justification came from seeing the significant changes in my students' reading and writing attitudes and competencies that I could tie directly to the reading aloud we did together. From Paulsen's "Tuning" in *The Winter Room,* my students learned about sensory language; from Angelou's "No Loser, No Weeper" in *Poems,* they comprehended the story that is a poem; from Randall's "Ballad of Birmingham" in his poetry collection *The Black Poets,* my students lived the gut-wrenching, vicarious experience of the Sunday school bombing in Birmingham, Alabama, in 1963; and from Marquis's *archy and mehitabel,* they listened to a great story from which they could learn the importance of punctuation as a tool for the reader. In each of these examples, the writers exemplify Mooney's words that the texts we share with children should be filled with "charm, magic, impact, and appeal." Additionally, read-aloud provided the opportunity for us to discuss the structure and significance of genre: story, poetry, drama, essays, journalistic articles, letters, and memoir. Read-aloud formed the foundation for future writing craft lessons, for discussion, for rethinking our choices, and for making us laugh and cry—listen and think.

Student Roles in Read-Aloud

In *I Know Why the Caged Bird Sings,* Maya Angelou says, "Words mean more than what is set down on paper. It takes the human voice to infuse them with the shades of deeper meaning." If read-aloud is so important and our voices are making a critical difference in the level of meaning making, how do we get ready for it? Many teachers tell me of administrators who have come to their classrooms to do observations/evaluations but have left preferring to return when teachers are "really teaching." The notion that read-aloud is somehow non-teaching may have arisen from the practice of reading aloud during "extra" time. Read-aloud is important instructional time and as such needs to be prepared for in the same way we prepare for any significant teaching moment: preparing our students for participating in the read-aloud; preparing ourselves to do an effective read-aloud; and making sure the environment is conducive for read-aloud.

Read-aloud is typically done by the teacher or other fluent reader while students actively listen and visualize the words they are hearing. Since students did not have the text during read-aloud time, I almost never chose novels as read-aloud selections. I usually saved novels I wanted to read in their entirety for shared reading (see Chapter 5) so that students would have the text in front of them and we could go back to the text for clarification, discussion, questioning, and rereading. I did, however, use excerpts from novels for read-aloud as a way to introduce students to new authors or titles and to show writer's craft or the beauty of language. I also used novel excerpts to show students what I was currently reading because so many students liked to read my book choices. However, novel excerpts made up a small percentage of our read-alouds. I usually read poetry, short stories, essays, Dear Abby letters, news or magazine articles, nonfiction pieces about word origins and inventions, and student writing.

I used the term *active listening* earlier in describing the students' role during read-aloud. I know some teachers worry that students just fade during read-aloud and therefore worry about wasting valuable class time. As you get more comfortable with reading aloud, careful observations can give you ample opportunity to assess student engagement because active listening has observable characteristics. I was observing in Mary Giard's first-grade classroom in Maine and noted the following types of active listening responses in one read-aloud session:

- Nonword responses—intake of breath, hands over eyes, body language (shivers and shakes)
- Comparisons to other works of literature—"These women aren't like the women in the other fairy tales we've read."
- Statements about language—"That's a funny word. What does *bold* mean?"
- Comments about physical characteristics of the book—"I don't like this version. There aren't enough illustrations."

- Offers of alternative versions of the plotline/book—"I think C. S. Lewis should have written this one [*Magician's Nephew*] first. I think I'll write a different ending."
- Opinions about characters and motivations—"That witch is mean . . . inconsiderate . . . has to have her own way . . . threatening."
- Mimicking of unique words—"trit trot," "whoopy once, whoopy twice"
- Statements of pleasure/displeasure with the ending of day's selection—"I knew it would end like that." "Oh, no, it can't stop here!"
- Asking important questions—authors' intentions; "I don't understand why the witch did that." "I wouldn't do that, would you?"
- Judgments about book—"I thought I wouldn't, but I liked this version better."
- Suggestions for extending the book—"We should make a play of that part."

As I watched the range of active listening responses by these first graders, I was newly struck by the contrast in responses between these children and those in our high school classrooms. When I questioned Mary, she mentioned several areas that she believed had set the stage for such enthusiasm during read-aloud. First, Mary had carefully chosen the book for read-aloud. She was reading a challenging novel to these first graders, and every student in the class knew that Mary expected they would understand and learn from their reading community.

Second, students knew they were expected to have personal interactions with the text. In discussions following their read-aloud time, students were all expected to contribute and extend the comments of others. When one student said, "He took my words," Mary responded by telling him that she would come back to him when he had had time to think about some other words he could share. With each student's comments, Mary modeled interreader connections: "Can you tell us anything else about what Nick has already offered?" Finally, students were doing enough reading that they had constant points of comparison to other texts, authors, and genres. All of these aspects are critical if we expect students to become active listeners during read-aloud. So, how do we inspire and support the same kind of text-related talk with our older students?

The first step for many students occurs when we use read-alouds that invite the reader to interact with the text. Such texts may require students to figure out mysteries or solve puzzles. Examples include lateral thinking books such as Sloane's *Lateral Thinking Puzzlers* and *Test Your Lateral Thinking IQ;* Sloane and MacHale's *Perplexing Lateral Thinking Puzzles;* Brecher's *Lateral Logic Puzzles.* Critical thinking puzzles such as those gathered by Hammond, Lester, and Scales and by Dispezio make rich listening and questioning read-alouds. Short mysteries also offer the opportunity for students to engage in the kind of active listening and questioning we would like them to carry over to the fiction and nonfiction. There are many of these collections, such as Gordon's *Solv-a-Crime* and *More Solv-a-Crime;* Treat's *Crime and Puzzlement;* and Logue's decks of illustrated mystery cards *Bella's Mystery Deck* and *An Eyeful of Mysteries.*

Teacher Preparation for Read-Aloud Choices

Teacher preparation for read-aloud actually occurs in several areas. The first is choosing a particular read-aloud based on students' interests, age, and needs as well as their reading and life experiences. Instructional preparation occurs in tandem with the choice of text. Then there are several points of preparation that will make the read-aloud experience richer for the teacher and students. Many years of reading aloud to students who were not interested in school or reading helped me develop a keen awareness of the steps I needed to take to grab their attention and make them want to keep reading:

- Practice reading the text prior to reading with your students.
- Choose texts you enjoy reading.
- Choose places where you might want to stop in order to build suspense, clarify words, or help listeners who get lost.
- Highlight words or situations that might need some explanation.
- Check for background information related to the author, time period, illustrator, or text *in case* students' questions lead in that direction.
- Choose a consistent time for read-aloud. Read-aloud is an effective transition into and out of a class period. It is also effective for transition from one activity to another.
- Choose a time for read-aloud that is as free from distractions as possible.
- Read the text with passion. Laugh and cry; wonder and question so that students see an authentic response from you, the reader.
- If the read-aloud is part of a larger unit or inquiry, be prepared to help students make the connection consciously.
- Provide time and opportunity for students to make connections to their lives.

Preparing Students and the Environment for Read-Aloud

Preparing the students for read-aloud is more difficult for the first few read-aloud experiences than it is after students have come to expect and demand read-aloud. Taking a proactive approach in these areas of preparation actually will save you class time in terms of management issues and gain time in terms of comprehension and response:

- Help students find comfortable places for read-aloud but establish the importance of these places not being areas of distraction.
- Establish clear expectations of student behavior during read-aloud. If you want students to listen with no activity, that needs to be established with

the first read-aloud. If, however, you are allowing students to doodle, create images, or take notes, establish parameters for those activities.

- Keep chart paper, overhead transparencies, and markers available in case student discussion leads to memorable talk.
- If the read-aloud has illustrations, change positions as you read so that all students have access to the illustrations.
- Find a way to help students stay focused during the read-aloud. If you think you're losing them, stop and say, "Is everyone with me?" in order to bring wandering students back into focus.
- Use artifacts (a hand, an empty box, a tangled chain) and lighting and music (if appropriate) as a way to draw students into the mood or tone of the text.

Finding Read-Alouds

Appropriate read-alouds are everywhere. The real issue is finding read-alouds that work for your students and your instructional purposes. When I first started daily read-alouds with my students, the choices were fairly random, and I was never quite sure which ones would work and which would fall flat. Over time I began to see a pattern of common characteristics for effective read-alouds. Looking at a few examples illustrates those commonalities. The following read-aloud is one of the most successful ones I have used. Originally printed in the *Columbus Dispatch* (1989) and then reprinted in *Reader's Digest* (July 1995), this humorous look at *Romeo and Juliet* by Mike Harden has reminded many students of the joy words can bring.

> *O Romeo, O, Like, Wow*
> At the end of the school year, my fourteen-year-old daughter's English class tackled Shakespeare's *Romeo and Juliet* and she had to give an oral report. Having listened to her talk on the phone, I can all too easily imagine just how it went.
>
> This is, like, a real super-sad play about this dude Romeo and this dudette Juliet. They had names like that 'cause it was, like, the real old days, before MTV. So, no one had cool names like Heather or Brandon or Shawna. They all had really geeky names like Benvolio and Tybalt and Mercutio.
>
> Anyway, these two families, see, the Montagues and Capulets, really hate each other. I mean, they can't even walk down the street without thrashing on each other, 'cause, like, that's what happens right at the beginning.

This dude, Sampson, who works for old man Capulet, he sees this other dude, Abraham, who hangs with Montague, and he bites his thumb. I mean, like, Sampson bites his own thumb, not Abraham's thumb, which in the old days was like saying "Your mama!" and Abraham says, "Are you dissing me?" So they start beating down. But it gets broken up before anybody's really messed, you know. And the Prince—he's like the principal of this whole town—he says, "Yo, next time you people get in each other's face, I'm gonna twist someone's head around so their cap's on straight."

So Romeo looks at the list, and there's all these names of dweebs, freaks, jocks, stoners, nerds, goods and motorheads. But then he sees Rosaline's name. She's this chick he thinks is really fly, so he decides to crash the party, which is like, easy, see, 'cause it's a masquerade party.

Meanwhile, Juliet's mom, she's trying to fix Juliet up with this guy named Paris. Is that a dorky name or what? I mean, I thought Dweezil and Moon Unit were weird. But Paris? I guess he's lucky he wasn't born in, like, Fort Wayne.

Romeo goes to the party even though he's totally bummed because he loves Rosaline and thinks she, like, doesn't love him. But Romeo's homey, Mercutio, tells him, like, "Chill. Just go. Party down. There's going to be some fly babes there."

So Romeo gets to the party and starts checking out the chicks. He sees Juliet and he goes, "Who is that babe?" and she goes, "Who is that hunk?" Which is bad, see, 'cause, like, Shakespeare already said they got "fatal loins," whatever that means, and they're "star cross'd," which means both of them are Aquarians, I think.

But that don't stop them. So Romeo starts hitting on her, and they hold hands for a while and, like, he goes, "O, then, dear saint, let lips do what hands do." And he kisses her, and it's, like, super rad, I mean totally awesome for both of them. But then Juliet's nurse pulls her away, 'cause, like, in the old days they really had a cow if they caught you sucking face.

Juliet's cousin, Tybalt, sees that Romeo is trying to ease in on a Capulet, even though he's a Montague, so Tyb says, "Yo, hand me that sword." But Juliet's dad says, "Be cool."

Then it's curfew or something 'cause everybody has to leave, but when Romeo is heading for his pad, he says, "Check it out, dudes, I'm gonna bail," and he jumps over this big fence into Juliet's yard. He's like creepin' in the trees and he looks up at Juliet's bedroom and goes, "Who left that light on?" or something like that, and she goes, "O, Romeo, Romeo, wherefore art thou Romeo?" And it's like, *duh,* 'cause he's standing right under her balcony. But maybe, like, she took her contacts out to go to bed.

So he goes, "Do you want to get married?" and she goes, "Yeah." So they do . . . only in secret.

But then, like, right after this, Juliet's pushy cousin Tybalt shows up again and starts getting in Romeo's face. See, he don't know they're married 'cause he didn't get an invitation or nothing. And, like, he should be happy, because he didn't have to buy an electric can opener or anything. He wants to kill Romeo. But Romeo won't fight him, so Tybalt jumps in Mercutio's face, and him and Mercutio start thrashing on each other. Mercutio gets killed, so Romeo kills Tybalt, which is, like, dumb, 'cause now him and Juliet ain't gonna get *any* wedding presents.

Then the Prince exiles Romeo, which is, like, being grounded but like in a whole nother state or something.

So Romeo and Juliet have to split for a while. Juliet goes, "O, think'st thou we shall ever meet again?" 'cause, like, some guys act like they like you a bunch at school but then they never call you up. You know?

Romeo leaves and Juliet is really bummin' 'cause her old man wants her to marry Paris. *Duh!* She's already married. But her parents are still planning a wedding, so it looks like she's going to get an electric can opener one way or another, or maybe even a microwave. But then this priest guy gives Juliet this stuff to drink so that everyone will think she's, like, dead until Romeo can get back from being grounded. But this stuff is so good that everybody thinks she really is dead, and they put her in this tomb thing, you know.

Then Romeo dreams Juliet has found him dead, and even though he's grounded in another state, he says, "Later. I'm outta here." He takes off to see Juliet, but he stops, like at a drugstore, for some poison. So he misses this letter that the priest sent that says, "Juliet isn't dead. She's like, sleeping."

But then Romeo sees Juliet and he goes, "Ah, dear Juliet, why art thou yet so fair?" 'cause, you know, if she was dead she ought to be green and starting to smell funny. And that totally bums him, so he takes the poison. *Duh!* Then you'll never guess this part. She wakes up and sees Romeo and goes, "O happy dagger!" and kills herself.

I mean, are these people serious, or, like, what?

Enjoyable? It certainly is, and since enjoyment is one of the primary goals of read-aloud, this text would meet that goal for many students (and their teachers). So, what is it about the text that works in terms of read-aloud? First, the text has interesting dialogue. In this case, we have contemporary dialect side-by-side with Shakespearean language, which makes all of the dialogue richer.

Dialogue gives you, the reader, the opportunity to make the text come alive, and this dialogue certainly offers that. The text offers listeners a fresh look at a story and text that seem old and traditional, and that fresh look makes the listener feels as if she has insider information. While this text is humorous, it also offers the opportunity for students to gain some content knowledge: Shakespearean language, the basic plot of *Romeo and Juliet,* character names (and some characteristics), conflict and resolution, and examples of anachronisms (contact lenses, electric can opener, microwave). Finally, the tone and voice of this piece invite the listener into the writer's thought processes. When students listen to this piece, they often feel as if the writer is inviting them to share a common joke. All of these components make this an effective read-aloud for *some* students. For younger students or students who have limited English fluency, this might not be the best choice. For teachers embarking on a study of *Romeo and Juliet,* this piece could serve as a segue into the text. It is the combination of interesting read-aloud characteristics, knowledge of your listening audience, and purpose for the read-aloud that make choosing texts for read-aloud a challenge.

I'm often asked where I find such great read-alouds. I read every day, and each time I find something I believe would make a good read-aloud, I make a note of it. I keep a binder of texts that I have copied to use as read-alouds, with notes about possible audiences and purposes. I have listed here a representative sample of read-alouds from my collection with a notation of why I might have chosen them. However, no matter what my instructional purposes might be, each passage is still chosen because it has interesting content, intriguing or unique points of view, humor, emotional impact, voice and dialogue that add to the message, and language that invites listeners into the experience.

For state or district-mandated test preparation:

The Sixth Grade Nickname Game, *(Korman)*
"We don't have anything to study," Jeff pointed out. "No practice questions no shortcut hints. Nothing."

"We've got everything we need," Cassandra insisted.

They just stared at her.

"It's so obvious!" she persisted. "It's a *reading* test!" She pointed to the shelves at the back of the room. "We've got books in the class, books at home; there are zillions in the media center, zillions more in the public library! How do you get ready for a reading test? By *reading*!"

"*Reading*?!" chorused half a dozen voices.

"Think!" ordered Cassandra. "If you play basketball, and you want to be a better foul shooter, what do you do? You take free throws—over and over and over. Well, that's how you get better at reading—by doing it!"

"You mean, like, *extra* reading?" asked Raymond. (78–79)

For making math real:

"Death by Algebra," from Speak *(Anderson)*

Mr. Stetman won't give up. He is determined to prove once and for all
that algebra is something we will use the rest of our lives. If he succeeds,
I think they should give him the Teachers of the Century Award and a
two-week vacation in Hawaii, all expenses paid.

He comes to class each day with a new Real-Life Application. It is
sweet that he cares enough about algebra and his students to want to
bring them together. He's like a grandfather who wants to fix up two
young kids that he just knows would make a great couple. Only the kids
have nothing in common and they hate each other. (83–84)

For when the going gets tough:

"Winners," from The Dog Ate My Homework *(Holbrook)*

I thought they had
something I lacked.
Until I learned,
winners fight back.

It isn't that
they never lose,
don't fall apart
or take abuse.

The trick is,
simply,
every round,
when they get hit?
Winners
don't stay down.

I would use each of these read-aloud texts for a different purpose in the
classroom. There are days when I just want students to enjoy the beauty of
language and days when I want the reading to help us move into a way to solve
our classroom community problems. There are also days when I want the read-
aloud to lead us into content and days when I want students to make significant personal connections to a text, an author, or a genre. These three texts
have the common traits already mentioned, and as you might suspect, each
would speak to some students more than others. The anthologies listed in
Appendixes B, E, and F have many read-alouds that would pull your class into
a literate community.

Points Worth Remembering

I have seen many teachers (and I've been guilty of this as well) take the enjoyment out of those few minutes of daily read-aloud time by turning it into a time of checking for understanding. In the chapters that follow, especially in Chapter 5 (shared reading), I talk about many opportunities for you to assess the attention, active reading behaviors, and comprehension of content of your students. But read-aloud should be a risk-free time in every classroom. Some students will connect with some readings more than others. Some readings will have students begging for more and others will fall flat. Read-aloud is the time for extensive reading so that students begin to develop reading tastes that will affect the choices they make during independent reading.

Reading aloud should be an integrated, predictable part of our lives with our students. On some days they should see the connection between the read-aloud and the theme or unit, and on other days they should understand that you're sharing this text because it is simply too good for them to miss. Donald Graves (1991) says, "As I read, the children compose their own images, but the feelings they create together create a literate bond that is unique in human existence" (79). Perhaps the bond created during these read-aloud times will be the one that sustains children as readers not only in school but also in their adult lives.

5

Shared Reading as the Heart of Reading Instruction

[Storying] very quickly becomes the means whereby we enter into a shared world, which is continually broadened and enriched by the exchange of stories with others. In this sense, the reality each one of us inhabits is to a very great extent a distillation of the stories that we have shared.

GORDON WELLS, THE MEANING MAKERS

Read-aloud time, where students do not have the text in front of them, extends quite naturally into shared reading, where students are invited to read along silently as the teacher reads the text. If engaging texts are chosen for shared reading and read fluently by the teacher, the experience of students seeing and hearing language in a meaningful text can be significant. Mooney highlights the instructional opportunities that shared reading can provide: "Presenting a variety of structures through the shared reading approach develops an attitude of familiarity and expectation about the elements of the various genres. This leads to children's becoming confident about taking more responsibility for the readings" (1991, 25).

A typical shared reading experience in elementary classrooms might include a big book with individual student copies. Shared reading in middle and secondary school classrooms can take a variety of forms depending on the purpose. It could include the reading of entire novels or short stories, excerpts from fiction and nonfiction, poetry or drama, recorded books, or texts used in literature circles. Students might have individual copies of the text, or the teacher might have the text on overhead transparencies or in Power Point presentations.

In a survey of over six hundred middle and high school students that I recently conducted, the area they cited as responsible for their greatest gains in reading achievement was shared reading. I was not surprised. In our classroom I found that shared reading had more potential for increasing students' reading ability than reading aloud to them because shared reading gave students the additional support of having the text in front of them during the reading. As readers encountered words that were new to them and they had both my voice support and the text in front of them, they became increasingly fluent. In addition, as a result of shared reading, students noted changes in their ability to choose appropriate and interesting books for independent reading as well as increased abilities in the areas of spelling, sentence structure, punctuation, and word choice. Ninth graders cited the following reasons why shared reading made such a difference to them:

- It's easier to understand when you are reading.
- This way we're all at the same place at the same time.
- You read fast and so our eyes move faster.
- We hear and see words we would not normally see.
- When I read alone, I have a hard time reading *and* thinking about the book.

While I consistently used read-aloud to demonstrate the breadth of reading, I used shared reading to illustrate its depth.

Tim, one of Nancy Roberts's students in Sarasota Middle School's Literacy Workshop, gives us a glimpse of what this time can mean for developing readers:

> Mrs. Roberts and I have seen it all. I've been in the strawberry fields with the Mexican migrant workers. I know people I've never talked to, I learned things I never knew. I've been on a Hippie bus with an old man named Dippy the Hippy. I've traveled through mines and dodged boulders. I've walked through Central High halls with Melba Beals and have seen with my mind the racism that was spat across her innocent face. Yea, I've seen it all without moving a muscle or going anywhere. Well, maybe to turn the page.

Whole-Group Shared Reading

Tim described the difference whole-group shared reading of novels made in his background knowledge during one semester in middle school. My students and I saw this type of shared reading as the heart of our curriculum. For Tim, the shared texts were both interesting and challenging, texts that students would want to read, and they were even more interesting and accessible because of the voice and reading support of the shared reading experience. As you may remember from your own student and teaching life, our experience with common texts doesn't always elicit such praise from students.

When I talk about the value of shared reading, a few teachers always ask, "But what if I spend all this time getting them to enjoy reading and then they get a high school teacher who doesn't believe in any of this—someone who just gives them boring books and tells them to read it for homework?" I always remind them that they can't control the kind of teachers or teaching students will have after they leave their classrooms, but they can control the kind of reading experience students have while they are with them. We don't need to give students negative reading experiences in order to get them ready for future negative experiences. We need to give them positive experiences so that they can develop reading strategies that can be transferred to any type of reading required of them at some future point in their lives. Shared reading is the place to demonstrate those strategies in a supported reading experience. Shared reading is not simply reading aloud to students. Shared reading is a purposeful reading of text designed to accomplish several purposes:

- Demonstrate fluent reading so students can experience the "charm, magic, impact, and appeal" of high-quality writing.
- Build bridges between reading and students' lives.
- Provide guided practice for strategies that made texts understandable.
- Model fluent reading behaviors for transfer to students' independent reading.
- Increase students' knowledge of the language, themselves, and the world.

Shared Reading Versus Round-Robin Reading

Shared reading is different from round-robin reading. In round-robin reading, where each student reads a few lines or paragraphs and then another student takes over, students are usually not taking the opportunity to use the support that comes with shared reading: eyes going past print with the support of a fluent reader's voice. One critical difference is that the voice support many readers can offer during round-robin reading is not fluent. Words are mispronounced, corrected, stumbled over. Sometimes entire sentences are left out and students stop the reading frequently to correct the reader or ask questions. The model of a fluent reading of the text is usually lost.

Second, students' eyes are often not on the text during round-robin reading. Students are counting and skipping ahead "trying to practice my own paragraph" and missing out on eyes passing print with voice support. Also, shared reading should be a time when the teacher is in control of the reading experience. As a teacher who is reading, I can stop to clarify or bring straggling or sleeping readers back to the text. I can occasionally ask questions that move students forward if they seem lost. I can stop to quickly make sure students have gained meaning from context. The student reader's goal is to get through the text—speed is often the most noted characteristic.

Finally, for most of us the task of oral reading remains a cognitive task. In Richard Lavoie's video *How Difficult Can This Be? The F.A.T. City Workshop,* which focuses on understanding learning disabilities, he makes the distinction between cognitive and associative tasks. Cognitive tasks are those that take all our concentration and focus; associative tasks are those that have become so automatic we could do several of them at the same time.

Have you ever had a speaker visit your classroom and watched the initial shock (and anxiety) as students entered the room? You can watch these visitors try to push themselves into a wall when the bell rings and students charge into the room asking, "Do I need anything to write with? What are we doing today? I was absent yesterday. Did I miss anything? Do we need our books? Are we having a sub?"

What scares these visitors is that we are able to answer all the questions almost at once: "Yes, you need something to write with. Look at the board. No, we decided not to learn anything until you returned—check the makeup notebook. Grab your books. I'm here, aren't I? Everyone ready?" And the class begins. All of this has occurred in about two minutes, and visitors think our ability to answer these questions with such rapidity is a sign of some abnormality. For the teacher who has answered those questions hundreds of times, the questions are now associative tasks. Many teachers aren't even listening to the questions; they just know what answers the students are waiting to hear. Answering those questions might become a more cognitive task on the day the teacher is being observed and evaluated for an annual review. Slowing down to consciously give positive feedback, delete sarcasm, monitor understanding, and clarify misunderstandings turns these questions into cognitive tasks. When that happens, we can answer only one question at a time.

Oral reading is like that. I have read "O Romeo, O, Like, Wow" (see Chapter 4) so many times that the reading has nearly become an associative task for me. I can read while gauging the audience's response, monitoring understanding of the language, controlling my reading speed, and so on. If, however, someone hands me something new and I'm asked to read it orally, I have to concentrate on the reading itself. My reading is not as fluent, and I might finish by wondering, "What did I just say?"

When all our cognitive focus is being used to decode, understand, create, or analyze (the meaning-making level), it interferes with reading fluency and the awareness of listeners' responses. If we are focused on basic decoding and pronunciation, meaning making is diminished. During round-robin reading, the person doing the oral reading is often the least able to comprehend the text and shape the reading to the listeners. By contrast, during shared reading, the decoding is done by the teacher (or tape), so student readers can focus their cognitive energies on the tasks of comprehension: visualizing, questioning, inferring, making word associations, predicting, connecting, and analyzing. As these comprehension tasks become automatic, they can be transferred to students' independent reading or a shared reading of more complex texts.

These incremental steps build developing readers' fluency through the modeling and support of the teacher's fluent reading. Shared reading offers support for students in terms of conditions for learning, resources, and instructional support for both *learning to read* and *reading to learn*.

Learning to Read	*Reading to Learn*
Reason for reading	Effective choice and use of strategies
Supportive environment	Activate or build background
Rich resources	knowledge
Extended time with text	Read text at multiple levels
Code knowledge	Establish purposes for reading
Guided choice	Use knowledge of text/genre to break
Personal connections	code
Active reading behaviors	Use appropriate study supports/
	resources
	Establish world knowledge connections
	Learn to manage text challenges

Shared reading provides the opportunity to move between these dual reading purposes that so often challenge students as they move from simple narrative to complex literary passages and expository texts. Each of these goals is established and reviewed in texts that students find meaningful, relevant, and worth revisiting.

Shared Reading and Independence

Why am I talking about shared reading in the context of independence? What I want to reference here is the use of recorded books to give the support of shared reading during times of independent reading. For many of my students, the engagement with books they experienced during our shared reading classes was lost when it was time for them to read independently. Each Monday and Friday (our independent reading days) there were always a few students who could not find a book in which they were interested that was also at their independent reading level. Those students would report reading everything from Golding's *Lord of the Flies* to Stephen King's Dark Tower series when I checked the status of the class, but after a couple of days, they abandoned those books in favor of some less difficult but also less interesting to them. These same students were also the ones who typically caused the most problems during this time of silent reading. In desperation, I finally began recording some of the students' favorite books so they could follow along with my voice support. As you might imagine, this was a task I could not possibly maintain for every student. Each day several students requested that I read their chosen books on tape. I quickly lost interest in sitting home every night recording books on tape.

Fortunately, I found several companies that were producing books on tape. After several purchases that proved problematic because the tapes did not match the text word for word, I discovered Recorded Books (see Appendixes A and D). This company not only offered a large young adult collection but also all the recordings were unabridged and therefore matched the texts students were reading. These recordings, together with the accompanying texts, afforded all readers the opportunity to read books at their interest level in spite of their reading difficulties. Using the published resources available allowed me the time to record many book *beginnings* on tape for those students who struggled with the challenges of the first chapter or two but who could then move on to independent reading. It also gave me time to record lots of picture books and nonfiction texts that were not available on tape. This process extended the support of shared reading into students' periods of sustained silent reading, providing yet another opportunity for increased reading fluency.

Shared Reading and Fluency

At the end of the first semester, I asked my students, How can teachers know whether students are becoming fluent readers? and What helps people become fluent readers? Their responses characterize several critical aspects of shared reading.

Characteristics of Fluent Readers
Reads a lot
Reads different kinds of books
Changes reading speed because of
    what they are reading and why
Reads for pleasure
Can talk about what was read
Knows what to skip when reading
Knows when having problems
Knows some solutions
Can use context to figure things
    out
Can reflect on reading
Makes personal connections to
    reading

What Creates Fluency?
Watching and listening to good
    reading
Time to read
Someone making reading sugges-
    tions (strategies)
Teachers and family reading
Someone showing different genres

The fluency and comprehension my students describe here are all directly or indirectly related to shared reading. Fluency is modeled for students each day as we come to the shared reading experience prepared to give students an opportunity to hear texts read in ways that can be interesting and meaningful to them.

However, having these productive reading experiences is not just a matter of grabbing a book and reading. Shared reading requires a great deal of preparation that ranges from purpose to practice. Questions I believe we need to ask (and answer) prior to any shared reading experience are these:

Why have I chosen this text for shared reading?

Why have I chosen to use the shared reading approach with this text?

What are the supports and challenges of the text?

How will I assess/build necessary background knowledge?

Are there words that are critical to text understanding that cannot be figured out using context clues?

Is the room arrangement supportive of shared reading?

Do students understand their roles as active readers during shared reading?

How will I help students maintain focus during shared reading?

Have I chosen appropriate places to stop?

How will I prepare for the shared reading experience so that I can give an engaging reading of the text?

How will I read the text and read the audience at the same time?

Do I have one or more strategies on which I'd like to focus before, during, or after this reading?

What will we do at the end of the reading? What connections will we make? How will transfer of learning be solidified?

I think the process of answering these questions can be illustrated using one of my favorite short stories. Following its reprinting here I describe my thinking and planning for using it as a shared reading experience.

"A Mouthful," from Uncovered! *(Jennings)*

Parents are embarrassing.

Take my dad. Every time a friend comes to stay the night, he does something that makes my face go red. Now don't get me wrong. He is a terrific dad. I love him but sometimes I think he will never grow up.

He loves playing practical jokes.

This behavior first started the night Anna came to sleep over.

Unknown to me, Dad sneaks into my room and puts Doona, our cat, on the spare bed. Doona loves sleeping on beds. What cat doesn't?

Next Dad unwraps a little package that he has bought at the magic shop.

Do you know what is in it? Can you believe this? It is a little piece of brown plastic cat poo. Pretend cat poo. Anyway he puts this piece of cat poo on Anna's pillow and pulls up the blankets. Then he tiptoes out and closes the door.

I do not know any of this is happening. Anna and I are sitting up late watching videos. We eat chips covered in sauce and drink two whole bottles of Diet Coke.

Finally we decide to go to bed. Anna takes ages and ages cleaning her teeth. She is one of those kids who is into health. She has a thing about germs. She always places paper on the toilet seat before she sits down. She is *so* clean.

Anyway, she puts on her tracksuit bottoms and gets ready for bed. Then she pulls back the blankets. Suddenly she sees the bit of cat's poo. "Ooh, ooh, ooh," she screams. "Oh, look, disgusting. Foul. Look what the cat's done on my pillow."

Suddenly Dad bursts into the room. "What's up, girls?" he says with a silly grin on his face. "What's all the fuss about?

Anna is pulling a terrible face. "Look," she says in horror as she points at the pillow.

Dad goes over and examines the plastic poo. "Don't let a little thing like that worry you," he says. He picks up the plastic poo and pops it into his mouth. He gives a grin. "D'licioush," he says through closed lips.

"Aargh," screams Anna. She rushes over to the window and throws up chips, sauce, and Diet Coke. Then she looks at Dad in disgust.

Dad is a bit taken aback at Anna being sick. "It's okay," he says, taking the plastic poo out of his mouth. "It's not real." Dad gives a laugh and off he goes. And off goes Anna. She decides that she wants to go home to her own house. And I don't blame her.

"Dad," I yell after Anna is gone. "I am never speaking to you again."

"Don't be such a baby," he says. "It's only a little joke."

It's always the same. Whenever a friend comes over to stay, Dad plays practical jokes. We have fake hands in the trash, exploding drinks, pepper in the food, shortsheeted beds, and Dracula's blood seeping out of Dad's mouth. Some of the kids think it's great. They wish their dads were like mine.

But I hate it. I just wish he was normal.

He plays tricks on Bianca.

And Yasmin.

And Nga.

And Karla.

None of them go home like Anna. But each time I am so embarrassed.

And now I am worried.

Cynthia is coming to stay. She is the school captain. She is beautiful. She is smart. Everyone wants to be her friend. And now she is sleeping over at our house.

"Dad," I say. "No practical jokes. Cynthia is very mature. Her father would never play practical jokes. She might not understand."

"No worries," says Dad.

Cynthia arrives, but we do not watch videos. We slave away on our English homework. We plan our speeches for the debate in the morning. We go over our parts in the school play. After all that, we go out and practice shooting baskets, because Cynthia is captain of the basketball team. Every now and then I pop into the bedroom to check for practical jokes. It is best to be on the safe side.

We also do the dishes because Cynthia offers—yes—*offers* to do it.

Finally it is time for bed. Cynthia changes into her nightie in the bathroom and then joins me in the bedroom. "The cat's on my bed," she says. "But it doesn't matter. I like cats.'" She pulls back the blankets.

And screams. "Aagh. Cat poo. Filthy cat poo on my pillow." She yells and yells and yells.

Just then Dad bursts into the room with a silly grin on his face. He goes over and looks at the brown object on the pillow. "Don't let a little thing like that worry you," he says. He picks it up and pops it into his mouth. But this time he does not give a grin. His face freezes over.

"Are you looking for this?" I say.

I hold up the bit of plastic poo that Dad had hidden under the blankets earlier that night.

Dad looks at the cat.

Then he rushes over to the window and is sick.

Cynthia and I laugh like mad.

We do love a good joke.

I have yet to see a group of students (or teachers) who did not enjoy this story, which brings me to my first point, about choosing this text for shared reading. This story is humorous and implies the pleasure of turn-around as fair play. Most students actually have a fairly keen sense of justice, and this story triggers that. This story will develop fluency because once students begin reading, they will want to continue with the text. Another reason I would choose this story is that this text has few challenges. Although this story is set in Australia, the language and context are familiar for readers. Thus, they will be able to return for repeated readings of this and other Jennings stories during their times of independent reading.

My planning for the use of this story as shared reading has several steps. The first is practicing the read-aloud so that the oral reading experience models fluent reading. Reading aloud requires practice, and that practice is even more critical when students are following the text with your support. The second step of preparation is identifying my purpose for using this story. Not only is this selection an enjoyable read, it also lends itself to predictions and confirmation or rejection of those predictions.

Having determined prediction as my strategy focus, I then plan the actual reading of the story. I would stop the reading in only a few places in this text because I wouldn't want to interrupt the fluency. The first place I would ask students to predict would be before beginning the text. This story offers a great opportunity for predictions based on the title of the short story and the cover of the book, *Uncovered! Weird, Weird Stories*. After predictions at this stage, I would read the beginning (from "Parents are" to "never grow up") and then ask students what they thought this father might be doing that would be so embarrassing to the daughter. "What things does your father do that embarrass you?" Students always give me an incredible range of ways their fathers have embarrassed them—everything from showing baby pictures and running around in their underwear to burping and asking friends to "pull my finger." Obviously, students are eager to take advantage of this opportunity to establish early, personal connections that will carry them through the story.

After their sharing of embarrassing parent stories, I would then continue reading the story with almost no further interruptions. At the point where the daughter describes the friend by saying, "She is *so* clean," I would ask students why they thought the author had put that word in italics. "Do you think he is trying to get us to make some guesses about what will happen next?" Most students would see the italics as an indication that her cleanliness would make what was going to happen even worse.

Maintaining focus with this story would not be an issue. For one thing, the text is relatively short; for another, it is so interesting students want to read it. It is almost impossible to interrupt the reading of this story for any kind of discussion because students will just continue reading. The story offers rich opportunity to go back through the text and look for ways the author led us to our predictions. Students will be asking for repeated readings of this as well as other Paul Jennings stories. This, of course, is one of the goals of effective shared reading.

In this shared experience, my strategy focus would have been on prediction as a way to active reading. There was no necessity for building background knowledge, but I would have wanted students to make that personal connection of dealing with aggravating parents early in the story. Had this been a novel, my instructional considerations would have been different. I would have taken into account several other areas represented in the list of shared reading questions: focus, pacing, vocabulary, background knowledge, and places to stop the extended reading.

In longer pieces, pacing is critical. Not every student can follow every word of the text, but I always ask them to do so. Those students who consistently followed with my reading were the ones who turned into readers more quickly, and they were also the ones with the most significant improvement on our district's reading test. Some students want to follow along but actually get lost after a few sentences. In order to help them, I use something I call RPMs to remind me to stop and help students who try to follow the text but get lost: R (recall), P (predict), M (move on) is a quick teaching strategy when you are reading and notice some students who can't find the place, have their books closed, or are "resting." When you get to an appropriate stopping point, say to the students: "I'm on the bottom of page 28. Who can tell me one thing that just happened (recall)? Who can tell me a prediction for our next three pages? OK, we're on the top of page 29. Everybody with me?" This abbreviated question and answer time lasts only a couple of minutes but it gives everyone the opportunity to make a fresh start at following the text.

A shared reading of this story has the potential to accomplish many reading purposes. We could have talked about local language ("pulling a terrible face"); use of italics for emphasis; prediction; foreshadowing; or story grammar characteristics (beginning, middle, end, rising action, turning point). Your reading goals and the natural language of the text that you have chosen provide the framework as you plan the reading curriculum. Finding and using appropriate texts is the key. When intriguing texts are chosen, the high levels of engagement and personal connection should move your students to accountable talk. This talk is one of the University of Pittsburgh's principles for learning and is characterized by certain features. Students engaged in accountable talk support their opinions, clarify and justify questions and comments, and actively extend and expand upon others' comments. I believe accountable talk is directly related to the quality of texts you make available to students during shared reading experiences.

Finding and Choosing Texts for Shared Reading

The kind of texts we choose as the resource for shared reading can make a critical difference in the success of this approach. In classes where students struggle with any reading, an independent reading of a novel can be overwhelming. For these students, I have found that some of the richest literary experiences came from the shared reading of entire novels. While many novels lend themselves to oral reading, I tried to choose novels that had rich dialogue, interesting characters, and intriguing conflicts as the focus for our shared reading. Choosing these novels or any other texts for whole-group shared reading is one of the most important and difficult aspects of teaching reading. Most of us have experienced the unsettling dilemma of planning an entire unit around the shared reading of a lengthy text and finding that students hate the book and view the reading experience as painful and boring. So, how do we avoid that trap?

Two knowledge bases are critical in choosing reading that will be successful as a shared experience: knowledge of your students and knowledge of resources.

I always recommend that teachers spend a good amount of time at the beginning of the year getting to know the students in their classrooms before starting their first shared reading of a novel. I used different beginning-of-the-year questions each year; some of those I found helpful in making choices for books are listed here. As I looked for patterns for each individual response, which assisted me in helping students with independent reading, I also put surveys together by class to establish patterns that would help me choose appropriate shared reading for each class. At any given moment in our year, each class might be reading a shared reading novel unique to that class.

> What books, plays, or other texts have you read in previous English classes that you have enjoyed? disliked?
>
> When you choose a book, what type of books do you choose (horror, suspense, adventure, westerns, biographies/autobiographies, contemporary realistic fiction, historical fiction, science fiction, fantasy, poetry, nonfiction, short stories, plays)? What are some titles you have read and enjoyed in one or more of these types of literature?
>
> What books have you read in the last year?
>
> Do you have a favorite author? If so, who?
>
> What are your favorite magazines?
>
> What are your favorite movies/television shows?
>
> What are your interests/hobbies?
>
> What school subjects interest you the most? the least?

These surveys are wonderful sources of information that give you significant amounts of background knowledge related to students' reading choices and authors; what makes reading difficult for them; what their previous reading experiences have been like; and perceptions of themselves as readers. The student who completed the survey shown in Figure 5.1 was able to identify his favorite author (R. L. Stine); his favorite reading (even though it wasn't included in the choices); his perceptions of reading difficulties; and what would make reading more enjoyable to him ("not having to get twelve points"). If I had an entire class of students who had similar responses in their surveys, my shared reading decisions would take the following areas into consideration in narrowing our selections: horror/suspense, adventure, shorter novels, hunting stories. Authors and titles I might include would be Sachar's *Holes,* Rawls's *Where the Red Fern Grows,* Spinelli's *Wringer,* Hobbs's *The Maze,* or Robb White's *Deathwatch.*

Another technique I used at the beginning of the year before choosing a whole-class novel was reading a lot of short works: short stories, excerpts from novels, articles, poetry. By gauging students' responses to content, length, readability, attention span, and interest level in these shorter works, I was able to make some fairly accurate predictions about longer works students would enjoy.

Male _✓_ Female _____ Age _12_

READING SURVEY

1. How often do you read? *1, 2, 3, times a day*

2. What types of books have you read this year?

___horror ___romance ___realistic fiction ✓ *sports magazines*

___westerns ___comedy ___mystery/suspense

3. Do you consider yourself a good reader? Why/why not? *I'm okay because I get enough pratice even though I don't read a lot.*

4. Do you remember being read to as a child? *yes*

5. What is the first book you ever read? *Morris goes to school*

6. What was the last book you read? *Flight to Fear*

7. Was the book listed in #6 assigned to you or did you read it just because you wanted to read? *I chosse to read it*

8. Who is your favorite author? *R.L. Stine*

9. Does anyone ever read to you? If so, who, and what do they read? *My dad reads the want ads to me*

10. Who is the best reader you know? *My Mom*

11. What do you think makes this person a good reader? *pratice*

12. Do you like to read? *Not really I like reading hunting magazines though*

13. What motivates you to read? Curiosity? Seeking new information? An assignment from a teacher? *Pictures (curiosity)*

14. In what ways could reading be more pleasurable for you? *Not having to get 12 points*

15. Do you have a public library card? *yes*

16. Tell me something about reading that I haven't already asked. *I read slowly so I can take in as much information I can get.*

Figure 5.1

Knowing resources is actually much more difficult than getting to know your students. With so many new books being published, it is difficult to keep up with everything that might serve as a beneficial reading experience in your classroom. Three critical components that will affect your ability to infuse a wide range of reading into your shared reading are time to read, finding a variety of readings, and keeping track for retrieval purposes. Time to read is not usually a difficulty for me. People always marvel at how many books I read each month, but I spend long hours in airports and flying. I always use that time as reading time. Of course, I use lots of time to read when I should be doing other things as well! Even when I was a full-time teacher, I had plenty of time to read because I always read with students during independent reading time, while supervising Saturday detention, and on long bus rides to basketball games. Reading during independent reading time gave me at least forty-five minutes per week in each of my classes (and more in my block classes). Most young adult novels can be read in a couple of hours so that time alone gave me the opportunity to read two to four novels per week.

For me, finding the books to read has never been an issue. I use several resources consistently. I go to an online bookstore a couple of times each month. I put in titles (*Holes* by Sachar), authors (Chris Crutcher), genres (short stories and young adult literature), or topics (juvenile detention centers, gangs) and follow the paths the bookstore creates for me. I read abstracts and follow leads by looking at "other people who ordered this also ordered" and "other books by the same author or authors like this author." I buy many more books than I should, but I use them not only for reading enjoyment but also for writing and sharing with teachers. I subscribe to journals that offer lists of books in each issue and buy reference books that provide me topical lists of books: high interest/easy reading, boys' or girls' books, and those suited for bibliotherapy (see Appendix A). I also keep a small notebook in my purse or briefcase in order to jot down titles others recommend to me in my travels. From all those resources, I have no problem finding books—the greater problem is paying for all I find.

Keeping track of what I've read has always been the biggest problem for me. I know the importance of developing a system for retrieving titles and authors because I have seen how having those names can make a difference in students' independent reading. I also know from many years' experience that I can't just remember the titles, authors, themes, and connections. I've tried most traditional forms of keeping track: reading logs, notecards, and journals. This year I have attacked the problem with new fervor and have started noting books I've read in a word-processed reading journal. Two samples from my journal are reprinted here. As you read them, you'll note I've made connections to shared reading (short stories to novels, novels to other novels) and overall interest. I've also cited passages I thought could make good models for writing.

Anderson, Laurie Halse. 1999. *Speak*. New York: Farrar, Straus, Giroux. 0-374-37152-0 (198 pp. Hardcover)
An incredible book! Told from Melinda's ninth grade pov, the story of Melinda's rape unravels. Melinda has all but stopped speaking for fear that she would speak the unspeakable. She is a school pariah in ninth

grade because she has called the police at the summer party where she was raped. When the police arrived, she ran home (didn't report the rape) and everyone thought she called the police just to get them in trouble. Tree metaphors throughout as Melinda finds her voice. There is great humor in the writing (especially related to teachers and classes) and a sensitivity that is uncommon, yet believable, in one so young.

Curtis, Christopher Paul. 1999. *Bud, Not Buddy*. New York: Delacorte Press. 0-385-32306-9 (243 pp. Hardcover)
Told through the wonderful eyes and ears of Buddy Caldwell, this story of loss and family is one of the best I've ever read. When Bud's single mother dies, he is left alone in Flint, Michigan. He is placed in a horrible foster home from which he escapes. Having nothing except a few signpost papers advertising a bandleader, H. E. Calloway, Bud sets out to find the man, believing this man to be his father. When he finds Calloway, he learns that Calloway is his grandfather. Set in the Great Depression. Bud has the same incredible sense of humor that we found in *The Watsons Go to Birmingham—1963*. **Chapter 6 (45–52) great read-aloud. p. 80/ good quote about talking too much about what stories mean.

If this method seems a bit extensive for your purposes (and it would have been for me when I was a full-time teacher), you might prefer the method shown in Figure 5.2. This is the table of contents from Gallo's *Time Capsule*, which I annotated as I read each story. As I read short story collections, poetry, or novels, I write

Figure 5.2

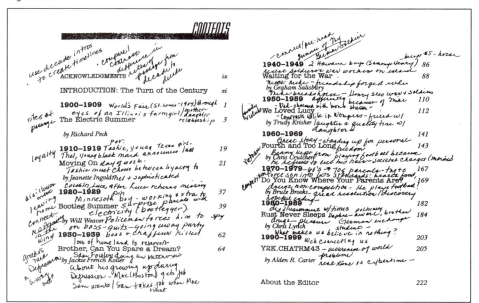

notes on the contents pages next to each short story, poem, or chapter title as a reference for later use. In this way, I can quickly go back to the book for reference.

The key is developing a system that works for you. I have spent hundreds of dollars on journals to keep with me so that I could log my reading. Each journal contains two or three book notes and is now stacked on a shelf. The journals didn't fit in my purse. I needed ones where the covers folded back for writing support. I couldn't use ones without lines. I know I'm not alone in this craziness. I've been in lots of teachers' home and seen similar stacks. Finding a quick, easy, accessible way to keep track of books is individual. I now jot things down directly in the book, stack the books by the computer, and enter one each time I sit down to respond to my e-mail. It works for me.

As I read novels, I make decisions about whether those novels are ones I would choose to share with students in a shared reading approach. For novels I plan to use with a whole class, I fill out a "guiding readers through the text" form. The example in Figure 5.3 is the first section of the guide for Fenner's *The King of Dragons* showing how many pages I plan to read, the strategy lessons, writing prompts, and follow-up. When the guide is completed, I place it into an individual notebook; each notebook has a cover and spine noting the title or theme.

These guides are not study guides for students nor are they comprehension checks; they are reminders for me of purposeful ways this text lends itself to the teaching of strategic literacy. As I'm reading and discover pieces of nonfiction, poetry, short stories, historical information, cartoons, or articles that would fit with the novel or theme, I put those pieces in the notebook with the reading guide. Poems and other short supplementary readings are put onto overhead transparencies so they too can be used for shared reading. This planning seems extensive, and it is, but these guides actually cover several weeks of instructional

Figure 5.3

Page Numbers	Possibilities to Explore	Additional Ideas
1 - 19	(1) prediction with first two paragraphs What questions do we have at bottom of page 1? (1) writing -- effective leads (2) new evidence for predictions (3) What have we learned about dad so far? (17) What do italics indicate to readers? (18) "Ralsky will help keep you alive. Learn something." Beginning list of things to learn (19) end of reading -- What do we know? (use guided literature response here).	

GUIDING READERS THROUGH THE TEXT
The King of Dragons

time and combine all the language arts. These are easier and richer to make when created with other teachers who plan to use the same novels for shared reading.

Lana Clark, a high school English teacher in Marion County, Florida, recently sent me an e-mail after discovering the value of developing a system for keeping artifacts that would enrich her students' shared reading experience with Hesse's *Out of the Dust*:

> I just thought I'd tell you what jumped from the old memory bank when my class started reading *Out of the Dust*. As we read, I remembered my great-grandma's scrapbooks that I have in the closet—from the 1930s, 40s, 50s. She had so much foresight! She clipped things from several newspapers that interested her and preserved them in scrapbooks. I remembered many articles on multiple births and the Lindbergh baby's kidnapping. When I got it out, I had a chronicle of the Dionne quintuplets from birth until one married and Marie died. I even found their doctor's obituary! I also had pictures of the Lindberghs before they married, when the baby was born, and several other interesting articles after the kidnapping. These were among the articles about 10- and 12-year-old girls having babies by 90-year-old men (Grandma was interested in many things.) I copied the articles and made a folder of news clippings to accompany the novel. Incidentally, the kids loved it! Two girls read the entire "book" on the first night.

Most of us have had the experience of finding the perfect poem, article, or short story that would have helped our students understand some aspect of a text but discovering it in a pile weeks after we finished the book. These guide notebooks provide a way to keep those resources together and accessible.

Finally, I create any writing connections or strategy lessons I would use in relation to this novel and include them in the notebook as well. Each guide leaves room for me to jot down new ideas my students and I have as we read this novel, and those resources are then available to me if I share this novel with another class. I would not use all the strategy lessons included in each novel notebook because students wouldn't always need them, but they are there for use when I do need them. These guides and strategy lessons are also great resources for small-group guided reading (see Chapter 6) with students who need extra support. The guides helped move me away from my role as assigner and comprehension checker and into my role as a *teacher* of strategic reading.

Modeling and Supporting Strategic Reading

Connecting the teaching of reading strategies to shared reading texts can seem like a difficult and counterproductive activity. After a particularly satisfying day of reading together, it somehow seems sad to turn the reading from pleasure to "work." Jip, in Katherine Paterson's *Jip, His Story,* knows what that experience is like. "Now Jip was just an ignorant boy and it wasn't his business, he knew, to try to tell a writer how to write a book, but it stood to reason that if you want to catch a reader tight, the trap needs to be plain and strong with no smell of the trapper lingering on it" (112). We don't want our strategy lessons to be so extensive and intrusive that students avoid reading because they see it as a trap!

In spite of not wanting to diminish the experience of reading, we do want students to leave the reading of a text with new knowledge and strategies for transfer of that knowledge to other texts. We also want them to take away from those experiences information and strategies that can be transferred to other learning opportunities that may or may not be text-based. Strategy lessons should support students as they move beyond the literal level (answers stated explicitly in the text) to the inferential level (answers implied by the text by combining several pieces of information, connecting personal background knowledge and knowledge of the world) and to the metacognitive level (students examine their thinking and learning processes). Researchers, teachers, and students have created a variety of ways to make these levels concrete, understandable, and transferable. Figure 5.4 shows how Ann Bailey's middle school students keep track of the strategies

Figure 5.4

they are learning. These lists stay on the wall as a reference for students as they move toward becoming more confident and competent readers.

Overcoming Text Challenges with Shared Reading

It might seem that I'm suggesting the importance of shared reading only for students who can't read well, but I am not. Shared reading provides access to texts too difficult for independent reading, and those levels of text can be increased and become more diverse as students' reading levels change. I usually spend a few hours each week in bookstores trying to find new books, and from the numbers of students standing at the *Cliffs Notes* rack, I can attest to the fact that thousands of our best students never read the assigned texts in the originals. For many students, these texts seem too challenging, so they never make it past the first chapter. They quickly discover they can manage with the *Cliffs Notes* summaries and the teacher's in-depth discussions of the assigned reading. In this manner, they are often dragged unwillingly through the secondary school literature curriculum, moving from Dickens to Twain and Faulkner to Ibsen with little noticeable change in their delight in or understanding of the beauty of language. In addition, many students do little or no reading while these works are taken up because they see themselves as studying a text rather than reading a text. I believe there are ways shared reading could make these reading experiences more effective and the literary experiences more meaningful.

One use of shared reading to overcome challenging texts is as an introduction to the text. Even if teachers plan to have students read a novel entirely as an independent reading experience (certainly an appropriate assignment for many middle and secondary students), the first chapter could be read together in a shared reading format. With students following the text as the teacher reads the first chapter, they can see and hear words or concepts that are integral to this novel and its setting. The first chapter usually has a lengthy description of setting, introduces many of the main characters, and often foreshadows the novel's conflicts. In addition, literary techniques such as flashback are often found in the first chapter.

If the first chapter is read with the shared reading approach, the teacher can fill in some of the geographic or descriptive gaps between students' reading and life experiences and the author's assumptions implicit in the writing. Students' questions and discussion will move the entire class into a different reading of the text than they might otherwise have had. Pronouncing difficult names or places as well as giving a voice to new characters can help students begin to create a mental image of the text. Students are then able to move on to the independent reading with a broader knowledge base than an individual reading might have provided.

Shared reading can also be used to build background knowledge that will support readers as they move into more challenging texts. A shared reading of Sara Holbrook's poem "Naked," from her collection *Chicks Up Front,* makes a lasting reader connection that leads students into Holocaust literature.

Naked
The first time I saw a man naked,
it was not my brother.
I was born without a brother,
which everyone knows
is like being born without green hair,
or a wart on the tip of your nose,
or the skin of a reptile.
Being born with no brother was a definite asset,
or so I thought until fifth grade, when I started to wonder.
I wondered why every time I would mention the word "it,"
in any context,
the boys would laugh—they'd fall on the ground.
Likewise, if I would say the word "them,"
in any context, the boys would laugh—they'd fall on the ground.
It was as if we were tuned into two different programs,
like they were tuned into cartoons
and I was watching a mystery.
I wondered.
And I wondered with the sense of urgency
of 4:30 in the afternoon and Mom says,
"No more snacks before dinner,"
and you're starving.
I wanted what I wanted and I wanted it now.

Prevailing neighborhood trade policies
provided for such things,
a look for a look, even up.
Worth considering,
until a permission slip came home from school.
There was to be a film about growing up.
Well, even I knew that was fiftiespeak for "naked."
My wonder swelled within me—
I had swallowed a balloon.
I couldn't breathe.
Breathless, until the film showed us diagrams.

Diagrams? Bones without the meat.
It looked like a direction sheet on how to assemble a bicycle.
Absolutely no help at all. I deflated gradually.
A couple weeks later, another film.
No permission slip this time.
Just a film about the war of our fathers, World War II.
Germany. Hitler youth. Wind up soldiers.
Waving train cars.
Pits of white, white limbs. Ovens, not for cakes.
Three men standing against a fence, heads shaved.
Their collar bones poking out like
coat hangers without the clothes.
The picture was cut off at the hollow places where
their bellies belonged.
Except for one man, standing in the background,
who stepped deliberately to the side.
Stripped of any sense of wonder or urgency,
he made no attempt to cover himself.
He faced the camera because he wanted me to see.

I dragged my feet a little on the way
home from school that day,
kicking aimlessly at the fallen leaves.
Not so much in a hurry.
After all, I had seen.
For the first time,
I had seen a man,
Naked.

Because shared reading gives students the opportunity to reread, they are able to return to the text to look at genre, text composition, figurative and literal language. Knowledge gained in these accessible ways helps students as they move into more challenging texts. The depth of the personal connection to such shared readings also makes students want to know more about the event.

Once your shared reading is complete for the day, students can also return to the text for extended thinking, questioning, noting of author's intentions, and searching for writer's craft. Strategies for using the shared reading approach as a vehicle for developing readers' strategies and language acquisition are detailed in Chapters 8, 9, and 10. The critical point here is that shared reading has made decoding an associative task for students because the teacher has taken on the task of decoding. This leaves readers' minds free to focus on deeper meaning, questioning, and critical aspects of point of view.

Sharing the Magic

On one of my last teaching days before leaving my high school classroom in Maine, I had elicited some student help in packing and labeling boxes. Some of my personal book collection was being left behind for other teachers, and other books were going with me to my new job in Florida. The bookshelves and racks were quickly emptied as I chose "go" or "stay" boxes. When one of the students in our Literacy Workshop came in the next morning, she burst into tears and said, "You've packed away all the magic." For the students in my classes whose previous connections with books had been anything but magical, this was a significant statement.

Tori's statement reminded me of the importance of shared reading as the core of our reading curriculum. I had built that portion of every week around the tenet that people repeat behaviors that are pleasurable. I had tried to choose texts for each shared reading session that would leave students with the sense that reading offers information in enjoyable ways, and I had tried to read them in a way that made the text come alive. I was not consumed with making sure that all our lessons were fun or easy; in fact, I would say that many of the texts were chosen because they were enjoyable *and* challenging. I did want students to leave each of these literacy experiences having lived the critical condition of engagement so that the motivation was there for them to return to books when I wasn't there.

Sarah's words always remind me of the liberating experience it must be when a student who has given up on books suddenly discovers a way to unlock that magical world.

> I disliked all my English classes. I never wanted to go. In Reading, I hated to read because I had a hard time to read. I was the one who would take forever to read a paragraph. Well books never really interested me. May be the books that we *had* to read were *boring*. When I got to my ninth grade reading class, well we can safely say I was not happy. But after a while I got comfortable. After hearing you reading out loud, maybe after the second book or so, I wanted to read my own fun filled book. After I read that one, I wanted to read more and more. Well, counting the books that were read out loud, I read about 17 books. Now the best books I've read, I've read in about two days and before, it took me weeks at a time!

Sarah and other students who participate in engaging shared reading have the opportunity to participate in the *experience* of reading—not just the skill of reading but the experience of words making us see the world in a different way. They experience what Charlotte Huck describes as the transforming power of literature: "to take us out of ourselves and return us to ourselves, a changed self" (1987, 69). Shared reading is the *heart* of the reading curriculum.

6

Guided Reading: "On the Run" Strategies Toward Independence

Ultimately, the test is whether the approach responds to the children's learning needs and helps them develop a self-extending reading system, one that fuels its own learning and enables the reader to continue to learn through the act of reading.

IRENE C. FOUNTAS AND GAY SU PINNELL, GUIDED READING: GOOD FIRST TEACHING FOR ALL CHILDREN

Fountas and Pinnell consider guided reading "the heart of a balanced literacy program" (1), but most of my students believed shared reading was the heart of our literacy program. I understand their favoring shared reading over guided reading. Certainly my favorite part of our literacy block was shared, rather than guided, reading. However, in a comprehensive literacy classroom, we don't have to choose one or the other. Each has its distinct purposes, and each meets the needs of certain types of readers. The first goal of shared reading is a relatively uninterrupted fluent reading of the text; the first goal of guided reading is establishing or reinforcing strategic processes by interrupting the text at key points.

Guided reading has generally been seen as benefiting to younger students who are emerging readers. The same benefits can be achieved with older readers as long as your schedule allows for time when you are able to work with individuals or small groups of students. Guided reading afforded me the greatest opportunity to reinforce reading strategies, introduce new strategies, and help students make critical connections between texts and readers. It also gave me time to do careful observations of readers *in the process of reading*.

The two questions I am asked most often about guided reading are How does guided reading differ from shared reading? and What is the difference between guided reading and what we have always done? Guided reading differs from shared reading in a number of ways. Teacher-led shared reading is most often done with the entire class; guided reading is typically done with a small group of students who have common strategy supports and challenges in place. While the shared reading text is read orally by the teacher, the guided reading text is read silently by students. Shared reading is a relatively uninterrupted reading of the text. Guided reading is done as the teacher directs students to read certain passages of text and then stops them for questioning, connecting, strategizing, predicting, and reinforcing.

How does this differ from the kind of reading and questioning typically seen in most language arts classes? I think the greatest difference is found by examining the purpose of guided reading. In *Reading To, With, and By Children*, Mooney describes the purpose of guided reading: "The aim of guided reading is to develop independent readers who question, consider alternatives, and make informed choices as they seek meaning. Guided reading is an enabling and empowering approach where the focus is on the child as a long-term learner being shown how and why and which strategies to select and employ to ensure that meaning is gained and maintained during the reading and beyond" (47).

When we look at the way teachers and students interact in a typical experience with text, we often find teachers asking lots of questions (often prepared in advance or found in guides) as a way of checking on students' understanding or extending the content of the text. These kinds of questions might be called product-oriented. We ask a question, get an answer, and move on. In fact, a student intern in my class recently asked a teacher about text-related discussions, and his advice was "Get in and get out before they have a chance to get off task." If we define our goal as checking for literal-level comprehension, that might be good advice. While some lively discussions may take place during these teaching moments, the discussions and rapid-fire responses often involve only a few students in the class. Further, the questions and answers usually focus on fact or motivation at a literal level. Teachers often see this kind of questioning as important because many students do not understand (or have not read) the text under discussion. This practice is often labeled "guiding readers through text" in teacher's guides and manuals, but it is not guided reading.

If we see our task as helping students bring to a conscious level how meaning is made from diverse texts and how those meaning-making strategies are transferred to other texts, then this "get in and get out" advice is not very helpful. For me, the most helpful way of thinking about guided reading has been to see it as bringing readers up to a conscious level of decision making to make sense of a text.

Perhaps the easiest way for me to illustrate the difference between guided reading and guiding readers through text at the secondary level is by looking at the way I would have taught differently depending on whether my goals were ones that could be accomplished with guided reading or ones that could be accomplished by guiding readers through text.

The piece I use here as an example is a short story by Edward M. Holmes titled "The Day of the Hunter" (see Appendix G), which I have used many times with middle and secondary students in guided reading lessons. If I had been guiding readers through text, I would have assigned the story to be read silently. When I assumed most students had finished the story, I would have begun asking questions. In this case, the questions would have been based on the basic plotline of the story, the main idea or theme, characters' motivations, the sequence of events, the impact of setting on the story, the conflict and the resolution of that conflict, and the author's style. Typically, the questions would have been asked by me and answered by a relatively small number of students. I would seldom ask students to go back to the text and support their answers, or ask them about the thinking processes they used to help them make sense of the story.

In contrast, the guided reading lesson that follows is from a session with an entire class of ninth-grade students who were not using several active reading processes: making predictions before and during reading; supporting opinions by using the text; and reading between the lines to try to understand the author's purposes and intentions. While guided reading is almost always carried out with only a small group of students in order to introduce or reinforce specific strategies, this entire class (fifteen students in Literacy Workshop) did not have these strategies as part of their reading repertoire. In addition, the difficulty of reading this text was low enough that the students were all capable of reading it with relative independence (or they would have skipped words they thought did not matter).

A Guided Reading Lesson

Setting the Stage

In guided reading the teacher is still responsible for introducing the story by activating and building background knowledge necessary for the content and helping students establish personal connections to the reading. Therefore, before we started reading the story, I explained to students the importance of making predictions or guesses so we could focus our thinking before and during reading. We discussed how we make predictions by creating a list of possibilities that lead us to those educated guesses. At this point, students had two items on their lists: what the book says and stuff we know.

I used their suggestions and asked them to make some educated guesses about this story's content based on the words in the title and "the stuff they knew." The title of the story, "The Day of the Hunter," and the title of the anthology, *Maine Speaks,* both served as good resources for prediction. When I told them that they could draw or write their predictions, they quickly went to work. Since the story was found in an anthology of Maine writing, many of the students made the deer hunting connection as their initial prediction.

"Probably about a guy who is out hunting for deer."

"He could be hunting something else."

"Yeah, like birds or rabbits or moose."

"Could be about the day he shot the biggest deer."

"Or his best experiences."

When I asked them to think of any other kind of hunting they had ever read about, several students mentioned a short story we had read together, Connell's classic "The Most Dangerous Game," as being about hunting, but about hunting a man. However, most of the students had made drawings or written predictions connecting hunting and animals, and most of them thought this story was about deer hunting.

I then asked them to think about why an author might title a story, "The Day of . . ." if this was an event as common as deer hunting. Again, most students went back to their original predictions that this was going to be about the biggest deer or the best deer hunting experience that this guy (or maybe anyone) had ever experienced. We listed the group predictions, and I asked them to keep the written/drawn predictions in front of them so we could come back and revise them at different points throughout our reading of the story.

Thinking Through the Story

I had copied the story and cut it into strips for this activity because I found that otherwise students would read quickly to the end of the story to "find out what happens." I wanted this close reading to help students develop thinking, questioning, and connecting strategies during the reading. Prior to the lesson, I had cut the guided reading text into strips, numbered and folded the strips, and asked students to take the strips from their envelopes one number at a time. Since then, I have started putting the guided reading texts on overhead transparencies. Each overhead has the text I want students to read independently, and a visual scan of the room can quickly tell me whether students are still reading. This method actually turned out to be the most successful in terms of keeping students engaged in the process of reading. The overheads take some time to create but if saved by covering with sheet protectors and numbered for order, they have the advantage of allowing the teacher to transcribe students' questions and notations about language, events, or words that led to their predictions directly onto the text during discussion. These can be wiped clean after the lesson and be ready to use for another class, group, or individual guided reading.

At that time, however, I was still using the numbered strips. The first strip contained the first paragraph of the story, a piece long enough to have meaning, yet short enough not to overwhelm.

Everyone in his home town somewhere east of the Penobscot River knew that, in or out of season, Lyle Hanscom and deer hunting were inseparable. Yet for years no one had been able to garner enough evidence to convict him. Once several casual spectators, stopping along the highway to watch three deer at the other side of a wide field, not only heard the shot that felled one of the animals, but saw a man run from a spruce grove and drag the game back into the woods. No one could quite recognize the man in the strange, drooping overcoat he was wearing, nor was anyone able to track him with success. Still, the town's rumor mill, talk of someone's cooperative dump truck—which circled the town for an hour or two with a dead deer lying in the back—and public confidence in Lyle Hanscom's unparalleled gall unofficially pinned the deed on him.

When students finished their silent reading of this paragraph, I asked them whether they thought it supported the predictions they had made. Since most of them had predicted deer hunting, they felt some immediate success. We then explored the ways the author was telling us about Lyle's character even before we actually met him. I asked them to take a minute and work with a partner to complete as much of the Knowing a Character chart as they could, supporting each item on the chart with specific evidence from the story. Students were able to gather the details shown here as ones that were supported by the text.

Character's Talk	*Character's Actions*	*What Others Say*
None heard yet	None anyone can prove yet	Lyle and deer hunting inseparable
		People had tried to convict him
		Suspected of poaching
		Suspected of driving around with a dead deer
		"Unparalleled gall"

Students had listed "unparalleled gall," so I asked them what it meant. No one had any idea. So we went back to the text to see if there were any clues. They thought it was something bad because it was in the same part about "the dump truck and rumors," but they didn't know what it was. I asked students what they had done when they came to that phrase while reading. They all said they had skipped over it. I gave them a few examples of unparalleled gall: "If the principal came in and told me I had to supervise students during noontime detention, and I told him, 'When pigs fly,' I'd have unparalleled gall." After several similar examples, students finally understood the magnitude of Lyle's disregard for the law. Then Derek asked, "If the author wanted to tell us this, why didn't he just come out and say it? Why did he try to ruin a good hunting story by hiding stuff on us?" Certainly this was a teachable moment about reading between the lines!

"So, given what we now know about unparalleled gall and what we suspect about Lyle, what do you think might happen to Lyle here?"

"Someday, I'll bet he's gonna mess with the wrong cop!"

I asked students to continue their reading of the story but this time I wanted them to see if they could find more evidence of Lyle's disregard for the law while they read.

> Small wonder, then, that the nearest game warden kept a sharp watch, as often as he could, on Hanscom. The time came when the officer felt he had something on his man. Somehow word had leaked to him that Lyle had sneaked home with fresh-killed meat. When the warden drove up to Hanscom's, he could see the suspect watching him from one of the front windows. Hanscom met the law at the door and admitted him without a search warrant.
>
> "I'd like to have a look around, if you don't mind, Lyle."
>
> "Don't mind a bit, Joey. Look all you want," Hanscom said. "There's just one thing I want to ask of you."
>
> "Ayeah?"
>
> "My mother in there in the bedchamber is sick. She's had a heart attack."
>
> "Is that so? I'm sorry to hear that."
>
> "Well, you can understand I don't want nothing done that would upset her. You can see that, can't you, Joey?"
>
> "I got to look in that room, same as any other, Lyle."
>
> "Oh, I know that. I just ask that you don't upset her none. Might bring on another attack."

As the students finished reading this portion of the story, I knew they were puzzled. "Now I'm confused," I said. "Lyle isn't what I expected. Anyone else thinking the same thing?"

"Why is he being so nice, anyway? I thought a guy like him would be a jerk."

"What was there in the story that made you think he was a jerk?"

"Well, he shoved it in people's faces that he could get away with poaching a deer."

"What did you read that made you think that?"

"It says right here that he put the deer right on the truck where everyone could see it."

"Hmm. . . . Can you think of any reasons why the author has him acting differently from what you expected?"

"I don't think he's trying to trick us. I think maybe people just misjudged Lyle."

"Is there anything in what you just read that surprised you?"

"He lives with his mother! How old is this guy anyway?"

"He's really worried about her."

"How do you know that?"

"'Cause he doesn't want the cop to bother her."

"I'm thinking about the relationship between Lyle and this game warden. Did any of you notice anything in there that could give us hints about that relationship?"

"Well, he calls him by his first name so maybe they know each other?"

"It says that the warden 'kept a sharp watch.' I think that means that he doesn't trust him."

"But he let him in without a search warrant. I don't think Lyle hates him or anything."

"Those are really good connections. Any predictions about why Lyle is being so nice?" Several students responded that they thought Lyle was just trying to get away with something. "So, should I worry on days when you're nice to me?" Students laughed as they took time to revise their predictions based on new information. I asked them to continue reading the story while looking for evidence that Lyle might be hiding something.

"I'll be careful," Joey said, and began making his search of the kitchen, the three small rooms, and the attic. He apologized to Mrs. Hanscom for intruding upon her, looked under the bed, and would have searched the closets if he could have found any. Back in the kitchen, Lyle sat in a rocking chair, smoking his pipe. "Guess I'll have to take a look in the cellar," the warden said.

"No, I guess you won't neither," Lyle said.

"How's that?"

"I let you in here nice as could be, Joey, and give you a chance to look around. You know as well as I do, I didn't have to. I even let you look in the room where my mother was laying sick, but I draw a line at the cellar. I don't want no game wardens nor nobody else poking around in no cellar of mine."

"You know I don't have to go above two miles," Joey said, "to get me a warrant."

"Then you'll just have to do it that way," Lyle said. "Call it a freak notion if you want, but I ain't giving no man permission to snoop in my cellar."

"I'm wondering what he's up to now."

"He's still being polite. He didn't have to let that warden in at all; I wouldn't have."

"Yeah, we all know why you wouldn't." The class erupts in laughter.

"What do you think? Do you all agree that Lyle is still being polite?" They nod, but I could tell they were increasingly unsure of Lyle's intentions.

"Well, he's not yelling at him or nothin' but he's getting his point across."

"What makes you say that?"

"'Cause he just tells him no and that's it."

"I think he's got that deer down in the cellar."

"If he does have it down there, now the warden knows because he won't let him go down there."

"He mentioned his mother's room again, but maybe he's just pointing out that he let the warden in when he didn't have to."

I told them that Lyle and the author both still had me guessing and gave the students time to revise their predictions. Most of their drawings now had something that looked like a deer head sticking out from under a house. Then I asked them to finish the story silently.

So Joey did it that way. When he came back, he presented Lyle with the warrant, and Lyle read it, every word, as slow as he could. "All right, warden, I see I'll have to let you look in the cellar if you're bound and determined to do it. You may have a mite of trouble, though: so far as I know, this house is built on cedar posts. I ain't crawled underneath lately looking for no cellar, but of course you might find one."

It was built on cedar posts, too, about a foot off the ground, and that was the end of that, except, of course, that Lyle Hanscom's mother has given him notice, if he ever puts a fresh-killed deer in bed with her again, heart attack or no heart attack, she will turn him over to the warden herself.

The class was filled with pandemonium. "I knew he had that deer hidden in the bed!"

"Why didn't the warden find it, then?"

"He had it in the cellar, then he dragged it in while the warden got the warrant."

"That's stupid. There isn't a cellar."

"You could do it. You could wrap it up and stick it under there."

I could barely make myself heard over their excited comments. "So, how did that author turn us around like that? What gave you your clues? Were your predictions confirmed?" As students listed their predictions (made after reading the third section), it turned out that there were two categories of predictions: the deer was hidden in the cellar or the deer was in bed with the mother. At that point I asked students to work with one or two other people who had the same prediction so that they could "track their predictions," trying to find evidence that supported their thinking throughout the story.

Making Conscious Connections for Transfer

By the time students finished this task, we were able to talk about the importance of reading between the lines and supporting our opinions with clues or facts given in the text. We also talked about the importance of making predictions, confirming or rejecting those predictions as we read, and then making new predictions based on information we find as the story evolves. We went back to our initial list of ways we can make predictions, and students now added several other supports: the tone of voice, knowing something about where it takes place, knowing how authors do things, knowing certain words can have more than one meaning.

This postreading processing gives the teacher and the readers an opportunity to reflect not only on the events of the story but also on the processes for making meaning from the story. As they process (and record in their academic journals) the strategies they used to find success in reading the story and new knowledge they constructed, word meanings are clarified and connections are made between this reading and other texts where those strategies would be beneficial. Concrete examples of literary techniques and author devices can be highlighted (and recorded in academic journals). Discussions of character traits and motivations, cause and effect, problems and solutions, and other aspects of story can be examined within the context of a text that has the critical characteristics Mooney cites: charm, magic, impact, and appeal.

Guided Reading—From Theory to Practice

I recently had the opportunity to work with fifty teachers who were in their first year of teaching. I said to them, "What would you like to ask me now that there is no one in the room who is evaluating you?" They had one heartfelt response to that question: "Why didn't anyone tell us what it would really be like? Why didn't someone tell us what would really happen to those perfect lesson plans we create?" I think guided reading is one of those approaches that needs the rest of the story told, especially for teachers in middle and secondary schools.

New Role for Students

Guided reading places new demands on students. Many students have adopted a routine for dealing with reading texts. Used to answering literal-level questions, they don't have much tolerance for process questions. For older students, often the only point of reading is finding out what happens in the end; therefore their only goal is getting to the end as quickly as possible. Students have even developed strategies for answering end-of-the-chapter questions without reading the text. They simply look for the most unknown word/phrase in the question and try to find that in the text. A frequent demand by middle and high school students is that teachers "put the questions in order." With these patterns in place, students need to see that guided reading has a different purpose than just finding out what happens at the end of the story. During guided reading, students are being challenged to make conscious connections between the text and their lives, to elaborate on the text by making connections and asking their own questions, and to make predictions, inferences, and conclusions as a way of deepening their understanding of how texts work. They are also being asked to get actively involved in understanding the purpose of these strategies and knowing when to use the strategies as a bridge between teacher-assisted reading and independent reading of new and unknown texts. These are active reading behaviors, and students who have seen reading as a passive activity are not initially excited about the prospect of extending what they already may not enjoy to something that takes twice as long. Most struggling readers see each separate reading incident as just that—separate and in no way connected to any previous or future reading. Guided reading is an approach that helps students make those connections at a conscious level so they can become automatic as they have more reading experience.

New Role for Teachers

Teachers who are using guided reading as a way to build and maintain reading strategies find that they experience new challenges in addition to those related to maintaining student interest. Guided reading has not often been used in middle and secondary classrooms. It takes practice to adhere to the purposes of guided reading and not let the lessons deteriorate into checking for comprehension questions. It also takes practice not to let them turn into shared reading lessons with the teacher doing the decoding in order to have everyone start and stop at the same time. Guided reading is an incremental step beyond shared reading in moving students toward silent, independent reading. In the absence of practice, it is easy to fall back to a shared reading approach, which seems easier and is more familiar to the students.

Teachers at Long Beach Prep Academy in Long Beach, California, have afternoon planning sessions every Wednesday. During those sessions, one of the things they practice together is how they would set up and conduct a guided reading lesson. Figures 6.1 and 6.2 show the first pages of two different guided readings they talked/read through together. One is fiction, Langston Hughes's "Thank You, M'am," and the other is a nonfiction account, "Hey Jew Girl, Jew Girl," by Livia Bitton-Jackson. These teachers have several pages of notes for each guided reading lesson. In these samples, we can see the struggle as they try to brainstorm questions that stay focused on process, and also how they support each other in learning to keep the questions guided rather than directed.

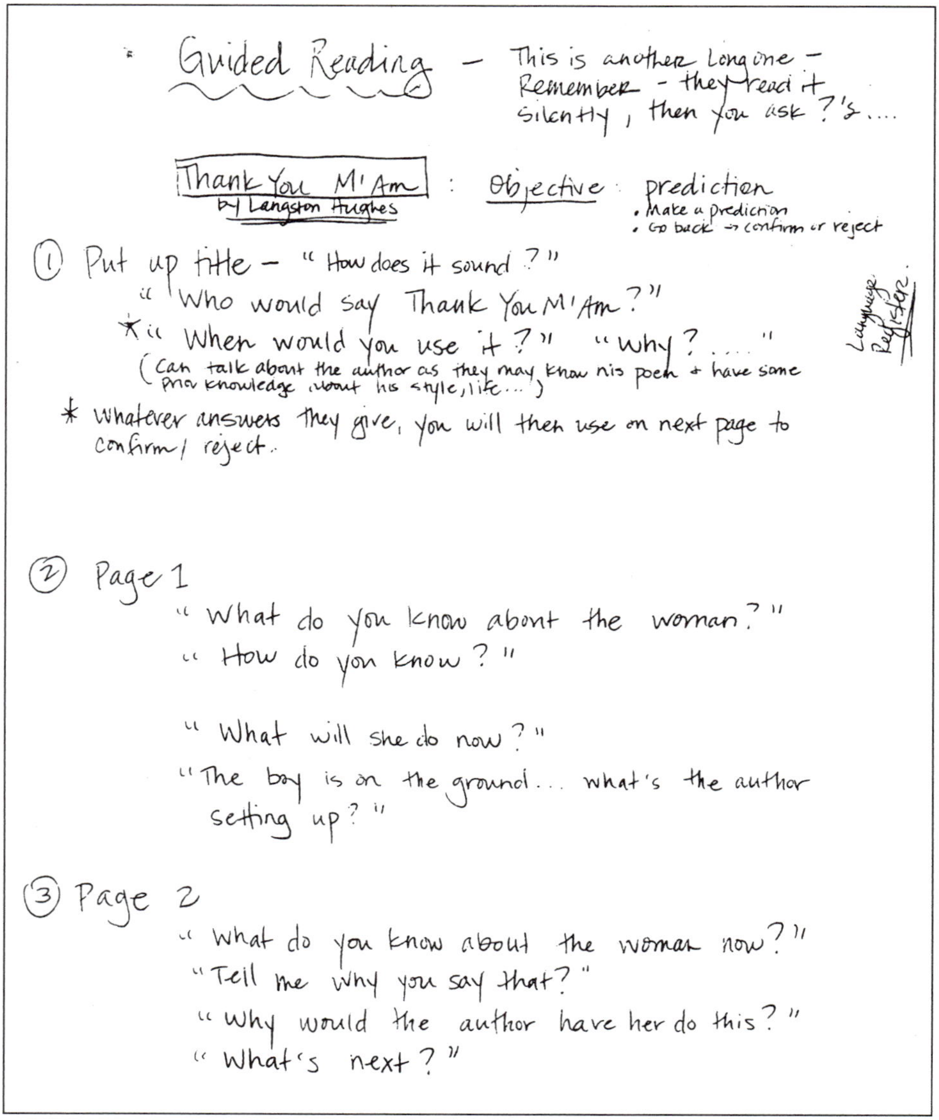

Guided Reading — This is another long one —
Remember — they read it
silently, then you ask ?'s ....

Thank You M'Am : Objective : prediction
by Langston Hughes   • Make a prediction
                                • Go back → confirm or reject

① Put up title — "How does it sound ?"
   "Who would say Thank You M'Am?"
   *" When would you use it ?"   "Why? ..."
   (Can talk about the author as they may know his poem + have some
     prior knowledge about his style, like...)

* whatever answers they give, you will then use on next page to
confirm / reject.

② Page 1
   " What do you know about the woman?"
   " How do you know ?"

   " What will she do now ?"
   " The boy is on the ground... what's the author
     setting up?"

③ Page 2
   " What do you know about the woman now?"
   "Tell me why you say that?"
   " Why would the author have her do this?"
   " What's next?"

Figure 6.1

These teachers have taken a very critical step by practicing the process of guided reading with engaging texts that are connected to students' interests, the content being studied, and strategies that need to be taught/reinforced rather than relying on textbook guides. We can see they are trying to determine ways to model fluency connections and questions: personal, metacognitive, critical, connection, and surface features. These process and fluency connections become their guide as

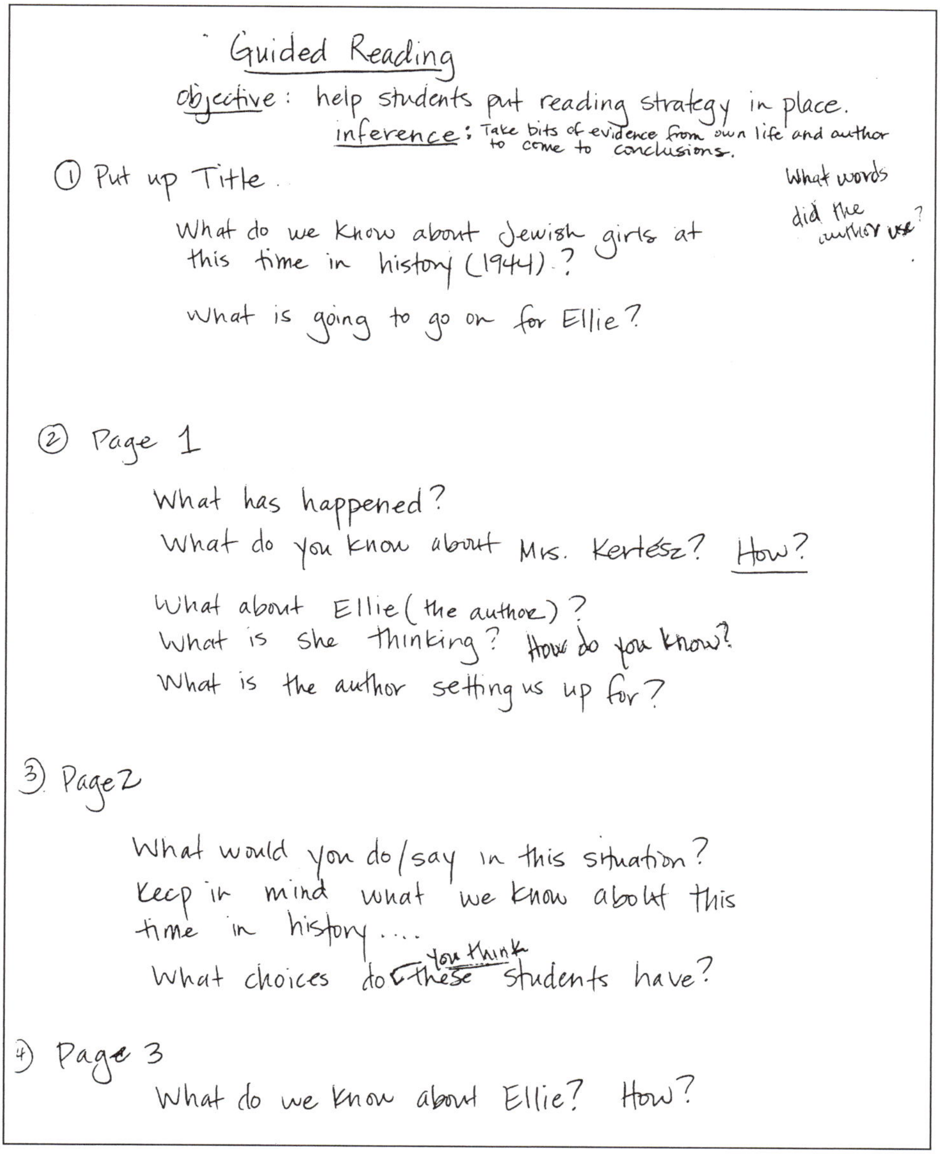

Guided Reading

<u>Objective</u>: help students put reading strategy in place.
 <u>Inference</u>: Take bits of evidence from own life and author to come to conclusions.

① Put up Title.

What words did the author use?

What do we know about Jewish girls at this time in history (1944)?

What is going to go on for Ellie?

② Page 1

What has happened?
What do you know about Mrs. Kertész? <u>How?</u>

What about Ellie (the author)?
What is she thinking? How do you know?
What is the author setting us up for?

③ Page 2

What would you do/say in this situation?
Keep in mind what we know about this time in history....
What choices do ~~these~~ you think students have?

④ Page 3
   What do we know about Ellie? How?

Figure 6.2

they work through the text rather than checking for right answers. Their questions have begun to focus on process: How do we know? What choices do you think the character had? Why would you say that? What do you think will happen next? What words did the author use that helped us discover that? They are working through the content of guided reading together but each will still have to deal with the logistical issues related to each class's schedule and individual student needs that call for guided reading. They will also have to learn how to wean themselves away from predetermined questions to questions that come directly from students' responses *during* the guided reading. They have, however, made a great start with guided reading plans for decreasing their decoding responsibilities and increasing students' responsibilities for understanding.

Finding Time and Planning Lessons

Finding time to do guided reading is a logistical challenge. Guided reading is usually done with small groups or even individual students (Allen 1995, 98–100), which means that all the other students have to be actively engaged for the teacher to be free to facilitate the guided reading lesson. While this type of grouping is common practice in primary classrooms, it is less common as we move to upper elementary, middle, and high school classes. In Chapter 8 I describe a structure for independent literacy exploration (ILE), which can leave time in each week's schedule for guided reading.

Another logistical issue, perhaps more critical, relates to grouping students for guided reading. Typical groups in middle and high school are student-chosen or formed because of interests or topics. Guided reading groups are formed by clustering groups of students who need more intense opportunity to develop specific reading strategies. In my teaching journal I noted three different guided reading lessons in one week. For the first lesson, I used a short story, "The Long Wait for Justice," from *Read* magazine in order to focus on predictions and confirmations of predictions. Four boys were in this group: Robbie, Gil, Cliff, and Trent. Another day, a new group was formed to reinforce questioning strategies. For this group, I used a poem that had simple language but abstract and complex connections. Robbie was also in that group, but this time Tabatha and Kerri joined him. I did a second guided reading group that same day to help students who were struggling to pass science learn the metacognitive processes necessary for successful textbook reading, such as monitoring understanding, clarifying information, and connecting the new to the known. Robbie was also in that group along with four other students who were in danger of failing science class. As you can see, these guided reading groups were not typical secondary school groupings; they were based on observed needs for in-depth strategizing.

Once the needs of the group have been established, the match between readers and text is critical. First, all students must be able to decode the text during an independent, silent reading time. If students are struggling with the surface features and the literal level of the text, then the text is too difficult for a guided reading lesson. Second, the text has to meet the needs and purposes of the students in the guided reading group. For example, if I am focusing on helping students make predictions; confirm or reject those predictions; make new predictions based on knowledge from further reading, then the story needs to be a predictable piece. On the other hand, if I am using the guided reading lesson to help readers establish questioning patterns of themselves, the author, and the text during reading, then I have to make sure that the text is interesting and challenging enough to elicit good questions. Finally, if I am using a nonfiction text in order to help readers learn to use the surface features of the text as reading support, then I need to make sure the chapter titles, headings, subheadings, glossary, pictures and graphs with captions, and the typographic features (bold, italics) are clearly present and predictably supportive and transferable to successful textbook reading.

A Different Kind of Questioning

Probably the most difficult aspect of guided reading for me was letting go of my predetermined questions in order to build my questions on students' responses. I had to become a better listener and a better questioner so that my questions could lead students' thinking in terms of their reading *processes*. Both the students and I were used to looking for *products* of our reading. I had to become less concerned with right answers and more concerned with good questions. I had to learn to model honest responses to the text with phrases that framed the approaches fluent readers take in order to understand new texts: "I'm confused . . . I got lost when . . . I was wondering if . . . I was shocked when . . .When I got to this part, I was thinking 'So what?' Did anyone else go down a dead end like I did?"

All questioning plays a significant role in a reader's experience with text. Unfortunately, much of the instructional time related to reading has been spent with teachers asking students questions. Questions are asked to assess background knowledge, guide and check comprehension, foster connections to prior knowledge, and assess new learning. I find that students are actually well schooled in *answering* questions. Finding ways for students to take on the guided reading behavior of *asking* questions is often far more difficult. As I looked over transcripts of my teaching, journals, and student responses, I realized that as I became more adept at modeling the kinds of questions fluent readers ask, the students' questions and responses became richer during our guided reading sessions.

The categories of questioning that ultimately made the most difference were based on appropriate points in the text before, during, and after reading and included five different *kinds* of questions. Those categories, with examples of questions I used to model each of them, are outlined here.

Personal Response Questions
What would I do if I were in that situation?
How would I react to that remark?
How would I feel under those conditions?
What would I be hoping for at this point?
Where would I turn next?

Metacognitive Response Questions
Does this make sense?
Why am I confused?
What did I miss?
Why did I think that was going to happen?
How did the author make me think . . .?

Connection Response Questions
What was the author intending when she did this?
How would my friends react to someone like this?
How would my parents react if I brought this person home as my date?
Would my friends put me in this kind of situation?
If someone were outside watching this, instead of inside living it, what
    would they think?

Critical Response Questions
What would have made this more interesting?
How does this compare to the last book I read?
If I were writing this book, how would I change it?
I wonder if a more effective ending would have been . . .?
If I could change one thing about this book, what would it be?

Surface-Features-of-Text Response Questions
Why are these words in bold/italics?
How does the title connect to the body of the text?
How do the chapter titles, headings, subheadings help me?
What is this extra white space supposed to tell me?
What are these graphs/pictures/charts for?

These questions can be modeled as a natural part of the language we use
during guided reading. Thinking aloud and using the language of questioning—
"I was wondering" or "I was thinking"—helped model for students the honest
questioning that fluent readers ask while they are reading.

One of the best professional supports I have read and reread in order to
understand the complexities of questioning our way to increased understanding
of the text and our own thinking is Chambers's *Tell Me: Children, Reading, and
Talk*. I refer to this text in Chapter 8, when I demonstrate a questions game, but
the general "Tell Me" framework in this book has really helped me make effective questioning a conscious act. It also helped me with the language of questioning. Rather than using questioning cues such as who, what, when, where—words
that often elicit one-word answers—I began using language such as, "Tell me
about" or "Let's think together about." Just changing my language effected
changes in the consideration students gave to the text.

Purposes of Guided Reading

I have discussed the general purpose for guided reading throughout this chapter, but I also want to look at the goals that might initiate a guided reading lesson for a specific group of students. In the course of one semester, I initiated guided reading lessons on all the topics listed here:

- Defining words in context
- Verbalizing/supporting opinions, attitudes, and reactions in accountable ways
- Accessing and building on prior knowledge
- Consciously connecting new to known
- Creating visual and mental images from text
- Predicting/confirming/rejecting new predictions
- Asking questions of self, author, text
- QRCM: questioning, rereading, clarifying, moving on
- Developing strategies for monitoring understanding
- Using text supports (charts, graphs, pictures, headings, titles)
- Understanding (not defining) literary techniques
- Transferring knowledge to new content
- Developing strategies for organizing facts/content
- Learning to read between the lines (understanding authors' intentions)
- Making personal connections

Some of these guided reading lessons were repeated several times with different texts and different students. For example, many students might need help internalizing a process for questioning themselves, the author, and the text during reading, but you can't use the same text in each guided lesson even though you are focused on the same strategy because the text has to be at the independent reading level of all members of the group. In a typical classroom of eighth- or ninth-grade students, I might have to reach this questioning goal with three different texts, based on students' independent reading levels. For example, all three of the following selections offer excellent opportunities for reinforcing self-questioning as an act of independent reading: Richard Peck's short story "Priscilla and the Wimps," Ogden's lengthy poem "The Hangman," and Chapter 12 of Chris Crutcher's novel *Staying Fat for Sarah Brynes*. Each, however, has different levels of complexity as well as different supports and challenges for readers. The focus of our guided reading lesson stays the same, but the text changes based on the needs and experiences of students.

Finding Texts

The guided reading lesson I described using "The Day of the Hunter" made it possible for us to focus on several strategies within the context of a story that had a great deal of appeal for my students. Other stories, poems, and pieces of nonfiction would be more appropriate for other strategies and other students. So, where do we find these great guided reading texts? It is often difficult to find a text that is short enough to meet the interest level and complex enough to meet the instructional purposes of middle and high school guided reading.

Although guided reading texts for students in grades 4–12 abound, they are not usually marketed in sets the same way guided reading packages are for primary classes. It is critical to pinpoint constellations of reading resources where new texts appropriate for guided reading might be found; otherwise, the task of finding just the right guided reading texts seems overwhelming. Appendixes A–E suggest various sources. As I read, I photocopy anything that I think would make good guided reading material (interesting, informative, short) and mark each photocopy with the strategy goals I believe this text would reinforce.

- *Read* magazine for students (articles, essays, short stories, plays, student writing, myths, fables)
- *Time Machine: The American History Magazine for Kids* (stories, articles, biographies)
- *FAIR: Fairness & Accuracy in Reporting* (articles on news that has been underreported by the media; some controversial topics)
- Teaching Tolerance (teaching kits *The Shadow of Hate* and *America's Civil Rights Movement* and other materials)
- *TeenInk (The 21st Century)* (newspaper with writing by teenagers)
- American Teen Writer Series (anthologies collected from student writing submitted to *Merlyn's Pen: The National Magazine of Student Writing.* Some are by grade level, such as *Eighth Grade: Stories of Friendship, Passage, and Discovery,* and some are thematic, such as *White Knuckles: Thrillers and Other Stories*)
- Short story collections (see Appendix E)
- The Scholastic series Horrible History, Horrible Geography, Horrible Science
- Poetry collections (see Appendix F)
- Newspaper/magazine articles (high-interest, current events)
- Excerpts from novels (Philbrick's *Freak the Mighty* for prediction; Spinelli's *Who Put That Hair in My Toothbrush?* for inference, author's intentions; Juster's *Phantom Tollbooth* for figuring out words from context)
- Micro-story collections (*World's Shortest Short Stories* (Moss), *Sudden Fiction: American Short-Short Stories* (Shapard and Thomas)
- Literature anthologies (discarded school anthologies, college anthologies, contemporary collections)
- *Chicken Soup for the Soul*

Regardless of where I find the text resource for the lesson, I try to keep in mind the importance of this time when I provide students with "support by assisting the reader to clarify meaning through utilizing problem solving strategies" (Smith and Elley 1994, 36). I view this time as a mediated step toward independence. These interactive guided reading and focused discussion sessions help students find their literary voices and refine their thinking. They are a very important step along the continuum toward reading independence. I recently found a quote by Lew Welch that said, "Somebody showed it to me and I found it by myself." For me, that is the essence of guided reading.

Creating (and Living with) Independent Readers

*What would make kids readers? A lot more reading and a hell of a lot
less writing! If you could just go to class without the teacher telling you
what to do, just let you read. There is never enough time to read,
always doing other work.*

Rene, grade 10

Perhaps John Goodlad's language would be a bit more refined than Rene's, but I think he would agree that if we want students to become more confident and competent readers, they need to spend more time reading. In *A Place Called School,* Goodlad reported that less than 2 percent of each high school day was being spent on actual reading. In spite of the research that supports independent reading time as a critical component in effective literacy programs because it affords readers the opportunity for "clocking up reading mileage," many administrators and teachers have difficulty creating effective independent reading programs.

Why Is Independent Reading Important?

I believe that the choices, attention, and purpose required during independent reading allow students to begin or continue the transition from teacher-directed reading in school to the kind of reading we do as adult readers. Allington and Cunningham highlight the significant differences between the teacher-selected reading of shared and guided reading and the student-directed choices of independent reading: "Authentic experiences begin with individual purpose and motivation. Authenticism is based on analyses of real world reading and writing where adults primarily determine what they will read and write and the level of involvement in the activities. As adults we decide which sections of the newspaper to read, which paperbacks to purchase, which manuals we need" (90). As these authentic experiences are nurtured in classrooms where students have access to diverse reading materials, students begin making the kind of choices we hope to see them make throughout their adult lives.

The International Association for the Evaluation of Educational Achievement (Elley 1992) reported that the most important factor in the development of literacy is access to books. The advantages seen when students have this access are significant in the reading development of students at any age. Many educators have found that extended time for independent reading affects reading fluency, world knowledge, word knowledge, motivation, and writing. Sadly, as students move from primary classrooms to middle and secondary classrooms and students lose or give up access to independent reading, many readers lose interest in reading. One of the most frequent questions I am asked by parents concerns the changes they have seen in their children's reading habits as they have moved through the grades. They wonder what happened to their children who loved to read in elementary school and now hate to read in middle/high school. I always tell them the things their children needed when they were younger readers are still important today. When the right conditions are in place, students will continue to read and reap the pleasures and advantages that come with reading.

Independent reading not only provides students with the opportunity to experience a range of texts but also gives them the opportunity to spend extended time on particular texts. Teachers often ask me what they should do if a student wants to reread an entire novel during independent reading, and I always tell them this is natural reading behavior that shows their literacy program is working. Independent reading allows students the opportunity to explore pictures, charts, graphs, borders, rereading, checking other resources— the very areas that often get limited time when all students have to finish a text at the same time.

There is much research in support of building independent reading time into the curriculum. Researchers certainly influenced my decision to make independent reading an appreciable part of our classroom time. However, it was the response of students in my classes who were experiencing independent reading for the first time in their lives that helped me continue and expand ways that students could be given reading choices.

> This class is pretty strange. Where I come from the english class was run a lot different. Our teacher was more concerned with our penmiship rather than our ability interpreting books and poetry. She thought that the key to life is in neat penmiship. We spent the first nine weeks on how to write neatly. To me this was a big waste of time. This class creates an atmosphere of mental control. Thus, the reader enters the book

and becomes part of what he/she is reading. It creates a feeling of solitude. Your no longer reading in a classroom, your living the story. What better way to understand a book than if you were there?

At a time when adolescents' lives are bombarded with demands on their time from extracurricular activities, both school-related and personal, schools and teachers must create a consistent space in the school day for the solitude and exploration that this student described when he was "living the story." In Daniel Pennac's engaging look at how a love of reading begins, *Better Than Life,* he offers us his "Reader's Bill of Rights." Two of those rights are the right to read anything and the right to escapism. I think hundreds of my students have discovered the value of reading because independent reading provided those rights for them. Given the advantages of independent reading, why don't we see that time in every classroom and school in the country?

Letting Go

Independent reading is a unique and sometimes challenging approach to reading instruction. Teachers often feel uncomfortable as they realize they have lost some control in terms of book selection and assessment. This can leave them uncertain about the role they should play during independent reading time.

Most teachers who do independent reading yearn for the day, the very first day, when every student in class will begin class reading independently—no requests for bathroom passes, no disruptions, no sleeping, and no complaining. In our high school classroom, that event always happened just when I despaired that students were ever going to begin reading independently. I remember one day in early March when students had settled and I was moving about the room offering to confer with them about their reading and writing.

"Mark, do you want to talk about the help you still need with your short story?"

"Not right now, Mrs. Allen. I'm reading."

I moved to meet with Ian, who had told me earlier that he needed help with his science textbook. "Ian, want to look at your science text now?"

"Not now, Mrs. Allen. I've almost figured out what the man in black is up to."

I sat down beside Traci and asked her if she wanted to work on her essays for her college application. "You scared the heck out of me! I'm not stopping this book [Beatrice Sparks's *Jay's Journal*] until I've finished."

I walked toward the back of the room, where Chris was stretched out on a couch reading Avi's *Nothing but the Truth,* to see if he still wanted to finish his "emergency" hat-complaint letter to the principal he had rushed in with at the beginning of the class. After I said his name softly a couple of times, he looked at me as if he were in another world but didn't bother to respond. Finally, I turned to go back toward the front of the room and tripped over Derek's feet. He erupted. "Mrs. Allen. Can't you go find a good book and sit down somewhere and read?"

Now that everyone in the class was really interrupted, I said, "Doesn't anyone need me?"

"No! Go read a book!" they chorused.

Ah, those independent readers we all fantasize about. In *Best Practice: New Standards for Teaching and Learning in America's Schools*, Zemelman, Daniels, and Hyde cite one of the qualities of best practice in teaching reading: "Reading is the best practice for learning to read" (31). These students were learning the value of sustained time with books of their choice. They had come to consider this their time, and I had tried to appropriate that time for teaching purposes.

Unfortunately, just providing time is not enough. Students need to know that they have real choices during this time. In "Choices for Children" Kohn supports the importance of such ownership for authentic learning: "If we want children to take responsibility for their own behavior, we must first give them responsibility, and plenty of it" (11). Independent reading time is the time students can begin to take responsibility for their reading habits and behaviors: learning to make good choices; learning when to abandon a book; discovering how to find books that support their author, genre, or theme tastes; and more important, how to find books that will help them know they are truly readers.

Mooney sees independent reading time as a "complement to the other approaches" (1990, 72). I see this time as both the umbrella and the foundation for shared and guided reading. Every year, with each new group of students, the two most important questions for me were how I could get readers to that point of independence and what my role should be once students didn't need me in the same way they needed me during times of more direct instruction.

Facilitating Independent Reading

As the teacher moves among instructional approaches ranging from read-aloud, when the teacher owns the responsibility for text selection, decoding, and fluent reading, to shared and guided reading, when the teacher is still responsible for text selection but students share the responsibility for decoding and meaning making during the reading, the ultimate goal for those practices is students' increased abilities during times of independence. In fact, I believe that an assessment measure for the effectiveness of read-aloud, shared reading, and guided reading is whether those approaches led to engaged readers who demand independent reading time in school and choose to read outside school hours. It is this competent and avid reading that is the mark of a lifelong reader. We all know, however, that most engaged and passionate readers have come to that point because of the reading apprenticeship they have experienced at the side of experienced readers. I believe there are several significant tasks for teachers in preparation for and during independent reading time that mediate and solidify the effectiveness of this classroom time.

Building and Using *a Classroom Library*

In the 1970s when I first began offering my students the opportunity to read independently, I quickly discovered a direct correlation between productive reading time and the quantity and quality of books available to them during that time. I do not believe that creating and maintaining an interesting classroom library takes away from the critical role of the media center's collection; I believe that each supports the other. The question for many is how to get those great collections started and how to get students reading the books once the room is filled with them.

One day, several years into my teaching career, a boy came in carrying a grocery bag filled with books. He told me his mother was going to throw the books away so he had asked her if he could have them for me. This was truly one of those students I would have suspected of having no books in his home. As I gratefully accepted the books, it occurred to me that if this student had books at home, then all of them probably did. I went to the principal and asked him if I could have a contest (and a party for a reward) to see which of my classes could bring in the most books for our classroom library. Permission was granted; one of the students whose father was a potato farmer donated five potato barrels for collecting our books, and we were on our way.

A description of the contest to my students was met with some reluctance. "Where are we supposed to get these books anyway?"

My reply, "You know that old saying, 'Anything you can beg, borrow, or steal,'" was one of those impromptu responses you live to regret.

"What do we get for this?"

"Does everyone in the class have to bring books or could one person bring them all?"

Rules were posted (everyone had to bring at least one book); charts were created; class numbers were painted on the potato barrels. Within three weeks, we had over three thousand books in our classroom. All the potato barrels were full; the custodians were complaining about the mess in our room; and the students felt they all deserved a party. I thought the problem of students' complaining there was nothing to read on independent reading days was solved.

When reading day came that week, I was stunned when students stood in the middle of the room (the only actual floor space left), glanced around, and said, "There's nothing good to read in here." There were books on the shelves, books in crates and barrels, books in piles around the perimeter of the room, and books inside each desk. There were books about every possible topic, including books I could have been fired for having in the room. And still they complained that there was nothing worth reading. It was then that I realized that choice isn't choice if you don't know what your options are. Nonreaders, especially those who have been in reading programs weighted toward teacher-selected materials, don't have any idea of what reading options are available or interesting to them. There were now too many choices in this room, and they had no idea how they could find the books that might be interesting to them.

I knew that I needed to do two things: weed out the book collection so that there were not so many choices, and give students some assistance in finding the books that were right for them. The first issue was easily resolved. I simply went through the three thousand books and took out those books that were overkill. (There must have been five hundred books with women on the front covers, head thrown back in ecstasy. Every well-balanced classroom library needs a few of those romance novels, but not five hundred of them.) I also took out books that were old, torn, smelly, and unimaginable reading choices for my students. I boxed those books and took them to a used-book store, where I traded them for ones more appropriate for the students in my classes. By doing this, I was able to fill in some of the noticeable gaps in our classroom library: science fiction, westerns, sports, and self-help books.

Even with fewer books in the room, however, the problem of getting students to sample and choose was still very real. I tried doing booktalks (Bodard) each week on books I thought students would enjoy. As I got more effective at booktalking, more students were enticed to read those books, but I found myself booktalking the same kinds of books each time—typically they were the books that I chose to read and booktalk. Booktalking continued to be an effective way for me to "sell" books to many students, but I was still interested in finding ways of helping students sample large numbers of books and make their choices from that sampling.

I originally saw the term *book pass* in *Ideas for Teaching English in the Junior High and Middle School* (Carter and Rashkis). The authors used this strategy as a way to help students find books in which they were interested and to increase reading speed. They included four columns on notebook paper (book number, title, author, and lines read). My purpose for the book pass differed from theirs in that my only goal was the sampling of diverse texts and making choices that would match student interests and independent reading levels. I modified the idea to meet the goals that I had for my students by creating a book pass form with columns for title, author, and comments. I devised a system of book passes that I presented every two or three weeks on a day preceding independent reading:

1. Organize students' desks or chairs in a circle.
2. Explain the purpose of the book pass by demonstrating how you sample a book before deciding to read it.

3. Gather books you want to include in the book pass and make sure you have one title for each student in the circle.

4. Give each student one book and explain to them that it does not matter which book they start with, as everyone in the circle will see all the books.

5. Choose a direction for passing the books so each student knows to whom she will pass each book.

6. After students receive a book, they should immediately list the title and author of the book they have received.

7. Allow one to two minutes for students to peruse each book. Students should look at the book covers, read the beginning of the book, and sample portions throughout the book.

8. At the end of one to two minutes, call "book pass." At that time students will make a quick comment about the book just sampled on their book pass form and pass the book to the next student.

9. Save a few minutes of class time at the end of book passing so some books can be highlighted through the use of quick questions: Who found a book he can't wait to read? Did anyone find a book that might get me fired? Did anyone find a book she would recommend to a friend as one she needs to read? Anyone find a book that will teach us something new?

10. After the book pass is finished, students put their completed forms in their working folders or academic journals as a reference for choosing books they might want to read during independent reading time.

The book pass was one of the most effective ways I found to help students sample the range of books available to them in our classroom library. Book passes in our classes served to get students looking at a variety of books, making their own judgments on the interest and readability of the books, and finding books they were willing to seek out on independent reading days. Initially, I chose from a variety of books to make up the book passes: all genres of fiction, nonfiction, poetry, informational, drama, picture books, and short story collections. I wanted students to sample the range of possibilities available.

One of the critical steps in the book pass is your demonstration of ways to choose books. I did this by thinking aloud with them my process of choosing books. I looked at the front and back covers and mused aloud about the reviews, what I picked up about the book's content, my knowledge of this author's writing, and any honors the book had received. I then read the first few lines and talked about what kind of leads caught my attention. I skipped through the book and talked about size of print, illustrations, and text supports such as maps, headings, and chapter titles. Finally, I talked about my reading mood. What did I want to read right now? Did I want another book by the same author because I wanted to read a series? Did I want to read more about teenagers who were living with abuse? Was I looking for an informational book that would help me plan my next vacation, or was I looking for a book that would help me escape?

In one class period students will be able to sample twenty to twenty-five different books. If your class numbers are large, form two circles so that you can still have a few minutes at the end of the book pass to talk about the books you have discovered. Many teachers are using this method as a way of getting students to use the media center's collections. After the arrival of book club orders or a weekend trip to garage sales and flea markets, book passes are a great way for students to explore the new books in the room. The sample in Figure 7.1 is a

Figure 7.1

New Books On Tape

Book Pass

Author	Title	Comment
Robert Lipsyte	The Contender	Kinda Hot Book 4
Mi Vida	Parrot in the Oven	Great Book 3
Katherina Paterson	Bridge to Terabithia	Blazin' 5
Marion Dane Bauer	On My Honor	Fair Book 3½
Walter Dean Myers	Darnell Rock Reporting	Hot Book 4
Katherine Coville	Short & Shivery	Okay Book 2
R.L. Stine	The Thrill Club	Fair Book 3
Gary Paulsen	Nightjohn	Great Book 3
Margaret Peterson Haddix	Don't you Dare Read This	Okay 2½
R.L. Stine	Bad Dreams	Great Book 3½
Ellen Raskin	The Westing Game	Blazin' 5
Matt Christopher	Michael Jordan	Okay Book 2
Paula Fox	The Slave Dancer	Okay Book 2
Matt Christopher	Grant Hill	3-Okay-Fair
Matt Christopher	Steve Young	3-& Fair
R.L. Stine	Double Date	4- Kinda Hot
R.L. Stine	The Dare	2-Okay
B.L. Stine	The New Boy	4-Hot
Anonymous	Go Ask Alice	2-OK
Caroline B. Cooney	The Voice On The Radio	5-Blazin

1=Poor 2=OK 3=Fair/Great 4.Hot/Kinda Hot 5=Blazin

recent one from Becky Bone's middle school literacy classroom. In this case, Becky had used the book pass as a way of introducing students to the new books on tape available to them during their independent reading time. This student has created her own rating system of 1–5, with 1 indicating a poor choice for her and 5 a "blazin'" choice. In this process, students discover many books they might otherwise never pick from the shelves.

Book passes can be used to help students choose books from a diverse selection or to match themes, historical projects, genre study, and classroom inquiries. Whether using your classroom collection or books borrowed from the media center, this is an effective means of involving students in lots of poetry collections if they are creating their own poetry anthologies. The possibilities for using the book pass are endless. If your students are stuck reading R. L. Stine and Christopher Pike books, you could use a book pass to introduce them to new suspense titles and authors. When you want to enjoy and learn from the beauty and complexity of picture books, a book pass can be a way to show students that picture books are not just for young readers.

This is also the method I used to help students make their literature circle choices. For example, when I wanted all the literature circles to explore the theme of survival, I bought six copies of several survival novels: *Hatchet* (Paulsen), *I Know What You Did Last Summer* (Duncan), *The Face on the Milk Carton* (Cooney), *Island of the Blue Dolphins* (O'Dell), *Teacher's Pet* (Cusick), and *Arly* (Robert Peck). Student desks were arranged in small groups with a copy of each title in each group. Students spent three to five minutes looking at the language, writing style, book topic, size of print, length of book, gender of main characters, and general interest level. At each book pass signal, students listed their pluses and minuses for each book in the comments column. When the book pass was finished (approximately twenty minutes), students made a first, second, and third choice for literature circle titles. It is important that students make more than one choice so that literature circles can be balanced. This also gives you the opportunity to put a student in a literature circle that is more suitable if the student has chosen a book only because her friends have chosen it.

Teachers have found a variety of ways to get students to choose books through recommendations from other students. Some use student-created book covers or bookmarks as advertising, posters, postcards, character sketches, debates between characters in books (e.g., Palmer in Spinelli's *Wringer* compares notes with Jonas in Lowry's *The Giver* about what it took to stand up for their beliefs), and readers' theater. Teacher's guides, education texts, and professional books related to young adult literature abound with such suggestions. A serendipitous event that led to student recommendations of books in our classroom occurred after our midyear examination. In each student's mandatory two-hour exam, I included a question or writing prompt related to the independent reading that students had done during the semester (see Chapter 12). I had used the same kind of assessment the previous semester and found that students enjoyed having exams unique to the work each had completed. At that time, I had typed all the questions on a page, cut the page into strips, and attached the appropriate strip to each student's exam. This time I didn't have time to cut the strips so I just ran off thirty copies of the entire questions page and stapled a copy to each person's exam. I told the students to find their names and respond to the particular question that was for each of them. Immediately after the exam, I noticed that students were checking those questions and then going to other students and asking for reading advice. For the first time, I began hearing students make comments to other students such as, "Hey, I've been wanting to read a Vietnam book. Which one is best?"

Some strategies work better than others, depending on your purpose and your student population. I want to highlight here three of many strategies that get students to make good book choices. When I owned all the books in my classroom, I encouraged students to write a one-line signed review of the book inside the cover. This writing could also be done on a 3 × 5 card attached inside the back cover of each book. I found this a great way to initiate students' seeking reading advice from other students. The year I had an entire class of ninth-grade girls, we had an amazing run on girls reading sports books because two of the stars of our basketball team were in my senior class!

In Ann Bailey's middle school classroom in Long Beach, California, students clamored to get their names on the waiting lists for popular books when Ann took an entire chalkboard, listed the books most in demand, and made a space for students to sign up to read those books. Many students who would never have chosen to read them were caught up in the frenzy of competing to get the books and in the process discovered books they enjoyed.

In my last three years of teaching, my students created computer logs for certain authors and titles. At that time of limited technology, each book log or author log was kept on a separate floppy disk. Students who were reading the same book would log on and write their comments about the book on the floppy. The next student would add comments and thus continue the conversation started by the previous entries.

In Nancie Atwell's *In the Middle,* she highlights the promise of independent reading libraries: "A classroom library invites students to browse, chat, make recommendations to each other, select, reject, and generally feel at home with literature. It also provides a crucial demonstration: supplying books for students to choose and read, creating a literary environment for them, are high priorities of their teacher and school" (37). We can know the value of sustained, self-selected reading experiences and classroom libraries and still struggle with the logistics of independent reading in our classrooms.

Dealing with Independent Reading Tensions

What about the kids who won't choose a book? What about those who refuse to read anything other than R. L. Stine? How do you keep track of books? Do you lose a lot of books? What about kids who fall asleep? What do you do when kids fight over where they'll sit during reading? How do you give them a grade? Did you ever get to actually read during independent reading, or were you too busy keeping kids on task? No matter where I am, teachers have lots of questions about the logistics of independent reading.

In *Seeking Diversity*, Linda Rief gives a humorous and touching account of her early forays into individualized reading when she tried to model her classroom after Nancie Atwell's. I have read this account many times to remind me that it is important for each teacher to find her own process for managing independent reading. There is an English proverb that says, "Only the wearer knows where the shoe pinches." This is certainly true as you design independent reading time. Finding what works for you and your students emerges from the tensions you and your students experience as you try to inspire the reluctant readers, support the struggling readers, keep up with the passionate readers, avoid censorship issues, and keep track of students' accomplishments for assessment and evaluation purposes. In other chapters, I discuss strategies for dealing with the comprehension issues of reluctant and struggling readers. During independent reading time, the key for these students is getting them started and ensuring that their experience with books becomes increasingly enjoyable and sustainable. I have found no better resource for this than the use of recorded books.

Using Books on Tape with Independent Reading

I was recently observing in a high school in southwest Florida where teachers were implementing a literacy workshop. The teacher was doing a shared reading of a short story, but one young man was sitting with headphones and the book and audiotape for Chris Crutcher's *Ironman*. The teacher asked if she should make him stop to participate in what everyone else was doing. "I kind of hate to make him stop. This is the first thing he has done all year."

I recommended that she just let him continue with the novel. Halfway through the period (block schedule), she took the class to the media center for some instruction on computer-based research. The young man brought along his book, tape, and tape player, sat away from the group, and continued reading his novel. When the media specialist tried to bring him into the group, the teacher told her not to disturb his reading. After about twenty minutes, he came to where we were seated and asked permission to go to the rest room. I took the opportunity to ask him about the book.

"What are you reading?"

"*Ironman.*"

"That's a great book. I love Chris Crutcher, don't you?"

He looked at me with a somewhat sullen look on his face and replied, "I hate to read."

"You're kidding. You don't look like you hate to read."

He seemed surprised and a smile lit his entire face as he responded, "I guess maybe I don't hate to read *this* book." The teacher said it was the first time she had seen him smile the entire semester.

For many readers, saying they don't like to read has become an acceptable response to allow them to escape many reading activities. Not wanting to appear to be schoolboys or schoolgirls, even students who like to read often won't admit it. Once readers say they don't like to read often enough, it becomes a habit and a belief. I found books on tape to be the most significant factor in overcoming that belief system in my own classroom and in the literacy project classrooms I visit around the country. Kyle Gonzalez and I wrote extensively about the logistics of using books on tape in *There's Room for Me Here*. It was amazing for us to see students develop such language fluency from reading books with audiotapes that they were able to wean themselves from the recordings. We watched them use the tapes for support as they chose increasingly more difficult texts, thereby compensating for the difference between their listening and reading vocabularies.

Many school districts have followed my advice and are now keeping audiotapes with books in their in-school suspension (ISS) programs. Most young adult books on tape range from one to six hours of listening time. Just imagine that for every day a student spent in ISS, he could read an entire book. I wouldn't dare hazard a specific statistic about the number of students who end up in ISS who are struggling or reluctant readers, but my guess would be a very high percentage. The administrator at one middle school in California told me the teachers wanted him to stop using books on tape in ISS because students wanted to go there to finish their books. That tells me those students need access to books on tape in their classrooms and in the media center so they can experience the same success without getting into trouble.

Keeping Track

I'm sure many of you are thinking, "This sounds too chaotic for me." Actually, after the initial confusion over where books/tape players/batteries are kept and after students get accustomed to how they (and you) are keeping track of their progress, students will quickly beg for extra independent reading time. Contrary to what you might expect, classrooms where books on tape are available for students who need them tend to be quiet places. I think Ian described our classroom very well in a note to me near the end of his high school career:

This has been a great class for me. I can remember me reading to my grandmother long before kindergarten. To some it's a chore to read but to me it's more like a privelage. Books help you learn how to make choices by seeing how others do it. I haven't seen anybody abuse the privelage of there own choice of reading. This is always the quietest class I have.

I believe there is a positive correlation between our keeping-track strategies and students' positive attitudes toward independent reading time, especially in the early weeks of any school year. In order for students to feel that this is important time in their week, they have to see that we also value the time. As they see us reading, keeping track, taking notes, and referencing the books they are reading during read-aloud, shared reading, and guided reading, they begin to see this as a legitimate use of their time.

I kept records of students' progress in several ways. I always tried to capture both their in-class reading progress and the outside reading they reported using a status-of-the-class form (Atwell 1987). The sample shown in Figure 7.2 is the first of three pages for one of my classes. I kept the list of names for each class on my computer so that I could add or delete as necessary, and simply ran off a new set each week. Students in this class ranged from tenth through twelfth grades and their reading interests encompassed westerns, sports, realistic fiction, suspense, and poetry.

I also took notes in a teaching journal so that I could track students' academic responses to the increasing independence they were demanding. My anecdotal notes for one class when I arrived late because of a hall crisis in the early fall showed me which students still needed my immediate support:

> Students came in angry—in conflict, nasty because I wasn't there immediately. No one reading—Matt stretched out on couch making snoring noises. Jason and Jay in easy chairs. Moved Matt to a desk where he asked for the new *Newsweek*. I told Jason he should look at the new book I bought for him (Time/Life) and he did. They were quietly reading when Jay picked up a copy of *Tex* and read all during the period (engrossed—didn't want to stop).

Other anecdotal notes taken later in the year indicated students' increased ability to accept responsibility for their own reading behaviors.

Students were also expected to keep an independent reading log (see form H.2 in Appendix H). This was a quick documentation at the end of class to keep track of their reading. Students then used those logs to write a more substantive response to the book when they had finished reading it. I found this an effective way for students to note their impressions and questions without feeling as though they had to write lengthy responses for every day they read. Additionally, they kept bookmarks in the books while reading. These bookmarks were either

		STATUS OF THE CLASS DIRECTED STUDY--1 3/10		3/11	3/12	3/13
Homework		3/9				
Sarah A.		working on project with Eva Quayle	Computer poetry	absent	Return of the Jedi 99	c/ writing
Boyd D.		Magic's Touch weeds 101	Magic's Touch 192	Magic's Touch Done	c/room response Magic Touch Devi Count	I never Loved Your Mind 20
Eva F.		project Goodbye Doesn't mean forever	Goodbye Doesn't mean 28 forever	Goodbye Doesn't mean 69 forever	112	Goodbye Doesn't mean forever 157
Clay F.		Dollar Man video-Tales from Darkside	Computer response Tales from a Darkside	response- Tales from a Darkside	Dollar Man 87	Dollar man 99
Phil H.		Gunslinger 38	Gunslinger 53	Shop McCluskey	Shop McCluskey	Field Trip play
Matt H.		The Book of Three Alexander 61	Book of Three 94	Book of Three alexander 135	179	Book of Three 212
Leasha H.		absent	BabyFace absent print	response BabyFace Senior Year	looking for a play	Senior year 18
Debra M.		absent Being tutored	absent ? tutored	absent tutored?	absent tutored	absent tutored
Ron M.		date - The Minnipins finished	Wonderful World of Henry Sugar	Henry Sugar 97	poster/ bulletin board	bulletin board Dahl
Andy M.		Trick or Treat 172	Trick or Treat finished	Listen to tape pg. 17	Lake next - T-Teacher tried	Gunslinger Tape 160

Figure 7.2

ones we created or ones I "borrowed" from publishers at conferences, and they were helpful when several students were trying to read the same book.

Final Thoughts on Independent Reading

Independent reading in our classroom was a sustained silent reading time. Students did not typically read magazines or newspapers at this time (although that happened occasionally) because it was a struggle for them to be sustained or silent with either of those reading choices. It was also not a time for students to do homework for other classes or read their textbooks. They read and listened to novels, short stories, poetry, drama, informational books, and picture books. And I read. Independent reading time was a time for all of us to read, and I was grateful for the time to keep up with the literature my students were choosing. In her chapter "Developing Lifetime Readers," Donna Alvermann points out the importance of staying abreast of student reading preferences: "Finally, regardless of which guiding principle (or sets of principles) are followed, teachers must keep abreast of students' reading preferences if students are to become lifetime readers" (34).

I did not confer with students during independent reading time. Most students became too easily distracted to read if conversations were happening around them. In a study of sustained silent reading programs, Wheldall and Entwistle report statistically positive effects of silence during SSR. "These continual distractions disturbed the silent readers and, as already suggested, proved cover for conversations" (65). I found the same to be true. If I spent my time having conversations, students felt they could spend their time the same way. I did spend several minutes at the beginning of the class getting students settled and a few minutes at the end of class to complete the status of the class. I also spent some "kid-watching" moments monitoring reading behaviors as a way to establish patterns that might indicate an intervention was needed. If I saw reading behaviors indicating the need for an intervention (sleeping, frequent bathroom requests, multiple book changes, distractability), I approached the student during independent literacy exploration (ILE) to make the necessary contact and offer support. If I noted students engrossed in their reading, asking for extra independent reading time, and asking not to be disturbed, I noted that (and the text) so that I could offer other books, authors, or genres that would seem to be at that student's current interest level.

During a typical fifty-minute class period, I probably read for thirty to thirty-five minutes. Wheldall and Entwistle noted the positive effects of such teacher modeling: "The on-task level was 20 percent higher than baseline levels during the final modeling phase, showing that modeling exerts an appreciable additional effect. It was clearly apparent, in all classes, that many children, during the initial intervention especially, would look up and watch the teacher reading and then resume their own reading. The teachers were providing effective concurrent models of the appropriate reading behavior which the children imitated" (65).

My experiences showed me that my reading during that time was a critical model for students—both in the books I chose to read and the level of my engagement with reading. One day I had started reading a novel, Joanna Lee's *Mary Jane Harper Cried Last Night,* during my second-period class. By lunchtime, when many students came to hang out in my room, I was almost finished. When the first students came into my room, I said, "If you come in here today, you'll have to be quiet. I'm almost finished with this book and I don't want any noise or I won't be able to read." They found quiet activities (some of them even read) and I finished my book. I was so angry after the last page, I threw the book across the room. When students accused and questioned my actions, I said, "I'm just so angry at what happened in that book. I can't even talk about it right now." From that day until the end of my teaching career at that high school, I had students who came to me every year asking for the book that had made me so angry I threw it across the room. Each year I ordered ten new copies, and each year ten copies were stolen. Our reading behaviors are powerful models for students.

Perhaps Adam summarizes the value of independent reading better than I: "A good English class is when you can come to the class and know you don't have to work your brains out on nouns, pronouns, adjectives, and verbs. That rots to high heaven! I like to come into class, sit down and read a good book." Adam was living the life of an assertive reader—a reader who could make choices because independent reading helped him discover what his reading options were.

8

Organizing for Choice:
Supporting Diversity in Reading,
Writing, and Learning

*Every teacher who is told what material to cover, when to cover it, and
how to evaluate children's performance is a teacher who knows that
enthusiasm for one's work quickly evaporates in the face of control.
Not every teacher, however, realizes that exactly the same is true of
students: deprive children of self-determination and you deprive them
of motivation.*

ALFIE KOHN, PUNISHED BY REWARDS

In classrooms where students have become accustomed to daily schedules that include mostly teacher-directed activities, students become resigned to the reality of teachers choosing for them. While these students say they wish they had more choices, they often flounder when given choices because they have not had a lot of experience with school choices. In some classrooms teachers give lists of books for students to read during "independent" reading days. One teacher told me that she just couldn't stand to have students "wasting time reading things that were clearly below their reading level." Many schools mandate specific titles for summer reading. Even choice-based time built into the curriculum for research projects is often taken over by limited "choices," with a significant portion of the grade coming from adherence to structures and guidelines.

Academic choice is a difficult concept for students and teachers who have been schooled in teacher-controlled or mandated-curriculum directions. In spite of those controls, some students have still become adept at making choices. I just wasn't always comfortable with the choices they made. When I told them their reading, writing, and learning choices were theirs, they believed me. These stu-

dents were my Calvins; if I couldn't find interesting things to teach, they certainly had some interesting areas to pursue.

You can imagine that I had some pangs when Kevin, after assuming he had real choices, chose to work on a "romance" novel that detailed his sex life, which prompted Karen and Wendy to do research on sexual lives of teenagers. Their honest questions and real choices led them to incredible amounts of reading: novels (especially romance and teenage pregnancy), pamphlets and articles, non-fiction texts, and medical books. Neither scenario is ideal: in traditional term paper classes, students had limited choices; in my classroom, students made unsupported choices. Both remind me that choice is like any other meaningful instructional goal in that it requires support.

In our classroom I found four components necessary for our move from my whole-class assignments to classes where students had more choices. We had to have daily and weekly schedules that allowed for days of choice, and I had to learn how to give incremental support so students could make realistic and productive choices during those times. Our classroom library and resources had to change because we had to find resources that supported individual and small-group choices. Finally, I had to let go of the notion that all students would have equivalent products at the end of a day, week, or grading period. Teachers who support choices for learners come to realize that they may have the same learning goals and standards for excellence for all students but students' choices for achieving those goals and demonstrating learning can be vastly different from one student to another.

Organizing for Choice

Independent reading is a time when all students have the opportunity to choose reading that is interesting and appropriate for them, so this time is a staple in classrooms that support choices. In our literacy project classrooms, students also have the opportunity during silent reading to choose to read the material independently or with the support of audiotapes. I strongly believe all students need the benefit of this sustained silent reading time where they are not interrupted by other students or by us for teaching. I also believe there are a wealth of learning activities and teaching opportunities such as instructional and peer conferencing, guided reading groups, literature circles, and independent research that cannot occur during silent reading or whole-class direct instruction. In order to accommodate these teaching and learning moments, I had to adjust our weekly schedule to create both a time and a structure where literacy explorations unique to the individual or small group could occur.

The schedule shown in Figure 8.1 demonstrates how I organized our classroom to allow for choices in classes where we had an extended block of time. In my case, this extended time was ninety minutes every day; other block schedules in classes where I work can be up to one hundred and twenty minutes per day.

Figure 8.1

A Typical Balanced Literacy Week (Extended Block)				
MONDAY	TUESDAY	WEDNESDAY	THURSDAY	FRIDAY
Independent Reading	*Read-Aloud and Accountable Talk (5–15 minutes)*			*Independent Reading*
	Shared Reading			
	• Here and now • Guided practice • Academic journals • Language collection	• Word of the day • Critical thinking and accountable talk • Questioning strategies	• Fluent reading of a variety of texts • Direct instruction for strategic reading	
	• Text-to-text, Text-to-self, and Text-to-world connections			
Independent Literacy Exploration	• Literal thinking	• Mini-mysteries		*Independent Literacy Exploration*
	Break			
	• Word Games	• Riddles/limericks		
	Shared Writing • Collaborative writing • Language experience activity • Usage mini-lessons • Guided writing • Extended writing • Fabulous phrases and scintillating sentences	*Putting the Art in Language Arts* • Art and literacy • Creative dramatics • Storytelling • Videos/recordings • Speakers • Readers' theater	*Writing Workshop*	
10 minutes • Exit slips • Sharing		*Closure* • Read-alouds • Review		10 minutes

A Typical Balanced Literacy Week (Single-Period Class)				
MONDAY	TUESDAY	WEDNESDAY	THURSDAY	FRIDAY
Read-Aloud				
Shared Reading • Here and now • Language collection • Guided practice • Critical thinking and accountable talk • Word of the day • Academic journals	• Fluent reading of a variety of texts • Direct instruction • Text-to-text, Text-to-self, Text-to-world connections	*Independent Reading*	*Writing Workshop* • Shared Writing	*Independent Literacy Exploration* • Guided reading • Conferencing • Literature circles • Plays • Research • Books on tape • Computer programs
• Academic journals • Word of the day		• Reading logs • Literary letters • Dialogue journals	*Sharing*	• End-of-week check-in • Continuous assessment

Figure 8.2

The schedule shown in Figure 8.2 represents a typical week in a class that has a traditional single period (usually forty-five to fifty-five minutes). Both schedules are labeled typical because my priorities for including all the approaches to reading and writing might not be the same as yours in terms of time. For example, both schedules are heavily weighted toward reading. I believe that it is the lack of reading that negatively affects students' writing, and both schedules reflect my belief that students' writing will improve with more reading time in conjunction with supported writing demonstrations. Also, projects, research, or special events sometimes took the place of what we would normally have done according to the schedule. A teacher recently told me she had been trying to stay on the schedule but found she had to modify it. I laughed as I told her that I had probably never managed to stay precisely on that schedule. The times varied every day in my classroom. Some days our read-alouds took five minutes and other days they took twenty. Text and purpose govern the amount of time you spend in any area. The critical aspect is making sure that all approaches to literacy are represented each week.

Both schedules include some literacy activities that may need explanation. Each of the reading approaches has been discussed at length in Chapters 3–7, and writing is discussed in Chapter 11, but I would like to highlight briefly some other areas as they relate to scheduling. On shared reading days, several activities occur that are related to the shared text. Some of those activities, such as Word of the Day, Here and Now, fluent reading of varied texts, and modeling of strategic reading, occur during each shared reading session. Other activities occur depending on students' needs and appropriateness with texts: guided practice for strategic reading, critical thinking and accountable talk strategies, academic journals, questioning strategies, language collection, and written or visual extensions. An umbrella goal for shared reading is always that students will begin or continue making text-to-self, text-to-text, and text-to-world connections (Keene and Zimmermann 1997; Harvey and Goudvis 2000). Use of graphic organizers, writing, visuals, questioning, and discussion are designed to lead readers back to those reader response connections.

Periods noted for shared writing have a range of writing opportunities depending on the needs and interests of the students: language experience activities, guided writing, collaborative writing, grammar and usage lessons, and highlighted student writing. Both shared reading and shared writing are essentially based in teacher-directed instruction. Writing workshop is student-centered, offering students time and opportunity to establish research, drafting, conferencing, revising, editing, and publishing priorities based on their writing agendas and class expectations.

All other periods during the week invite students to make choices for their learning. Independent reading, independent literacy exploration, writing workshop, and arts in the classroom all have student choice at the core. In this way, the organizational structure is in place for choice. Unfortunately, it didn't take me long to learn that student choice requires more support than just building in time for it to happen.

Supporting Realistic and Productive Choices

After several years of trying to figure out how to create a time for choice without students' seeing it as "free time," I finally came up with the idea for an independent literacy exploration (ILE) period each week (see Figures 8.1 and 8.2). It sounded ideal when I thought of it over the summer, and it still seemed like a great idea as I considered it during our day of preplanning. Lots of ideas seem great at first but need more thought before they can be implemented.

During the first week of school, I told my students that we would have a time each week called independent literacy exploration (ILE) when they would be free to choose whatever they wanted to work on as long as it related to literacy. So it was with high hopes that on our first Friday together we began ILE time. Students slept, talked, asked to go to the bathroom and their lockers and even other classes. No amount of cajoling could get them moving toward any literacy behaviors. I told them we wouldn't be able to have ILE time if they couldn't be more responsible. They could barely hear my voice over the noise. ILE as a concept was over for me.

On the following Thursday, students said, "Are we doing ILE tomorrow?" You can imagine the amount of tact I used in telling them they had abused the concept of ILE—of course we weren't having it. The following week, students once again asked about ILE. So I started a chart on the board and labeled it ILE Possibilities. Each day when we did something together in class, I wrote what we had done on the board and explained to students where they could find other materials like the ones we had used if they wanted them during ILE. If we read a play out of *Scope* or *Read,* I showed them how each issue of these magazines was filed in a cabinet by the main topic of the issue (drugs, drinking, prejudice, etc.). If we did art and writing projects, I explained where the paper and supplies were kept and listed that activity on the board. Finally, we had a substantial list of possibilities on the board, and students were asking every day, "Are we ever going to do ILE again?"

After about five weeks of planning, labeling, organizing, and listing, we finally tried ILE again. This time it was all that I had imagined because students now knew a range of possible options for this time in their week. During the course of the year, if students chose to do something not on our list, I asked them to add it to the list of possibilities in case someone else might want to do the same on another ILE day. Students began using the board to leave ILE messages: "Anyone want to read a play Friday?" or "I want to read *The Face on the Milk Carton* out loud. Anyone want to read it with me?"

ILE is always the most difficult to explain during workshops and the most critical for implementation if teachers plan to give students individual choice as well as individual attention. Once everyone had made an ILE commitment (see Figure 8.3, indicating a range of ILE activities I documented during one class period), I was free to confer with students about their reading, writing, research, or goals. I could also work with individuals or small groups of students who needed the extra support of a guided reading lesson. Once the structure for independence and choice is in place, there are always opportunities for students to receive extra support and to pursue research interests unique to the individual.

Ongoing assessment during ILE gives the teacher an opportunity to ascertain areas where the entire class might need support in order to make productive choices during times of independence. Thus, the ILE assessments influence teacher planning for subsequent classes on days of shared reading and writing. Research was one of the first areas I noted that students found overwhelming as an independent activity. Lots of students wanted to do research, and they often had important and intriguing questions, but they had no idea how to begin the research process. I found myself spending an inordinate amount of time with these students giving them instruction on research methods: forming questions, interviewing, collecting data, searching resources, organizing information, refining questions, and so on. I knew this was something that I didn't have time to do on an individual basis, so I designed a collaborative research project for students

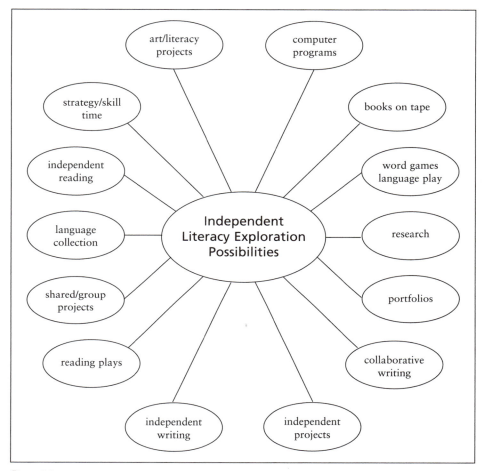

Figure 8.3

that would give them opportunities to learn the strategies and presentation of research. This research unit came out of my observations and conferences during ILE and influenced the direct instruction during our shared writing time. The impetus for much of what is done during whole-class instruction comes from the ongoing assessment of student needs discovered during times of independence. That whole-group direct instruction then affords students more choices during ILE because they have strategies and skills for that independence. These are reciprocal effects in a comprehensive literacy program.

With time and experience, I became more adept at seeing how to support students' choices with suggestions, direct teaching, needs- or interest-based grouping, and appropriate resources. I learned when I needed to pull the class back together for a shared experience that would extend their range of independent choices. I learned to intervene when students became lost or when they were making choices because they wanted to please me. The students and I learned how to manage time so everyone could get personal attention. Fortunately, some of those learnings transferred to the days when we worked together so that students began taking on some of the teaching responsibilities rather than waiting for me to make sure everyone was learning.

Resources That Support Choice

At the end of each school year, our classroom looked like a museum with a disorganized curator. There were books everywhere. Where class sets of novels and independent reading novels had previously taken up most of the space, now hundreds of reference books and nonfiction titles lined the shelves. There were still class sets for shared reading, but there were also several other sets of books. There were baskets with five to seven copies of single titles for literature circle groups. There were text sets (baskets of books all related to a common subject such as Vietnam or pregnancy), and there were author baskets (books by a single author for author studies). Some books were in boxes by genre (poetry collection, short story collection, myths and fables, tall tales and fairy tales for genre study). Student products were on the walls, hanging from the ceiling, and on racks.

Students played a crucial role in building resources to support choices. When the librarian asked for lists of books and resources to order for the library, students spent time with catalogs suggesting materials. When we had money left for ordering materials in our department, students made suggestions for films, videos, recordings, documentaries, and books. Students even created their own version of the library's vertical files by hanging large envelopes on hooks under the chalk tray. Each envelope was labeled for the pamphlets, newspaper and journal articles, and artifacts related to the topic of the envelope: drinking and driving, drugs, pregnancy, obituaries, drivers' education, hunting, Dear Abby letters, fishing, snowmobiling, drag racing, wrestling. As students read things they thought would interest others, they added them to current envelopes or created new ones. I sometimes joked with students that their off-task behavior was reading because they so often stopped to read on their way to doing something else.

Reflections on Classrooms of Choice

With so much emphasis on curriculum guides, published units for novels, textbook teacher's guides, and content standards, it is easy to lose sight of the fact that students do have questions about themselves and the world in which they live. Even students in middle and high school who have come to expect a standardized curriculum still have real questions. I asked a middle school social studies teacher in California to ask her students what questions they had that they would like to learn more about in their social studies classes. I thought their questions were incredibly interesting and fantasized about how much more these students would enjoy their classes if the curriculum could come from the real questions they had. Some of their questions (and there were hundreds of them) are the following:

How did people become people?
Were people here before plants?
Did any living or dead people live when dinosaurs lived?
Where did water first come from?
Why do we have different religions?
Why are there wars?
Why was Cambodia poor of money?
Why were books invented?
How did Jackie Robinson die?
Were cats really important or not in Egyptian times?
Why did Daniel Shay have a rebellion?
Why did they start naming streets after people?
What major ideas went into shaping the American government?
Back in the ice age did the year start with 1?
Who invented history?
Where did music come from?
Who made up overheads?
Who invented desks?
What was the real meaning of the Bill of Rights?
How did they find the name for things like president? Why couldn't it have
    been dog or something else?
Did we ever recreate the exact Egyptian language?
Was Malcolm X Muhammad Ali's best friend?
Who discovered Long Beach?
Why did it take so long for all states to celebrate Martin Luther King day?
Why are science and history so different?
Why is the world round?
Why is there violence?
Who thought of inventing schools?

I was amazed at the range of questions students asked. As I read through their questions, I couldn't help but imagine a room filled with hundreds of books and computers and walls covered with students' questions. Students could categorize their questions, and as they found answers, they could add their answers to the question wall and write their new questions—independent social studies exploration (ISSE). Perhaps that will be this teacher's next step toward a classroom supporting choices. When I wrote about ILE, I was referring to a reading/language arts classroom, but this could happen in any class. Imagine the rich learning lives students would have if they had an ILE experience in all their content classes where they were supported in discovering answers to questions that really matter to them—questions about math, science, history, or health.

In Steven Levy's *Starting from Scratch: One Classroom Builds Its Own Curriculum,* he gives support for making independent learning a critical part of our time with children. "When students learn by discovery, they are much more likely to understand, remember, and apply their knowledge to other situations. . . . The challenge is always to give them a chance to discover it for themselves" (78). Learners need these times of independence—times when they make choices and live with the consequences of those choices—while they still have our support. Neither independent reading nor independent literacy exploration function effectively without the scaffolding of a knowledgeable teacher.

Two of my students spent almost six weeks of ILE time with the research question Can you have sex and not get pregnant? This was probably the most important thing they could have learned during that six weeks of their lives. They talked with doctors and nurses; read pamphlets and books; read young adult literature with main characters who had become pregnant; visited community service programs on planned parenthood; interviewed students who had children, church youth group leaders, and their own parents. One student read Diane Duane's short story "Midnight Snack," and this led her to explore the existence of unicorns. After reading Sparks's book about religious cults, *Jay's Journal,* three students explored religious cults. Voigt's *The Runner* led another student to an incredible research study about the Vietnam war. Had I been planning curriculum for these students, I would never have chosen those books or those topics. Independent reading leads to independent research, which leads them back to more reading.

Their research products were modeled after the I-Search paper format (Macrorie 1988). If you haven't considered using this method of research with your students, it is an exciting, personal, and resourceful way for students to document their reading and research paths. Essentially, students document their search in four areas:

- Finding your question . . .
  What do you really want/need to know in your life?
- Searching . . .
  What paths did you take to find answers to your questions?
  What happened or how did that lead you to your next source?

- Findings . . .
  What answer(s) did you find?
  What did you find that would lead you to other questions?
- Now what?
  Good I-Search papers end with new questions. If you were to start a new
  paper and you already knew the information you have here, what new
  questions would you have?

I-Searching students usually begin their research by going to live sources. They document the search by using "I" and they cite sources. Finally, the papers end with questions that lead them to new reading and further research. When students are searching for answers to real questions, the investment in research is dramatically more significant than just "doing research on Whitman."

Nehring relates, in *"Why Do We Gotta Do This Stuff, Mr. Nehring?"* how he tried to get his students involved in asking questions and doing research that would be significant to them. "With all respect, Mr. Nehring," said one, "I don't think students should have to go out of their way like that." When Mr. Nehring asked him why, the student replied, "We're just kids, after all. We're not real researchers." Mr. Nehring asked when they would become real researchers, and the students replied, "After we're done with school. Or maybe never, if we like go into advertising or something" (135–136). I believe the time for students to become real researchers— not those who copy information about a British author who lived in the 1900s but learners who do research when they have real questions—should occur while they have the support of knowledgeable mentors. Learning how to question and find answers to those questions; learning how to make good choices and establish priorities are critical life skills for each of us. Independent reading and ILE help students make the transition from school learning to life learning.

One of my high school students gave me the gift of a poetic reminder about the importance of independent learning in our classroom. Jasmine came into my class because she had failed English during the previous school year. My class was to count as makeup credit for that failure. When I explained my beliefs about the importance of students learning to make choices, she was visibly skeptical. After several days of grumbling that it wasn't her job to find the work she needed to do, she settled in and started reading. Her reading led to lots of writing. She went back and read the books and plays she had refused to read in the class she had failed. She did vocabulary programs on the computer and wrote her own poetry calendar. Each day she seemed to be into something new, so I questioned her about the range of choices she was making. She said, "I kept waiting for you to change your mind and say, 'This is really what you have to do to pass.' But, you didn't. This class has been like Christmas dinner where you get to taste and taste until you finally get your fill and then you settle down for seconds with the food you liked the most." On Friday afternoon, I found the note she left me as a response to what she had learned that week.

Shopping for Christmas
Shopping for Christmas
I saw an old man
He asked for a penny
To lend him a hand

He walked away grinning
I had made his rough day
Seem easier than before
And I went on my way.

Before I could stop
At one more store
I was struck by a feeling
I'd not felt before
A feeling of hope
In the midst of despair
Helping to cope
With the smog in the air

At the ripe age of twelve
I knew it all
At least so I thought
Until my visit at the mall

Sheltered by love
Eased in with care
I knew nothing of hate
Caught up in a snare
Knew nothing of how rare
To find people who care

I found myself staring
At the black man in rags
He was begging for mercy
As they spit—hit, he lagged

Finally behind
This bunch of wise fools
Where did they learn to hate?
At our public schools?
It was in those few minutes
It was after this show
I realized I'd learned
Everything I needed to know

I don't know where Jasmine is today. I do know that wherever she is, she is able to make choices in a world filled with interesting things to learn. I also know that our choice-based classroom was the place where she made the transition from active not-learning to passionate explorer. Schools should be places where we expect such transitions.

"Am I the Only One Who Can't Make a K-W-L Work?" Literacy Paths to Content Knowledge

Crucial to comprehension is the knowledge that the reader brings to the text. The construction of meaning depends on the reader's knowledge of the language, the structure of texts, a knowledge of the subject of the reading and a broad-based background or world knowledge.

RICHARD DAY AND JULIAN BAMFORD, EXTENSIVE READING IN THE
SECOND LANGUAGE CLASSROOM

Content literacy brings special challenges to most students, even those considered successful by traditional measures. These challenges typically fall into the categories Day and Bamford highlight: lack of background knowledge, structure of texts, management of the reading task, and inability to make personal connections to the content. Because of these text and cognitive difficulties, many students walk away from content classes feeling lost.

When students at one middle school were asked to complete the prompt "To me, reading my science (history/geography) book means . . ." their responses included the following sentence completions: death, total boredom, agony and pain, reading a lot of stuff, reading stuff I don't care to learn, too much stuff at once, torture, nothing because it makes no sense, hard work, boring time because there are no good parts, and work. When questioned further, some students had positive comments about the maps, pictures, graphs, experiments, and unusual places, but they didn't actually see those as part of the reading they did. Those were the extras they looked at on their own time.

Content area reading is more difficult than reading fiction. Textbook reading is the most difficult kind of reading and is the one most often given to students to read independently. Fiction depends on readers' identifying with interesting plots, dynamic characters, exciting resolutions, and memorable descriptions to hold their interest. Textbooks rely on graphs, charts, pictures, historical events, and scientific descriptions to sustain the reader's attention. In fiction many of the same words are repeated; in textbooks several specialized and technical words may be introduced in every chapter. Fiction is more likely to provide entertainment; nonfiction, information. Finally, an entire work of fiction might revolve around a single theme whereas textbooks are dense, requiring readers to hold multiple concepts in their heads throughout the reading. All of these characteristics of textbooks lead us to see the importance of two approaches to content literacy: supplementing textbook instruction with understandable and interesting texts that build background knowledge and personal connections, and scaffolding reading experiences to provide students with strategies for understanding text structures and managing the reading experience.

Prereading: The Role of Background Knowledge and Personal Connections

Meltzer (1994) cites the importance of scaffolded historical experiences: "The danger of providing young people with myths rather than history is that mythology makes it easier for the people who wield political power to get away with platitudes and pieties they feed to the public so they can carry out their policies at home and abroad. If we do not learn how to ask probing questions about the past, how will we meet the challenges of the present?" If we want students to ask probing questions, search for their own answers, and transfer that learning to other events, we have to begin with print and nonprint sources of information that invite readers to make such explorations.

Using literature in these ways in content area classes supplements textbook instruction by giving students information in a narrative format and allowing them to explore events more extensively than is afforded in most textbooks. In

Jean Fritz's autobiography, *Homesick*, she talks about coming to the United States and encountering social studies textbooks for the first time: "I skimmed through the pages but couldn't find any mention of people at all. There was talk about dates and square miles and cultivation and population growth and immigration and the Western movement, but it was as if the forest had lain down and given way to farmland without anyone being brave or scared or tired or sad, without babies being born, without people dying" (153).

At this point you might be saying, "But I don't have time to provide so many experiences for each event. I have to cover the entire text." I think this is one of the things that has left most of us with such sketchy understandings of historical events: someone tried to *cover* all the events rather than help us *understand* the social and political concepts several events might have shared. F. M. Newman cites the pressure of content coverage as a contributing factor to this lack of deep understanding:

> We are addicted to coverage. This addiction seems endemic in high schools . . . but it affects all levels of the curriculum, from kindergarten through college. We expose students to broad surveys of the disciplines and to endless sets of skills and competencies . . . the press for broad coverage causes many teachers to feel inadequate about leaving out so much content and apologetically mindful of the fact that much of what they teach is not fully understood by their students. (346)

When I first started attending reading conferences and workshops, I was struck by the number of strategies teachers and researchers were using to help students build and activate background knowledge. In my English education courses the only reference we had made to background knowledge was talking about giving students historical information about time periods and authors. Even then we didn't talk about this information as facilitating the reading of difficult texts; we talked about its being critical to knowledge of literary movements.

In reading education the importance of activating and building background knowledge has long been established as critical to the reading process. Frank Smith summarizes that importance: "The implication for anyone involved in teaching reading should be obvious. Whenever readers cannot make sense of what they are expected to read—because the material bears no relevance to any prior knowledge they might have—then reading will become more difficult and learning to read impossible" (1988a, 81). Establishing background knowledge that will lead readers into texts and support their understandings of texts as they read is the mark of scaffolding content reading experiences. Those prereading scaffolding experiences require teachers to ask (and answer) several questions that have teaching implications concerning the most effective steps for helping learners develop language, factual information, and emotional connections that will carry them into the content-related reading, writing, and research:

What is the major concept?

What background knowledge will students bring to this concept or event?

How can I help students make a connection between this concept and their lives?

How could we use the titles, headings, and subheadings as a way to build knowledge and predict content?

What could we do to replicate these events or show similar events in contemporary times?

Are there *key* concepts or specialized vocabulary that need to be introduced because students could not get meaning from context?

How could we use the pictures, charts, and graphs to predict or anticipate content?

How can I provide prereading experiences for students that will make them care enough to want to know more?

What supplemental materials to I need to provide to support reading (maps, artifacts, diaries, videos, news clips, music, art)?

Will the textbook be used as one of many sources of information, or will it be the sole source?

What support will students need to access textbook information (shared reading, recordings, questioning guides)?

I would come to see the importance of background knowledge in a different light after the lesson my students taught me as we prepared for our read-aloud one day. I intended reading Maya Angelou's poem "No Losers, No Weepers" as our beginning-of-class read-aloud. Just before class began, I discovered that we had a set of *Reading Road to Writing* workbooks that contained a brief biography of Angelou. I decided that students might connect more if they had some knowledge of the poet, so I read the bio to them before reading the poem. However, as soon as I finished reading the bio, I thought I had to ask them some questions or the time would have been wasted. (Where do we get these ideas?) The "conversation" that follows documents my foolhardy attempt at activating background knowledge (Allen 1995, 113–114):

JANET: What do you think they're talking about when they say, "She did what her ancestors could only wish for"?

MELVIN: She freed the slaves.

JANET: Did we have slaves when Maya Angelou lived?

TAMMY: No.

JANET: When did we have slaves?

MAC: With Columbus?

TERRI: In the 1500s?

DEREK: 1700s.

TANYA: World War II.

By this point I was becoming more exasperated than I wanted to admit. The class was in pandemonium.

JANET: Wait . . . Stop . . . What war was fought to get rid of slavery?
TORI: World War II.
DIANA: World War I.
MAC: Revolutionary War.
JANET: This is pathetic. What war was fought over slavery?
MELVIN: The Silver War.

This wasn't horseshoes; close was good enough.

JANET: That's close, Melvin. The Civil War. Now, who was president at that time?
TERRI: Abraham Lincoln.

A smart teacher would have stopped there; I finally had a right answer.

JANET: Great, now we're getting somewhere. Now, what two parts of the country were fighting?
TANYA: England and the West.
JANET: Now, let's try and get these facts straight.
TAMMY: Just tell us if it's a, b, or c. It's a, right?
JANET: The point is not whether it's a, b, or c; the point is learning something. This needs to make sense.
TAMMY: It would make sense if we just wrote down the right answer.
ANNE: I know the answer. The Civil War was fought between the North and the South.
MAC: I thought that was the Revolution War.
JANET: What was the Revolutionary War fought for?
DIANE: Freedom.
JANET: For whom?
TORI: Jews?
MELVIN: Blacks?
MAC: Italians?
JANET: Arghh!

I realized at that moment (once I calmed down) that students are often asked to read and write about concepts, themes, and events of which they have no working knowledge. In addition, these events and the people in them seem distant enough to be fantasy for many students. Fletcher recounts advice from his writing teacher: "The bigger the issue, the smaller you write. Remember that. You don't write about the horrors of war. No. You write about a kid's burnt socks lying on the road" (49). As I sat at home that night transcribing our tortuous lesson, I wondered what I would have done had my students really needed accurate knowledge of the wars for our learning that day. As it was, none of those historical events actually had anything to do with what we were doing in class that day. After all, this had only been the segue into our daily read-aloud. At the time, I wasn't quite sure how I could quickly build background knowledge so that students could connect historical events with their lives. Literature can provide both the content knowledge and the emotional connection that leads to personal response and social consciousness.

Structures That Support Connections and Questions

I had seen many content literacy workshop leaders demonstrate the use of K-W-L (Know, What to Know, Learned) (Ogle 1986), but I never had much success when using it. For example, I would put the K-W-L up on the overhead projector and say to my students, "What do you know about the civil rights movement?"

"Nothing."

"OK, what do you want to know?"

"Nothing."

I would remove the K-W-L transparency and think, "Well, that didn't accomplish much." I always thought I was just not using the K-W-L correctly until I thought about the amazing amount of misinformation and lack of connection to the historical events my students evidenced in our Maya Angelou "discussion." It helped me realize that many learners need some background knowledge *before* they know enough to want to know more. Also, the background had to have an emotional impact in order for my students to make personal connections. With those goals in mind, I created the Writing to Learn and B-K-W-L-Q graphic organizers (see Figures 9.1, 9.2, and 9.4), which I adapted from Ogle's K-W-L in order to meet the needs of learners in my classes.

Writing to Learn can be used with any number of reading, listening, viewing, and tactile experiences as long as each experience builds on previous learning and leads students to develop their own questions. The use of this organizer builds on research about the significant relationship between reading and writing. Tierney and Shanahan highlight this connection in their discussion of how reading and writing contribute to learning new ideas: "The more content is manipulated, the more likely it is understood and remembered. In accordance with this thesis, a number of researchers have hypothesized that writing will have an impact upon what is learned because it prompts learners to elaborate and manipulate ideas" (266).

The student samples of Writing to Learn (Figures 9.1 and 9.2) were completed by students at a California high school during their reading of *The Watsons Go to Birmingham—1963* (Curtis). The teacher had read aloud to students from

H.3 Writing to Learn

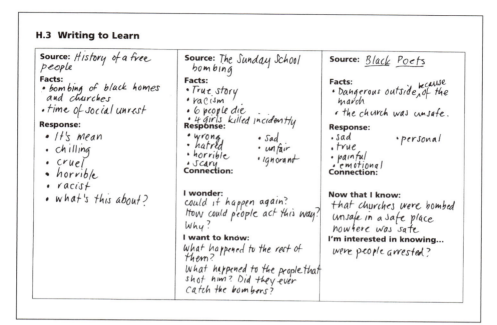

Source: *History of a free people*	Source: *The Sunday School bombing*	Source: <u>Black Poets</u>
Facts: • bombing of black homes and churches • time of social unrest **Response:** • It's mean • chilling • cruel • horrible • racist • what's this about?	**Facts:** • True story • racism • 6 people die • 4 girls killed incidently **Response:** • wrong • sad • hatred • unfair • horrible • ignorant • scary **Connection:** **I wonder:** could it happen again? How could people act this way? Why? **I want to know:** What happened to the rest of them? What happened to the people that shot him? Did they ever catch the bombers?	**Facts:** • Dangerous outside, because of the march • the church was unsafe. **Response:** • sad • personal • true • painful • emotional **Connection:** **Now that I know:** that churches were bombed unsafe in a safe place nowhere was safe **I'm interested in knowing...** were people arrested?

Figure 9.1

H.3 Writing to Learn

Source: *History of Free People*	Source: *The Sunday School bombing*	Source: *Black Poets*
Facts: Bombing of black homes & churches Social unrest **Response:** • What the hell are these people doing? The Bible says that thou shall not kill or Murder. • Black hard times • Racial tension	**Facts:** • 6 people killed • They were all black • biggest church in Alabama (negro) **Response:** • 4 kill'd incidently • 2 kill'd purposely **Connection:** These people suck **I wonder:** I wonder if we can live in peace. if racism can stop Why a church **I want to know:** Did the 17 injured die? What happened to the others Did they get caught. Why can't they control themselves	**Facts:** • Didn't want kid to march. • Thought kid would be safe in church. **Response:** My response is that the kid was try'n to be safe sad·frightening **Connection:** **Now that I know:** These people suck **I'm interested in knowing...**

Figure 9.2

three sources, giving them the opportunity to jot down any facts they heard. When she finished reading, she gave students a few minutes to write their responses to the reading. From an American history textbook called *History of a Free People* (McCutchen) the teacher read, "In Birmingham, Alabama, police dogs and electric cattle prods were used against black demonstrators. Black homes and churches were bombed" (743). This is not an excerpt from a larger body of information but all the information in that book for this pivotal event in the civil rights movement. These students have listed "bombing of black homes and churches" as factual notes. While the facts based on the limited information are the same for both students, their responses showed evidence of personal connections: "What the hell are these people doing?" "What's this about?"

The teacher also read an article from *Bridges and Borders: Diversity in America*. This collection of articles appearing in *Time* magazine from the 1930s to the 1990s highlights major historical events that had an influence on American history. The article (see Figure 9.3) has many more facts than the textbook, and it also evoked an incredible emotional response. Students noted the number of people killed, the significance of the bomb site, and the racial tension in their factual notes. After their responses in this column, students were asked to note something they were still wondering about or would like to know. These students wondered if we can live in peace, if racism can stop, and why a church was chosen. They wanted to know why people could act this way and could it happen again. It is clear from their responses that they now care about the people involved in this event and have transferred that caring to contemporary times.

Finally, the teacher read Dudley Randall's poem "Ballad of Birmingham" from his collection *The Black Poets*:

Ballad of Birmingham
"Mother dear, may I go downtown
instead of out to play,
and march the streets of Birmingham
in a freedom march today?"

"No, baby, no, you may not go,
for the dogs are fierce and wild,
and clubs and hoses, guns and jails
ain't good for a little child."

"But, mother, I won't be alone.
Other children will go with me,
and march the streets of Birmingham
to make our country free."

"No, baby, no, you may not go,
for I fear those guns will fire.

The Sunday School Bombing   SEPTEMBER 27, 1963

SUNDAY MORNING, Sept. 15, was cool and overcast in Birmingham. Sunday school classes were just ending in the basement of the yellow brick 16th Street Baptist Church, the city's largest Negro church and the scene of several recent civil rights rallies. The morning's lesson was "The Love That Forgives," from the fifth chapter of Matthew. Four girls—Carole Robertson, 14, Cynthia Wesley, 14, Addie Mae Collins, 14, and Denise McNair, 11—left the classroom to go to the bathroom.

At 10:22 the bomb exploded, with the force of ten to 15 sticks of dynamite. It had been planted under the steps behind the 50-year-old building.

Great chunks of stone shot like artillery shells through parked cars. The blast shattered the windshield of a passing car, knocked the driver unconscious. A metal railing, torn from its concrete bed, lanced across the street into the window of the Social Dry Cleaning store. Next door, customers at the Silver Springs Restaurant were knocked to the floor. In nearby Kelly Ingram Park, pieces of brick nipped the leaves off trees 200 ft. from the blast.

BENEATH THE ROBE. Inside the church, a teacher screamed, "Lie on the floor! Lie on the floor!" Rafters collapsed, a skylight fell on the pulpit. Part of a stained glass window shattered, obliterating the face of Christ. A man cried: "Everybody out! Everybody out!" A stream of sobbing Negroes stumbled through the litter—past twisted metal folding chairs, past splintered wooden benches, past shredded songbooks and Bibles. A Negro woman staggered out of the Social Dry Cleaning store shrieking "Let me at 'em! I'll kill 'em!"—and fainted. White plaster dust fell gently for a block around.

Police cars poured into the block—and even as the cops plunged into the church, some enraged Negroes began throwing rocks at them. Rescue workers found a seven-foot pyramid of bricks where once the girls' bathroom stood. On top was a child's white lace choir robe. A civil defense captain lifted the hem of the robe. "Oh, my God," he cried. "Don't look!" Beneath lay the mangled body of a Negro girl.

Bare-handed, the workers dug deeper into the rubble—until four bodies had been uncovered. The head and shoulder of one child had been completely blown off. The remains were covered with shrouds and carried out to waiting ambulances. A youth rushed forward, lifted a sheet and wailed: "This is my sister! My God—she's dead!"

The church's pastor, the Rev. John Cross, hurried up and down the sidewalk, urging the milling crowd to go home. "Please go home!" he said. "The Lord is our shepherd, and we shall not want." Another Negro minister added his pleas. "Go home and pray for the men who did this evil deed," he said. "We must have love in our hearts for these men." But a Negro boy screamed, "We give love—and we get this!" And another youth yelled: "Love 'em? Love 'em? We hate 'em!" A man wept: "My grandbaby was one of those killed! Eleven years old! I helped pull the rocks off her! You know how I feel? I feel like blowing the whole town up!"

The Birmingham police department's six-wheeled riot tank thumped onto the scene and cops began firing shotguns over the heads of the crowd while Negroes pelted them with rocks. Later, Negro youths began stoning passing white cars. The police ordered them to stop. One boy, Johnny Robinson, 16, ran, and a cop killed him with a blast of buckshot. That made five dead and 17 injured in the bomb blast.

"I CAN'T." Several miles away, on the worn-out coal-field fringe of Birmingham, two young Negro brothers, James and Virgil Ware, were riding a bicycle. Virgil, 13, was sitting on the handle bars. A motor scooter with two 16-year-old white boys aboard approached from the opposite direction. James Ware, 16, told what happened then: "This boy on the front of the bike turns and says something to the boy behind him, and the other reaches in his pocket and he says *Pow! Pow!* with a gun twice. Virgil fell and I said, get up Virgil, and he said, I can't, I'm shot."

And so six died on a Sunday in Birmingham.   ■

Figure 9.3

But you may go to church instead,
and sing in the children's choir."

She has combed and brushed her nightdark hair,
and bathed rose petal sweet,
and drawn white gloves on her small brown hands,
and white shoes on her feet.

The mother smiled to know her child
was in the sacred place,

but that smile was the last smile
to come upon her face.

For when she heard the explosion,
her eyes grew wet and wild.
She raced through the streets of Birmingham
calling for her child.

She clawed through bits of glass and brick,
then lifted out a shoe.
"O, here's the shoe my baby wore,
but, baby, where are you?"

From this reading, students understood that it was dangerous even outside the march and that even churches could be unsafe. They now had many unanswered questions related to the events, the aftermath, and the arrests/prosecutions. They were particularly interested in knowing if anyone was arrested.

After students have had the opportunity to build factual knowledge and develop personal connections to this historical event at the individual level, the class can come together to document class understandings using the B-K-W-L-Q (see Figure 9.4). The resources used to build background knowledge for this event were all read-alouds (texbook, article, poem) but a wide range of resources would have accomplished the same purpose: Spike Lee's documentary *Four*

Figure 9.4

H.4 B-K-W-L-Q (Adapted from Ogle 1986)

Build background	What do I know?	What do I want to know?	What did I learn?	What new questions do I have?
• Textbook • article • Poem	• Time of social unrest • True story • 6 people died • Bombing of black homes and Churches	• Could it happen again? • How could people act this way? • Did they ever catch the bombers? • Can we stop racism?		

Little Girls; other poetry; "The Long Wait for Justice," a 1998 article in *Read.* The teacher could have gathered news articles, interviews, and news clips. This B-K-W-L-Q graphic organizer can then take the students to other resources where they might find answers to their questions and develop new questions to carry over into future reading and study.

Two teachers in Alabama's Hewitt Trussville Middle School used the same resources for Writing to Learn prior to their classes' reading *The Watsons Go to Birmingham—1963.* Following these reading, writing, and reflecting experiences, they took their students to the 16th Street Baptist Church and the Civil Rights Institute. Then the students wrote and drew their responses to these events and contributed those responses to a collection they created, *We Remember . . .*, not because they had a class assignment but because they had been so moved by their experiences. Joey, a student in Tara Bensinger's class, wrote a poem from the perspective of one of the four girls killed in the Sunday school bombing, Carole Robertson:

Carole
If you were Carole,
What would you do?
Would you miss your parents
or your tiny white shoe?

She didn't know she was going
to die that day;
she just went to church
to sing and to pray.

She was getting dressed
above the bomb that day,
then BOOM! She didn't have
Time to get away.

Now she and three of her friends
are just sweet memories,
and now her mother
has no one to please.

These students' lives and their reading have been changed because of the layers of experience and perspectives these teachers have given the learners in their classrooms. Building background knowledge in memorable ways does take more time than simply assigning chapters to read, but students remember the events and take these understandings into new learning moments. Ralph Waldo Emerson said, "The things taught in schools are not an education but the means of an education." Each of these in-depth learning experiences leads students one step closer to independent lifelong learning.

During Reading: Managing the Reading Task

Once students have some background knowledge that will help them move into textbook or other expository text reading, our teaching roles take on some additional responsibilities. We have to help students manage the task of reading. Management of reading actually requires that students develop understandings in several areas: understanding the structure of informational texts; determining the purpose of passages; selecting meaning-making strategies appropriate to the text; understanding the subtleties of text (tone, style, voice) as predictors of meaning; monitoring understanding; and how and when to use all these understandings to support effective reading. This is an area where emerging readers often falter in their development as readers: they try to read informational texts and textbooks using the same reading processes they would have used to read narratives. They find themselves lost and often attribute this confusion to the fact that they "just don't enjoy reading anymore." Informational texts offer readers a variety of supports (text features and conventions that assist the reader in making meaning) and challenges (text features and conventions that get in the way of reading). The teacher's job during reading is assisting students as they manage the reading task. This assistance can take many forms:

- Asking questions or creating prompts that help students experience the problems or events from the perspective of primary involvement.
- Helping students maintain reading focus with strategies such as RPMs (Recall-Predict-Move on).
- Modeling and expecting student questions during reading as a way of maintaining purposeful reading.
- Using charts and graphic organizers to organize, document, and display group thinking, questioning, and learning.
- Using comparison/contrast to help students connect new to known.
- Helping students infer and question their way through the text.
- Demonstrating fluent reading processes by monitoring reading and stopping when reading does not make sense.
- Giving students opportunities to document changes in thinking as new material is presented.

With each of these critical teaching moments, students must be actively involved in coming to new understandings of the ways that texts work to provide information, pleasure, and impetus for further reading.

Understanding Text Structure

Long after most students in my classes were reading with fluency in our classroom, they were still struggling to pass some of their content classes. Many students loved the hands-on aspects of science but could not or would not read the required textbook. In social studies classes where the teachers used lots of supplementary materials (videos, newspapers, storytelling), these students were successful. In social studies classes where grades depended on information gained from textbook reading, they failed.

It was during this time that I discovered Davey's textbook activity guide (TAG) in a *Journal of Reading* article. Davey developed strategy codes (P = predict; WR = provide a written response; Skim = read quickly for stated purpose; Map = complete a semantic map; and PP = predict with partner) to guide students through the text with a focus on the strategic processes and self-monitoring strategies they used to understand their reading. After reading the article, it occurred to me that part of the problem my students experienced was seeing the textbook as overwhelming. They didn't know how to break the text into the manageable chunks. They saw everything in the textbook as equally important (or unimportant) and therefore viewed the textbook not as a reference with predictable reference tools but as a long, long novel without any interesting characters or action. They were stymied before they even began.

In my reading classes I decided to help them develop strategies for reading their textbooks effectively by creating a TAG that would show them the supports and strategies readers use to get meaning from textbooks. Unfortunately, the guides I created for my students' textbooks didn't survive the move, but I have created many since then for students in the classrooms where I consult. The one discussed here was created for middle school students in Long Beach for use with their Houghton Mifflin social studies textbook, Level 6. Students complete the TAG with their learning partners. To explain the construction of the guide, I'll discuss each question and the texts supports I wanted students to notice and use in the process of completing the TAG.

The first four questions relate to the process of skimming:

1. (201) Skim Use the timeline to determine the years of the New Kingdom.
2. (199–203) Skim With your partner, list all the headings and subheadings found in this section.
3. (199–203) PP, WR Based on these subheadings, create two prediction questions. For example, if I look at the subheading "A Better Calendar," my prediction question might be, "I wonder if the book will tell me how the Egyptian calendar is different from the one that existed before this?"
4. (199) P Discuss with your partner the way the word *pharaoh* changed in meaning. Write the two meanings below.

Teaching students how to skim is often more difficult than sitting though a root canal. Skimming is based on quickly determining main ideas and concepts. To do that, fluent readers use conventions they can trust: titles, headings, subheadings, thesis sentences, bold and italicized words, captions, and side bars. Struggling or inefficient readers see all words as equally important and do not use the supports available to them in the textbook. In this case, students could quickly identify title, headings, and subheadings by looking for larger font and bold type. I didn't want them simply to know where to find those supports (although that would be a good place to start for many readers) but wanted them also to realize the predictive support those titles and headings provide for them. Therefore, question 3 asks students to use those headings to write prediction questions. To answer question 4, students would have to pay attention to the use of bold type **pharaoh** and let it clue them in to the importance of a word they would encounter several times in the reading of the text. Students sometimes believe these key terms are random rather than seeing them as significant to the text in terms of repetition or context. These four questions have "right there" answers yet still move students in the direction of using the text supports available to them.

Questions 5–10 ask students to continue using text supports to do a close reading of certain passages:

5. (200–03) Map Work with your partner to complete a graphic map that compares and contrasts the accomplishments of Hatshepsut and Thutmose III.
6. (200) WR Write a note to yourself about why there were no pyramids built during this period.
7. (199–201) Map Create a Map that shows the order of rulers during the New Kingdom.
8. (200–201) PP, WR Predict with your partner the response of the Egyptian people when Hatshepsut wouldn't let Thutmose III rule the Kingdom. Create newspaper headlines for that day's newspaper: one headline for an interview with Hatshepsut and one headline after interviewing a man and woman on the street and one headline after interviewing Thutmose III.
9. (199–203) Map Create two obelisks with one representing Hatshepsut's reign and one representing Thutmose III's reign. Your words and drawings should be specific enough so we could match the obelisk with the ruler.
10. (All) P, WR Discuss with your partner the lasting gifts we have received from the rulers and people living during the New Kingdom age. Write a summary sentence that would help us remember those gifts.

These tasks now extend readers' strategies into predicting, inferring, analyzing and applying new information, and making personal connections. To respond to questions 5–10, students would have drawn on the following text supports: bold, italics, borders, captions, side panels of information, glossary/key terms, pronunciation guides, maps and legends, headings and subheadings, timelines and side bar questions with arrows that indicate where readers would find answers to those questions.

Questions 7–9 are designed to have them map their discovered information or create visuals for themselves as reminders of what they are learning from this experience. In the original TAG, Davey used self-monitoring codes for students to indicate their understanding of the information being presented: I understand; I'm not sure I understand; and I do not understand and need to restudy. Questions 6 and 10 ask students to assess their own knowledge level by summarizing and writing notes to themselves related to the critical aspects of their reading and study.

While these TAGs are intended for use with textbooks, my colleagues and I have found them useful when working with genres that have distinctive text features that students often miss. For example, students often skip all the stage directions and parenthetical information when reading drama. This information should be assisting them as they read the dialogue. Lee Corey, while teaching at Oak Ridge High School in Orlando, created a TAG to help students focus on those aspects prior to each act of *Romeo and Juliet*. Two of the TAG prompts for Act V follow:

> Skim, PP, Map (Act V): Read through the stage directions in Act V prior to reading the dialogue. Predict the action you think will take place in Act V based on information you learned from the stage directions. Map that information by using a chain diagram for Events 1–2–3.

> WR, P (Act V): Use the parentheticals that show the emotion attached to Romeo and Juliet's dialogue to examine their speeches for characteristics of a crush or characteristics of true love. Create a Venn diagram that compares and contrasts these traits.

The distinction I make between this type of guide and traditional study or question guides is that the TAG tasks lead students to look at processes for learning new information. The products of using these processes then require students to use effective reading and learning strategies to internalize information and then make connections to their prior knowledge of content. Finally, I always try to embed monitoring questions in the TAG so that students are encouraged to use the monitoring behaviors of fluent readers: *taking note*; *making clear* with organizing and summarizing; *making connections* with comparing, contrasting, and categorizing; and *showing* ways to demonstrate their understandings to others.

Readability

Another aspect of understanding text structure is having a working knowledge of readability. So many books now come with a readability level imprinted on the back cover or on the citation page that many students and most teachers are aware of those numbers. In fact, in one classroom the teacher had arranged her library to reflect those grade-level numbers and students had to read books that "matched" their individual grade-level reading scores. This was a well-intentioned teacher who really wanted her students to gain fluency by reading books that were at their independent reading levels. Unfortunately, she didn't know readability levels' shortcomings in terms of predicting student success with texts.

The Fry graph shown in Figure 9.5 is one of the most commonly used methods for determining readability for textbooks and trade books. This readability is based on determining the numbers of sentences and syllables in a one-hundred-word passage. The instructions with the graph suggest taking three different one-hundred-word samples and averaging the scores from those in order to obtain an estimated readability. Passages with multisyllabic words and longer sentences have higher readability scores; those with shorter words and sentences, lower readability scores. While the Fry graph does take into account word and sentence length, it doesn't account for several other factors that influence readability: specialized vocabulary, text coherence, organizational structure of text, reader's interest, background knowledge for content, concept density (several concepts introduced in a small amount of text), languages other than reader's first language, and text supports. As a result, some texts with very low readability scores are actually quite difficult for students to read, and some texts with high readability scores are quite easily understood.

Figure 9.5

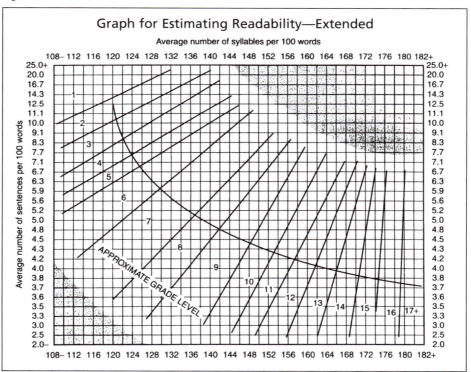

In her ninth-grade classroom, Lee Corey asked students to examine the readability of the texts they were reading during their independent reading time as a way of discussing text choice. Students were given Fry readability graphs and asked to determine readability based on the graph. They were then asked to analyze that readability and discuss whether they felt the readability was accurate in terms of content, supports, and challenges in the text. One student who was reading a Christopher Pike suspense novel determined that the text passage was at the sixth-grade level based on the Fry graph (see Figure 9.6). However, he didn't see the text as suitable for sixth graders because of the mature content: "It deals w/a person being murdered" and "It mentions Michael's sexual apatite." Based on students' discussions of their books after analysis, they came up with several conclusions that have instructional implications for teachers:

- The same book can have different readability scores depending on the passage you choose to analyze—have to think about the whole book not just one hundred words.
- Books about stuff like killing might be easy to read but they shouldn't be read by kids who are too young.
- Stuff like punctuation or unusual vocabulary can make a book harder to read even if the words are short words.

Figure 9.6

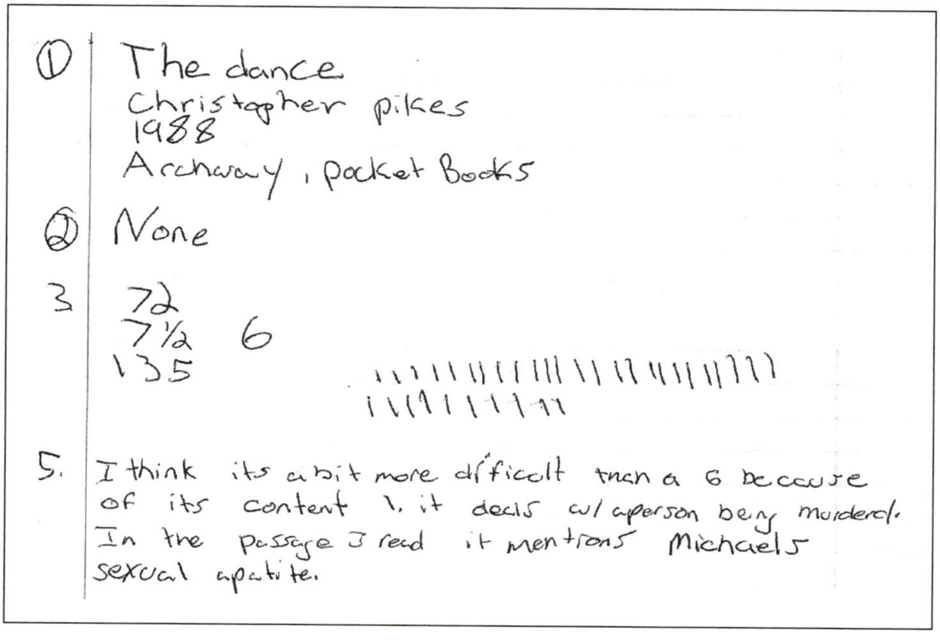
① The dance
Christopher pikes
1988
Archway, pocket Books
② None
3 72
7½ 6
135
5. I think its a bit more dificolt than a 6 because of its content 1. it deals w/ a person being murdered. In the passage I read it mentions Michaels sexual apatite.

- Sometimes we can read hard books (high readability) because we are really interested (like my X-Files book) but we couldn't read low books if we weren't interested.
- Sometimes the teacher talking through the book helps and sometimes it makes the book harder to read (looking for stuff all the time and can't remember what the book is about).
- If we're not familiar with what the book is about, it's harder to read.
- Names can make a book harder to read.
- Seeing the movie makes a book easier to read.
- If the book uses everyday words (even if they are long words), the book is easier to read.

When students' comments are combined with text structure areas, the list becomes comprehensive in terms of factors to consider related to readability. While a readability formula can be a broad guide for level of difficulty, we can't put our faith only in that readability number when matching readers and texts. Perhaps one of the boys in this ninth-grade class said it best: "You can put any number on the back of the book, but if I want to read it, I'll find a way, and if I don't, there's nothing you can do to make me."

After Reading: Owning and Transferring New Learning

In Brooks and Brooks's *In Search of Understanding: The Case for Constructivist Classrooms*, the authors cite the aspect I think is most critical in terms of continuing to scaffold the reading experience after the reading is completed: "Traditionally, learning has been thought to be a 'mimetic' activity, a process that involves students repeating, or miming, newly present information. Constructivist teaching practices, on the other hand, help learners to internalize and reshape, or transform, new information" (15). For students who have had years of experience "miming" new learning, the necessity of scaffolding the reading experience through demonstration of learning is clear. As with prereading and during-reading scaffolding, postreading support can be given in a variety of ways that extend and connect readers' experiences:

- Provide opportunities for personal response so students can connect the text to their lives.
- Assist students in creating timelines or event charts to show cause and effect.
- Use strategy lessons such as the questions game (Chambers), text highlighting (Chambers), or think-pair-share so that all students can have a voice in discussion.

- Use graphics and visuals so students can collaborate and share new understandings.
- Develop questions and research projects to extend thinking.
- Provide students with the opportunity to create text sets related to a topic, event, or phenomenon.
- Develop oral presentations such as readers' theater or debates that demonstrate knowledge of topic or events.
- Provide study guide models so students can create study guides for other students. Questions/prompts would focus on three levels of understanding: searching and recalling (define, match, select, name, describe); making sense (summarizing, organizing, classifying, identifying cause/effect or problem/solution); and evaluating/applying (planning, applying to new situations, forming new questions, forming opinions).

There are many creative teachers who give students the opportunity and modeling for demonstrating their learning in unique ways. Jill Perry's geometry students in Pasco County, Florida, each took a chapter of the geometry text and rewrote that chapter giving readable explanations, diagrams, word problems, and support for the developing mathematician as a way to demonstrate end-of-the-year learning. My students created alphabet picture books for chapters of their science and social studies books (*Life Cycles from A to Z* and *Zeppelin to America: Music of the Times*). Students spent a great deal of time discovering the connections that would make their texts logical. I would like to highlight the work of two teachers and their students who used their knowledge of content and texts to demonstrate connections and new understandings.

In Julie Joynt's drama classes at Titusville High School, students had used readers' theater to make short stories come to life. When discussing how boring their textbooks were, they decided to try making their textbooks come to life by using the same readers' theater techniques. Students formed groups and brought the textbooks from their content classes. Each group chose a chapter they were currently studying and decided on the main concept of that chapter. They then took notes and gave explanations and examples to everyone in the group until the concept was learned, and then the entire group brainstormed a "script" idea. They wrote the entire script, making sure they had a narrator who introduced everyone; a script that taught the concept idea or lesson; and a review/wrap-up at the end. The first script that follows was created by students for finding the value of X. Students made large cards with all the parts of the equation (one with X, one with 3, one with +, etc.). They stood on the stage holding up the cards in the order of the equation. As they read through the script and decided what X had to do in order to have value, each "character" in the equation moved. At the end of the script, they were sitting in the order that showed the equation solved.

The Story of the Lonely X

Narrator	Lauren
+	Erin
X	Heather
=	Cathy
3	Nazra
4	Stevie

N: Our readers' theater is for Algebra 2—finding the values of X, and I am Lauren, the narrator. (*Everyone else introduces himself or herself.*)

N: This is the story of the lonely X. Once upon a time there was a variable X who was sad and lonely because unlike all the other numbers in her equation she had an unknown value.

X: Why can't I have a value like the other numbers, or a use like the signs? I'm just a dumb nobody.

N: And to make the matter worse, some numbers were mad at the X for making the equation unknown.

4: That's right; you are a nobody. You make your equation unknown. Without you, we would be a simple problem. But now no one knows how to solve our equation. We are going to be like this forever!

+: I put two numbers together. Without me in this equation you would not be able to add anything together. I am important, but what do you do?

3: Don't worry about your values; they are just unknown. Someday you'll show them all what value you have. We just have to find someone who knows how to solve our problem.

N: After many days of not knowing if the equation would ever find its value, the wise old equal sign spoke up.

=: I know how to fix your problem. It's simple—just make the equation equal to X.

All: Wow.

+: But how do we do that?

=: Simple—just subtract 3 from each side. That would make our equation say X equals 4 minus 3.

4: Wait, you mean you are going to subtract 3 from me?

3: Yep, to get X by itself you must subtract 3 from that side of the equation.

=: And everyone knows that if you do something to one side of the equation you must do it to the other side.

=: So that makes X equal 4 minus 3!

X: 1! I'm equal to 1!

N: So all the numbers worked together to get the job done, and they lived happily ever after and especially that variable X who now knows that she wasn't just any old number, she was number 1!

Another group of students used their science textbooks and demonstrated their understanding of the scientific method currently being studied:

The Scientific Method

We did ours on the scientific method. It involves Amy as *Amy the book smart super nerd; Monia as *Monia the not-so-bright high school student; Suzanne as *Suzanne the narcoleptic girl who likes to sleep a lot; Tammy as *Tammy who's also dense and not quite smart; and then there is me, Jennifer and I play *Jennifer the lady who works in the morgue. And now with that said and out of the way we'll begin our story..

It takes place on a pleasant sunny day in the spring. Tammy, Amy, and Monia were walking down a path in a nearby forest. All of a sudden they spot their friend Suzanne, who is lying rather still on the ground.

TAMMY: Hey! There's Suzanne!

MONIA: What's she doing on the ground?!

TAMMY: Ohmigod, she's dead!!

MONIA: What do we do?!

AMY: Let's do the *Scientific Method*!!!

TAMMY: Hmmmm. What's that?

AMY: A systematic approach to problem solving! We've already done the first two steps—identifying the problem and gathering information! Let's move on to the next step—form a hypothesis!

MONIA: How many steps are there?

AMY: Six. Anyway, the third step is to form a hypothesis, which means to form an educated guess. What do you think caused her death?

TAMMY: Well, I think that it could be the mushrooms lying there next to her. I think she ate one.

AMY: Good! OK, so how will we do step 4—testing the hypothesis?

MONIA: Here, I'll eat one!

Monia eats a mushroom and dies.

TAMMY: Now Monia's dead!

AMY: And that gets us step 5—results. Obviously the mushrooms are poisonous. Now let's take them to the morgue!

All of a sudden, Suzanne wakes up.

SUZANNE: Hey, where are you guys going?

TAMMY: Aren't you dead?!

SUZANNE: Does it look like I'm dead?! I was sleeping!

AMY: Well then you can come with us to the morgue to do step 6—come up with a conclusion.

At the morgue

JEN: Yup kids! You were right! It was the mushrooms that you thought killed Suzanne but really killed Monia 'cause she ate one and Suzanne was just sleeping! Congratulations for using the Scientific Method correctly! Amy, what are those wonderful steps again?!

AMY: The Scientific Method consists of six steps: identifying the problem, gathering information, forming a hypothesis, testing the hypothesis, observing and recording data, and arriving at a conclusion.

The End

Julie's students were learning that textbooks can come to life when we move from passive to active learning. These students made some conscious choices about strategies they could use to remember concepts from their academic classes. I believe they learned that content is not something you learn just for school. They learned that the information and knowledge they discovered could be used to solve or analyze real problems. Content in these classrooms was used for literacy and life purposes.

In *The Having of Wonderful Ideas,"* Duckworth says, "Having confidence in one's ideas does not mean 'I know my ideas are right'; it means 'I am willing to try out my ideas'" (5). It seems to me that our content classrooms ought to be rich places where we try out our ideas—places where we read, write, think, question, and learn about things that will matter as we move from school to adult lives filled with choices and consequences that require "trying out our ideas" in larger arenas.

10

Help for the Most "Tangled" Readers

Horace Mann, the leading American educator in the nineteenth century,
told teachers they needed to learn to respond to the most difficult
pupils like physicians who find challenge in solving difficult cases.
LARRY BRENDTRO, MARTIN BROKENLEG, AND STEVE VAN BOCKERN,
RECLAIMING YOUTH AT RISK

As I read these words, I think how fortunate physicians are in dealing with the most difficult cases one at a time. Many teachers deal with difficult students thirty to forty-five at a time. Even in classes tracked for teaching and learning with students who have experienced severe academic failure, the numbers are only reduced to fifteen or twenty. What physician would try to find a solution to twenty difficult cases all presenting themselves at the same time, each with a unique set of symptoms?

I know many teachers have overwhelming feelings of frustration and failure as they try to figure out ways to make a difference in such students' lives. I experienced those same feelings when I encountered students who seemed so lost. In spite of my many years teaching, at the beginning of each year, when I faced the at-risk students who had been selected for Literacy Workshop classes, I always felt my enthusiasm and hope wane. I started each day confident that these students and I would have an incredible learning experience together—then the students arrived. Jennifer's first-day writing is an example of the kind of writing that augured difficulties ahead:

The first day of school was horable. My first class I hated the teacher plus some of the students were seniors that's all right but I didn't like the seniors I got. Next was the class I hated to think about because all the dumb student or as you would say low students are in. If you ask me their no girls in here that are not skums except for Kelly and I. All the boys are ugly and don't talk. I do like the teacher. But I would like to drop the class. Dad said if I do good they will put me in a other class.

149

That bull. My fourth period class is gym which I like but I don't like my teacher. He is I don't know I just don't understand him. Lunch is alright. I like going off school grounds. 5th period class is Health I like my teacher he is cool. The student are ok except for one. I seem like a picky person huh I not I just don't like school. Six French I hate everything about that. And finally World Geography. Borring.

Boring classes, boring teachers. Peer pressure and self-esteem problems. Embarrassment and uncertainty. These are difficult problems for any adolescent. When you add to these issues the cumulative effect of several years' experiencing reading failure, the problems can seem insurmountable. The Jennifers of our classrooms—unhappy with themselves and everyone around them—often create walls that leave them feeling alone while teachers focus on helping those students who show promise of making the most growth.

Jennifer's problems seemed unique to her. Those of us who have been working with struggling and reluctant readers know that her problems, and many that are even worse, are shared by thousands of other students. When I asked the students in her class to tell me what they thought had caused them difficulties in their academic subjects in previous years, Jennifer quickly saw that she wasn't alone. Their list is a concrete reminder that older students who are struggling readers have accumulated an appreciable number of negative school and learning experiences:

- Classes too noisy
- Being left-handed
- Being different
- Bad weather
- Teachers with no patience
- Belt (punishment when someone called home)
- Not enough time
- No one to talk to when I had trouble
- Frustration
- Too much pressure
- Boring classes
- Worksheets
- Boring, boring stuff to read
- Useless stuff
- Teachers who said, "Because I said so!"
- Always being the one who didn't finish
- Being embarrassed (reading out loud, stuttering)
- Always having to do the same thing

Amazingly, not a single student attributed difficulty in school to reading or learning problems.

At least these students could articulate the difficulties they had in school. There were no second language barriers or handicapping conditions to block our communication. Many students have language issues or learning disabilities in addition to personal, developmental, social, and failure issues. These students' feelings often echo those of Jorge in "Invisible," from Jane Medina's collection *My Name Is Jorge on Both Sides of the River* (1999, 8):

Invisible
If I stay very still
And breathe
     very quietly,
the Magic happens:
     I disappear
     —and no one sees me
     —and no one hears me
     —and no one even thinks about me
     And the teacher won't call on me.

It's very safe
     being invisible.
     I'm perfect!
I can't make mistakes
     —at least
     nobody sees them,
     so nobody laughs.

We have all known and worked with students like Jorge—students who live in the silence so they won't be embarrassed, whose names we struggle to remember when recalling class lists, who somehow do just enough to move from grade to grade. In primary classrooms, where the focus is often on the individual student, most Jorges find support. In many secondary schools these same students sometimes get lost, moving in silence from class to class. The problems they initially experienced with language and literacy have now been exacerbated by years of failure, silence, and decreasing time with texts. How do we help these students who seem to have fallen through the cracks?

Freebody and Luke categorize the four roles of readers as code breaker, meaning maker, text user, and text critic. In *There's Room for Me Here* (Allen and Gonzalez 1998, 22–34), we discussed the components we felt were necessary for tangled readers: time, choice, resources, support, and connections. In this chapter I would like to highlight one of those components, support, by detailing strategies for direct interventions that help students attain solid and consistent gains in the four literacy roles mentioned by Freebody and Luke.

Code Breaker

In much of the professional literature, *code breaking* has a distinct definition related to systematic phonetics. I'm using the term here as a set of strategies and skills necessary to break the code of a text. Global text knowledge occurs in conjunction with word knowledge. When students lack basic understandings of text, it is essential that we get them to visualize and anticipate the predictable characteristics of text: story grammar, genre supports, literary devices, and nonfiction supports. This code breaking requires many understandings in order to lead to reading competence and fluency: text supports (titles, headings, subheadings, cover information, citation page information); text subtleties (voice, tone, symbolism, literary devices); text conventions (italics, bold, paragraphing, punctuation); text asides (glossary, captions, graphs, charts); text patterns (genre, fiction/nonfiction, story grammar); and text language (word families, rhyme, word parts, word order).

I created opportunities to introduce these elements in the context of meaningful, relevant texts, not in workbooks, because I wanted my students to understand that these supports are not discrete reading exercises but supports that *all* readers use to make sense of text. Once students have a desire to read, each of these aspects of code breaking takes on an importance for students' own purposes.

My students also needed a way to keep track of these supports so they could refer to them in the process of learning to make the strategies automatic. In her classroom Kyle Gonzalez used a strategies banner that hung from the ceiling for students' reference. In our classroom I used individual student academic journals in order to help students document their emerging understandings of language and literature. These journals were not personal journals detailing students' conflicts and conquests; these journals had an academic focus. These academic journals were kept in the classroom and used each day as we worked together as a whole group or in individual and small-group settings. Sections of the journals included the following:

- Things We Do Together in Class
- Things I'm Learning How to Do
- Things I Know How to Do
- Language Collection
- Spelling

As we developed charts and lists, collected words from reading or for writing, conferred about their next learning steps, established goals, or used graphic organizers to make learning visual, everything was documented in students' academic journals. Students were allowed to use their academic journals each day in class, even during exams. For students who have struggled with ways to organize for academics, these journals were a great support.

Building Oral and Print Connections

At some point most children have experienced the rhythm and rhyme of language. For many, this occurred on a daily basis from before birth into their school years. Many caregivers connect oral language to print early in children's lives. For others, the rhythm of language may have been picked up from an oral culture, television, or music, and they have not made the connection between oral experiences and the printed word. Repeated reading of poetry, picture books, and excerpts from novels with descriptive and lyrical passages help students experience the pleasure of language. Offering the first reading as a read-aloud experience and then inviting students to join in by giving them copies of the text or putting the text on overhead transparencies or charts solidifies the connection between sound and print. A beginning list of texts that are rich resources for these shared experiences follows. Selections other than poetry are noted.

- Arnold Adoff, *My Black Me*
- Laurie Anderson, *Speak* (novel excerpts)
- Maya Angelou, *Poems*
- Jo Carson, *stories i ain't told nobody yet*
- Sandra Cisneros, *The House on Mango Street* (autobiography)
- Roald Dahl, *Revolting Rhymes*
- Sharon Draper, *Buttered Bones*
- Paul Fleischman, *Joyful Noise: Poems for Two Voices*
- Ralph Fletcher, *I Am Wings*
- Eloise Greenfield, *Night on Neighborhood Street*
- Karen Hesse, *Out of the Dust* (novel)
- Sara Holbrook, *I Never Said I Wasn't Difficult*
- Paul Janeczko, *Stardust Hotel*
- Norton Juster, *The Phantom Tollbooth* (novel excerpts)
- Gordon Korman and Bernice Korman, *The D- Poems of Jeremy Bloom*
- Richard Lederer, *Anguished English*
- John Marsden, *Prayer for the Twenty-First Century* (picture book)
- Alice McLerran, *Roxaboxen* (picture book)
- Angela Medearis, *Skin Deep and Other Teenage Reflections*
- Jerry Spinelli, *Who Put That Hair in My Toothbrush?* (novel excerpts)
- John Steinbeck, *Of Mice and Men* (novel, setting passages)
- Michael Strickland, *Poems That Sing to You*

Reinforcing predictable language patterns is an excellent way to help struggling readers begin to anticipate words in reading and to use those words in their writing and talk. This can be done with both literature and nonfiction (or textbooks). For example, the David Harrison poem that follows is from his collection

The Boy Who Counted Stars. Putting this poem on a chart or transparency so that all students can predict the words helps students look for patterns of language (in this case, language that is rhyming and conceptually oppositional).

> **The Trouble with My House**
> I haven't any windows
> And I haven't any <u>doors</u>,
> I haven't any ceilings
> And I haven't any <u>floors</u>,
> I haven't got an attic
> And I haven't any halls,
> I haven't got a <u>basement</u>
> And I haven't any <u>walls</u>,
> I haven't got a roof
> And that's the reason, I suppose,
> Why rain keeps pouring on my head
> And dripping off my <u>nose</u>.

Underlined words can be omitted during the first reading, and students can try to figure out the pattern of the missing words and insert words that fit. As students read and reread Harrison's poem and the version they created, they are reinforcing sight words (I, haven't, why, any) and perhaps learning new words (reason, pouring, dripping).

The same technique can be used to support students in finding patterns and therefore anticipating language once they have developed sufficient background knowledge of a text, characters, or actions while reading short stories or novels. For instance, this activity can be done during the reading of Lois Duncan's *Ransom*. Students work collaboratively to fill in the blanks with language that makes sense in the context of the story and what they know about the characters. This then serves as an opportunity for the class to talk about what kinds of words these characters would use, dialect, language patterns, and sentence structure.

> *Ransom*
> The kidnapping took _____ on a _____.
>   "If it had been Friday," Jesse said _____, "I wouldn't have taken the _____ at all. I would have _____ in the library and _____ until Mother _____ me up after _____ Committee meeting."
>   _____ were a lot of ifs.
>   "If my car _____ not been in the _____," said Glenn.
>   And Marianne Paget thought: If I had _____ that _____ with Rod when he _____ it to me, when he drove _____ the way _____ to the high school just to _____ me up.
>   But she had not. She had _____ onto the bus _____ the others, swinging her hips a _____ so that _____ plaid skirt _____ about her,

holding her _____ shoulders _____ straight _____ the blue _____ jacket.

I have hurt him, she thought, and the _____ was _____ satisfying. I have hurt him, and by hurting him, I _____ shown Mother _____ all of them.

When she _____ her seat, she leaned _____ and looked _____ the window to _____ Rod was standing _____ his car, _____ in a defeated _____ at the door she had just _____.

One of the difficulties teachers discover as they work with developing readers is that lack of reading experience leaves students unable to make a distinction between literal and figurative language. When this happens, students are confused and lose reading confidence. Some texts give us the opportunity to make dialect, local language, or idiomatic expressions understandable because of the larger meaningful context. Teachers in Ocala, Florida, used sentences and phrases from their shared reading of Ruth White's *Belle Prater's Boy* to help students understand local language and idioms in the context of what they knew about the characters and their speech. Discussion of these expressions within the context of surrounding text was helpful for showing students how authors make creative use of language.

Understanding Local Language

(3)   . . . Woodrow, lived way far in the head of a long, isolated <u>holler</u> called Crooked Ridge . . .

(16) He and Mama were gone to Abingdon to see some of Porter's <u>kin</u>...

(23) They were both loaded down with <u>pokes</u> that were crammed full, and Woodrow was so tickled he couldn't stop grinning.

(25) That was a real <u>knee-slapper</u> but Woodrow didn't seem to mind our laughing.

(26) It seemed there was a lot of chattering and <u>guffawing</u>, but when we walked in, they got quiet and looked at us.

(28) "They don't want no haircuts. They're just <u>chewing the fat</u>."

(31) "And don't forget you gotta <u>unplait</u> your hair and wash it before the party."

(50) "He made it up!" Buzz Osborne chimed in. "'<u>Pon my word of honor</u>," Woodrow said.

(61) ". . . if folks heard me carrying on about a place in the air, they'd think I was <u>addled</u> in the head."

(76) "They have money. And I bet if the truth was known, a bunch of 'em were <u>borned uglier than a mud fence</u>."

(82) "I don't care about it but the kids are <u>champing at the bit to go</u>."

I found that many of my most tangled readers struggled with text at the word (and even the alphabet) level. There were always students in my classes who didn't know the alphabet, and this got in the way of many common activities and use of resources (index, dictionary, word study, use of files with alphabetized copies of high-interest reading). The "listening" activity that follows reinforces alphabetic awareness and highlights commonly confused words such as *reverse, remove,* and *replace.* Students listen to your directions as you read one step at a time, and they attempt to get from the word at the beginning to a word at the end.

From the First to the Last. . .
1. Print the words GEORGE WASHINGTON as one word at the top of your paper.
2. Eliminate from your word the vowel that appears as the second vowel in the alphabet.
3. Remove the last letter of your word and put it in front of the first letter of your remaining word.
4. Find the fifth consonant in the alphabet and remove those from your word.
5. Put the remaining letters in your word in pairs *in the order they appear* in your word. You should have one letter without a partner.
6. Reverse the order of the letters within each pair of letters.
7. Remove any remaining *n*'s from your word.
8. Remove the letter that is the fourth vowel in the alphabet.
9. Replace the first letter in your word with the last letter of your word.
10. Reverse the order of the letters in your middle pair of letters.
11. Determine the third vowel in the alphabet and remove it from your word.
12. You should be left with something you leave at the curb.

This activity was one of my students' favorites. This list was created by my students after we did several of these together. We were able to weave in new words such as *determine* and *eliminate* in each new listening activity we created.

Text Supports

From book interviews I conducted with my students, I found that almost all of them chose books randomly. Further, they had no idea where to look in a book to find information that would help them make choices. It was amazing how few of my students even knew where to look to find the author's name on a novel. Lack of basic knowledge in using text supports hampers students not only in choosing appropriate books but also in reading them successfully. For struggling readers, these supports are often a mystery and as such require step by step shared discovery. These scaffolding experiences can range from helping students discover predictable language and word patterns to developing awareness of predictable patterns of genre and text structures.

Textbook supports are very different from supports we might find in literature, and students typically overlook all supports, including the most basic supports of titles and headings. This same process of asking students to anticipate and reconstruct the supports can be used with textbooks. In the example in

Figure 10.1, students have been given a sample of text from *Heath Earth Science* (Spaulding) with many of the text supports blocked out. This lets the teacher predict with students the kinds of supports they should be able to expect as they read their textbooks. This lesson can then be extended by discussing and documenting the function that each of these text supports perform. In this case, the chapter number and title in the running head, the number and title of the section, the photographs and drawings with captions and labels, and the pronunciation guides in the text have been blocked out. Based on how much background knowledge of textbooks students have, they might have to look at a complete example first before trying to reconstruct the supports that would/should accompany this text. This textbook has excellent supports, including italic and bold words, but students could also suggest other supports that would be helpful to look for when reading textbooks (table of contents, glossary, index).

Figure 10.1

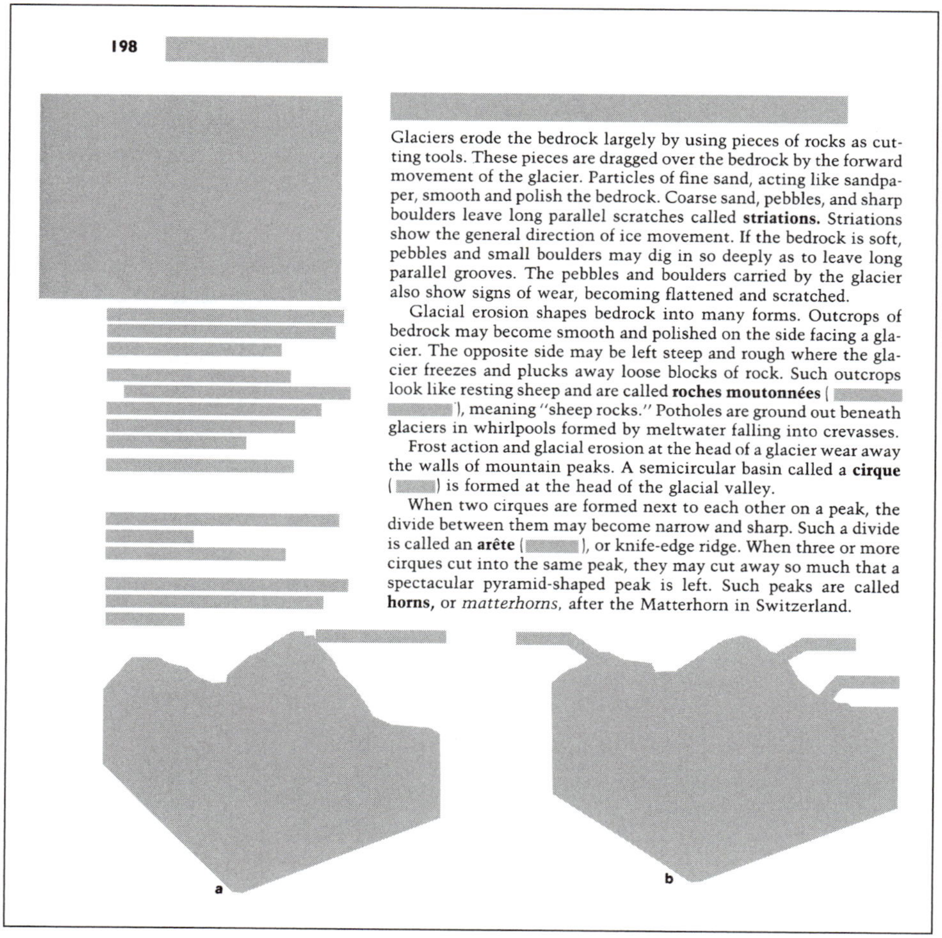

198

Glaciers erode the bedrock largely by using pieces of rocks as cutting tools. These pieces are dragged over the bedrock by the forward movement of the glacier. Particles of fine sand, acting like sandpaper, smooth and polish the bedrock. Coarse sand, pebbles, and sharp boulders leave long parallel scratches called **striations**. Striations show the general direction of ice movement. If the bedrock is soft, pebbles and small boulders may dig in so deeply as to leave long parallel grooves. The pebbles and boulders carried by the glacier also show signs of wear, becoming flattened and scratched.

Glacial erosion shapes bedrock into many forms. Outcrops of bedrock may become smooth and polished on the side facing a glacier. The opposite side may be left steep and rough where the glacier freezes and plucks away loose blocks of rock. Such outcrops look like resting sheep and are called **roches moutonnées** (▓▓▓), meaning "sheep rocks." Potholes are ground out beneath glaciers in whirlpools formed by meltwater falling into crevasses.

Frost action and glacial erosion at the head of a glacier wear away the walls of mountain peaks. A semicircular basin called a **cirque** (▓▓) is formed at the head of the glacial valley.

When two cirques are formed next to each other on a peak, the divide between them may become narrow and sharp. Such a divide is called an **arête** (▓▓), or knife-edge ridge. When three or more cirques cut into the same peak, they may cut away so much that a spectacular pyramid-shaped peak is left. Such peaks are called **horns**, or *matterhorns*, after the Matterhorn in Switzerland.

a   b

Understanding that words should form pictures in our heads may be a basic concept for us, but for many of our students words have never translated into images. Using story or chapter maps to help students begin making those connections concrete lets students create memorable images from the language and then use those images as a way to reconstruct the text. This recursive process is demonstrated in Figure 10.2. While reading M. E. Kerr's short story "I've Got Gloria," this literacy teacher modeled for students the images the words created for her as she read this story. At the end, she was able to go back and ask students what they would have titled each section of the story map if each of the squares had been a chapter. Students titled the first square Revenge at Last and the second one Mrs. Whitman Crumbles. The third and fourth squares relate to Scott's talk with his father and his subsequent guilt, A Father-Son Saturn Moment and Letting Mrs. Whitman off the Hook. The final panels describe Scott's dilemma when he arrives home to find that Mrs. Whitman has traced his call and his summer school experience is looming: The Tables Turned and Not Mrs. Whitman Again!

From this conversation, students suggested literary elements critical to moving the story forward in an interesting way: problem, characters, action, and endings that make you guess at what might happen. The teacher modeling and discussion related to "I've Got Gloria" can then be extended to guided practice. Ann Bailey's students Trinh and Sokhary created their storyboards for Richard

Figure 10.2

Peck's "Priscilla and the Wimps," labeling their visuals for the elements that built excitement and led this story to its conclusion (see Figure 10.3). These visuals and text represent their collaborative visualization, retelling, and predictions for this incredibly funny short story. Each of these stages moves students closer to making independent meaning from text because their text connections can lead

Figure 10.3

them to personal connections. Once students begin making those connections, they have moved into meaning-making roles.

Meaning Maker

For many years I commiserated with my colleagues about the abysmal apathy some students exhibited toward reading. After some time I came to realize that I was contributing to this lack of personal response. A pattern was evident in our classroom: when we read books with which students felt no connection, they were apathetic; when we read books that angered them, made them laugh or cry or argue, they certainly were full of personal response.

Why does it take so long to find the patterns in our classrooms? Probably because the concentration needed just to keep a classroom filled with multiple personalities moving forward doesn't allow much leftover time for close observation and thoughtful reflection. I had started keeping a teaching journal as we were reading Stevenson's *Kidnapped*. An entire class of students sat before me looking as though they were drugged. When we abandoned that book and moved to Avi's *Nothing but the Truth,* the students woke up and interrupted the reading at every turn to express opinions and argue over school policies.

Over time I had avoided some fiction and nonfiction that I thought would be too controversial because of days that had ended in class brawls. In Blume's collection of short stories *Places I Never Meant to Be: Original Stories by Censored Writers,* Katherine Paterson says, "When our chief goal is not to offend someone, we are not likely to write a book that will deeply affect anyone" (70). The same is true for students as we want them to gain personal meaning from texts. It is very difficult for developing readers to learn the importance of asking personal and text questions while reading if the literature doesn't prompt them to question. Poems such as Fletcher's "Justin and Frank" (*I Am Wings*) and Draper's "Band-Aids and Five Dollar Bills" (*Buttered Bones*) cause students to raise questions about the way they are living their own lives and the impact of their actions on those around them. Works of nonfiction such as Sparks's *Jay's Journal* and *It Happened to Nancy* push students to question the pressures they are experiencing as adolescents and to look for meaningful ways to solve those problems. However, giving students meaningful texts is only the first step toward supporting their independent meaning-making strategies.

Inference: Reading Between the Lines

Once your shared reading is complete for the day, you can return to the text for extended thinking, questioning, noting of author's intentions, and searching for writer's craft. Inferential thinking in response to reading is often challenging for students who have struggled with the text. One ninth-grade boy told me, "I sit and listen to the teacher talk about all the *hidden* stuff in the poems and think, 'It sure is hidden from me.'" Students sometimes have no idea how classmates or the teacher came up with character analyses, motivations, or predictions. In fact, terms such as *infer, clarify,* and *monitor* are fairly abstract for many readers. As I became better at understanding the process of helping these students, I saw that I was usually leaving out several critical meaning-making steps along the way. Graphic organizers often help students make those steps more visible.

Lynnette Kaiser teaches eighth grade at Stonewall Jackson Middle School in Orlando, Florida. She has found that graphic organizers are extremely useful in helping her students look beneath the surface level of texts. The graphic Fleshing Out a Character (see Figure 10.4) helped her students look at Max's self-concept

Figure 10.4

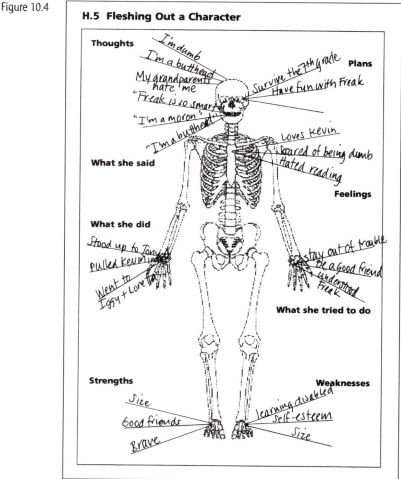

and motivations in Philbrick's *Freak the Mighty*. Lynnette read the book to the class in shared reading, and the graphic helped them pull their ideas together to read beneath the plotline. The organizer helped students focus on the text in their collaboration prior to class discussion. Students found quotes that showed the influence of Max's self-talk on his self-esteem as well as areas where Max changed throughout the story. This focus led to a richer discussion when students combined the best of their ideas.

Another activity after the supported initial reading of Sachar's *Holes* asked students to choose a character they would follow throughout the text as they reread it. After reading was finished each day, students were asked to go back and discover the person inside of the name for the character each had chosen to follow. They looked for indications of the person by noting what he said, others' descriptions of him, his actions, opinions from another character, and the character's own perspective (see Figure 10.5). One of the students chose to follow Zero's growth throughout the book by looking for these characteristics. His "peeling the layers" note taking is shown in Figure 10.6. Organizational structures such as these help students negotiate that difficult territory from concrete to abstract thinking and learning.

Another organizer that has helped Lynnette's students infer and predict their way through the text is shown in Figure 10.7. I first developed this organizer when I saw two girls come to class after a lunchtime fight. Of course, they brought the conflict into class, and the teacher wanted to get it stopped so she could continue to teach. She asked one girl, "What happened?" When the other

Figure 10.5

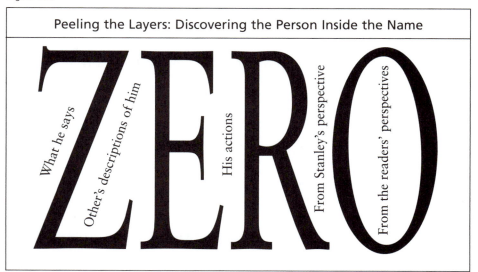

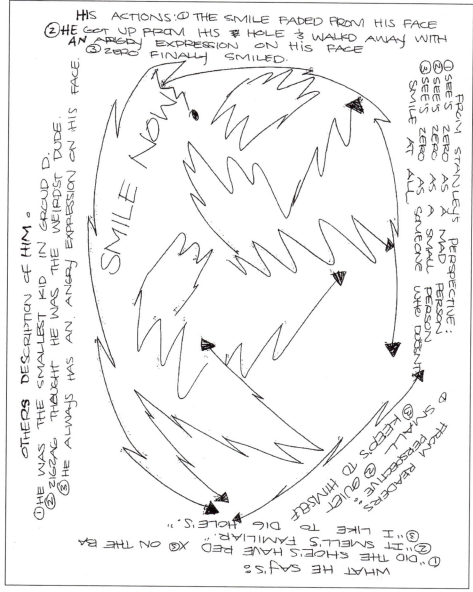

Figure 10.6

girl responded that the first girl had hit her, she quickly screamed, "I had to. She said something bad about my mother." As I listened to this argument, I realized that most early adolescents believe there is only one option for every problem. They see life in these black-and-white frames that leave them little room to make healthy choices.

Figure 10.7

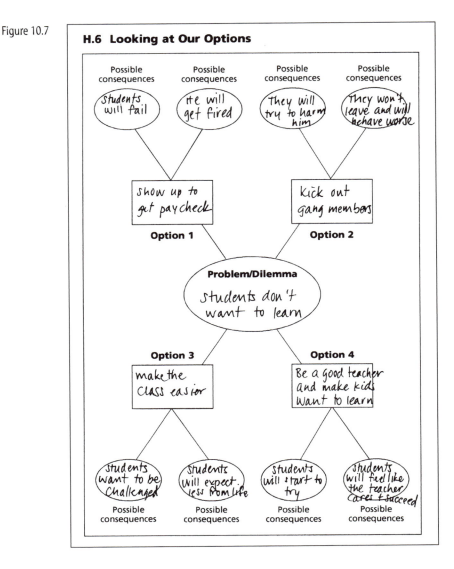

Lynnette's students have used this organizer as a way to frame their discussion of the teachers' possible responses to the fact that students did not want to learn in Andrew Clark's *Stand and Deliver*. Students had to figure out the main problem or dilemma in the story and postulate some options that the teachers might use to solve that problem. They suggested that the teachers could just show up at school and collect their paychecks, kick out the gang members, make classes easier, or make the students want to learn. In the discussion they then inferred what might happen at that school if the teachers employed each of these options.

Many teachers and administrators are using this organizer across content areas. In social studies the organizer could help students collect their thinking about causes of the Civil War or the consequences of internment camps for Japanese-Americans during World War II. In one middle school math class, students get into their thinking-learning groups and use the organizer to help them read word problems. They try to determine what the core problem is and then figure out what options they might try for solving the problem. Consequences for each option are determined as students actually use each option for problem solving.

The most creative use I have seen of this organizer has helped students read between the lines but is not related to reading. Some middle school administrators and counselors have been using this for counseling purposes. When students get into trouble, they are given this graphic organizer prior to meeting with a counselor or dean. They have to write down the problem, what they did to try to solve the problem, what they think the consequences should be for those actions, and at least one option they might have used that would have gotten them into less trouble but still might have solved the problem. Counselors have found this very effective in helping students gather their thoughts enough to think and talk through a problem. A significant aspect of predicting and inferring is questioning, and this unfortunately remains a struggle for many students.

Questioning

Learning to ask questions is a difficult task for most struggling readers. One of the contributing factors is that many readers struggle so much at the word level that their cognitive energy is used up. Then, after years of that struggle, even when they have significant response and questions to texts that are meaningful to them, their questions stay at the literal level they have come to expect. As we neared the end of our reading of Hunt's *The Lottery Rose,* I asked students to generate a list of things they questioned or were wondering about. Tracy's questions are representative:

> Why did Georgie have to stay in bed for a while?
> Where did Georgie finally plant his rosebush?
> Why was Georgie scared of what Mrs. Harper would do?
> What did the judge give the school?
> Why did Molly change her mind and decide to let Georgie plant his rosebush in her garden?
> What was it that Georgie came down with?

These are all questions to which Tracy already knew the answers. After reading through one hundred similar questions from this class, I was discouraged. I realized these students had posed questions to which they already knew the answers because to them these questions represented teacher or school questions (the very kind they wanted to see on tests). It was time for a questioning intervention.

At the end of our next day's reading, I said, "I'm wondering what will happen to Georgie? Is anyone else wondering that? Oh, I'm also wondering if Mrs. Harper is going to get attached to Georgie." Student questions and "I wonders" erupted. Their original context for questions had been literal, and without modeling of other kinds of questions that is where their questioning stayed.

The most effective strategy I have ever used to scaffold questioning for students has been the questions game. This questioning strategy was developed by Frank McTeague and described in Aidan Chambers's *Tell Me* (115). This book is filled with support for teachers who are trying to help students make the transition from literal to inferential questioning. Directions for the questions game as I have used it follow. Times given are approximate and vary depending on students' reading abilities as well as length and complexity of texts.

- Each student reads the poems or any other text and writes down three questions he or she would like answered. (10 minutes)
- Students choose a partner, exchange questions, and try to answer each other's questions. I usually have students try to do this in writing before they share. (5 minutes)
- Partners then sit together to discuss answers to each other's questions. At the end of the discussion time, these partners form three new questions. These questions can be extensions of questions they had in their original sets, questions that remained unanswered, or new questions that came out of their discussion. (10–15 minutes)
- Each two-person team exchanges questions with another two-person team. The partners discuss the questions they have received and attempt to answer them. (10 minutes)
- The two two-person teams that have exchanged questions combine into a four-person group. The four readers discuss the six questions represented in their group. (10 minutes)
- When time is called, each four-person group comes up with one question that is still unanswered or that they would like to bring to the whole-class discussion.

This strategy works well with poetry, short stories, novels, nonfiction, and even textbooks.

The two following poems are ones that I like to use together for the questions game with readers who need more support. Typically, I give students the two poems with the titles omitted and read each poem aloud to the students. I have found that their questions are richer when they are trying to establish their own contexts for these poems. The titles actually narrow the context and therefore narrow the range of questions that students propose.

She had raised the window
higher

than her head; then
paused

to lift wire spectacles,
wiping

sight back with a wrinkled
hand-

kerchief. She wanted to watch
the old

place until the train's passing
erased

the tarpaper walls and tin roof;
she had

been able to carry away
so little.

The fingers of her left
hand

worried two strings
attached

to a baggage tag
flapping

from her
lapel.

Dinner was cold: one boiled potato,
a can of Vienna sausage
and rice with cinnamon & sugar.
Outside the fence
a dog barks in the cricket-filled night.
You stay in your horse stall,
sitting on a mattress stuffed with straw
and stare at white grass
growing up through the floor.
Hay, horse hair and manure
are whitewashed to the boards.
In the corner
a white spider is suspended
in the shadow of a white spider web.

When students finish the questions game, I usually begin by asking them what they think the context is for these two poems. One group of students' predictions, both historical and contemporary, are represented in the following list:

- Homelessness
- Runaways
- Moving from Oklahoma to California
- Abuse
- Concentration camps
- Migrant workers
- Depression (hobos)
- Military (POW)
- Aging person taken from home (being sent to a nursing home)

Given the varied contexts these poems have created for students, their questions are predictably varied. Interestingly, no students in this class actually established the context as the internment camps for relocation of Japanese-Americans during World War II. Both poems are by James Mitsui and written from his family history of having been forced to live in an internment camp. The first is titled "Destination: Tule Lake Relocation Center, May 20, 1942" and the second is titled "Holding Center, Tanforan Race Track, Spring 1942."

One set of questions from students in a ninth-grade reading intervention class is given here as an example of the refinement that occurred in the process of the questions game. The first six questions represent two individual students with their first questions.

1. Why do you think the person is in a horse stall?
2. Are these poems about the same people or the same thing?
3. Why aren't there titles on the poems?

1. Do these poems go together?
2. Why has the person been able to "carry away so little"?
3. Why does she have a baggage tag on her lapel?

After these two students discussed their six questions, they generated these three questions to exchange with another partnership:

1. We are wondering if the baggage tag has been put on her so she won't get lost because she is old and has Alzheimer's?
2. We wonder if there is a reason for the "white" in the second poem?
3. Why is the person eating this awful food and living in a horse stall?

The pair of students with whom they exchanged questions had given them the following questions after their discussion:

1. Why would someone be living in a horse stall?
2. Why has she left so much behind? Has she been forced to go somewhere?
3. What is the significance of the baggage tag attached to a person instead of baggage?

The discussion with this four-person group was animated as each partnership had moved the other back to some of the original questions. In the end, two of these questions (baggage tag, forced moving) ended up being the one question brought to the larger group by two different groups. This format took the readers back into the text many times as they searched for answers to their own and others' questions. With each exchange, both in the questioning and answering, students were moved to articulate more complex questions and to continue with the questions that are still nagging at them.

One of the areas where readers struggle the most with questioning is lacking enough background knowledge to ask questions that move them forward. This questioning activity has given students enough background knowledge to move them into more reading from a variety of text types that will continue their predicting and questioning. In the graphic organizer Multiple Sources, Multiple Perspectives (see Figure 10.8) students then encounter other texts that build on the foundation of background knowledge they already have gained from the poem. The new texts then give them opportunities to see how others tell the same (or different) accounts of this event to extend both their inferring and questioning abili-

Figure 10.8

H.7 Multiple Sources, Multiple Perspectives

Sources	Factual information	Reading between the lines information	Questions
"Destination: Tule Lake Relocation Center" (poem)	May 20, 1942 People forced to leave Could take only a little	→ (baggage tags) scared "worried two strings"	What would someone take? How would I feel?
"Holding Center, Tanforan Race Track" (poem)	Spring 1942 kept in horse stalls not good food	did this in a hurry (whitewashed grass, manure)	What was the hurry? How did this make people feel?
"Home Was a Horse Stall" (magazine)	Dec 7, 1941 Japanese attack Pearl Harbor people forced to leave people got $ 1988	no respect (stay away from fence) "didn't hesitate to use weapons" Called JAPS	Is $20,000 enough for all they lost? How could this happen?
"In Response to Executive Order 9066" (poem) Dwight Okita	must relocate Executive order 9066 made Japanese go to "camp"	people thought all Japanese - enemies "I didn't know what to say"	Why did they say camp - not prison?
The Invisible Thread Yoshiko Uchida part of novel	prisoners in own homes no $ to live	mad at mother for being kind	How could U.S. do this? Why were we afraid? What do history books say?

ties. Their new questions take on a higher level of connections: personal (How would I feel?) and world (How could the U.S. do this?). They also begin to examine and question the justice aspects both in terms of the event and the subsequent reparations. At this point, students had enough information to make those critical text-to-self, text-to-text, and text-to-world connections. Such connections lead students into using a variety of texts for their personal and academic purposes.

Text User

Text using presents a double-edged sword for most older tangled readers. These students come to texts not having read enough to build a background of world knowledge, language patterns, word families, genre characteristics, or strategies for making sense of text. Additionally, they often do not have the confidence or fluency to continue with independent reading of texts that interest them. Charts such as those found in Mooney's *Developing Life-Long Readers* that list characteristics of emergent readers typically highlight attitudes such as keen interest in hearing and using new language and expectations that books will "amuse, delight, comfort and excite" (1991, 8). They list understandings such as book language, story patterns, and awareness that background knowledge is important. When we encounter older readers who have not had successful early reading experiences, they are often not even at that emergent stage. These students need time built into every day when reading is interesting, easily accessible, and supported. Langer believes, "Literature can serve as an important entry into schooling. It can contribute toward each student's development of meaning, sense of self-esteem, engagement in thoughtfulness, and literacy development" (99). In order for students to enter an independent text-using role, they need these initial *experiences* with text.

I believe the single most significant event for tangled readers is more *supported* time with texts. After reading Mooney's characteristics of emergent, early, and fluent stages of literacy (1991, 8–11), I developed a list of goals I wanted to accomplish as I supported students' moves into using texts independently. I titled this list Developing a Set for Literacy because that is how I visualized my responsibility at this stage of students' reading development.

Developing a Set for Literacy—What Can I Do?
- Help students see that text has meaning.
- Help students understand that books offer enjoyment and information.
- Help students gain pleasure from the rhythm and rhyme of language.
- Help students develop language play.
- Make students eager to hear and tell stories.
- Help students see that books can amuse, delight, comfort, excite, raise questions, and give answers.

- Help students develop self-winding strategies by developing personal questions during reading.
- Develop readers who want to read and reread.
- Develop readers who make time to read.
- Develop students who see themselves as readers and writers who are eager to extend books by writing and sharing with others.
- Help students understand that texts have challenges and develop confidence in taking risks to overcome those challenges.
- Help students develop skills as listeners, thinkers, and responders.
- Help students move from passive to active roles in reading (challenging, questioning, disagreeing).
- Help students focus on meaning first.
- Help students see new meaning with rereading.
- Help students understand that texts have predictable components.
- Help students understand that texts have codes that can be broken with skillful, strategic reading.

These literacy goals became the foundation for read-aloud, shared reading, and guided reading in my literacy classrooms. The specific strategies for the goals that are skills- and strategy-based are described in the foregoing sections Code Breaker and Meaning Maker. Here I want to highlight the approaches and text choices that make text using appealing and profitable for students.

Using Texts to Create Readers Who Are Eager to Hear and Tell Stories

I always suffered when students responded like Shannon at the end of Williams's *The Glass Menagerie*: "The mistake Tom made was not putting a contract out on that mother long before now." In contrast, each time we read Steinbeck's *Of Mice and Men*, students were eager to talk and write about the friendships and losses they had experienced in their own lives. When we were halfway through Hilton's *Goodbye, Mr. Chips*, Warren said, "God, Mrs. Allen, just shoot us now and put us out of our misery." But when I read MacCracken's *Lovey*, they spent days talking about teachers who had made a difference in their lives. While I would never argue that students shouldn't be exposed to classic literature, some texts are just not developmentally appropriate for the readers in our classrooms. Choosing the right texts is critical to making students eager text users. In Appendixes B, E, and F I have listed my suggestions for nonfiction, short stories, and poetry I believe will engage the most reluctant readers. My students became increasingly eager to hear and tell their own stories when the texts I shared with them connected to their personal lives, their sense of justice, and their sense of humor.

I remember Gordon Korman, speaking at an ALAN workshop at NCTE, asking the audience, "How many dead canines do students need to encounter in their reading experience?" He was talking about the need for weaving into the reading curriculum more books that are humorous. As I listened to the panel, I jotted down the books I had used for whole-class shared reading the previous year:

- Avi, *Nothing but the Truth*
- Betsy Byars, *The Summer of the Swans*
- Caroline Cooney, *The Face on the Milk Carton*
- Richie Tankersly Cusick, *Teacher's Pet*
- Lois Duncan, *I Know What You Did Last Summer; Killing Mr. Griffin; Ransom*
- Irene Hunt, *The Lottery Rose*
- Mary MacCracken, *Lovey*
- Arthur Miller, *The Crucible*
- Gary Paulsen, *Hatchet*
- John Steinbeck, *Of Mice and Men*

I was shocked to look though my list and see that while some of those books had amusing scenes, essentially they were focused on characters going through life traumas and painful events. Students loved these books, yet looking at the list reminded me of the need to balance the books we read aloud to students so they leave the reading experience knowing that readers also turn to books when they want to be amused or delighted.

Sharing Texts That Comfort and Give Answers

I truly believe that one of the deepest attractions of reading is finding comfort in books. In my years in the classroom, I found that most of the time the students who were skipping other classes in order to read books were those who had discovered the comfort of books. However, it is impossible to predict which books will bring that comfort.

There was no way I could have predicted that my reading of Angelou's poem "No Losers, No Weepers" would comfort Traci when her boyfriend left her for his former girlfriend. Nor would I have guessed that reading excerpts from Arundel's *The Longest Weekend* would have caused Russell to skip automotives so he could read the book and try to understand why his pregnant girlfriend wanted to try making it on her own. I certainly would not have anticipated that Tammy's own abuse would make Krupinski and Weikel's *Death from Child Abuse . . . and No One Heard* an appealing book for her, yet reading about abuse that was "worse than mine" helped her cope. Rachel's reading of Miller's *The Crucible* helped her deal with her sadness at realizing she might never get to date

Adam because he "is so upper-class and I'm nobody. Still, I can't help but 'think softly on him from time to time.'" Sharing a variety of texts in ways that make them accessible to all students (read-aloud and shared reading) offers students lots of options for finding comfort in an unsettling and scary world.

We found lots of evidence of a relationship between sharing books that elicited emotional responses (laughter, tears, questions, and anger) and students' taking on the role of text user in the literacy classroom.

- Students began making independent choices for reading.
- Students became more willing to follow teacher-read texts during shared reading.
- Students demonstrated increasing degrees of self-confidence related to their opinions about books and interpretations of text.
- Students referred to books in conversations.
- Students began taking an interest in books available in the classroom and the media center.
- Students began to choose reading as an activity when the opportunity for choice was given.
- Students saw books as places to go for writing ideas (words, characters, situations, or story starters).

These were not behavioral objectives we established for students; rather they were the behaviors we noted as a result of the "text user" literacy work we did together. Sometimes, I think, we become aware of how far struggling readers are behind their peers and we attempt to make up for those differences by jumping into programs heavily weighted toward strategies and skills. While many of these skills and strategies are necessary for successful reading and writing, it is interest and motivation that have to be fostered before students can realize there is anything worth reading. The older the student, the more difficult it is for him to admit to reading problems. For students to take that risk, there has to be something interesting and appealing on the other side—a "literacy club" (Smith 1988a) that they *want* to join. Once that desire is there, these readers become ready for code breaking.

Text Critic

Children who are exposed to a variety of texts actually become text critics at a very early age. If you have spent your evenings reading books such as Carle's *Brown Bear, Brown Bear* or *The Very Hungry Caterpillar* to your two-year-old and you decide to switch from picture books with colorful illustrations and predictable texts to picture books with lengthy narratives and subtle illustrations, you will quickly see your child in the role of text critic. Children know intuitively which texts capture their interest and which don't. The problem for us is that in their inability to articulate what they like as readers, we often continue to make the same ineffective choices.

Older readers suffer from the same problem. They often refuse to abandon texts that have helped them build reading confidence (predictable characters and plots, limited vocabulary) for unknown authors and more challenging texts. Their lack of experience in reading has not given them a repertoire of incrementally more challenging and interesting texts, so they often see books as totally interesting or totally not worth opening.

When these students are asked to move into the role of text critic, they often have very limited comments: "It sucked!" or "Borrrring." Helping students move beyond those colorful criticisms to ones with a bit more substance is directly related to our modeling of text-to-text comparisons. One of the reasons students are reluctant to move beyond comfortable books even when criticizing them is that they don't have many points for comparison. Quite typically, they either love or hate a plot, and that is all they address at the text critic level. Readers need the same support here as they did in their roles as code breakers, meaning makers, and text users.

A way to provide this support is through the use of comparing/contrasting multiple texts related to a common subject. In this way students can see the ways in which each text addresses the topic. Lynnette Kaiser has used a simple Compare and Contrast organizer to help students develop the cognitive habit of text-to-text connections (see Figure 10.9). She documents their comparisons and asks them to take a critical stance by citing challenges they experienced with the texts. In Andrew Clark's *Stand and Deliver,* the students felt, the characters didn't come alive, and in "The Last Spin," they felt, the story starting in the middle was confusing. This gave Lynnette the opportunity to talk about flashback, engaging dialogue, and effective characterization as critical points.

Lynnette also uses text sets as a way for students to compare texts in terms of their promise as resources for information. She has put together several sets of books related to World War II prior to students' reading Holocaust literature. Students then sample each book in the set and offer critical comments about the readability and interest for them. The two book passes in Figure 10.10 show students' comments related to text supports, readability, illustrations, emotional impact, and interest level. They highlight features that would make them want to read the book such as the illustrations (or lack of) and how informative the book is. Part of text criticism is knowing the kind of text that you are able to read and would want to read.

One of the reasons students in this situation have moved into the role of text critic is that they have been exposed to multiple kinds of texts through read-aloud, shared reading, and independent reading. They have also had the opportunity to explore different genres that each have unique supports and challenges.

Figure 10.9

H.8 Compare and Contrast

Title	
Stand and Deliver	The Last Spin
Setting	
a school in Los Angeles	In a room in a building in the city.
Time period	
1980s	Current time
Conflicts	
students and gang members don't want to learn	Gang members are playing Russian Roulette to solve a fight between 2 gangs.
Resolution	
Mr. Escalante does a great job teaching and the students learn and pass a test.	Two gang members of opposite gangs end up friends, but dead because of the game.
Development of main character	
Students learn to believe in themselves.	Gang members started to realize the importance of real friendship and the dangers of gangs.
Challenges	
The characters didn't come alive. Not enough dialogue.	Story begins in the middle. A little confusing.

Sometimes struggling readers do not have many types of books at their reading interest and abilities. In some classrooms, students read from high interest/low readability kits where the books all look the same.

Students enjoy text sets, and they have been wonderful additions to classrooms, but students need to see lots of other kinds of books they could read each week. These books should be all shapes and sizes, fiction and nonfiction, picture books and short stories. These books should offer students a range of text supports: illustrations, graphics, text type, point-of-need word explanations, historical contexts, primary source documents and photographs, authors' notes and

H.9 Book Pass

Title	Author	Comment
The Artists of Terezin	Gerald Green	The pictures are real cool since they were from real people.
When the Soldiers Were Gone	Vera W. Propp	Its real interesting because it shows the Holocaust from a childs point of view.
A Midnight Clear	William Wharton	I like it because war stories interest me. Also its about something more than just war.
Upon the Heat of The Goat	Aranka Siegal	This book is cool since its written by a survivor of the Third Reich
HEROS	Ken Mochizuki	This book is kind of good. I really like the illustrations
Farewell to Manzapar	Jeanne Wakatsuki Huston James D. Houston	I think its sad because they get sent to camps.

H.9 Book Pass

Title	Author	Comment
Hanna and Walter (a love story.)	Hanna and Walter Kohner with Frederick Kohner	I think this book would only be informative about the holocaust in Hanna Kohners point of view.
From Anna	Jean Little	I think this book will give information about people who got to escape the holocaust.
The Morning Glory War	Judy Glassman	This book seems to be more focused on Jeannie and her penpal than info. on the holocaust.
Flowers on the Wall	Miriam Nerlove	I think this book would be a great source of info. on the holocaust. It gives important events and tells about what the little girl wants to do.
Kinderlager	Milton S. Nieuwsma	I think that this book gives alot of information on many of the death camps in Poland. Great source of information.
Terezin	Naŝe Vojsko	I think it would be a very emotional book to read. It tells about the ghettos and death camps.

Figure 10.10

contemporary connections. I recently discovered two sets of books I recommend in every place I visit. The first set is truly the best social studies series I have ever seen: A History of US, by Joy Hakim, is an eleven-volume collection of United States history. I purchased the entire set, but each volume can be purchased individually. Book 11 is a sourcebook of primary source documents that can be used in conjunction with the texts. The text of the books is so readable that it reads as narrative. In book 10, *All the People 1945–1998*, Chapter 28 is titled "Lyndon in Trouble." The chapter begins:

> Lyndon Johnson was miserable. He knew he was losing his dream of a Great Society. But he didn't know how to stop the war in Vietnam. He did seem able to admit that he had made a mistake. He had started with that fib about an attack in the Gulf of Tonkin. But you know how those things go: one lie usually leads to another, and sometimes another, and another.

What reader wouldn't want to read this text? In addition to this very engaging text, the books offer informative and interesting text supports: caricatures, fine art, cartoons, photographs, timelines, poetry, quotes, colorful side bar glossary, and points of contemporary interest (McDonalds arches and the history of slime).

Penguin Putnam has published a Whole Story series where the same kind of text support is offered for classic works of literature. The books I have from the series are *The Adventures of Tom Sawyer, Around the World in Eighty Days, The Call of the Wild, Frankenstein, Heidi, The Jungle Book, Little Women,* and *Treasure Island.* These books are not adaptations; rather, they offer complete, unabridged texts but each classic is annotated with extended captions, historical and geographical notes, art and science connections, historical customs, and photography. The illustrations are varied, and some date from the time the story was written. Students will choose these readings of classics over and over again.

Readers in Action

Our ultimate goal as we support readers into the roles of code breaker, meaning maker, text user, and text critic is the creation of readers who want to read, reread, and share their experiences. I can still remember the silence that occurred at the end of the first day of independent reading when I said, "Who would like to share something about the book they read today?" I knew fairly quickly that no amount of wait time was going to help this situation. Students' lack of experience as readers had made them uncomfortable and vulnerable. Over time and with weeks of book passes, read-aloud, shared reading, direct instruction, individual support, and group strategies, students felt more confident in taking reading risks. They had developed their skills not only as readers but also as listeners, thinkers, and responders. They knew (at least most of the time) how to challenge and question without being disagreeable. They knew how to criticize texts and support their opinions. Most important, they knew what made a good book and how to use the supports available to enjoy those good books.

11

Reading the Way to Writing

What people somehow (inadvertently, I'm sure) forgot to mention when we were children was that we need to make messes in order to find out who we are and why we are here—and, by extension, what we're supposed to be writing.

Anne Lamott, Bird by Bird: Some Instructions on Writing and Life

During my last year of graduate school, I spent many days in Mary Giard's first-grade classroom observing the teaching and learning that was occurring there. When it was time for writing workshop, Mary would turn on a classical music tape she had put in the tape player that morning. As students heard the music, they gathered up their writing folders, found a place, and began to write. Mary alternated between crafting her own writing and conferring with student writers. Comparing those moments to the chaos that often occurred at the beginning of writing workshop in my classroom, that time always seemed somewhat magical. It led me to examine both my role as a teacher (not an assigner) of writing and the role of reading in providing examples of effective writing.

Students know that writing is important. At the beginning of each year, I always asked my students how important they considered writing to be in their lives, and I also asked them to rate themselves as writers. In one class all students except one felt that writing was important in their lives. However, all claimed to be average or below average writers. They did not see themselves as writers, yet they believed it was important to be a good writer. In an effort to systematically change the years of failure these students associated with writing, I used the same classroom structure as with reading: shared and guided writing with students and independent writing by students. These approaches to writing gave students a great deal of support so that they could take increasing risks with their writing.

Shared Writing

In shared reading the teacher (or other fluent reader) takes responsibility for activating and building background knowledge prior to reading the text, decoding the text, and helping students make the act of learning something from the text a conscious and transferable act. Shared writing puts the teacher in the same role: he uses a variety of texts to lead the students into writing; transcribes students' ideas so that the class can see their words in print; and helps students see how they might use the text models in their own future writing.

We often talk about the importance of scaffolding a reader's experience with the text, and I learned that emerging writers need the same kind of scaffolding to increase their fluency and range of writing options. As I found ways to support students as writers, I discovered the truth of Fletcher and Portalupi's words in *Craft Lessons*: "The writing you get out of your students can only be as good as the classroom literature that surrounds and sustains it" (10). In my work with students and teachers in elementary school through college, I have found that scaffolding has many components:

- Sharing diverse examples of effective writing
- Demonstrating multiple ways to begin writing
- Showing writers how to establish audience and purpose
- Creating word banks
- Using language experience activities (LEA) to demonstrate language choices
- Creating opportunities to write often
  - Self-selected and prompt-driven
  - Writing to learn
  - Writing to demonstrate learning
  - Patterned writing and free writing
  - Writing for personal purposes (enjoyment and questioning)
  - Writing for public purposes
- Providing craft lessons
- Providing timely and specific feedback
- Demonstrating revision techniques
- Creating, modeling, and using editing checklists
- Building language and usage resource notebooks
- Modeling self-questioning and self-assessment techniques
- Sharing responsibility for evaluation

Each of these activities provides support for the developing writer. In this chapter, however, I want to focus on those scaffolding techniques that begin with reading literature and end with students' writing: sharing diverse examples of effective writing, creating word banks and language resource notebooks, patterned writing, and craft lessons. These scaffolded writing experiences give us the opportunity to "make messes" in order to find our way as writers.

Sharing Diverse Examples of Effective Writing

I began using multiple texts as a way of demonstrating effective writing when I finally listened to how often students said, "I don't know what to write. I don't have anything good to write about. I don't know how to get started. What do you want this to look like?" I knew they did have interesting things to say and write; they just didn't have them when it was time to write. When I read aloud to them, they often had opinions and ideas related to the read-alouds. When we had class discussions, their strong opinions nearly gave way to classroom brawls. When I conferred with them, they often commented they had forgotten about the questions I had asked them last time we talked about the possibility of writing about their snowmobile races or their difficulty living alone. I realized that my students needed support in keeping track of their writing ideas and shared suggestions. This led quite naturally to extending our read-aloud time into writing purposes.

Each day I read something aloud to the students. After that reading, we took just a few minutes to focus on some aspect of the piece I had just read to them: personal connections, writing ideas, writer's style, genre/form, interesting language, and so on. Students kept a log in the front of their academic journals (see form H.10 in Appendix H) as a resource for the writing they did for homework or during writing workshop and ILE (see Chapter 8). These notes for writing gave them their own prompts when they were ready to write—prompts that came from their own experiences and connections. Students recorded the read-aloud each day and noted if it had made a writing connection for them.

Interestingly, I began seeing notes on the Ideas form based not only on our read-alouds and conferences but also on their independent reading. Brendon noted his reading of Hemingway's *The Old Man and the Sea* and next to it he had written "old man's face" on his Ideas form. A few days later he gave me his poem "Take the Old Man Home."

> The old man's weathered face
> whispers of past struggles.
> Each line has a different tale
> Each scar tells of a separate battle
>
> He lay sleeping now
> Curled on his newspapers
>   scattered on a stained and dirty mattress.
> I wonder when God
> will look down and find mercy for this poor old soul
> Take him to the other ocean where he can fish
> Never with any tragic stories of struggle
>   Or toil
>   Or battles for survival.

See this poor man lying here now.
Tarrying on until death comes.

Even still, many of his great fish
are only in his dreams.

One of the first shared writing assignments in our classroom was writing life stories. At one point in my teaching, I gave students a different personal history journal topic each day for twenty days with the notion that at the end of the twenty days students would have a wealth of material out of which they could carve one finely crafted snapshot of their lives. Instead, the journal topics most often produced a collage—writers were hesitant to leave out any of the pieces they had spent time writing. Some students even numbered each day's entries and then just typed them all in the same order as the twenty daily journal topics. These prompts hadn't served to help them discover the story within the story; they had only served to help them create a linear story of every remembered event in their lives.

It took me several years to realize that students did not have enough concrete models for ways in which authors can tell a life story without telling the whole story of their lives. As I was comparing my pictures with those taken by a photographer friend, it occurred to me that writing was much like taking a good picture. Troy and I had stood in exactly the same spot and used essentially the same photography equipment and film, yet his photograph of one flamingo and its reflection was breathtaking. My photograph of fifty flamingos was a blur of pink; I hadn't missed a single flamingo. When I complained about how much better his photograph was than mine, he simply pointed out that one flamingo could capture the moment and represent all the others. I realized that writing is a lot like that and rethought my twenty journal prompts.

The next year I made three major changes in supporting students' writing during our life story writing. First, I used the two photographs as a concrete example of finding the story that represents one significant aspect of our lives. Second, we used the main character in the novel we were reading and wrote his life story (Georgie from Hunt's *The Lottery Rose*) as a shared writing experience. Finally, rather than giving students a writing prompt each day, I gave them a reading prompt. These books were read with a writer's ear as students listened for strategies and forms these authors used to share their lives with readers. Graves points out that a reader "takes what he understands from each, just as he did when he acquired language as an infant" (1983, 67). At this point, we were no longer reading these pieces just for story, essay, or poem; we were reading them as examples of writer's craft and choices. In this way, students had a constantly expanding notion of ways to tell a story or capture a moment. Some of the books in the following list are those I used with my students, and some I have found since then and used in my writing classes. With all the great books being published each year, teachers have access to an incredible variety of constantly changing models of writing.

Life Story Texts That Capture a Moment
- Aliki, *The Two of Them*
- Maya Angelou, *I Know Why the Caged Bird Sings*
- Forrest Carter, *The Education of Little Tree*
- Jan Cheripko, *Imitate the Tiger*
- Sandra Cisneros, *The House on Mango Street*
- Pam Conrad, *My Daniel*
- Robert Cormier, *I Have Words to Spend*
- Roald Dahl, *Boy*
- Roald Dahl, *Going Solo*
- Annie Dillard, *The Writing Life*
- Amy Ehrlich, *When I Was Your Age*
- Ralph Fletcher, *I Am Wings*
- Jean Fritz, *Homesick*
- Robert Fulghum, *All I Really Need to Know I Learned in Kindergarten*
- Nikki Giovanni, *Sacred Cows and Other Edibles*
- Donald Graves, *Baseball, Snakes, and Summer Squash*
- Sara Holbrook, *Chicks Up Front*
- Lee Bennett Hopkins, *Been to Yesterdays*
- Michael Jordan, *I Can't Accept Not Trying*
- Patricia MacLachlan, *All the Places to Love*
- Gary Paulsen, *Sentries*
- Robert Newton Peck, *A Day No Pigs Would Die*
- Cynthia Rylant, *The Relatives Came*
- Cynthia Rylant, *When I Was Young in the Mountains*
- Gary Soto, *A Summer Life*
- Jerry Spinelli, *Who Put That Hair in My Toothbrush?*
- Sue Townsend, *The Secret Diary of Adrian Mole, Aged 13¾*
- Alice Walker, *To Hell with Dying*
- Bailey White, *Mama Makes Up Her Mind*

Once students have seen and heard a range of possibilities for writing, they have more options for telling their own stories. Most students were able to find a genre that matched their voice and their story because they had such a wide range of possibilities. For students who have experienced a limited repertoire of writing, their only writing style is often the bed-to-bed story, which even ends with The End or as one of my students wrote at the end of his life story, "More later when I've lived longer."

Graves says, "Writers who do not learn to choose topics wisely lose out on the strong link between voice and subject" (1983, 21). A way to help students find their own topic—the one flamingo among many—is to show them how other writers have found a focus. With these writing models, the students' products show the same range. Ian's and Brandi's memory pieces reflect the models that spoke to them as writers based on the works we shared together. Ian's rough draft of a memory piece about high school came after my reading of Fulghum's *All I Really Need to Know I Learned in Kindergarten*:

> It seems that in my high school career, I haven't learned all that much. I know that it's mostly my fault. I think that the school should take some of the blame. It's awful easy for a kid to slip through the cracks. I came here three years ago and I think I learned more in the halls, at the tournament games, at the dances and on dates than I did in the classrooms. In the classrooms I got smarter, outside I learned to be a person. I think I've learned a lot and I've dealt with some things a person shouldn't have to deal with. Now, I don't know if I did it the right way or the scared way but I dealt with it. I learned how to deal with problems in school. I learned not to kiss the teachers. I got three days in-house suspension for that. I've learned that girls can be nothing but a pain in the butt and that girls come and go but your friends are forever. Is that all I need to know? I don't think so because life's a classroom and it's one that you can't jig.

Brandi's poem was written after several poetry read-alouds that contained childhood memories:

At the End of the Rainbow
"Darrell! Wade! Look at the rainbow!"
"Get your boots!"
"Wait for me!"
The chubby fingers
grabbed at boots and sneakers
jackets and sweaters.
The children raced across the yard
squealing, laughing,
anticipating, hoping…
In the potato field
we raced toward the rainbow
where our dreams lay as coins of gold.
"Help me, I'm stuck!" yelled Wade,
and Darrell and I helped pull his feet
from the muck
losing his boots,
but still we wrenched him free.
We lost little things along the way:
A shoe here
A jacket there, buttons, bows.
We had each other
And stumbled along the way together.

Seeing the pot of gold within reach,
We peered in
And found what we had lost
Along the way.
In the reflection
We saw innocent faces with chubby cheeks.
Santa Claus and the Easter Bunny
Dukes of Hazard and the Muppets
floated under our fingertips.
. . . color books, red crayons
the playroom
Bugs Bunny lunch boxes
Snow angels and moon books
Swing sets and ponies.

"Goodbye to us," we said
and we wrapped those memories up
and preserved them between yellow pages
and placed them in musty trunks with moth balls
to search for the rainbow another rainy day.

Memories of school, home, growing up, and growing older began to fill our
classroom whereas past years had brought us hundreds of papers with answers
to my prompts. Romano says, "It is human beings who create those first words,
false starts, scratched-out lines, and messy pages that eventually become polished
writing published in books and magazines. And those human beings are not so
unlike the freshmen in your final class of the day" (41). As students like Ian and
Brandi hear the stories of others and begin to sort through their own truths, we
begin to see glimpses of those published writers.

Creating Word Banks

Baker, Simmons, and Kameenui cite research that shows "reading is probably the
most important mechanism for vocabulary growth throughout a student's school-
age years and beyond" (7). This research comes as no surprise to those of us who
know how reading can increase the language we are aware of and use on a daily
basis. Unfortunately, many developing readers read texts that have a fairly narrow
range of vocabulary, or they skip the unknown words in more complex texts. I
began using language collection with my students as a way to help them become
more aware of language and find words they could appropriate for their own use.

Many students just do not have a bank of words sufficient to express themselves in writing or in speech. Many developing readers and writers do not read
enough to build extensive word banks. I wrote extensively about the use of word
walls in *Words, Words, Words* (Allen 1999, 70–71) as a way to build classroom

word banks. Essentially, language collection is a way for students to create personal word walls in their academic journals so they can have them for use in their writing.

My students usually gathered these words from the texts we read together in class. During shared reading, each student had a Post-it or flag that he moved through the reading of the book. Each day during the reading, students put their flags on words they wanted to discuss at the end. Each day we talked about a few of the words students had marked. Interestingly, students often chose the same words as being interesting or intriguing words. Sometimes we just discussed the words or generated lists of them, but other times we spent more time looking at the structural analysis of the word or making connections to other words or concepts we had learned.

Shared reading provides decoding support so that students can spend more time focusing on interesting language. Using the postreading time to gather those words they have collected gives students the opportunity to explore far more words than they otherwise would. These words can be collected in predetermined categories or from the random interesting words students choose. The word list shown in Figure 11.1 represents students' combined word collection

Figure 11.1

Language Collection					
Who Put That Hair in My Toothbrush?					
Action		*Emotion*		*Speech*	
scooting	groveling	goochy	snickered	breezily	
rammed	sniveling	sensational	peeped	snapped	
gushing	mashed	glaring	squealed	snickered	
dashed	jolt	sympathy	booming	hissed	
stormed	jabbed	trifle	howled	booming	
swooned	flinched	bitter	bleat	squeaked	
gawking	scramble	astounded	whimpered	snorting	
breezed	barged	antsy	cackled	peeped	
smacked	brawled	horrified	sneered	gulped	
whirled	gaping	sheepish	piped	chuckled	
staggered	twitching	survive	shrieked	groaned	
startles	jerking	infuriates	mocked	ranted	
plopped	disintegrate	fascinated	whined	snarled	
badger	splattered	hysterical	screeched	hissing	
prowled	lunged	disgusted	sneered	swooned	
smirky	frantically	worships	blurting	howling	
recoiled	yanking	roaring (mad)	snapped	hoots	
lurching	smearing	relief	screeched	roared	
lured	hammered	gruesome	mocking	whooped	
swooning	slinging	cheerful	shyly	yahoo	
scrunched	stomped	desperate	adorably		
winced	pried	pitiful			
staggering	wretched				
waggled	wobbled				
slither	slobbering				

during their shared reading of Spinelli's *Who Put That Hair in My Toothbrush?*
Students have collected action, emotion, and speech words that will later support
their writing related to this and other texts.

Shared reading also provides the impetus for in-depth study of words and
synonyms. The Word Questioning graphic organizer in Figure 11.2 is adapted to
fit the word *unpredictable,* which students discovered in our reading. We had
spent lots of time talking about and making predictions, but students had not
made the connection between prediction and predictable/unpredictable behav-

Figure 11.2

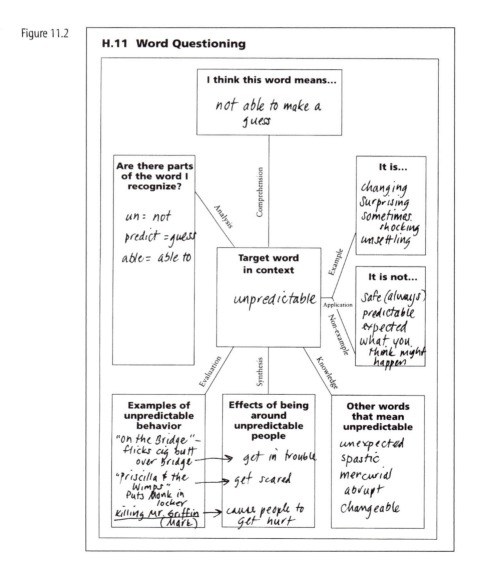

iors. After our discussion of unpredictable behaviors and the effects of being around unpredictable people, students actually were more aware of what their brains were doing as they predicted their way through a text. By generating a list of words (with help from the thesaurus) that might mean unpredictable (unexpected, mercurial, changeable, abrupt, spastic), students were able to add some new language to their word banks. The examples of unpredictable behavior and the consequences of that behavior came from literature we were reading (Strasser's "On the Bridge," Peck's "Priscilla and the Wimps," and Duncan's *Killing Mr. Griffin*).

On some days as we read together, I asked students to move their Post-it flags to certain categories of words if they heard them. At the end of our reading, we made collections of words, which students transferred to the Language Collection section of their academic journals. These words were then available to them as they wrote each day. The text was read for information and enjoyment first and then students had the opportunity to go back and find the words they wanted to contribute. Words collected from several days of reading are gathered on the Language Collection form (see Figure 11.3). Words/Images That Make Me Smile or Laugh came from a reading of "Vocabulary" in Korman and Korman's *The D- Poems of Jeremy Bloom*; Tears to My Eyes, from *I Never Saw Another Butterfly* (Volavkova); Words That Paint a Picture, from Paulsen's *The Winter Room*; and Action Words, from Paulos's *Insectasides*, "dedicated to don

Figure 11.3

H.12 Language Collection

Words/images that make me smile or laugh	Smells, sights, sounds that bring tears to my eyes	Words/phrases that paint a picture
glurd flice sveen wazzle perfuffle kazyme terflape	*"thirty eyes seeking quietness" "bald heads that gape from out of the prison" "anguish deep in my soul" "tears inspired by grief" "heavens shriek with blue"	gold with bits of hay dust Coleman lantern full moon on snow dawn

Words that make noise	Forbidden words	Action words
		saittle whisk secrete linger determine shake recline (a shimmy) browse chant trek slink explore

Figure 11.4

marquis." Students also created individual language collection pages for words or concepts that interested them (see Figure 11.4).

Our most daring language collection lesson plan came from a day spent with language choices. Students in my classes were placed in in-school suspension (ISS) or suspended from school so often that they missed entire novels. One day I became so frustrated with the situation that I asked students to generate a list of all the reasons they were suspended. The list was fairly predictable: fighting, swearing (bad language), and skipping classes. I knew I couldn't do much about the fighting and skipping classes, but we could work on the bad language. I closed the door, drew two columns on the board, labeled one "What you said" and the other "What you could have said." I said a prayer that no one was listening on the intercom system, and we began to generate a list of all the bad language that students had said that got them kicked out of class/school. When the list was "complete," we came up with alternative things they could say that might not get them in as much trouble. For example, instead of "You suck!" they

Figure 11.5

H.13 Language Choices

Instead of saying...	I could say...
Said	recited uttered exclaimed pronounced blurted out screamed cried mumbled proposed cited announced

---

came up with "You need some work—some major work!" While many teachers would hesitate to record such language, not a single student in that class was kicked out of class for bad language for the rest of the year. We also used the Language Choices chart several other times when we encountered overused words in the books we were reading, for instance, things to say instead of *said* (see Figure 11.5) or *nice*. Each chart (except the bad language one) was copied into students' academic journals for continued reference.

A similar activity occurred with the Language Register chart (see Figure 11.6). Halliday's work with language register supports teaching students that our language varies depending on audience and purpose. The first time it occurred to me that it was my responsibility to make these language distinctions clear for students was after reading Cullum's *The Geranium on the Window Sill Just Died, but Teacher You Went Right On.* As a result of the reading, students were quick to make fun of "being fake" because of the way I changed my language when the principal came into the room. I started to get defensive and then realized they were right. It was a perfect opportunity to talk about the ways we can change our language that might be communication tools. I talked with them about language register, and we started keeping track of the way we might say things to our friends and the way we could change that language if we wanted to

Figure 11.6

H.14 Language Register

Everyday voice	Formal language
"Can I go to the can?"	"Do you have a restroom available?"
"Duh..."	"That's good but I'm wondering if you've considered..."
"I was RFS last night."	"I may have had too much to drink."
"Give me that before I take your head off."	"Would you like to reconsider that decision?"

---

impress, persuade, motivate, manipulate, or entertain a wider audience. Perhaps I was making them all candidates for a doublespeak award, but I know visitors to our classroom were impressed when met with such obvious displays of effective language.

Baker, Simmons, and Kameenui state, "Learning something new does not occur in a vacuum. Rather, new learning always builds on what the learner already knows." Language activities such as language choices and language register help students move from their natural speaking to a wider repertoire of language. They also begin to move learners from reader roles and into writer roles.

Patterned Writing

Patterned writing has often been criticized as limiting student writers because of the constraints of the pattern. I'm not writing here about patterned copying, such as the gum paragraph that a middle school student gave me as her example of why kids hate writing:

THIS ASSIGNMENT IS GIVEN INSTEAD OF AN AFTER-SCHOOL DETENTION. YOU <u>WILL NOT</u> BE STAYING AFTER SCHOOL. THE DETENTION FORM <u>MUST</u> BE SIGNED BY A PARENT OR GUARDIAN AS REQUESTED.

GUM PARAGRAPH

WRITE <u>FIVE</u> (5) TIMES

I SHOULD NEVER CHEW GUM DURING HOME ECONOMICS CLASS FOR MANY REASONS. I MIGHT CHOKE ON MY GUM DURING AN ACTIVITY, OR MY GUM MIGHT FALL OUT OF MY MOUTH AND STICK TO VALUABLE AND EXPENSIVE EQUIPMENT USED FOR MY HOME ECONOMICS CLASS. THE NUMBER ONE REASON FOR NOT CHEWING GUM IS BECAUSE I KNOW IT IS A SCHOOL RULE <u>NOT</u> TO HAVE GUM ON SCHOOL GROUNDS. IN ORDER FOR ME TO BE THE BEST STUDENT I CAN POSSIBLY BE, I <u>WILL NOT</u> CHEW GUM AGAIN WHILE I AM IN HOME ECONOMICS CLASS. I REALIZE I MAY NOT GET AN "N" IN CONDUCT FOR THE NINE WEEKS AS A RESULT OF RECEIVING THIS DETENTION; AND IF I HAVE GUM AGAIN THIS SEMESTER, I WILL RECEIVE A REFERRAL(S) TO THE OFFICE AND VERY PROBABLY A "U" IN CONDUCT ON MY REPORT CARD.

I am writing about choosing pieces of literature and expository text that students can replicate as their first steps in composing a variety of texts. For many student writers, patterned writing can be their first writing to be successful.

We often ask students to use poetry as a pattern by following a rhyme or form pattern: cinquain, haiku, bio poems, I Am poems, limerick. Some teachers also ask students to follow the theme or opening lines of a poem such as "When I Was One and Twenty," where students simply change the first line to match their ages (e.g., "When I was four and ten") and then proceed to personalize the poem. Students also enjoy using the visual pattern of concrete poems, using the image of the words as the pattern for the shape and content of the text.

Song lyrics also make fine patterns for students to follow. After reading Hunt's *The Lottery Rose* and viewing *I Know My First Name Is Steven* (Echols), the story of the kidnapping of Steven Stayner, my students and I listened to Suzanne Vega's song *Luka*. We read the lyrics as we listened to the music. When we had finished listening to it for the second time, one of the students said, "Georgie could have written that." I agreed with them and asked them to write what they thought his song would be. April was one of the students who chose to write song lyrics from Georgie's perspective in *The Lottery Rose*:

Georgie
My name is Georgie.
I live in Florida.
I live in a mean house
Yes, I think you've seen me before.
If you hear something late at night
Some kind of snapping or crashing
Just don't ask me
Just don't ask me
Just don't ask me what happened.

I think it's because I'm clumsy
I try not to scream
Maybe it's because I'm bad
They hit me until I cry
And after that you don't ask me
About the scars.
I just won't talk
I just won't talk
I just won't talk to you.

Yes, I'm hurting
I fell down the stairs
If you ask, that's what I'll say
And it's not your business anyway

I would like to be alone
With things broken and things scarred
Don't even ask me how I am
Just don't ask me how I am
Because I'll look at you and yell

Now before the crying begins
I'll finish packing
I'll runaway far—
Far away.

Traci chose Steven's perspective (*I Know My First Name Is Steven*) for her point of view piece based on Vega's lyrics:

Steven
My name is Steven
I live with Parnel
I am a stolen child
Yes, I know you know me
If you see me, please come and get me but
You don't ask me who I am
You don't ask me who I am
You don't ask me who I am.

I think it's because I'm unhappy
I try not to cry so much
Maybe it's because I miss my mommy
I try to act myself
Maybe because I am not
I hate my new daddy
I wish I could be with my mommy

I think I am going to die or
Maybe I should just cry.

The connection between literature and writing in patterned writing is critical. Writers can use the pattern of the writing as a way to communicate their discoveries, emotions, and thinking about the characters and events in their reading. These are fine assessment tools, but they are also forms of writing that allow students to work with a framework of support.

Picture books can also make excellent patterns for student-written picture books. Many of my students reveled in creating their own versions of Viorst's *Alexander and the Terrible, Horrible, No Good, Very Bad Day,* and I was delighted when they also saw the humor in Charlip's *Fortunately.* The following text represents one student group's own version of *Fortunately.* I can assure you this text was not in line to win our district writing contest; however, it was the first writing students had actually enjoyed that year and as such made a great point of departure for lots of other writing.

Fortunately (NOT)
Fortunately we have a nice English teacher
Unfortunately she's making us write a story
Fortunately our pencils broke.
Unfortunately the teacher gave us new ones.
Fortunately Jed had some dope
Unfortunately it was rag weed
Fortunately Robert had some good weed
Unfortunately we got busted
Fortunately they let us go
Unfortunately not for a week
Fortunately they made us go back to school
Unfortunately they made us go back to English
Fortunately they changed the assignment
Unfortunately they still made us write—
　　The story!

Essays can also form the basis for patterned writing. I know the writing wave sweeping schools in anticipation of state writing tests is the hamburger paragraph for the five-paragraph essay. What I am advocating here is extending that to a variety of essays (yes, there are essays that do not have five paragraphs). A *Newsweek* essay, "Inside the Classroom" (Butson), provided a patterned writing sample for my students. The article said, "What America needs is a desk's-eye view of what really goes on day after day, year after year," and in response to the media focus on the plight of America's schools, Butson detailed her day as a teacher from her arrival at school until the last bell. Her final line, "And I have to do it again tomorrow," precipitated an excellent reading and writing experience for my students. The pattern of the essay supported students' writing because they were able to use the key cue words in the paragraphs (then, next, finally) as well as the structure the author had used by going through each class period of her day.

Patterns help struggling writers generate text in depth and breadth in ways they have never accomplished in the past. The pattern provides a safety net when they run out of ideas about what to write and where to go next. For many students, patterned writing is a mediated step between teacher dependence and independent choice of ideas and forms.

Guided Writing: Focused Craft Lessons

I was recently talking with the person sitting next to me on a long flight to California. Once he discovered that I was a teacher, he was quick to tell me that I would "probably disagree with him but he was glad we were finally getting back to the basics." Having heard that phrase enough to last me several lifetimes, I was not hesitant in asking him what he meant by the basics. "Readin', writin', and 'rithmetic—everyone knows what the basics are." I asked him what he meant by the basics of writing. He was the owner of a large company, and his stance was "For my money, the basics of writing are spelling, grammar, and punctuation." I think many people see these as the basics of writing; I see them as the basics of editing. For *my* money, those are two very different things. I found that literature could provide the resources for helping students discover concrete examples of both our definitions of basics: craft and editing.

For years I did not know what to do to help my students make their writing more effective. I could help them discover spelling errors and give them tips for finding those errors themselves. I could pick out most punctuation errors, but they made the same errors again in the next piece of writing. I could sometimes help them with more effective words, but they were my words, not theirs. One day when I finished just such a writing conference with Chris, he said, "I guess you could use my paper as a nonexample of writing." I realized anew just how demoralizing those writing conferences were for students. His words stayed with me, and I started thinking about ways we could use examples/nonexamples as tools for discovering rules or patterns of effective writing. I searched for patterns of writing that would help all students move to new places in the critique and revision of their own writing. We came up with what we called extended writer's craft lessons. Fortunately, I knew that I wanted the lessons to begin with literature.

Literature can be a valuable resource for all aspects of the writer's craft: topic development, organization, details, sentence variety, effective leads and ends, and characterization. In *Craft Lessons,* Fletcher and Portalupi provide an incredible range for exploring writer's craft, from structure and organization to literary devices such as flashback and symbolism. I would have given anything for this resource when I was trying to decide what would make a piece of writing even more effective.

The range of options for these lessons is wide. For example, the beginning of Carolyn Coman's *What Jamie Saw* gives writers a sense of the effectiveness of repetition in pulling the reader into the emotion of the situation: "When Jamie saw him throw the baby, saw Van throw the little baby, saw Van throw his little sister Nin, then they moved" (7). In a similarly effective manner, John Neufeld in *Almost a Hero* offers readers a very satisfying ending:

"Am I too heavy?"

"No way," I told Jennie.

I swung my leg over the bike and put my hands on the bars around her.

"It's uphill," Jennie warned.

I smiled. "Not all the way."

Neufeld's ending helps us see one way writers draw closure by pulling the pieces together in a way that leaves the reader not feeling cheated.

So, with all the writing paths available to us, what were the back-to-the-writing basics in our craft lessons? In two years my students and I explored the following writing lessons through extended time with texts and their own writing:

- Getting started
- Finding the right word
- Crafting effective beginnings
- Making transitions from one idea/event to another
- Using a variety of sentences
- Using strong verbs
- Adding effective details
- Writing in ways that are kind to the reader
- Finding our writing voices
- Daring to take writing risks
- Knowing when and how to ask for help

This was a huge accomplishment for us. I spent a great deal of time searching for just the right texts to extend our thinking in these areas. Given that the only two leads my students seemed to know were repetition of the prompt sentence or a "once upon a time" variant, our first extended craft lesson was on effective leads. I know that some students will pick up these writing tools just from seeing them; students in my classes needed the support of a graphic organizer and their notes to keep track of their discoveries. This was our process for our lesson with effective leads.

First I asked students the purpose of effective leads in fiction. They decided the purpose was to hook them as readers and get them to want to read more. So I took the beginnings of several works of fiction such as the following ones and put one lead on each overhead.

On the night Jimmy Chavez escaped from prison, his daughter, Andrea, was playing her flute at Melody Mountain Music Camp's Sunday evening concert. By the time the concert ended, Jimmy and four other convicts lay face down under the flapping tarp of an open flatbed truck headed south on the interstate. Meyer, *Wild Rover*

It's not that I hated Billy Blanchet, though at times I thought I did. "Somebody made a mistake," Uncle Raz had told Keo and me. "That boy belongs on another planet." Salisbury, *Blue Skin of the Sea*

I used to think if you fell from grace it was more likely than not the result of one stupendous error, or else an unfortunate accident. I hadn't learned that it can happen so gradually you don't lose your stomach or hurt yourself in the landing. You don't necessarily sense the motion. Hamilton, *A Map of the World*

The windshield wipers are flapping, slap, slap, slapping:
"You/screwed/up/good./
"You/screwed/up/good./
"You/screwed/up/good./ Many, *These Are the Rules*

Most people are kind of surprised when they find out I stabbed a guy, once. I can't really blame them. I mean, I look pretty normal. They're even more surprised when they find out it happened when I was just thirteen and in eighth grade. When it happened, I still had my backpack slung over my shoulder with my uniform skirt stuff in it. I don't think the guy was really hurt, although I never found out for sure. He had a leather jacket on, and it was pretty thick. . . .The day started off normally enough . . .Testa, *Dancing Pink Flamingos*

We wanted to wreck Jeffrey Pratt. That was Theo's word for it. Wreck. We didn't want him hurt, we didn't want him dead, we didn't even care if he got expelled from William Tecumseh Sherman Junior High. We simply wanted Jeffrey Pratt *destroyed*.
   Like, take the kid and—
   Shatter his mind.
   Burst his soul.
   Wreck the kid, once and for all. Skinner, *The Wrecker*

It's only half an hour since someone—Robyn I think—said we should write everything down, and it's only twenty-nine minutes since I got chosen, and for those twenty-nine minutes I've had everyone crowded around me gazing at the blank page and yelling ideas and advice. Marsden, *Tomorrow, When the War Began*

The air was clogged with heat. Through open windows streamed the dusty sunlight of another city afternoon. An undercurrent of fretfulness rippled around the room. The children were irritable and restless, and Mrs. Henrey couldn't stand them in the classroom any longer. Thomas, *The Runaways*

Around 5:00 a.m. on a warm Sunday morning in October 1953, my Aunt Belle left her bed and vanished from the face of the earth. White, *Belle Prater's Boy*

We read each of the leads together so we could hear how they sounded. After each lead was read, students decided whether the lead was effective or ineffective at making them want to continue reading. If effective (+), they generated these reasons: short, suspenseful, something happens right away, everyday language, vivid verbs, interesting characters; if ineffective (–), they cited these reasons: formal language, abstract, nothing happens, long sentences, no characters (see Figure 11.7). Based on our examples, we wrote a class definition for effective leads.

Figure 11.7

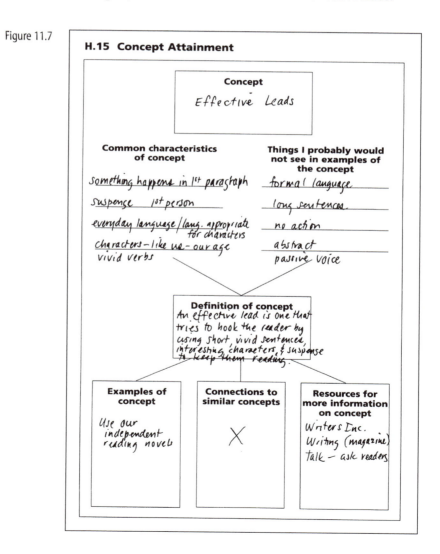

H.15 Concept Attainment

Concept
Effective Leads

Common characteristics of concept
something happens in 1st paragraph
suspense   1st person
everyday language/lang. appropriate for characters
characters – like us – our age
vivid verbs

Things I probably would not see in examples of the concept
formal language
long sentences
no action
abstract
passive voice

Definition of concept
An effective lead is one that tries to hook the reader by using short, vivid sentences, interesting characters, & suspense to keep them reading.

Examples of concept
Use our independent reading novel

Connections to similar concepts
X

Resources for more information on concept
Writers Inc.
Writing (magazine)
talk – ask readers

Students then worked in groups to examine the leads in books they were reading during independent reading. They decided that sometimes books got better after the leads but some students said if a book didn't get them in the first few sentences, they changed books. Each group came to consensus on the most effective lead in the books represented in their groups and wrote the lead on an overhead transparency so we could see if we needed to modify our definition. Finally, students took one piece of writing they had worked on during the semester and attempted to make the lead in that piece more effective. This form of guided writing was specific enough not to be overwhelming for students. In fact, some students used the same piece for several lessons in order to make the entire piece more effective.

Sometimes we spent our time looking at making language more powerful; other times we explored the kinds of decisions writers have to make. One of the most effective lessons of this type occurred when I brought in a suspenseful short story to read to them. Instead of starting the story at the beginning, I began reading just before the turning point and stopped just after that point. Students immediately started to argue over what happened before that led to that point and how the story would have ended. This led to a discussion of the range of choices writers have to make early in the story and how that range continues through the end. Figure 11.8 shows the categories of decisions students believed writers had to make.

When readers begin to think like writers, and writers begin to write with readers in mind, the lines that separate the teaching of reading and writing disappear. As we pull examples from literature for these writing craft lessons, we can use the examples as opportunities for students to create their own language resource notebooks. In our classroom, we did not use grammar books or writing manuals as anything other than points of reference. Instead we used a variety of texts as sources for examples and nonexamples of effective writing. We then documented those so they would be available as resources for future writing by creating our own language resource notebooks. Together we discovered the truth of Richard Peck's words: "We writers reach for our readers where they live, hoping to lead them into the wider world of storytelling. And we are inspired by other storytellers. Nobody but a reader ever became a writer."

Figure 11.8

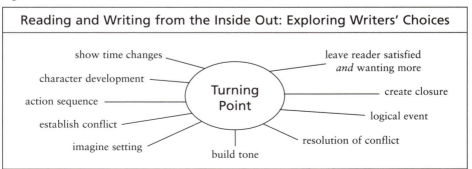

12

Full Circle: Assessing, Evaluating, and Starting Again

Learning is hard to measure. The best kind of learning—the kind that stays with you for the rest of your life—is maybe impossible to measure. This is a source of great frustration to small minds that are compelled to measure all and discard all they cannot measure.

James Nehring, The Schools We Have, the Schools We Want

Learning is indeed hard to measure. The measures that teachers give in anecdotal reports of success often leave politicians and school leaders asking for "hard data." The results of the hard data gathered in most state assessment tests leave teachers feeling shortchanged. I was working with a group of teachers in Florida after our state test was finally over this year. I asked them how it felt to have the test finished, and one teacher's reply summarized the feelings of many in the group: "I feel cheated—kind of let down. All the hype—all that work—and then it was over and I knew that the scores still wouldn't tell me if kids in my class now enjoyed or were even good at reading. I thought of all the great things I did in the past that I didn't have time to do this year, and it made me sick. Too much for too little, I say."

If our state-mandated tests leave us feeling as though we don't have enough information to inform our teaching, I think it is even more critical that we design and publish demonstrations of learning that are meaningful to us as well as to students, parents, school leaders, and the community. Tom Robbins in *Jitterbug Perfume* says, "The gods have a great sense of humor, don't they? If you lack the iron and the fizz to take control of your own life, if you insist on leaving your fate to the gods, then the gods will repay your weakness by having a grin or two at your expense. Should you fail to pilot your own ship, don't be surprised at what inappropriate port you find yourself docked" (84–85). Learning to trust my judgment for literacy assessment and evaluation has been one of the most difficult aspects of teaching for me. Lack of confidence often left me looking for answers in "inappropriate ports" as I tried to document students' progress toward literacy.

Why Assess?

It is obvious to all educators that assessment plays a critical role in education. Unfortunately, we are now spending so much time, energy, and money in high-stakes assessment tests that the literacy needs of some children are getting lost in the process. It's important to remember that measuring your height doesn't make you grow any faster and weighing yourself doesn't make you lose weight. If we continue to let assessments that least inform classroom practice take a dispro-portionate amount of teaching and learning time, progress in the very areas the assessments supposedly measure will decrease from lack of high-quality instruc-tional time. This emphasis on high-stakes assessment has stolen the time and energy we need for teaching and for developing assessment practices that will inform our teaching.

Assessment should serve many purposes in schools and communities. It should inform everything from daily classroom practice to long-range district planning. When a variety of assessments is used, it can serve to give important feedback to many interested members of the school community:

- Learners
- Parents
- Other faculty
- Support personnel
- Teachers
- Administrators
- Alternative programs
- Community support programs
- Curriculum planners
- Community members
- Boards of education
- Higher education groups
- State policy makers

I believe there is a distinction between assessment and evaluation and the distinction is critical for classroom teachers. I define assessment as the ongoing redefinition of starting points. Evaluation is the assigning of value (letters, num-bers, mastery levels) to work. Multiple assessments should be used in order to come to a fair evaluation. When teachers in workshops ask me, "What about assessment?" they are usually asking, "How did you grade?" For me, those are two different questions.

Our individual and whole-group assessments each day should inform our teaching and show us where to start again. Some teachers are required to submit lesson plans from one to three weeks in advance, so they often applaud when I say ongoing assessment precludes such detailed planning. While general plans, such as topic and resources for a thematic unit of study, can be stated in advance, our assessment today dictates what we should do tomorrow. This is one of the reasons I am such a proponent of exit slips.

I know many teachers who use exit slips each day to help them and their students plan next steps. Exit slip prompts may be content-specific or related to the processes and cognition of learning in any class. Exit slips can serve as closure for a day's class so the information can be used for planning. Students can also use the slips at the beginning of the next class to generate common class questions or to form study groups. Some teachers use strips of paper (a different color for each class or day), and others ask students to respond to the prompts in their academic journals. In her Literacy Workshop classroom, Kyle Gonzalez asks the exit slip question, "Tell me something new you learned today," at the end of class, and students respond orally as they exit the class. Some generic exit slips prompts are these:

Write about something new you learned today.
What made learning easy/difficult for you today?
What was left unanswered?
Where should we begin tomorrow?
How did what we learned today connect to the work we did last week?
If you were teaching this topic/theory/concept, how would you help students understand?
How will I know when you have mastered this concept? What will you be able to do that will show me you understand?
Why do you think we are studying this?
What new questions do you have?

This type of assessment has at its core the shared responsibility of active learning. I attempted to forge this connection in each of the types of literacy assessments we used in our classroom. These multiple assessments then led to evaluation and ultimately to grading.

Lines of Assessment

I like to think of each type of assessment as a line of assessment because each line led us to a different aspect of understanding of both process and product literacy knowledge. I didn't want students to see assessment and evaluation as random, so I tried to co-construct many of the assessments with students and gave them opportunities to modify assessments that didn't seem to give us productive information.

I'm sure there are many other literacy assessments, but the ones highlighted here are ones I used with my students. Some of these assessments could be used in one class that had fewer students than my other classes; other assessments are ones I used in larger classes. In each case, I asked three things: What are the students doing? What makes this "doing" useful? How can learners demonstrate their knowing? The examples I've used here to support each of the lines of assessment come from my classroom and from elementary and secondary classrooms where I have worked as a consultant. They are examples of assessment (ways of knowing), not examples of evaluation (ways of grading).

Surveys and Sentence Completions

Writing samples completed at the beginning of the year were always more intimidating for my students than survey forms or sentence completions. No matter how specific I made the baseline assessment writing prompt, students who were struggling readers and writers always found it overwhelming and wrote only a few words. After several relatively unsuccessful writing samples, I realized I could gain more knowledge by using formats that were less open-ended. From April's fall survey (see Figure 12.1), I am able to assess literacy attitudes, background, and behaviors in place for April. I can see that she enjoys suspense and realistic fiction and that she believes reading and writing are important. I can see her learning preferences and her commitment to her own learning. For several years I looked only at the individual responses in relation to the individual student. In my last year of teaching, however, I realized that the information on the surveys could also be instructive when I looked for class patterns. When I looked at the results of this survey for one class, I discovered several areas that influenced my planning:

- Most students disliked content classes and enjoyed gym.
- Students saw important teacher qualities as respectful, listening, and patient.
- Favorite categories of books were suspense and realistic fiction/nonfiction.
- Qualities they looked for in books included truthful discussion of life, interesting writing, talking about feelings, important information.

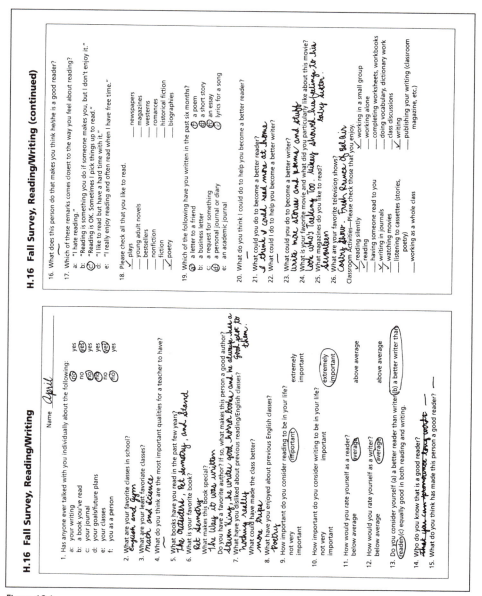

Figure 12.1

- Reasons they had disliked reading/English included too much reading work, reading in front of the class, boring, reading out loud, bad grades.
- Students believed classes would be better with less homework, doing a variety of things, doing stuff that doesn't have anything to do with reading, and not having so many worksheets.

- Almost all students saw reading and writing as important in their lives.
- Most students (70 percent) didn't know anyone they considered a good reader.
- They believed that people became good readers when they had time to read and practice a lot, knew a lot of words, and could pronounce long words.
- Most students (70 percent) had no idea how I could help them become better readers; the others thought that they would become better readers if I read a lot to them, gave them interesting books, and made them read.
- Most students enjoyed working alone or in small groups, listening to recorded books, having someone read to them, and reading silently.
- Most students disliked doing vocabulary, worksheets, journals, oral reading, and whole-class work.

I would never have learned this much about the students as individuals or as a learning group if I had used a writing sample.

Sentence completions served the same informative purpose in our class. From Craig's early sentence completion (see Figure 12.2), I can see that we have

Figure 12.2

H.17 Sentence Completions

Please respond to the following sentence completions by writing the first honest, coherent thought that completes the sentence for you.

1. Today I feel _great_
2. When I have to read, I _hate it_
3. I get angry when _I have homework_
4. To be grown up _I be my self_
5. My idea of a good time _is act like me_
6. I wish my parents knew _I didn't act this way_
7. School is _terrible_
8. I can't understand why _we go to school_
9. I feel bad when _I have school_
10. I wish teachers _would stop giving homework_
11. I wish my mother _gave me her check_
12. Going to college _might be fun_
13. To me, books _suck_
14. People think I _am weird_
15. I like to read about _comic books_
16. On weekends, I _do nothing_
17. I don't know how _to be normal_
18. To me, homework _is hard_
19. I hope I'll never _have to go to school again_
20. I wish people wouldn't _be mean_
21. When I finish high school _I will be done_
22. I'm afraid _of college_
23. Comic books _are pretty good_
24. When I take my report card home _I am scared_
25. I am at my best when _I am average_

a challenging year ahead of us. He hates reading, school, homework, and grades. He thinks he is at his best when "I am average." Paul's first sentence completion was much like Craig's. His second-semester completion (see Figure 12.3) still showed that he was struggling with reading, writing, and school but that he knew he could improve if he worked at it.

Short-answer, topic-specific questions also proved to elicit more helpful information that general questions about attitude or understandings of literacy. These seven questions in the reading strategy questionnaire ask students very specific questions about reading strategies:

Figure 12.3

H.18 Sentence Completions

Please respond to the following sentence completions by writing the first honest, coherent thought that completes the sentence for you.

1. When someone assigns a book for me to read, I _read it_

2. When I'm asked to write in a journal, I _write in a journal_

3. When I think of school, I think of _Hell_, _Hell_, _Hell_ and _Hell_

4. If someone asked me if I were a good reader, my response would be _No_

5. When I am asked to write on a topic I choose, the process I use to decide what to write about is _thinking_

6. The way I choose a book to read for independent reading is _picking one up_

7. If I were asked to summarize my past reading experiences, I would say _Not good_

8. The things I think I do well as a reader are _Nothing_

9. The biggest problem for me when I try to read is _Skip hard words_

10. The hardest type of reading for me is _in front of a class_

11. Given my future plans, I feel that reading and writing _is not important_

12. Some believe that writing is a gift; others believe that everyone can be a good writer. In my opinion, _you can be a good writer or reader if you work at it._

13. I think that what would make me a better reader is _read more_

1. What can each one of us do to become readers?

2. When we're reading a novel and there is extra white space between passages, what might the author be telling you that would help you as a reader?

3. Why do people often have trouble with the beginnings of novels? What strategies do you have for overcoming those problems?

4. Where you're reading and a few of the words are in *italics*, what might that tell you about those words?

5. We've talked about word composition as it relates to writing and art. Tell me what it means to have good composition in both a piece of writing and a picture.

6. When you come to a word you don't know, tell me four options you have to find out the word's meaning in that context.

7. In what ways could making a diagram or writing a character list/map help you in reading a novel, play, or short story?

Paul's responses indicated that he knew the purpose of several text conventions (white space, italics); had fix-up strategies when confused (diagram, listing, concept density, unknown words); and knew part of the responsibility for becoming a better reader rested with him ("read more often"). In contrast, Craig was still struggling with some of the same concepts. He didn't have strategies for overcoming difficulties with beginning of books or unknown words. He was even still confused in his belief that "learning big vocab words" would make him a better reader. This assessment told me I needed to spend some individual time with Craig during independent literacy exploration (ILE) reinforcing reading strategies with some texts he would find interesting.

Interviews and Inventories

My students and I found interviews a rich source of information for both assessment and ongoing reflection. Reading interviews with my students became important for me at several levels: individual student perceptions and progress, information about our curriculum, and building a classroom research-based, theoretical perspective for literacy. The reading interview that follows is an excerpt from a longer interview with Sarah, who was in the tenth grade at the time.

J: Today is November 8th and I'm interviewing Sarah. Sarah, can you tell me in your own words a little bit about what school has been like for you? Try to remember back as far as you can from the time you started school. Anything you want to tell me.

S: OK, well, when I started kindergarten, I can barely remember it, but I was always fighting with people—you know. But when I moved up here to Presque Isle from Warwick, Rhode Island, it was like totally different, you know. It was like I was a year behind, or something like that. I don't really know. Anyway, I had to stay back a year.

J: What grade were you in then?

S: First grade. My parents wanted to get me out of the city before I became a weird child. But, *all through that school year my spelling, English, reading, and all of that situation wasn't very good for me.* I sure wasn't the best student in school. But since I got up to the high school my grades just kind of got bigger—you know? This year in high school has been really good. I've been reading a lot better. When I was in eighth grade I didn't want to read out loud or even read at all, but now I think reading is fun. In fact, I saw the movie *Pet Sematary,* and then I read the book, and I thought the book was better than the movie. There are a lot of good books in here. I just never thought I would like reading, but now I do. [sounds puzzled]

J: When you were in reading in the elementary grades, what was your reading class like? Did you have reading groups? Did you have a reading book?

S: Hmmm . . . I don't know. Well, yeah, I remember the reading groups—I was always in the lower reading group, sitting around a table. We would all get a big book and have to read the same story at the same time. Like he would give us a day to read this big story. You know I'm not a very fast reader and it takes me a while to read something.

J: So, you'd all have to read the story silently?

S: *We'd have to read the story silently and I'd be like halfway through the story and the rest of the kids would have finished. That's when I got messed up with my reading. I wouldn't have read the whole story and so I'd only get half the questions right.* Hmmm . . . Let's see. [long pause] I think that when they give us a reading assignment . . .

Sarah's interview yielded information about Sarah as a reader: need for extra time, perceptions of what causes reading success and failure, and aversion to reading out loud. This interview also made me question several aspects of the instruction in our classroom. I made notes on the transcript at the first italicized portion, asking, "Do students who can't spell believe they can't read and write?" I also bracketed that entire paragraph and wrote at the end, "Attribution theory? Is reading out of my control?" Finally, in Sarah's last response (italicized), I asked, "What does she want me to learn from this?" Sarah's responses to the interview had assessment value for Sarah and also for the other students in the class because her responses led me to think about the way learning was structured in our classroom.

I know such interviews can seem daunting, but they don't have to be completed with all students in order to make a difference in our understanding of how students learn to read. If you interview two students each semester (one struggling and one successful), you will gain a wealth of knowledge about reading processes, environments that support literacy, what gets in the way of success, and what resources students need. The cumulative impact of these interviews on my thinking was significant. I used the interviews to make individual modifications for students in the class and also began looking at the interviews at large to see how students described their reading changes.

By December the close assessment and resulting purposeful teaching was starting to show in students' increasingly sophisticated personal knowledge of reading fluency. At that time, the students generated the following lists of literate attitudes, understandings, and behaviors they noted as characteristic of fluent readers:

Attitudes	*Understandings*	*Behaviors*
Want to read	Books and words should make sense	Read a lot
Comfortable expressing myself talking or writing	Certain ways to say things that help make it make sense	Write on my own
Confident		Think critically
Enjoy hearing words	Resources to help solve problems	Solve problems
See books as good places to get information	Good readers have strategies that help them when reading	Ask questions
		Search for answers
		Support opinions
Reading and writing aren't just school things	Have to connect what I'm reading to what I know	Fix mistakes
Reading helps me understand myself better	Reading shows different points of view	Motivate myself
Reading helps me understand why people do things	Have to change the way I read when my purpose changes	Talk about reading
OK to take risks		Show organization
Pride for success		Read several different things (make transitions)
Want to learn		
Have to make a place in my life for reading		

Observations, Anecdotal Records, Checklists, and Progress Notes

I always think of my dad's saying to me as we left for our adventures together, "Let's just see what we can see." At certain times each quarter, I used observational checklists for specific purposes, but more often I simply found a few minutes of quiet in our learning time together to "see what I could see." Some weeks I found only five or ten minutes for focused observations; other weeks I found small chunks of time every day. Both the observational checklists and observations that led to anecdotal notes gave me insights into students' development and learning, but each offered something not in the other.

On days when we had independent literacy exploration (ILE) time, I often had some time to do observations. My anecdotal notes were simply written on sheets of self-stick address labels that were kept on a clipboard. As I did observations, I simply circulated from student to group taking notes on the labels. I wrote the student's initials on each sticker and jotted things I noted about the student. These were then peeled off and placed on the back of each student's quarterly record form. These narrative notes took longer than a checklist but offered more depth of assessment. Checklists, however, often offered broad information that told me which students needed more support. These then led me back to careful observation of one or two students. I believe both narrative and checklists give us a deeper understanding of students and their learning.

Whether using a checklist to note strategies and skills that meet district standards or to highlight missing or incomplete assignments, the strength of the checklist can be in its significant saving of time. The checklist in Figure 12.4 is one I used to make sure that unproductive behavior that might signal a need for my intervention wasn't getting overlooked in the group dynamics that occur when many learning activities are happening simultaneously. I made copies of this checklist and labeled one for each student. Each Monday and Friday (our ILE days), I tried to focus on two or three students as a way of assessing their abilities to find and commit to learning that would challenge and sustain. After completing the checklist for the behaviors I had noted, I looked for patterns in behaviors that I had noted during my anecdotal notes from whole-class observations.

The students I focused on first were the students I had noted in my class observations and anecdotal notes as ones who seemed to be having some trouble. For example, my observational notes on November 13th showed that Mac seemed to be picking up only the surface level of a film we were watching, *The Late Great Me* (Scoppettone).

MAC: She's so ugly!
KERRIE: Shut up!
MAC: Now she's really drunk.
JOHNNA: No, she's not.
MAC: Then why is she talking to a dead cat?
JOHNNA: She's depressed because the only one she could talk to is gone.
(*Everyone is engrossed. No one is writing notes or talking. Mac is fidgeting.*)
MAC: Ha—potato face!

My suspicions of Mac's problems were reinforced and fleshed out as I closely observed him during ILE. The first thing I noted was that I had had him on my list for two weeks before I could do a focused observation because he was always on his way "somewhere" or just getting ready to do "something" but seldom showed a sustained interest in *anything*. Sound familiar? Students like Mac are often overwhelming because it is difficult to know where to start to get them on

Figure 12.4

H.19 Observational Checklist: Independent and Commitment to Learning

Yes	No	Observable behaviors
___	___	Monitors own behavior
___	___	Shows (leadership) capacity *in negative ways*
___	___	Helps others
___	___	Works well independently
___	___	Doesn't give in to peer/group pressure
___	___	Maintains focus
___	___	Asks for help after independent attempts
⊂══⊃	___	Shows high level of concentration — *only w/break dancing & monster truck books/mgs*
___	___	Evaluates own work for completion or work needed
___	___	(Articulate in group/class discussion) — *usually in distracting ways*
___	___	Does additional work (home, study, pursues research)
___	___	Makes good decisions about next steps
___	___	Tries to understand *and* complete work
___	___	Chooses challenging material and tasks
___	?	Daydreams frequently
✓	___	Easily distracted (auditory) visual, tactile)
✓	___	Reacts negatively with structure or challenging tasks
✓	___	Needs reminders or task
___	✓	Shows pattern of tardiness or absenteeism
✓	___	Often submits incomplete or "sloppy" work
✓	___	Interferes with others in small or whole group — *draws Craig in*
___	✓	Needs frequent praise or questions to stay committed
✓	___	Misses directions or needs individual directions
✓	___	Fools around during group learning
✓	___	Takes role of class clown *"can't find my work"*
✓	___	Interferes with others' learning
✓	___	Has trouble with organization (materials, time, goals)
___	✓	Doesn't work well with others (difficult, aggressive) — *doesn't like isolation*
___	✓	Uses work of others rather than own
✓	___	Rushes through assignments *(Sporadic — works in "mad" spurts)*
✓	___	Makes poor choices
✓	___	Needs structure (time, limited choices, brief tasks)

Assessment notes:
- Needs fewer choices
- Needs short works (nonfiction) on tape
- Help set goals. Help organize/do agenda

give Craig a different task

the right track. I admit that my initial instinct was disciplinary; however, I knew that I had to figure out what was getting in the way of literate activities for him. The disruptions were only the symptoms. Using the observational checklist helped me pinpoint the areas where I might begin to help Mac.

I decided that Mac needed some support in making good decisions and I could help with that by giving him fewer choices and making his choices less open-ended and of higher interest. I realized all the books on tape in our room were fiction; Mac needed his nonfiction books recorded so he could have support for *his* reading interests. Finally, Mac was one of those students who needed an agenda and organization. Each of these modifications was something I could do quickly, and the difference was immediately noticeable. This tool was a necessity for me so I could sort through disruptions and get to the issues in the way of Mac's success.

The observational checklist in Figure 12.5 is one I developed with content teachers for use when students were working in cooperative groups reading their textbooks. The teachers told me they wanted to help students use their textbooks more efficiently, so they put them in groups and gave them study guides to com-

Figure 12.5

H.20 Observational Checklist: Group Learning (Nonfiction)

articles & textbooks – Holocaust

Yes	No	**Strategic reading behaviors: text supports**
____	✓	Used table of contents or index to narrow search
____	✓	Previewed reading using titles, headings, captions, art
✓	____	Predicted using some of the following features: title, pictures, tables, diagrams, first and last sentences, headings, captions, key words, chapter summaries, or prereading prompts
____	✓	Checked for advanced information/organizers
✓	____	Used glossary, key words, parentheticals as support

Yes	No	**Strategic reading behaviors: active reading**
✓	____	Reread when appropriate (difficult text, clarifying)
____	✓	Evaluated and revised predictions
____	✓	Used skimming to summarize and clarify
____	✓	Prepared for reading by having necessary resources (Post-its, highlighters, dictionary, atlas, graphic organizers)
____	✓	Made appropriate decisions related to skipping sections
✓	____	Used resources in appropriate ways (knowledgeable others, other texts)
✓	____	Adjusted reading rates for text difficulty or purpose
____	*some*	Used questioning to monitor, summarize, and clarify

Yes	No	**Strategic reading behaviors: demonstration of learning**
✓	____	Able to summarize
____	✓	Shows learning by formulating personal questions
✓	____	Responds to reading with opinions, agreement/disagreement
____	✓	Creates mind maps to solidify reading connections
✓	____	Takes notes in ways that support discussions and connections
____	✓	Shows ability to distinguish between central and peripheral information
✓	____	Discriminates fact from opinion
✓	____	Annotates when appropriate for information retrieval

plete. When I asked them what they observed during this process, they admitted honestly that they didn't know what they should be looking for. I took them back to their original goal, "to use their textbooks more efficiently." We decided what efficient use would look like and then created a checklist for observing which students were using those strategies.

The checklist in this figure was completed as a middle school social studies teacher sat with two different groups of students: one at the beginning of the task and one as students neared the end of the task. In this way, she noted the getting-started behaviors as well as active reading and learning behaviors. From this observation, she could see students were adept at some things such as predictions and use of glossary words. She could also infer the necessity of spending more time in certain areas: modeling effective focus and background knowledge behaviors before reading as well as monitoring/clarifying behaviors while reading. This checklist showed her the strategy lessons she needed to demonstrate for students with their next assignment. I haven't been back to this classroom, but I assume she was able to further refine her content reading lessons as she saw students transferring the lessons to their independent and cooperative group reading of texts.

Reflections and Self-Assessments

In *Assessment: Continuous Learning*, Bridges notes the critical role of reflection in learning: "The essence of education may well be the ability to look back on the learning experience and evaluate what worked and why, and what didn't work and why. Self-reflection—or knowing you know—helps students discover what they have learned, how they learned it, and what they should do next to extend and refine their learning" (30). Many students struggle with the process of reflection and self-assessment. Daniel, a student in Kelly Stevenson's literacy class at Immokalee High School in Florida, used the graphic organizer shown in Figure 12.6 to keep track of his accomplishments and his planned next steps on a weekly basis. He used the Assessment: Continuous Learning graphic organizer (see form H.22 in Appendix H) to figure out areas where he was having difficulty. These organizers were a way for him to document both his reading and writing at the end of the week. Keeping track of products and activities in this way created a scaffold for Daniel so he could begin noting his questions and predictions during independent reading of Beatrice Sparks's *Go Ask Alice*. His use of the Monitoring Our Reading Process (see Figure 12.7) organizer helped him see the importance of making new predictions after further reading.

Formal Tests

At this point you might be wondering if I ever gave my students tests. Even had I wanted to avoid tests, my students would not have tolerated it. They saw tests as

Figure 12.6

H.21 End-of-Week Check-in

Things I accomplished this week	I learned	I still need help with...	I'd like to spend more time learning about...
• Wrote a diary on Tears of a Tiger • Wrote a poem • chose The Outsiders for SSR	• how to write poems • how to write a diary	• writing	• writing

something that proved to them they were becoming successful. In spite of how students enjoyed my praise, individual time, and written feedback, it was the "objective" test grades that gave them a comparison band for measuring success. Even our tests, however, went through a change process in order to move students away from the notion that the only value for tests was an end grade.

When I first began teaching, my tests were like those in my own student days: lots of matching of characters and quotations; fill-in-the-blanks questions about details of the literary work; matching vocabulary and definitions; and a few lengthier pieces of writing. I did the same things many of you have done in order to change the form and content of testing: allowed students to generate test questions; embedded questions in games and word searches; and generated creative applications to check content knowledge. But we were still left with a test that determined right answers. Further, we tended to move on regardless of how many right answers we had.

It was after I began working on our state-mandated test, the Maine Educational Assessment (MEA), that I began to really question the tests I had been giving. The administrators at our school had been resourceful in obtaining computers for our school, so by the late 1980s we had one computer for every two or three students. In 1987 all teachers at our school began using our computer rooms as writing labs. The state guidelines for the MEA were that students would be tested in the manner they were taught, so we lobbied that students should be

Figure 12.7

H.23 Monitoring Our Reading Process

Go Ask Alice by Anonymous	What confuses you? What words do you focus on?	What predictions do you make about topics/events?	What rethinking do you do?
Title	Who is Alice? Who face? Ask Alice, what? Why black ground?	This got to be about Alice.	I still believe that she is going to move
First paragraph	Smashed down upon my head	I think that Alice get picked at school.	She becomes with drawn
Continued reading	Alice love to date boys.	I think that Alice will get pregnant.	I do think she will become clean.
End	I have joel and my new super striaght friends and they will help me.	Alice will stay of drug because the new friends.	I can't believe that she kill her self.

allowed to respond to the writing portion of the test by generating writing on computers. We were successful in our request, but the action made me realize how seldom my own students were tested in the manner in which they were taught.

As is typical after such flashes of insight, I went too far in the other direction. Since I had essentially constructed all the test items, I decided to stop that practice and let students show me that they had learned something. Students were totally lost. "What do *you* want?" became the plaintive cry. Some students felt it was my job to figure out the tests, and others thought I believed they were too stupid to take tests.

At the time, our committees working on the MEA were considering multiple, multiple-choice questions as part of the MEA. We never did implement that as we moved directly from multiple-choice to open-ended questions, but the discussions about the value of students seeing multiple right answers gave me the impetus for changing our tests. Building on the early success my students had found with sentence completions, I decided to give sentence starters that could elicit a variety of responses to help me assess students' content knowledge and underlying meanings, their application and transfer of reading strategies, and their personal connections to the text. Paul's *Of Mice and Men* test (see Figure 12.8) demonstrates his knowledge of the Depression and its effects on people living during these times. The test also gave me the opportunity to assess Paul's abilities to predict, visualize, infer, question, and clarify. The results of reading strategy lessons that had been part of our class goals could be assessed within the context of our shared text by asking students to predict the outcome, picture characters and settings, infer background and events in characters' lives, and question the plot and character motivations. I could also assess the effectiveness of using this book as a shared reading with the sentence starter, "Hearing this book read aloud. . . ." Given as a midbook test, this assessment had value for students as a way to synthesize, clarify, and question their thinking. It also had instructional value for me because I could determine any misinformation they held about the times, historical events, relationships among characters, and cause/effect situations.

This success had several positive spinoffs. Students began talking about reader response and how it is possible to "read the same words and get different stuff." They also internalized the sentence starters as part of their language when responding to books they were reading for independent reading. Their responses began to be filled with statements such as, "At this point I'm wondering/questioning . . ." or "One thing I've learned so far . . ." or "This character reminds me of . . ." In a sense, they began taking on the language of active readers.

The other positive outcome was that I began rethinking our traditional semester final exam practice. Our school had mandatory two-hour exams for all students at the end of each semester. The exams were supposed to be cumulative, and the grades were averaged with students' quarter grades to achieve the semester grade. These exams were a nightmare for my students. Many teachers gave up the notion of cumulative exams and just attempted to measure knowledge on the most recent material covered. I tried everything I could think of to create an exam that would last two hours. Some students will sit for two hours responding to a single essay question; my students were not among those who would do that. After I began allowing students to use their academic journals, their time on task and their abilities to make text-to-text connections increased, but I still felt I was only giving value in terms of testing to the whole-class work we did. Two ninety-minute blocks each week were devoted to independent reading and independent literacy exploration. When I gave generic prompts such as "Write about

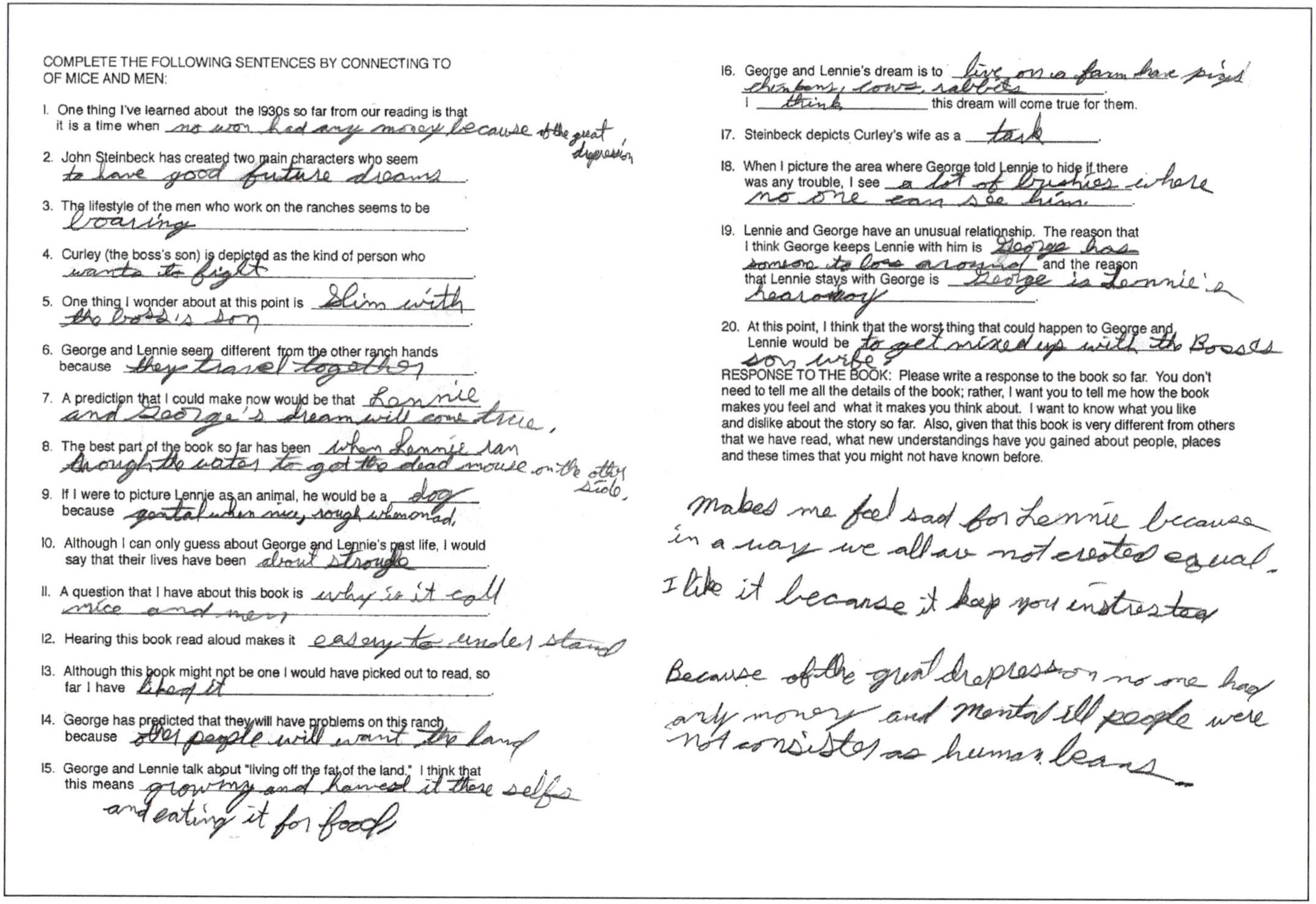

COMPLETE THE FOLLOWING SENTENCES BY CONNECTING TO OF MICE AND MEN:

1. One thing I've learned about the 1990s so far from our reading is that it is a time when _out men had any money because of the great depression_

2. John Steinbeck has created two main characters who seem _to have good futures ahead_

3. The lifestyle of the men who work on the ranches seems to be _boring_

4. Curley (the boss's son) is depicted as the kind of person who _wants to fight_

5. One thing I wonder about at this point is _Slim with the brake men_

6. George and Lennie seem different from the other ranch hands because _they have a future_

7. A prediction that I could make now would be that _Lennie and George's dream will come true._

8. The best part of the book so far has been _when Lennie ran through the water to get the dead mouse on the other side._

9. If I were to picture Lennie as an animal, he would be a _dog_ because _gentle in my rough element_

10. Although I can only guess about George and Lennie's past life, I would say that their lives have been _about both_

11. A question that I have about this book is _why is it sad_

12. Hearing this book read aloud makes it _easy to understand_

13. Although this book might not be one I would have picked out to read, so far I have _liked it_

14. George has predicted that they will have problems on this ranch because _the people will want the land_

15. George and Lennie talk about "living off the fat of the land." I think that this means _plowing and having it there self and eating it off of it_

16. George and Lennie's dream is to _live on a farm here and drink_ this dream will come true for them.

17. Steinbeck depicts Curley's wife as a _tart_

18. When I picture the area where George told Lennie to hide if there was any trouble, I see _a lot of together where no one can hear_

19. Lennie and George have an unusual relationship. The reason that I think George keeps Lennie with him is _George had someone to live with_ and the reason that Lennie stays with George is _George is Lennie's family_

20. At this point, I think that the worst thing that could happen to George and Lennie would be _to get mixed up with the Boss_

RESPONSE TO THE BOOK: Please write a response to the book so far. You don't need to tell me all the details of the book; rather, I want you to tell me how the book makes you feel and what it makes you think about. I want to know what you like and dislike about the story so far. Also, given that this book is very different from others that we have read, what new understandings have you gained about people, places and these times that you might not have known before.

makes me feel sad for Lennie because in a way we all are not created equal.

I like it because it keeps you interested.

Because of the great depression no one had any money and mentally ill people were not considered as human beings.

Figure 12.8

a book that you've read that has made a difference in your thinking," I received tired responses or a summary of the book read most recently. So those areas were ignored for my exam purposes because I couldn't figure out how to assess their independent work during a standard examination.

Just prior to exams one year, I was looking over status-of-the-class forms and recording the range of books read during the quarter. It occurred to me that I could actually create individualized test questions fairly quickly simply by pulling together patterns of reading, writing, and research students had done. In this way, I believed, students would see their independent literacy as having equal value to our whole-class work. If students had pursued similar literacy tracks, I used one question for those students. Several of the individualized questions follow.

Dean, Ed, and Jason: You've all read (and watched videos) of S. E. Hinton's books during this semester. Write a response discussing the contributions to young adult literature that S. E. Hinton has made. Discuss why you think her books are so popular, making them among the most widely read books in this country. What did you like/dislike about them? What would have made the books stronger or more effective? Use specific examples from the books/videos to support your answers.

Nikki, Kim, and Jennifer: You've read several books related to education (or lack of education) during this semester and you've each done education-related independent studies. What new understandings do you have (or what old understandings have been reaffirmed) about what it takes to be a good teacher? Support your responses with statements from your reading and your independent studies.

Denise, Dawn, and Chris: You have read several books this semester that all fall into the category of horror/suspense. Based on the wide variety of books you've read, what specific elements do you see making up this type of writing? What do these books all have in common? What do you think makes these books so interesting? What would be the difference between a good horror/suspense novel and a bad one? Cite specific examples from the books you've read this semester to support your responses.

Tony: You've read several books this semester that deal with loss/dying (*Stone Fox, A Day No Pigs Would Die, Rumblefish*). Using these books, as well as any others you have read, write a response to the ways you think people cope with loss in their lives. Use specific examples from the characters you've read about this semester as well as from your own life.

Aaron: Although you've read several different types of books this semester, it seems like the book that has made the biggest difference to you has been *The Island*. Many of us have our own islands. Using Paulsen's writing style in *The Island* as an example, write about your own day on your own island—either real or imaginary.

Scott: Two of the books in which you seemed the most engrossed during this semester appeared to be *Jay's Journal* and *So Much to Tell You*. Using these two books as examples, discuss the psychological/social problems that confront young adults today.

Angel and Clarina: You've done an incredible amount of reading this semester, most of which has been realistic fiction about young adults today. Based on your reading and your own life experiences, discuss the problems you feel are most difficult for young people. Choose any books you wish as you support your responses.

Brian: You've done a lot of creative writing this semester, and it seems as though you especially like to write poetry. Write a poem (or any other genre you choose) based on one of the books you've read this semester. It might be a poem written from one of the character's points of view; it might be a poem that pulls together people and events in S. E. Hinton's books. The choice/format/ideas are yours!

Troy: You've read several books this semester related to the broad theme of survival: *Castaway, Hatchet, Elephant Tree*. What have you learned about the characteristics it takes to survive? Use specific examples from your books to support your response.

Dee: You've read several Gary Paulsen books this semester. Write a letter to Gary Paulsen highlighting your opinions of the books, the things you've especially liked, and any questions you might have for him based on what you've learned through his writing. Be sure to cite specific books in your letter.

Students were visibly moved that each of them was getting a test unique to the learning each had pursued independently during the semester. In all my years in the classroom, I had never seen students so engaged in giving such high-quality demonstrations of learning during exams. The range of their responses was astounding as they chose to make their exams individual and unique. Some students wrote essays or created ideal classrooms. Many wrote letters and poems. Jennifer's poem response to what she had learned about effective teaching was only one of many that were equally passionate.

Hell's Bells
Sometimes I cannot write.
Why, I wonder, does it fight
Whenever I'm uptight.
There is no problem to make light

School is there and so am I.
Filling us with truths, but more often lies.
You do not think so? Believe what I say
When your mother calls you a liar
When you return from school today.
Arguments over who was who
and who did what during 1952.
But the worst is when
she comments about education today
Retaliating against
all the taxes she pays.
I feel like saying,
I understand!
I know what you mean
about China and Japan.
Against the rote learning system
Who am I to rebel?
Just a lone student
in one in a million cells
Just one lone student
lonely as hell
because there's no one to listen
To what we have to tell.
All of us different
but we must ring your bell
waiting for appreciation
for what we have learned
we get denial and frustration
always, in return.

In the past, semester exams had ended a semester and students didn't refer to them, or the first semester's learning, again. These exams carried over from first to second semester. Many of the students chose to continue working on the drafts of pieces they had written for the exam. They liked what they had written in that limited time and wanted to put more thought and work into revising during the second semester. They also started using the exams as resources for their independent pursuits during the next semester.

The first semester I used these individualized tests (combined with common questions representing our whole-class learning), I simply made a copy and cut individual strips, which I stapled to each person's exam. The second semester I ran out of time and simply made thirty copies of the whole page of questions and stapled the entire set of questions to each exam. So all students had each other's questions. That had some surprising results. Students kept the exam questions in their folder and began using other students in the class as resources. Instead of seeing me as the only book-finding source in the room, students began going to other students for book titles and questions about their independent study projects. Assessment had once again led us to a place of starting over. These individualized exams were easy to create and the responses interesting to read—a good reminder for me that teachers have to live with *reading* hundreds of common essays we give students. In this case, I actually enjoyed reading these unique responses.

Performance Tasks

Exams are not the only demonstrations of learning. Projects and other performance tasks have been a major part of assessment and evaluation in most classrooms for years. I seldom meet a teacher whose grading is based solely on classroom tests. Most teachers use a combination of performance tasks to determine a fair evaluation of the students' progress. These performance tasks can range from asking students to demonstrate their ability to transfer learning of a specific strategy or procedure, to teacher-designed, collaborative, project-based learning, to student-designed independent studies. I believe that all three categories have value for assessment and evaluation purposes.

In elementary classrooms content-specific performances can occur several times each day. In middle and high school classrooms, these performances occur several times a week. Following a lesson on prediction strategies, the teacher might ask students to predict the content of the next shared reading novel and cite the support used to make the prediction. In social studies a teacher might ask students to complete a graphic organizer to represent the sequence of thinking that a president might have used prior to declaring war. Figure 12.9 shows how a ninth-grade student in our intervention class used an organizer to demonstrate his ability to read between the lines during our reading of Speare's *Sign of the Beaver*. These performance tasks ask students to synthesize and document learning from the content they have studied.

In the broader definition of performance, which typically includes a more substantial production and a larger audience than a teacher, students are given the opportunity to establish a level of expertise for a range of tasks such as organization, content knowledge, and ability to communicate. The following collaborative explorations of literature are ones I designed for students. Each of the creative reading, writing, and research projects ended in a class performance: readers' theater, art shows, oral reading and acting out of tall tales, illustrated writing, or graphic representations of information.

You have been selected as the best in your field by the archeological society to study the remains of a newly discovered civilization. Examine the

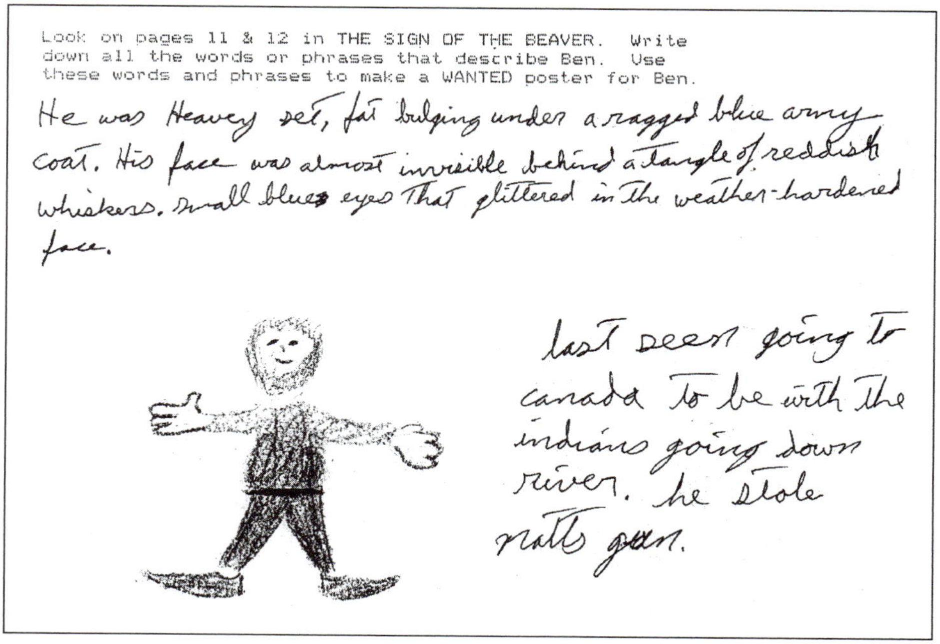

Look on pages 11 & 12 in THE SIGN OF THE BEAVER. Write
down all the words or phrases that describe Ben. Use
these words and phrases to make a WANTED poster for Ben.

He was Heavey set, fat bulging under a ragged blue army
coat. His face was almost invisible behind a tangle of reddish
whiskers. small blues eyes that glittered in the weather-hardened
face.

last seen going to
canada to be with the
indians going down
river. he stole
natts gun.

Figure 12.9

materials that have been found, and then write a scenario, "A Day in the Life of _____." In your examination of these artifacts, you should try to figure out religious beliefs, customs, family structure, leisure activities, monetary systems, methods of government, and work habits before attempting to write your scenario. Make sure you give your society a name and a time of existence. We'll look forward to your performance as you bring this lost civilization back to life for us!

Read and use the variations of Cinderella that you have been given in order to create a chart that gives viewers the following information:

1. What characteristics do most Cinderella stories have in common?
2. What characteristics did you find that were unique?
3. How are these unique aspects representative of culture?

Now create your own contemporary Cinderella story, which you can perform in any manner that fits your production: storyboard, skit, dramatic confrontation, readers' theater.

As you can see from the books in your kit, our first version of a story may not be the only version. Read the Roald Dahl versions of fairy tales found in *Revolting Rhymes*. Then choose a fairy tale from the ones you know or ones in the collection to create your own "revolting rhyme."

We'll look forward to your performance of this rhyme. Feel free to create or use appropriate music to support your performance.

Read the short story "Ethan Unbound" found in your kit. After reading through the directions for readers' theater, create your own readers' theater version of this short story. We'll be eager to watch and hear your performance!

Use the variations of tall tales and legends that you have been given in order to create a chart that gives viewers the following information:
1. What characteristics do tall tales/legends have in common?
2. What reasons can your group give for why our culture continues to enjoy tall tales?
3. As a group, try your hand at choosing a contemporary person who might be the "stuff" of tall tales. Create a tall tale for that person.
We'll look forward to learning more than we ever wanted to know about someone who is larger than life!

These collaborative explorations are easy to create and can be kept in boxes with the needed materials (books, bags of artifacts, art supplies) and directions. When students complete a project, they sign up for a performance time, which gets scheduled into the weekly plans. In this way, everyone does not have to finish at the same time, so students are not sitting in class watching several performances one after another on the same day. Each of the performances requires students to use some core literacy and learning strategies: reading, writing, researching, creating, mapping/graphing, organizing, analyzing, and communicating. Assessment in each of these areas can then provide valuable information relative to students' progress toward independence.

Some of Holly Lang's students at St. Cloud High School chose to explore the Cinderella literature project. As Holly observed and worked with the group, she noted that students had to examine and research a variety of areas in order to complete the project. She was able to assess their developing understanding of parts of a book, literary elements, archetypes/stereotypes, cultural values/differences, editing/proofreading, readability of text (audience), writing to a specific genre, and effect of setting change on story.

Student-designed independent studies often come out of the positive experiences students have when given choices for demonstrating their learning. At some schools all students are required to design and complete an independent learning project prior to high school graduation. In our classroom independent study was not a requirement, but it was always an option during students' ILE time. The study sometimes came from books the students were reading or interests that had developed as part of a unit of study.

After reading all of Torey Hayden's and Mary MacCracken's books as well as Avi's *Nothing but the Truth* and Conroy's *The Water Is Wide,* Kim decided she wanted to do an independent study working in an elementary classroom with children who had special needs. She researched the possibilities within our school community, wrote a letter to the principal of an elementary school, and designed a schedule for her assistantship that included two ILE periods each week as well as her study hall time. She designed forms for her field notes and her reflective journal. Her final product included all those documents as well as the following reflections about her learning and the impact of that learning on her goals, and a slide show for fellow students detailing her work and her independent study design.

Over the past half year, the books I have read and the subject I have focused on have been education. I have come to the conclusion that education is about the most delicate and complex subject for a person to deal with. I have read many books dealing with education and the way teachers handle situations. I have decided that most teachers have good methods as well as bad ones and are not usually all good or all bad.

I think that before this it would have been easy to say, "If I were that teacher, I would have . . ." but who really knows how she would handle a situation. By being the bystander, I have had the chance to observe the situation and weigh the results of the outcome as to how the teacher handled herself. I guess the qualities I've discovered to be successful in teachers are the ones I would try to instill in myself. A teacher that takes the time to listen to what her students are saying and then tries to act on that are my favorites. Everyone feels that if they are at least given the chance to voice their opinions, taken into consideration, then they were thought about. That teacher cared to know how they felt.

I think that confidentiality is most important. A student should be able to tell a teacher something without worrying that the teacher is going to run to the teachers' lounge for daily gossip hour. A teacher who has her students' trust has the key to their minds. Nine times out of ten they'll let you in. A good teacher realizes that all students are different. They can't be generalized into one group and be expected to think and respond on those levels. Students all have different interests and so need a wide variety of methods of teaching as well as materials.

These are observations that I have made watching other teachers, reading books on education and helping a teacher firsthand. If I were a teacher, I would use creative books and a lot of one-on-one time with my students. Someday I would like to teach a class for children with learning problems. I really like kids and I find the program interests me because the schedule is open. Books can be worked into the program and your own methods are more easily worked in. I think that everyone should learn about the ups and downs of education because we are learning every day.

I did learn something really important. If a person wants to be a teacher but can never reach that goal, she should put her mind to rest. In our own little ways everyone is a teacher. We teach ourselves, our children, the people around us. I also know that how well we teach depends on our own education.

This piece serves to synthesize and illustrate several critical aspects of assessment. First, Kim has given me multiple points for assessing her progress in literacy and learning. She has demonstrated organization and organizational strategies. She has created several written products as well as oral and visual presentations. Her products demonstrated several writing modes: letter, resume, field notes, reflective journal, and essay. Each of these lines of assessment let me assist Kim in learning skills and strategies and assess her progress toward them. These assessments then led to evaluation and grading.

Reading Portfolios

During my last year of teaching, I began developing reading portfolios with my students as a way to document their progress as readers. I have expanded that early work with middle school and high school teachers and students in classrooms in Florida and California. When I began the process in 1991, I knew very little about portfolios, and those I had encountered were essentially writing portfolios. I wanted my students to develop literacy portfolios with an emphasis on reading as a way for us to document, assess, and evaluate their literacy progress. I didn't want all the portfolios to have the same products (a short story, a poem, a favorite piece). Valencia, Hiebert, and Afflerbach in *Authentic Reading Assessment: Practices and Possibilities* note the temptation of template portfolios. "Unless goals and purposes are kept foremost in educators' minds, authentic assessment will probably have an end no different from standardized tests" (8–9). Hoping not to fall into that trap, we devised what I called "show me" portfolios as a way for students to show me or anyone else the reading progress they were making.

I believe purpose should govern what goes into a portfolio. My umbrella goal for these portfolios was letting students show how they had changed as readers, writers, and thinkers. I had established reading goals for the year, so it was a logical next step for us to use those goals as critical components of our portfolios. Each quarter I asked students to find examples of work that would "show me" they were making progress in certain areas. Typically, I gave students five "show me" prompts each quarter, and they chose to demonstrate their progress in three of those areas. Some of the prompts I used during my first year with this process are these:

Show me that you know how to choose interesting, challenging reading.

Show me that you know how to predict, reevaluate those predictions, and make new predictions when you have more information.

Show me that you make personal connections to your reading.

Show me that you can assess your own reading progress.

Show me that you know how to use reading to learn new things about the world in which you live.

Show me that you use reading to develop and support your writing ideas.

Show me that you know how to critique an author's work.

Show me that you understand the roles of a strategic reader (questioning, inferring, connecting, monitoring, clarifying).

Show me that you know how to communicate to others the value of reading in your life.

Show me that you vary your reading depending on purpose and interest.

In each case, students chose to demonstrate the work by pulling examples of work from their academic journals and their working folders, or they created something new that showed their competence for that goal. Their samples ranged from poetry to class notes, from photographs to storyboards. For each they wrote a brief reflection telling why the piece had been chosen for that goal as well as what they wanted me to notice in the work they chose. Their choices and reflections gave me insights into our progress toward established goals; the progress (or lack of) then made me reflect on both the direct and indirect instruction occurring in our classroom.

From Assessment to Evaluation and Grading

I believe that moving from assessment to evaluation and grading is as individual a process as any act of teaching and learning. In classrooms where teachers give homework, classwork, quizzes, tests, and project grades with a percentage allocated for each, the process of grading seems easier because there are fewer individual pieces. It certainly is a clearer process than what I am about to describe. But even with that clarity there is always room for individual interpretation. "Yes, he only has sixty-four points, but he has improved so much. That should count for something." Or we decide too many students are failing because of homework (or lack of) and so weight quizzes and tests more heavily than in previous classes. Modifications and "rule-bending" occur on a daily basis in most classes.

The demands for me to give fair grades that I could justify were the same then as they are for us today. I wish I could say I had found a magical process for making the whole thing easier and less guilt-ridden, but I hadn't. I did discover there were ways to bring students into the process, to establish and maintain progress toward standards of excellence, and to allow for individual forays into learning without using the same grading system for everyone. In Lavoie's video *F.A.T. City: Frustration, Anxiety and Tension—What It Feels Like to Be Learning Disabled*, he talks about the difference between fair and equal. Fairness isn't giving everyone the same thing; fair is giving each individual what he or she needs. I think the assessment and evaluation system I developed worked because it moved in the direction of giving students and their caregivers information about their initiative, progress, and accomplishments.

My grade book for work completed by the entire class looked the same as any other grade book. There were lists of grades for tests, class projects, class work, and writing assignments. The test grades I gave were nothing new: twenty questions, five points per question. The grades for projects were based on the usual criteria: quality of work related to the parameters established by the teacher. These can be grades with scoring guides or rubrics. Class work, including whole-group writing, was usually checked for completion. I weighted the categories differently each quarter depending on our focus. I'm sure all of this sounds very familiar.

What may be new is how to take into account the independent work students engage in or complete. Forty percent of our week was spent with students pursuing individual learning. That learning had to be documented so that "credit" could be given. The sample in Figure 12.10 represents Kim's accomplishments during the third quarter of her senior year. There was a similar form for all students on which I could document their products and accomplishments, our conferences, and areas for concern or improvement. This same form would show different areas completed for other students, and Kim might have focused on other areas during other quarters. In this quarter, she spent lots of ILE (and personal) time reading and responding to that reading. She also spent time with me planning her independent study. The final products of that study weren't completed until the fourth quarter, but the progress she is making is documented here. I've noted some spelling errors from her writing and her confusion about their/there as things I want to point out to her. I've also highlighted an area of writing improvement for our next conference. Each form was kept in a cumulative notebook by class so that when I looked at Kim's form for the third quarter, I could also look back at her accomplishments during the previous two quarters.

All students also had access to this information as they completed their self-evaluations (see form H.24 in Appendix H). This form invites students to evaluate themselves in terms of goals, commitment, accomplishments, and areas for improvement. I averaged the grades in the grade book for in-common work and added to that our collaborative evaluation of the student's independent learning. As you can see, there is lots of room for subjectivity on both the students' and my parts at that independent level of work. I was always pleased at how honest students were in these evaluations and that helped with the level of subjectivity.

NAME *Kim* PERIOD *4* QUARTER *3*

READING

NOVELS

The Night of the Moonbow (R-√+)

Somebody Else's Kids - great response

Jemmy - (R-√+)

Macbeth (D - Essay √+)

Macbeth (T-96)

Mac - R - √+

Water Is Wide √+

SHORT STORIES

Dicey's Song / Homecoming } R-√+

PLAYS/POETRY

- Macbeth - questions (noted literary/genre characteristics)

WRITING

CREATIVE/INFORMAL

time line (Dicey)

FORMAL

SKILLS

SPELLING

guesse for guess

conscience

VOCABULARY

their/there

OTHER

working on revised face survey -

A/V

VIDEOS

Conrack - created test for 9th gr.

TAPES/RECORDINGS

taped picture books for elem students

PROJECTS

education project (*goals*, *Carl T. Folsom*, *resume*, *Mary*, *persuasive letter*)

WORD GAMES

AREAS FOR DISCUSSION/IMPROVEMENT/CONCERN

• Writing → move from retelling to critique

Figure 12.10

Reflective Teaching Leads to Starting Again

In Newkirk's *Workshop 4: The Teacher as Researcher,* he talks about the importance of continually questioning our practice. "When we ask new questions about our classrooms (and ourselves), we admit the possibility of real self-transformation. To ask if things might be done differently is to loosen the hold of routine and habit" (7–8). Assessing, evaluating, and starting again are critical steps for students *and* for teachers.

One of the most important things I learned during this time related not only to my ways of knowing students but also to my responsibility in helping students know *themselves* as learners. Eisner has said, "The surest way to create semiliterate graduates from American secondary schools is to insure that many of the most important forms through which meaning is represented will be enigmas to our students, codes they cannot crack" (128). I think assessment and evaluation are two of the most puzzling aspects of education for many students. Rubrics and scoring guides have made a noticeable difference in helping students understand criteria for effective demonstrations of learning, yet many students still feel that grades and teachers' comments are cloaked in mystery.

In *Winnie-the-Pooh on Problem Solving,* Roger Allen reminds us of the importance of choosing the right problem to solve. "'I think,' said Pooh, 'that if you don't pick the right problem, it's the wrong problem which means that you still have to solve the right problem after you've solved the wrong problem, if you do. Right?'" (47). From my perspective, solving the right problem with assessment and evaluation is not finding new models for scoring guides or rubrics or computerized grading systems. Solving the right problem is finding multiple ways of determining and documenting what students are able to do and using those discoveries to guide us in our teaching decisions. Ultimately, we will have moved closer to solving the right problem when students are able to make and act upon those judgments independently.

13

Living the Professional Life

The silver shoes have wonderful powers. And one of the most curious things about them is that they can carry you to any place in the world in three steps.

L. Frank Baum, The Wonderful Wizard of Oz

If only our teaching and learning paths were as easy as taking three steps in silver shoes! When I walked out of the doors of the university and into my secondary English classroom in 1972, I thought I knew everything I needed to know about being an English teacher. I had taken survey courses in American, British, and World literature and specialized courses on Chaucer, early British poets, and history of the theater. What else could I possibly need to know to teach English to high school students? It only took one day, with one hundred and fifty students in five general English classes, to teach me how wrong I was. It took me only one semester to realize there were questions I hoped never to have to answer again.

Questions I Hope I Never Hear Again
I was absent. Did we do anything I need?
What? What do you want? What are we doing anyway?
Can I go over to shop class since we're not doing anything anyway?
How long does this have to be? Pen or pencil? One side or two?
Why did you give me a "C" when I did most of my work on most of the
    days I was here?
Do you want us to read the whole thing?
Can we go to lunch early?
Can we have a free day?
Do teachers get paid for weekends and vacations?
What do you mean I have makeup work? Those days were excused
    absences!

In the absence of early professional support, I managed to produce a blend of classroom activities that made students happy most of the time; a workload that hovered just at the edge of chaos; a plan book stuffed with more memos than plans; a grade book with enough grades to justify the numbers that were more fiction than fact; and a set of slightly sarcastic answers to those horrible questions. My criteria for choosing our learning activities were several well-known educational variables: the weather, available resources, impending pep rallies, students' tolerance levels, amount of necessary correction time (learned slowly), approaching winter carnivals and basketball tournaments, and occasionally even broadly defined educational value. We began and ended our activities at the same time whether or not students had actually finished. My teaching and the students' learning were actually measured by the passage of time rather than by changes or progress. We spent many days in the breakdown lane of our yellow brick road.

It took me a long time to realize that the wizards who could make learning happen in new ways were sitting (or standing or sprawled on the floor) in my classes. Dorothy never did realize that as she journeyed along the yellow brick road. She and her friends stayed on that road with a singular focus—getting to the wizard at the end of the road. Dorothy had many examples along the way of exactly what the wizard told them at the end of their journey: they themselves had the strengths they needed all along. They already possessed the brains, heart, and courage to get them to new places. So, what do we all know about the teaching and learning of reading that could help us move away from our search for the wizard and onto our own paths toward successful reading classrooms?

Teaching with Our Brains

Holt has said, "There are two ways to get to the top of an oak tree. You can climb the branches or sit on an acorn and wait." I think one of the most undermining phrases in U.S. education today is, "Why reinvent the wheel?" Those words lead us to believe that someone else can do it better than we can (or they have already done it better than we ever could) so we might as well "sit on an acorn and wait" until somebody tells us what to do. I believe it is time for each of us to acknowledge that we have, or know how to acquire, the expertise that will help us meet the challenges of the students who come to us each year.

If we don't take on both the rewards and responsibility of that professional commitment, we risk teaching in environments and with resources that are counterproductive for the reading work we need to accomplish. One superintendent's words to me captured the prevailing "sitting on an acorn" trend in our country: "Janet, I love the way teachers feel and how excited they are about their work when they leave these sessions. But I can't replicate this experience with all my teachers. I've got so much pressure that I just want to buy a program—a package—so I can put any fool in that classroom and I can guarantee reading success. I can hold the program's statistics up to the board and say, 'I know what we were doing wasn't working, but now we've found a program that is guaranteed to work.' Before we can see whether or not it works, the board has moved on to something else." I know he isn't alone in these thoughts.

I believe we are on dangerous ground when we abdicate our responsibility to connect theory and practice in rich and new ways. It might be cheaper and easier to use someone else's wheel, but there is incredible value in reinventing one for yourself and your students. You might create a new, more effective wheel. You might come out with the same wheel, but your method of getting there might be better. You might discover something in the process that no one has ever considered and you had not imagined. In the process of creating the wheel, you might develop creative strategies that can transfer to many other learning moments. Our knowledge base related to how children learn to read is changing every day, and it is teachers who will expand on that base with ongoing research and reflection.

Those of you who, like me, are fans of Juster's *The Phantom Tollbooth* may remember the Dodecahedron explaining that if a beaver two feet long with a tail a foot and half long could build a dam twelve feet high and six feet wide in two days, all you would need is a beaver sixty-eight feet long with a fifty-one foot tail to build the Boulder Dam. When Milo complains about the absurdity of this, the Dodecahedron says, "If you want sense, you'll have to make it yourself." I think the successful teaching of reading is a lot like this. If you want learning to make sense in *your* classroom, you'll have to make it yourself.

Postman and Weingartner state in *Teaching as a Subversive Activity,* "There is no learning without a learner. And there is no meaning without a meaning maker" (81). As individual teachers, we are responsible for making the meaning in our classrooms. Given the hectic schedules of most teachers, how do we use our brains in new ways to take advantage of the resources that are available to us?

In spite of the individual and often lonely journey that is the professional life, we *can* find support: workshops, inservice programs, professional books and journals, and sharing ideas with colleagues. Most new professional books provide extensive lists of resources in the body of the text and in the appendices. The resources listed in Harvey and Goudvis's *Strategies That Work,* for instance, could support several years of classroom and independent reading.

In one school where I work, teachers meet every Wednesday and plan all their lessons cooperatively. They each bring professional books and resources they have found so they can plan from a wealth of options. In many middle schools, the schedule allows teachers common planning time. In our schools here in Orlando, Wednesdays are early release days so that teachers can have staff development and do cooperative planning. At an elementary school in Mapleton, Maine, teachers discovered they were each at individual stages of questioning their spelling practices. They applied for a grant to support their study, created individual questions around the central question of spelling, and crafted their own staff development opportunities that supported their research. The results of their collaborative research, writing, and new understandings are described in *Spelling Inquiry: How One Elementary School Caught the Mnemonic Plague* (Chandler et al.). This book well demonstrates the individual strengths we each bring to the journey. Making wise use of our time, resources, and the support of those around us gives us more time for our own lives.

Local collegial support and planning are critical, but state and national connections are also beneficial. Web sites for literacy organizations such as the International Reading Association and the National Council of Teachers of English offer ideas, research, and avenues for political voices. Appendix C lists Web sites that support lesson plans and classroom instruction.

The Internet also provides varied resources. As I was working on a packet of material related to the Triangle Shirtwaist Fire for use with social studies teachers, I found political cartoons, news articles, a factory worker's journal, and photographs of the event from Cornell University's archives. What would have taken us weeks and months to research in the past can now be obtained in minutes.

Taking Heart

The young man mentioned in Chapter 1 who pushed my thinking by telling me, "It's time for a change," led me to see that the heart of education is in our students' voices. In *The Schools We Have, the Schools We Want*, Nehring says, "One voice has been noticeably absent from the chorus of school-reform literature: students. We hear from scholars and policy makers, task forces and think tanks, sometimes even teachers. But what about kids?" (129). I often spent a lot of time creating resources and planning curriculum that proved counterproductive to my students' reading lives. When I finally learned to ask the right questions and listen to my students' answers, it moved me to the heart of changes I needed to make in the classroom. The same is true for me today.

When I began writing this book, I knew that I wanted to include students' voices as support for the methodology and as impetus to continue our study. I designed a survey questioning students about what reading instruction works for them and what gets in the way of success. I gave the survey to teachers who had previously been involved in professional development with me and asked them to give the survey to students in their reading intervention classes. Their answers are rich resources for us as we consider where our next professional steps might be with the struggling readers in our schools.

Students mentioned several areas in terms of impediments to reading success:

- Not having the big picture when trying to do smaller pieces
- Not knowing words
- Reading and answering questions at the end of each chapter
- Hating reading
- Filling in circles on tests
- No comprehension at the end
- Not being given enough time to finish
- Workbooks
- Not understanding what is read
- Getting distracted
- Reading out loud
- Remembering what is read
- Boring stuff to read
- Too noisy
- Stopping to sound out every word

These students also had several insights about methods that were helping them improve:

- Extra reading time
- Books on tape
- Someone who pushes me to read
- Following along while the teacher reads
- Having reading buddies
- Helping me change my attitude toward reading
- Feeling successful
- Strategies that help me with comprehension and remembering
- Interesting books to read
- Giving me things to read at home
- Letting me take tapes home to continue reading
- Showing me what I'm doing better
- Helping me decide what to read next

This survey was only administered to a few hundred students in two states, but their input has led me to develop my next research steps. Some of the students took the time to write letters giving me advice about what teachers should do to make reading classrooms more effective places. Those recommendations ranged from making more things into games to giving students more opportunities to do hands-on, collaborative work. My favorite letter told me that I should make sure that teachers love reading if they are supposed to teach it. Asking your students these kinds of questions will help you make critical decisions about expanding certain aspects of your reading plan and eliminating others. They can be our best teachers as they remind us that all of teaching is about relationship—with our mentors, our texts, and most of all, our students.

Finding Our Courage

My friends would say I am addicted to the British comedy *Are You Being Served?* In this sitcom, Mrs. Slocombe, the matronly clerk at Grace Brothers' store, often offers her dissenting opinion with this caveat: "Speaking for myself, and I am unanimous in this . . ." I've learned a few things about which "I am unanimous": one is to trust my instincts when working with adolescent literacy. At a time when so many are looking to programs to "fix" students, I continue to search for ways to help teachers expand their repertoire of strategies so they can make informed *daily* choices. I don't encourage administrators to buy programs for students; I encourage them to buy books, resources, videos, and time for their teachers to continue their professional growth. I have had the joy of working with a gifted administrator in Long Beach, California, for the past year. When I asked her how she went about finding the right people, she said, "I look for three things: teachers with heart, determination, and a willingness to learn. If they bring that, I can provide everything else they need."

The International Reading Association's Commission on Adolescent Literacy recently developed a position paper listing the principles for supporting adolescent literacy:

1. Adolescents deserve access to a wide variety of reading material that they can and want to read.
2. Adolescents deserve instruction that builds both the skill and desire to read increasingly complex materials.
3. Adolescents deserve assessment that shows them their strengths as well as their needs and that guides their teachers to design instruction that will best help them grow as readers.
4. Adolescents deserve expert teachers who model and provide explicit instruction in reading comprehension and study strategies across the curriculum.
5. Adolescents deserve reading specialists who assist individual students having difficulty learning how to read.
6. Adolescents deserve teachers who understand the complexities of individual adolescent readers, respect their differences, and respond to their characteristics.
7. Adolescents deserve homes, communities, and a nation that will support their efforts to achieve advance levels of literacy and provide the support necessary for them to succeed.

As I look back, I realize that one of the most difficult things for me to learn was the importance of asking the tough questions that would have supported these principles. There were times in my teaching when I didn't know what questions to ask and times when I didn't dare ask the questions that needed asking. Today I tend to ask those important questions, not to be obstructionist but because I need to hear the thinking of others in order to clarify and solidify my own. Your questions might not be mine. My guess is we could come up with hundreds of questions that deserve to be asked. At the moment, these are the questions Lorri Neilsen would call the "stones in my shoe."

Questions I Wish I Had Known (or Dared) to Ask

Why can't we read this book?

Do you have a copy of the research that supports that, please? I'd like to read it before we have our next meeting.

Why are we doing it this way?

Who is going to read my comments, and how will they be used?

Why isn't there money for interesting books for these students?

Why can't students get elective credits for taking an extra class in reading?

Who *can* tell me why we are spending this much money on testing?

What are we doing with test results besides putting them in the newspaper?

Why do *all* students need . . .?

If *you* can't, who can?

So, this journey ends where all journeys end—at another beginning. My poet friend Sara Holbrook and I were talking tonight. She told me she had left a performance and driven home in tears because she was so overwhelmed with the collective pain and violence the teenagers in the group that day had experienced in their short lives. I have come to believe that no time is easy if we live in the real world, but I know that the world becomes much more difficult for adolescents who have to struggle to make sense of the world without being able to read. So I leave you at the end of our journey, perhaps to begin another with the readers in your care. *Educate* is derived from the Latin *educare,* "to lead forth." If you don't lead them, who will?

Resources

Bridges and Borders: Diversity in America
Time Education Program
PO Box 85026
Richmond, VA 23285-5026
1-800-882-0852

This is an excellent resource for building background knowledge for major historical events. Includes articles that appeared in *Time* magazine from the 1920s through the 1990s.

Merlyn's Pen
PO Box 910
East Greenwich, RI 02818
1-800-247-2027
www.merlynspen.com

Published annually, *Merlyn's Pen* features top stories, essays, and poems by American teen writers. Visit their excellent Web site to see their full range of resources for student writers, including the American Teen Writer series.

MindWare
2720 Patton Road
Roseville, MN 55113
1-800-999-0398
Fax 1-888-299-9273

This company offers a variety of critical thinking books, puzzles, and manipulatives. The decks of mystery cards, Mind-Bending Puzzle Cards, lateral thinking puzzles, and Plexer books can all be ordered from this company.

Read *Magazine*
Weekly Reader Corporation
3001 Cindel Drive
PO Box 8007
Delran, NJ 08075-9978

1-800-446-3355
Fax 1-856-786-3360
www.weeklyreader.com/wrstore

This magazine for students publishes eighteen issues per year and includes articles, essays, short stories, plays, student writing, myths, and fables.

Recorded Books, Inc.
270 Skipjack Road
Prince Frederick, MD 20678
1-800-638-1304

This company provides various children's, young adult, and adult titles of unabridged recorded books.

Teaching Tolerance
Southern Poverty Law Center
400 Washington Avenue
Montgomery, Alabama 36104
334-264-0286
Fax 334-264-3121
www.splcenter.org

This educational project of the Southern Poverty Law Center makes videos, teaching guides, texts, and posters available to classroom teachers to provide resources that promote cultural understandings. The two teaching kits, with illustrated texts and award-winning videos, include *America's Civil Rights Movement* and *The Shadow of Hate*. These resources are free to classroom teachers when you fax your request on school letterhead.

TeenInk (The 21st Century)
Box 30
Newton, MA 02461
1-800-363-1986
www.TeenInk.com

This nonprofit foundation publishes a newspaper with only student submissions. An excellent source for your students to publish their own writing and read the writing of other teens.

Time Machine: The American History Magazine for Kids
PO Box 2879
Clifton, NJ 07015
1-800-742-5402

This magazine is an excellent source of historical and current events. The articles are reader-friendly, well illustrated, and connected to history.

APPENDIX B

Literature Supporting Content Literacy

Critical Thinking and Puzzles

Brecher, Erwin. 1994. *Lateral Logic Puzzles*. New York: Sterling.

Dispezio, Michael A. 1997. *Great Critical Thinking Puzzles*. New York: Sterling.

Gordon, A. C. 1972. *Solv-A-Crime*. New York: Scholastic.

———. 1978. *More Solv-A-Crime*. New York: Scholastic.

Hammond, D., T. Lester, and J. Scales. 1983. *More Plexers*. Palo Alto, CA: Seymour Publications.

Logue, Mary. 1995. *An Eyeful of Mysteries*. Roseville, MN: MindWare.

———. 1997. *Bella's Mystery Deck*. Roseville, MN: MindWare.

Sloane, Paul. 1991. *Lateral Thinking Puzzlers*. New York: Sterling.

———. 1994. *Test Your Lateral Thinking IQ*. New York: Sterling.

Sloane, Paul, and Des MacHale. 1997. *Perplexing Lateral Thinking Puzzles*. New York: Sterling.

Treat, Lawrence. 1991. *Crime and Puzzlement*. New York: Henry Holt.

Math

Barry, David. 1994. *The Rajah's Rice: A Mathematical Folktale from India*. New York: Scientific American Books for Young Readers.

Blum, Raymond. 1991. *Mathemagic*. New York: Sterling.

Brown, Kurt, ed. 1998. *Verse and Universe: Poems About Science and Mathematics*. Minneapolis: Milkweed.

Enzensberger, Hans Magnus. 1997. *The Number Devil*. New York: Henry Holt.

Guedj, Denis. 1996. *Numbers: The Universal Language*. New York: Abrams.

Isdell, Wendy. 1993. *A Gebra Named Al*. Minneapolis: Free Spirit Publishing.

Juster, Norton. 1961. *The Phantom Tollbooth*. New York: Random House.

Lasky, Kathryn. 1994. *The Librarian Who Measured the Earth*. Boston: Little, Brown.

Pappas, Theoni. 1989. *The Joy of Mathematics: Discovering Mathematics All Around You.* San Carlos, CA: Wide World Publishing/Tetra.

———. 1991. *More Joy of Mathematics: Exploring Mathematics All Around You.* San Carlos, CA: Wide World Publishing/Tetra.

———. 1993. *Fractals, Googols and Other Mathematical Tales.* San Carlos, CA: Wide World Publishing/Tetra.

———. 1994. *The Magic of Mathematics: Discovering the Spell of Mathematics.* San Carlos, CA: Wide World Publishing/Tetra.

———. 1997. *Math for Kids and Other People Too!* San Carlos, CA: Wide World Publishing/Tetra.

Sachar, Louis. 1989. *Sideways Arithmetic from Wayside School.* New York: Scholastic.

———. 1994. *More Sideways Arithmetic from Wayside School.* New York: Scholastic.

Science

Ardley, Neil, et al. 1984. *Why Things Are: A Guide to Understanding the World Around Us.* New York: Simon & Schuster.

Caney, Steven. 1985. *The Invention Book.* New York: Workman.

Feldman, David. 1988. *Why Do Clocks Run Clockwise? And Other Imponderables.* New York: Harper & Row.

———. 1989. *When Do Fish Sleep? And Other Imponderables of Everyday Life.* New York: HarperPerennial.

Goldwyn, Martin M. 1979. *How a Fly Walks Upside Down . . . and Other Curious Facts.* Secaucus, NJ: Carol Publishing Group.

Horrible Science Series. New York: Scholastic. Includes *Chemical Chaos* (1997), *Fatal Forces* (1997), *Nasty Nature* (1997), *Disgusting Digestion* (1998).

Isdell, Wendy. 1996. *The Chemy Called Al.* Minneapolis: Free Spirit Publishing.

Levithan, David. 1998a. *In the Eye of the Tornado.* New York: Scholastic.

———. 1998b. *In the Heart of the Quake.* New York: Scholastic.

Myers, Jack. 1991. *What Makes Popcorn Pop? And Other Questions About the World Around Us.* Honesdale, PA: Boyds Mills Press.

Quinlan, Susan E. 1995. *The Case of the Mummified Pigs and Other Mysteries in Nature.* Honesdale, PA: Boyds Mills Press.

Trefil, James. 1992. *1001 Things Everyone Should Know About Science.* New York: Doubleday.

Voorhees, Don. 1995. *Why Does Popcorn Pop? And 201 Other Fascinating Facts About Food.* Secaucus, NJ: Carol Publishing Group.

Social Studies

Aron, Paul. 1997. *Unsolved Mysteries of American History: An Eye-Opening Journey Through 500 Years of Discoveries, Disappearances, and Baffling Events*. New York: Wiley.

Booth, David. 1996. *The Dust Bowl*. Toronto: Kids Can Press.

Fact or Fiction? Series. Brookfield, CT: Copper Beech Books. Includes *Spies and Traitors* (1995), *Bandits and Outlaws* (1995), *Pirates* (1995), *Cowboys* (1995), *Conquerors and Explorers* (1996), *Knights* (1996).

Greenfeld, Howard. 1993. *The Hidden Children*. New York: Ticknor & Fields.

Gregory, Leland H. 1998. *Presumed Ignorant!* New York: Dell.

Hansen, Joyce, and Gary McGowan. 1998. *Breaking Ground, Breaking Silence: The Story of New York's African Burial Ground*. New York: Henry Holt.

Haskins, Jim. 1995. *Black Eagles: African Americans in Aviation*. New York: Scholastic.

Knight, Margy Burns. 1993. *Who Belongs Here? An American Story*. Gardiner, ME: Tilbury House.

Lorbiecki, Marybeth. 1997. *My Palace of Leaves in Sarajevo*. New York: Dial Books for Young Readers.

Maruki, Toshi. 1980. *Hiroshima No Pika*. New York: Lothrop, Lee & Shepard.

Meltzer, Milton. 1992. *The Amazing Potato: A Story in Which the Incas, Conquistadors, Marie Antoinette, Thomas Jefferson, Wars, Famines, Immigrants, and French Fries All Play a Part*. New York: HarperCollins.

News Series. Cambridge, MA: Candlewick Press. In newspaper format. Includes *The History News: Explorers* (1997), *The Greek News* (1996), *The Egyptian News* (1997), *Revolution* (1999).

Palacios, Argentina. 1994. *Standing Tall: The Stories of Ten Hispanic Americans*. New York: Scholastic.

Pratt, Richard. 1999. *Castle Diary: The Journal of Tobias Burgess, Page*. Cambridge, MA: Candlewick Press.

Scieszka, Jon. 1999. *It's All Greek to Me*. New York: Viking.

Sis, Peter. 1998. *Tibet: Through the Red Box*. New York: Scholastic.

Thomas, Velma Maia. 1997. *Lest We Forget: The Passage from Africa to Slavery and Emancipation*. New York: Crown.

Web Sites Supporting Lesson Plans and Classroom Instruction

Lesson Plans

AskERIC Lesson Plans: Language Arts.
http://ericir.syr.edu/Virtual/Lessons/Lang_arts/Reading/index.html
  A variety of lesson plans for English/language arts noted by grade level.

Blue Web'n Lesson Plans. http://www.kn.pacbell.com/wired/bluewebn/
  Posts outstanding education-related Web sites where teachers can find lesson plans, unit plans, and Web-based learning lessons for all content areas.

Busy Teachers' Web Site K–12. http://www.ceismc.gatech.edu/busyt/
  Provides teachers of all content areas with lessons, materials, and activities.

The Chalkboard. http://thechalkboard.com/
  Lists free educational resources for teachers, such as materials, grants, lesson plans.

Collaborative Lesson Archive. http://faldo.atmos.uiuc.edu/CLA/
  A collection of over 10,000 lesson plans, grouped by grade level as well as by content area.

CyberGuides. http://www.sdcoe.k12.ca.us/score/cyberguide.html
  Based on the California Language Arts Content Standards, this Web site includes supplementary units of instruction for specific pieces of literature at all grade levels. Each lesson includes a student edition, a teacher edition, and standards that correlate to each lesson.

Education Place. http://www.eduplace.com/
  Web site created by Houghton Mifflin provides elementary teachers with ideas and lessons for all content areas.

Internet School Library Media Center/English Language Arts.
http://falcon.jmu.edu/~ramseyil/yalit.htm
> A variety of resources to support the English/language arts curriculum on many topics, such as African-American literature, Asian-American literature, Young Adult literature, humor and wit, ESOL, drama, vocabulary, reluctant readers.

Kathy Schrock's Guide for Educators. http://school.discovery.com/schrockguide/
> Sponsored by the Discovery Channel, this is a detailed list of Internet sites, by subject area, that enhance teacher professional growth.

Learning Strategies Archive.
http://www.muskingum.edu/~cal/database/database.html
> This Web site contains databases on general-purpose and content-specific learning strategies that can be used with students of any age or level.

Outta Ray's Head. http://www3.sympatico.ca/ray.saitz/lessons3.htm
> A collection of literature, writing, poetry, and library lesson plans.

Pedagonet. http://www.pedagonet.com/
> A database of lesson plans and learning resources for all content areas.

Teacher Talk Forum. http://educ.indiana.edu/cas/ttforum/lesson.html
> A wide variety of lesson plans arranged by content area.

Teachers Helping Teachers. http://www.pacificnet.net/~mandel/
> Provides a forum for teachers to discuss topics of interest in all subject areas. Also includes an excellent collection of lesson plans from all disciplines.

Media and Technology Literacy

Just Think Foundation. http://www.justthink.org/
> Shows students how to understand the media's influence and teaches them to think for themselves. Provides a lesson bank as well as projects and resources students can use to study media.

Literacy and Technology.
http://campus.fortunecity.com/newton/40/literacy.html
> Promotes literacy by helping teachers integrate technology into the curriculum. Provides many computer- and technology-specific links to help teachers and students become more successful in all disciplines.

Media Literacy Online Project.
http://interact.uoregon.edu/MediaLit/HomePage/

A general media literacy Web site with many links to other Web sites. This site also provides a teacher's desk, which contains lesson plans at all grade levels, as well as a parent corner with materials parents can use at home to teach media evaluation skills.

Virtually Yours/Midlink Magazine.
http://www.ncsu.edu/midlink/vy/virtually.yours.html
Provides creative lessons that integrate technology into the curriculum in all content areas.

Reader's Theatre and Read-Alouds

Aaron Shepard's Web site. http://www.aaronshep.com/
This author discusses the books he has written and provides directions on how to integrate Reader's Theatre into the classroom, as well as scripts to utilize.

Do's and Don'ts of Reading Aloud.
http://161.31.208.51/ched/johnson/guidelin.htm
A detailed list of things to remember when reading aloud.

Dramatic Storytelling in the English Classroom.
http://www.aspa.asn.au/Projects/english/rtheatre.htm
Explains the purposes and procedures for incorporating Reader's Theatre into the classroom.

Gander Academy Reader's Theatre. http://www.stemnet.nf.ca/CITE/langrt.htm
Defines Reader's Theatre and provides instructions for performing it and evaluating.

Read Aloud Strategies. http://clerccenter.gallaudet.edu/Literacy/readit45.html
A set of seven strategies to utilize when reading aloud.

Reader's Theatre/Language Arts Home Page for Teachers.
http://hometown.aol.com/rcswallow/index.html
Provides a variety of Reader's Theatre scripts arranged by title.

Reader's Theatre Poetry Project. http://www3.sympatico.ca/ray.saitz/rdrsthr.txt
Includes a detailed lesson plan for using poetic Reader's Theatre in the secondary classroom.

Scripting for Reader's Theatre.
http://www.humboldt.edu/~jmf2/floss/rt-notes.html
Detailed steps for producing Reader's Theatre scripts.

Children's and Adolescent Literature

Bookhive. http://www.bookhive.org/bookhive.htm
A database of children's book reviews.

Booktalks Quick and Simple. http://rms.concord.k12.nh.us/booktalks/
A listing of over 300 short booktalks arranged by subject, interest level, title, and author. Also provides tips on giving booktalks.

Carol Hurst's Children's Literature. http://www.carolhurst.com/
A very detailed site of children's literature that includes information in the following categories: reviews of books, genre and subject area books, authors and illustrators, professional resources, and a free newsletter of children's literature.

Children's Literature Web Guide.
http://www.acs.ucalgary.ca/~dkbrown/index.html
Provides many resources for parents, teachers, and students using children's literature. Includes information on the following topics: award-winning books, author and illustrator biographies, teaching ideas, research guides, and children's publishers.

Database of Award Winning Children's Literature.
http://www2.wcoil.com/~ellerbee/childlit.html
A detailed database of high-quality and award-winning children's literature.

Index to Internet Sites: Children's and Young Adults' Authors and Illustrators.
http://falcon.jmu.edu/~ramseyil/biochildhome.htm
Aids teachers and students in finding biographical information about authors as well as critical reviews of authors' works. Site includes author biographies, autobiographies, birth dates, and interviews for many of today's popular children's and young adult authors.

Kay Vandergrift's Young Adult Literature Page.
http://www.scils.rutgers.edu/special/kay/yalit.html
A site that defines and defends the use of the Young Adult novel in the classroom. It also provides research and lists of books that teachers can use in the teaching of Young Adult literature.

Notes from the Windowsill.
http://lib.nmsu.edu/subject/childlit/reviews/notes/notes.htm
Provides critical book reviews of popular and classic children's literature.

Grammar and Writing

AskERIC Lesson Plans: Writing/Composition.
http://ericir.syr.edu/Virtual/Lessons/Lang_arts/Writing_comp/index.html
A variety of writing lesson plans and activities for grades K–12.

Common Errors in English.
http://www.wsu.edu:8080/~brians/errors/errors.html
This site provides a collection of common grammatical errors and remedies to correct them.

Creative Writing for Teens.
http://kidswriting.about.com/teens/kidswriting/index.htm?COB=home&PID=2773
Provides many activities and links to get young adults writing and publishing their work.

Grammar Bytes. http://www.chompchomp.com/
An interactive site that provides grammar exercises, quizzes, and rules for students and teachers.

Guide to Grammar and Writing.
http://webster.commnet.edu/HP/pages/darling/grammar.htm
Provides many resources for writing and grammar, including information on the following topics: the parts of speech, the essay, the paragraph, sample letters, interactive quizzes, grammar Q & A's, grammar and writing resources.

Outta Ray's Head Writing Lessons.
http://www3.sympatico.ca/ray.saitz/writing.htm
A variety of writing lesson plans that can be used at all levels.

Sue Palmer's Language Live.
http://www.nuff.ox.ac.uk/users/martin/languagelive.htm
A whimsical collection of stories and poems to use to teach various punctuation marks and parts of speech.

Teacher's Desk Writing Plans.
http://www.knownet.net/users/Ackley/writing_plans.html
A collection of lesson plans on various topics to get students at upper levels interested in writing.

Write Environment. http://www.writeenvironment.com/linksto.html
Provides many resources to help teachers guide student writers. Topics include lesson plans, reference materials, activities, publishing, professional resources.

Write Site. http://www.writesite.org/default.htm
Sponsored by ThinkTVNetwork, this writing site encourages student journalists to incorporate reading, writing, and technology to tell a story.

Spelling and Vocabulary

Amanda's Mnemonics Page.
http://teenwriting.about.com/teens/teenwriting/gi/dynamic/offsite.htm?site=http:
//www.frii.com/%7Egeomanda/mnemonics.html
Includes mnemonics for a variety of subjects and topics, including arithmetic, history, spelling, grammar, geography, biology.

AskERIC Lesson Plans: Spelling.
http://www.indiana.edu/~eric_rec/bks/lhome.html
A collection of spelling lesson plans and activities for grades 1–6.

AskERIC Lesson Plans: Vocabulary.
http://ericir.syr.edu/Virtual/Lessons/Lang_arts/Vocabulary/index.html
A variety of vocabulary lesson plans and activities for grades K–12.

Education By Design: Learning to Spell.
http://www.edbydesign.com/spelling.html
Discusses an individualized approach to spelling lists as well as strategies to help students learn to spell on their own.

Everyday Spelling Reference Room.
http://www.public.asu.edu/~ickpl/learningvocab.htm
Recommendations for the spelling curriculum for grades 1–8 based on findings from Research in Action. Provides a variety of word-attack strategies, including pronouncing for spelling, creating memory tricks, steps for spelling new words.

Spelling Lesson Plans.
http://teenwriting.about.com/teens/teenwriting/msub150.htm?iam=dp&terms=
spelling+strategies
A collection of lesson plans and activities for teaching spelling at various grade levels.

Teacher's Desk Spelling and Vocabulary Plans.
http://www.knownet.net/users/Ackley/spell_plans.html
A variety of lesson plans, which can be used at various grade levels, to teach spelling and vocabulary.

Teaching Strategies for Children with Spelling Disabilities.
http://www.psych.westminster.edu/psy411ws/learning_disabilities/
spelling_strategies_links.htm
> Provides a variety of activities and lessons to help the spelling-disabled student, including individual instruction, dialogue journals, speech synthesis, and games.

Virtual Thesaurus. http://www.plumbdesign.com/thesaurus/
> An unusual visually stimulating thesaurus that combines the concepts of word-webbing, parts of speech, synonyms, and antonyms to define words.

Vocabulary Enhancement Strategies.
http://www.smsu.edu/ids117/new/vocabulary.html
> Includes a variety of strategies and activities for students to use to create a lifelong development of vocabulary.

Vocabulary Learning Strategies.
http://www.public.asu.edu/~ickpl/learningvocab.htm
> This collection of learning strategies helps improve vocabulary development by providing a variety of mnemonic strategies, semantic mapping strategies, and real-life practice strategies.

Vocabulary University. http://www.vocabulary.com/
> Utilizes a variety of activities such as comic strips and election campaign puzzles to teach Latin and Greek roots as well as vocabulary in context.

Books on Tape

These books on tape (as well as many others) are available from Recorded Books, Inc. If I were starting a classroom library of recorded books, I would order the following titles as a beginning collection. Any of the books listed for grades 4–9 would be appropriate in a 10–12 collection as well. Those books listed in the 10–12 list might be controversial for younger readers.

Grades 4–6

Avi	*S.O.R. Losers*
Bauer, Marion Dane	*On My Honor*
Bunting, Eve	*Our Sixth-Grade Sugar Babies*
Byars, Betsy	*The Pinballs*
Christopher, Matt	*Baseball Pals*
Cleary, Beverly	*Dear Mr. Henshaw*
	Ribsy
DeClements, Barthe	*Nothing's Fair in Fifth Grade*
Farmer, Nancy	*The Ear, the Eye, and the Arm*
Gantos, Jack	*Heads or Tails: Stories from the Sixth Grade*
Gardiner, John Reynolds	*Stone Fox*
Jacques, Brian	*Redwall*
Park, Barbara	*Mick Harte Was Here*
Paterson, Katherine	*Bridge to Terabithia*
Peck, Robert Newton	*Soup*
Robinson, Barbara	*The Best School Year Ever*
Rowling, J. K.	*Harry Potter and the Sorcerer's Stone*
Shreve, Susan	*The Flunking of Joshua T. Bates*
	The Goalie
Soto, Gary	*The Skirt*
Spinelli, Jerry	*Crash*

Grades 7–9

Avi	*The True Confessions of Charlotte Doyle*
Cooney, Caroline B.	*Flight #116 Is Down*
Curtis, Christopher Paul	*The Watsons Go to Birmingham—1963*
DeFelice, Cynthia	*Weasel*
Duncan, Lois	*Killing Mr. Griffin*
Hesse, Karen	*Out of the Dust*
Hinton, S. E.	*The Outsiders*
Hunt, Irene	*The Lottery Rose*
Lipsyte, Robert	*The Contender*
Lowry, Lois	*Number the Stars*
Myers, Walter Dean	*Scorpions*
O'Dell, Scott	*Island of the Blue Dolphins*
Paterson, Katherine	*The Great Gilly Hopkins*
Paulsen, Gary	*Hatchet*
	Nightjohn
	Sarny
San Souci, Robert D.	*Short & Shivery*
	More Short & Shivery
Rowling, J. K.	*Harry Potter and the Sorcerer's Stone*
Sachar, Louis	*Holes*
Salisbury, Graham	*Blue Skin of the Sea*
Soto, Gary	*Taking Sides*
Spinelli, Jerry	*There's a Girl in My Hammerlock*
	Who Put That Hair in my Toothbrush?
	Wringer
Stine, R. L.	*The Dare*
Taylor, Mildred	*Roll of Thunder, Hear My Cry*
Voigt, Cynthia	*Dicey's Song*
White, Robb	*Deathwatch*
Yolen, Jane	*The Devil's Arithmetic*

Grades 10–12

Anonymous (Sparks)	*Go Ask Alice*
Cooney, Caroline	*Driver's Ed*
	The Face on the Milk Carton
	Whatever Happened to Janie?
Cormier, Robert	*The Chocolate War*
	We All Fall Down
Crew, Linda	*Children of the River*

Crutcher, Chris	*Athletic Shorts*
	Ironman
Duncan, Lois	*Don't Look Behind You*
	Killing Mr. Griffin
Haddix, Margaret	*Don't You Dare Read This, Mrs. Dunphrey*
Hinton, S. E.	*Rumblefish*
	That Was Then, This Is Now
Hobbs, Will	*River Thunder*
Lowry, Lois	*The Giver*
Martinez, Victor	*Parrot in the Oven*
Paulsen, Gary	*The Crossing*
Powell, Randy	*Is Kissing a Girl Who Smokes Like Licking an Ashtray?*
Sachar, Louis	*Holes*
Stine, R. L.	*Bad Dreams*
Wiesel, Elie	*Night*
Woodson, Jacqueline	*I Hadn't Meant to Tell You This*

Short Story Collections Supporting Read-Aloud, Shared, Guided, and Independent Reading

Asher, Sandy, ed. 1996. *But That's Another Story: Famous Authors Introduce Popular Genres.* New York: Walker.

Avi, et al. 1999. *Second Sight: Stories for a New Millennium.* New York: Philomel.

Blume, Judy, ed. 1999. *Places I Never Meant to Be: Original Stories by Censored Writers.* New York: Simon & Schuster Books for Young Readers.

Cameron, Ann. 1981. *The Stories Julian Tells.* New York: Knopf.

———. 1986. *More Stories Julian Tells.* New York: Knopf.

Carlson, Lori M., and Cynthia Ventura, eds. 1990. *Where Angels Glide at Dawn: New Stories from Latin America.* New York: HarperCollins.

———. 1994. *American Eyes: New Asian-American Short Stories for Young Adults.* New York: Henry Holt.

Cofer, Judith Ortiz. 1995. *An Island Like You: Stories of the Barrio.* New York: Orchard Books.

Courlander, Harold, and George Herzog. 1974. *The Cow-Tail Switch and Other West African Stories.* New York: Henry Holt.

Coville, Bruce, ed. 1993. *Book of Monsters: Tales to Give You the Creeps.* New York: Scholastic.

De Jesus, Joy, ed. 1997. *Growing Up Puerto Rican: An Anthology.* New York: Morrow.

Deary, Terry. 1995. *True Ghost Stories.* New York: Penguin.

Duncan, Lois, ed. 1996. *Night Terrors: Stories of Shadow and Substance.* New York: Simon & Schuster Books for Young Readers.

———, ed. 1998. *Trapped! Cages of Mind and Body.* New York: Simon & Schuster.

Fraustino, Lisa Rowe, ed. 1998. *Dirty Laundry: Stories About Family Secrets.* New York: Viking.

Gallo, Donald R., ed. 1984. *Sixteen: Short Stories by Outstanding Writers for Young Adults.* New York: Dell.

———. 1987. *Visions: Nineteen Short Stories by Outstanding Writers for Young Adults*. New York: Dell.

———. 1989. *Connections: Short Stories by Outstanding Writers for Young Adults*. New York: Dell.

———. 1992. *Short Circuits: Thirteen Shocking Stories by Outstanding Writers for Young Adults*. New York: Dell.

———. 1993a. *Join In: Multiethnic Short Stories by Outstanding Writers for Young Adults*. New York: Delacorte Press.

———. 1993b. *Within Reach: Ten Stories*. New York: HarperCollins.

———. 1995. *Ultimate Sports: Short Stories by Outstanding Writers for Young Adults*. New York: Delacorte Press.

———. 1997. *No Easy Answers: Short Stories About Teenagers Making Tough Choices*. New York: Delacorte Press.

———. 1999. *Time Capsule: Short Stories About Teenagers Throughout the Twentieth Century*. New York: Delacorte Press.

Gilson, Kristin. 1998. *Tales Too Scary to Be True: A Baby-Sitter's Nightmare*. New York: Harper Trophy.

Gorog, Judith. 1996. *When Nobody's Home: Fifteen Baby-Sitting Tales of Terror*. New York: Scholastic.

Jennings, Paul. 1985. *Unreal! Eight Surprising Stories*. New York: Puffin Books.

———. 1990. *Unbearable! More Bizarre Endings*. New York: Puffin Books.

———. 1995. *Listen Ear and Other Stories to Shock You Silly!* New York: Penguin.

Kantor, Susan. 1998. *One Hundred and One African-American Read-Aloud Stories*. New York: Black Dog & Leventhal.

Levine, Ellen, ed. 1993. *Freedom's Children: Young Civil Rights Activists Tell Their Own Stories*. New York: Avon.

Lindsay, Janice. 1998. *The Milly Stories*. New York: DK Publishing.

Lyons, Mary, comp. 1991. *Raw Head, Bloody Bones: African-American Tales of the Supernatural*. New York: Scribner.

Mazer, Harry, ed. 1997. *Twelve Shots: Outstanding Short Stories About Guns*. New York: Delacorte Press.

Minnesota Humanities Commission. 1991. *Braided Lives: An Anthology of Multicultural American Writing*. St. Paul: Minnesota Council of Teachers of English.

Monroe, Jack. 1995. *True Survival Stories*. New York: Penguin.

Mooser, Stephen. 1991. *The Man Who Ate a Car and Tons of Other Weird True Stories*. New York: Bantam Doubleday Dell.

Myers, Walter Dean. 2000. *145th Street*. New York: Delacorte Press.

Pearce, Q. L. 1995. *More Super Scary Stories for Sleep-Overs*. Los Angeles: RGA Publishing Group.

Peck, Richard. 1998. *A Long Way from Chicago*. New York: Dial.

Pullman, Philip. 1996. *Clockwork*. New York: Scholastic.

Rau, Margaret. 1994. *World's Scariest "True" Ghost Stories*. New York: Sterling.

Rochman, Hazel, and Darlene McCampbell, eds. 1993. *Who Do You Think You Are? Stories of Friends and Enemies*. Boston: Little, Brown.

Rylant, Cynthia. 1985. *Every Living Thing*. New York: Bradbury Press.

Schwartz, Alvin. 1991. *Scary Stories: More Tales to Chill Your Bones*. New York: HarperCollins.

Singer, Marilyn, comp. 1998. *Stay True: Short Stories for Strong Girls*. New York: Scholastic.

Skinner, David. 1999. *Thundershine: Tales of Metakids*. New York: Simon & Schuster Books for Young Readers.

Smith, Geof. 1997. *Above 95th Street and Other Basketball Stories*. Los Angeles: Lowell House Juvenile.

Soto, Gary. 1990a. *Baseball in April and Other Stories*. San Diego: Harcourt Brace Jovanovich.

———. 1990b. *A Summer Life*. New York: Bantam Doubleday Dell.

———. 1993. *Local News: A Collection of Stories*. San Diego: Harcourt Brace Jovanovich.

Spinelli, Jerry. 1997. *The Library Card*. New York: Scholastic.

Stearns, Michael, ed. 1993. *A Wizard's Dozen: Stories of the Fantastic*. New York: Scholastic.

Sussex, Lucy, comp. 1994. *Altered Voices: Nine Science Fiction Stories*. New York: Scholastic.

Thomas, Rob. 1997. *Doing Time: Notes from the Undergrad*. New York: Simon & Schuster.

Turner, Megan Whalen. 1995. *Instead of Three Wishes*. New York: Greenwillow.

Weiss, M. Jerry, and Helen S. Weiss, eds. 1997. *From One Experience to Another*. New York: Tor.

Welch, R. C. 1995. *Scary Stories for Stormy Nights*. Los Angeles: RGA Publishing Group.

Wynne-Jones, Tim. 1994. *The Book of Changes*. New York: Orchard Books.

———. 1999. *Lord of the Fries and Other Stories*. New York: DK Publishing.

Yep, Laurence, ed. 1993. *American Dragons: Twenty-Five Asian American Voices*. New York: HarperCollins.

Yolen, Jane, ed. 1991. *2041: Twelve Stories About the Future*. New York: Bantam Doubleday Dell.

Poetry Collections

Comprehensive Anthologies

Adair, Virginia Hamilton. 1996. *Ants on the Melon*. New York: Random House.

Agard, John, and Grace Nichols, eds. 1994. *A Caribbean Dozen: Poems from Caribbean Poets*. Cambridge, MA: Candlewick Press.

Alexander, Rosemary. 1983. *Poetry Place Anthology*. New York: Scholastic.

Angelou, Maya. 1994. *The Complete Collected Poems of Maya Angelou*. New York: Random House.

Baker, Russell, ed. 1986. *The Norton Book of Light Verse*. New York: W. W. Norton.

Berry, Wendell. 1985. *Collected Poems 1957–1982*. San Francisco: North Point Press.

Bly, Robert, and David Lehman, eds. 1999. *The Best American Poetry*. New York: Scribner.

De Regniers, Beatrice Schenk, Eva Moore, Mary Michaels White, and Jan Carr. 1988. *Sing a Song of Popcorn: Every Child's Book of Poems*. New York: Scholastic.

Dickinson, Emily. 1960. *The Complete Poems of Emily Dickinson*, ed. Thomas H. Johnson. Boston: Little, Brown.

Dillard, Annie. 1995. *Mornings Like This: Found Poems*. New York: HarperCollins.

Giovanni, Nikki. 1996. *The Selected Poems of Nikki Giovanni*. New York: Morrow.

Halpern, Daniel. 1994. *Selected Poems*. New York: Knopf.

Heaney, Seamus. 1998. *Opened Ground: Selected Poems 1966–1996*. New York: Farrar, Straus, Giroux.

Hughes, Langston. 1993 [1932]. *The Dream Keeper and Other Poems*. New York: Knopf.

Kerouac, Jack. 1992. *The Pocket Poets Series #48 Kerouac*. San Francisco: City Lights Books.

Kherdian, David, ed. 1995. *Beat Voices: An Anthology of Beat Poetry*. New York: Henry Holt.

Laurence, Mary Sanford, comp. 1993. *Best Loved Poems to Read Again and Again: The Most Moving Verses in the English Language*. New York: Galahad Books.

Levertov, Denise. 1987. *Poems 1968–1972*. New York: New Directions.

Major, Clarence, ed. 1996. *The Garden Thrives: Twentieth-Century African-American Poetry*. New York: HarperPerennial.

Miller, E. Ethelbert, ed. 1994. *In Search of Color Everywhere: A Collection of African-American Poetry*. New York: Stewart, Tabori & Chang.

Mosley, Ivo, ed. 1996. *Earth Poems: Poems from Around the World to Honor the Earth*. New York: HarperCollins.

Nye, Naomi Shihab, and Paul B. Janeczko. 1996. *I Feel a Little Jumpy Around You*. New York: Simon & Schuster.

Parini, Jay, ed. 1995. *The Columbia Anthology of American Poetry*. New York: Columbia University Press.

Rosenberg, Liz, ed. 1996. *The Invisible Ladder: An Anthology of Contemporary American Poems for Young Readers*. New York: Henry Holt.

Rubin, Robert Alden, ed. 1993. *Poetry Out Loud*. Chapel Hill, NC: Algonquin Books.

Sword, Elizabeth Hauge, and Victoria F. McCarthy, eds. 1995. *A Child's Anthology of Poetry*. New York: Scholastic.

Walker, Alice. 1991. *Her Blue Body Everything We Know: Earthling Poems 1965–1990 Complete*. San Diego: Harcourt Brace Jovanovich.

Washburn, Katharine, and John S. Major, eds. 1997. *World Poetry: An Anthology of Verse from Antiquity to Our Time*. New York: W. W. Norton.

Wilbur, Richard. 1988. *New and Collected Poems*. San Diego: Harcourt Brace Jovanovich.

Humor

Bagert, Brod. 1992. *Let Me Be . . . the Boss: Poems for Kids to Perform*. Honesdale, PA: Wordsong/Boyds Mills Press.

———. 1995. *Elephant Games and Other Playful Poems to Perform*. Honesdale, PA: Wordsong/Boyds Mills Press.

Ciardi, John. 1991 [1966]. *The Monster Den; or, Look What Happened at My House—and to It*. Honesdale, PA: Wordsong/Boyds Mills Press.

Cole, Joanna, and Stephanie Calmenson, comp. 1990. *Miss Mary Mack and Other Children's Street Rhymes*. New York: Morrow.

Cole, William, comp. 1981. *Poem Stew*. New York: HarperCollins.

Dahl, Roald. 1983a. *Dirty Beasts*. New York: Farrar, Straus, Giroux.

———. 1983b. *Revolting Rhymes*. New York: Knopf.

Florian, Douglas. 1994. *Bing Bang Boing*. New York: San Diego: Harcourt Brace Jovanovich.

Foster, John, ed. 1991. *Dragon Poems*. New York: Oxford University Press.

———. 1993. *Dinosaur Poems*. New York: Oxford University Press.

———. 1995. *Monster Poems*. New York: Oxford University Press.

———. 1997. *Magic Poems*. New York: Oxford University Press.

Harrison, David. 1996. *A Thousand Cousins*. Honesdale, PA: Wordsong/Boyds Mills Press.

Harrison, Michael, comp. 1989. *Splinters: A Book of Very Short Poems*. New York: Oxford University Press.

Moss, Jeff. 1989. *The Butterfly Jar*. New York: Bantam.

Prelutsky, Jack. 1984. *The New Kid on the Block*. New York: Scholastic.

Silverstein, Shel. 1981. *A Light in the Attic*. New York: HarperCollins.

Smith, William Jay. 1980. *Laughing Time: Nonsense Poems*. New York: Dell.

Snyder, Mike. 1998. *Swimming in Chocolate*. San Clemente, CA: Beetle Bug Books.

Westcott, Nadine Bernard. 1994. *Never Take a Pig to Lunch: Poems About the Fun of Eating*. New York: Orchard Books.

Illustrated Classics

Carroll, Lewis. 1987. *Jabberwocky*, illus. Graeme Base. New York: Abrams.

Eliot, T. S. 1987. *Growltiger's Last Stand; with The Pekes and the Pollicles; and, The Song of the Jellicles*, illus. Errol LeCain. New York: Farrar, Straus, Giroux/Harcourt Brace Jovanovich.

Frost, Robert. 1978. *Stopping by Woods on a Snowy Evening*, illus. Susan Jeffers. New York: Dutton.

———. 1988. *Birches*, illus. Ed Young. New York: Henry Holt.

Kipling, Rudyard. 1987. *Gunga Din*, illus. Robert Andrew Parker. San Diego: Harcourt Brace Jovanovich.

Koch, Kenneth, and Kate Farrell, comp. 1985. *Talking to the Sun: An Illustrated Anthology of Poems for Young People*. New York: Metropolitan Museum of Art/Holt, Rinehart & Winston.

Longfellow, Henry Wadsworth. 1983. *Hiawatha*, illus. Susan Jeffers. New York: Dial Books for Young Readers.

Poe, Edgar Allan. 1987. *Annabel Lee*, illus. Gilles Tibo. Montreal: Tundra Books.

Service, Robert. 1986. *The Cremation of Sam McGee*, illus. Ted Harrison. New York: HarperCollins.

———. 1988. *The Shooting of Dan McGrew*, illus. Ted Harrison. New York: David R. Godine.

Sullivan, Charles, ed. 1989. *Imaginary Gardens: American Poetry and Art for Young People*. New York: Abrams.

Math

Hopkins, Lee Bennett, comp. 1997. *Marvelous Math: A Book of Poems*. New York: Simon & Schuster.

Pappas, Theoni. 1991. *Math Talk: Mathematical Ideas in Poems for Two Voices*. San Carlos, CA: Wide World Publishing/Tetra.

Music and Poetry

Goldstein, Bobbye S., comp. 1992. *Inner Chimes: Poems on Poetry*. Honesdale, PA: Wordsong/Boyds Mills Press.

Harley, Avis. 2000. *Fly with Poetry: An ABC of Poetry*. Honesdale, PA: Wordsong/Boyds Mills Press.

Janeczko, Paul, comp. 1990. *The Place My Words Are Looking For*. New York: Bradbury Press.

Shange, Ntozake. 1994. *I Live in Music*. New York: Welcome Enterprises.

Strickland, Michael R., comp. 1993. *Poems That Sing to You*. Honesdale, PA: Wordsong/Boyds Mills Press.

Rites of Passage/Growing Up

Adoff, Arnold. 1995. *Slow Dance Heart Break Blues*. New York: Lothrop, Lee & Shepard.

Adoff, Arnold, ed. 1994 [1974]. *My Black Me: A Beginning Book of Black Poetry*. New York: Dutton Children's Books.

Angelou, Maya. 1987. *Now Sheba Sings the Song*. New York: Dutton.

Cisneros, Sandra. 1994. *Loose Woman*. New York: Knopf.

Fletcher, Ralph. 1994. *I Am Wings: Poems About Love*. New York: Bradbury Press.

————. 1996. *Buried Alive: The Elements of Love*. New York: Atheneum.

Giovanni, Nikki. 1985. *Spin a Soft Black Song*. New York: Hill & Wang.

Glaser, Isabel Joshlin, comp. 1995. *Dreams of Glory: Poems Starring Girls*. New York: Atheneum.

Gordon, Ruth, comp. 1995. *Pierced by a Ray of Sun: Poems About the Times We Feel Alone*. New York: HarperCollins.

Graves, Donald. 1996. *Baseball, Snakes, and Summer Squash: Poems About Growing Up*. Honesdale, PA: Wordsong/Boyds Mills Press.

Greenfield, Eloise. 1978. *Honey, I Love, and Other Love Poems*. New York: HarperCollins.

Holbrook, Sara. 1995. *Nothing's the End of the World*. Honesdale, PA: Wordsong/Boyds Mills Press.

———. 1996a. *Am I Naturally This Crazy?* Honesdale, PA: Boyds Mills Press.

———. 1996b. *The Dog Ate My Homework*. Honesdale, PA: Boyds Mills Press.

———. 1996c. *I Never Said I Wasn't Difficult*. Honesdale, PA: Wordsong/Boyds Mills Press.

———. 1996d. *Which Way to the Dragon? Poems for Coming-on-Strong*. Honesdale, PA: Boyds Mills Press.

———. 1998. *Walking on the Boundaries of Change: Poems of Transition*. Honesdale, PA: Boyds Mills Press.

Hopkins, Lee Bennett. 1995. *Been to Yesterdays: Poems of a Life*. Honesdale, PA: Wordsong/Boyds Mills Press.

Hudson, Wade, comp. 1993. *Pass It On: African-American Poetry for Children*. New York: Scholastic.

Janeczko, Paul B. 1993. *Stardust Hotel: Poems*. New York: Orchard Books.

Marcus, Leonard S., comp. 1993. *Lifelines: A Poetry Anthology Patterned on the Stages of Life*. New York: Dutton Children's Books.

Prather, Hugh. 1972. *I Touch the Earth, the Earth Touches Me*. New York: Doubleday.

Rylant, Cynthia. 1990. *Soda Jerk*. New York: Orchard Books.

Soto, Gary. 1991. *A Fire in My Hands*. New York: Scholastic.

Strickland, Michael R., comp. 1997. *My Own Song, and Other Poems to Groove To*. Honesdale, PA: Wordsong/Boyds Mills Press.

School-Related

Abeel, Samantha. 1994. *Reach for the Moon*. Duluth, MN: Pfeifer-Hamilton.

Dakos, Kalli. 1990. *If You're Not Here, Please Raise Your Hand: Poems about School*. New York: Four Winds Press.

———. 1995. *Mrs. Cole on an Onion Roll*. New York: Simon & Schuster.

Florian, Douglas. 1999. *Laugh-eteria*. San Diego: Harcourt Brace Jovanovich.

Glenn, Mel. 1982. *Class Dismissed! High School Poems*. New York: Clarion Books.

———. 1991. *My Friend's Got This Problem, Mr. Candler*. New York: Clarion Books.

———. 1996. *Who Killed Mr. Chippendale? A Mystery in Poems*. New York: Lodestar Books.

———. 1997a. *Jump Ball: A Basketball Season in Poems*. New York: Dutton.

———. 1997b. *The Taking of Room 114: A Hostage Drama in Poems*. New York: Lodestar Books.

———. 1999. *Foreign Exchange: A Mystery in Poems*. New York: Morrow.

Harrison, David L. 1993. *Somebody Catch My Homework*. Honesdale, PA: Wordsong/Boyds Mills Press.

Hopkins, Lee Bennett, comp. 1993. *Extra Innings: Baseball Poems*. San Diego: Harcourt Brace Jovanovich.

———. 1996. *Opening Days: Sports Poems*. San Diego: Harcourt Brace Jovanovich.

Kennedy, Dorothy M., comp. 1993. *I Thought I'd Take My Rat to School: Poems for September to June*. Boston: Little, Brown.

Korman, Gordon. 1996. *The Last-Place Sports Poems of Jeremy Bloom: A Collection of Poems About Winning, Losing, and Being a Good Sport (Sometimes)*. New York: Scholastic.

Korman, Gordon, and Bernice Korman. 1992. *The D- Poems of Jeremy Bloom: A Collection of Poems About School, Homework, and Life (Sort of)*. New York: Scholastic.

Lansky, Bruce, ed. 1997. *No More Homework! No More Tests! Kids' Favorite Funny School Poems*. Minnetonka, MN: Meadowbrook Press.

Mathis, Sharon Bell. 1991. *Red Dog, Blue Fly: Football Poems*. New York: Viking.

Shields, Carol Diggory. 1995. *Lunch Money and Other Poems About School*. New York: Dutton.

Singer, Marilyn. 1996. *All We Needed to Say: Poems About School from Tanya and Sophie*. New York: Atheneum.

Thurston, Cheryl Miller. 1987. *Hide Your Ex-Lax Under the Wheaties: Poems About Schools, Teachers, Kids, and Education*. Fort Collins, CO: Cottonwood Press.

Science

Aska, Warabe. 1990. *Seasons*. New York: Doubleday.

Carle, Eric. 1991. *Dragons Dragons and Other Creatures That Never Were*. New York: Scholastic.

Esbensen, Barbara Juster. 1986. *Words with Wrinkled Knees: Animal Poems*. Honesdale, PA: Wordsong/Boyds Mills Press.

Fleischman, Paul. 1985. *I Am Phoenix: Poems for Two Voices*. New York: Harper & Row.

———. 1988. *Joyful Noise: Poems for Two Voices*. New York: Harper & Row.

Florian, Douglas. 1998. *Insectlopedia*. San Diego: Harcourt Brace Jovanovich.

———. 2000. *Mammalabilia*. San Diego: Harcourt Brace Jovanovich.

Heard, Georgia. 1992. *Creatures of Earth, Sea, and Sky*. Honesdale, PA: Wordsong/Boyds Mills Press.

Paulos, Martha, ed. 1994. *Insectasides: Great Poets on Man's Pest Friend*. New York: Viking Penguin.

Rogasky, Barbara, comp. 1994. *Winter Poems*. New York: Scholastic.

Social Issues

Carson, Jo. 1991. *Stories I Ain't Told Nobody Yet*. New York: Theatre Communications Group.

Feelings, Tom, illus. 1993. *Soul Looks Back in Wonder*. New York: Dial.

Johnson, Angela. 1998. *The Other Side: Shorter Poems*. New York: Orchard Books.

Medearis, Angela Shelf. 1995. *Skin Deep and Other Teenage Reflections*. New York: Macmillan Books for Young Readers.

Sones, Sonya. 1999. *Stop Pretending: What Happened When My Big Sister Went Crazy*. New York: HarperCollins.

Social Studies

Adoff, Arnold. 1995. *Street Music: City Poems*. New York: HarperCollins.

Gunning, Monica. 1998. *Under the Breadfruit Tree: Island Poems*. Honesdale, PA: Wordsong/Boyds Mills Press.

Hopkins, Lee Bennett, comp. 1994. *Hand in Hand: An American History Through Poetry*. New York: Simon & Schuster.

Joseph, Lynn. 1990. *Coconut Kind of Day: Island Poems*. New York: Lothrop, Lee & Shepard.

Marsden, John. 1997. *Prayer for the Twenty-First Century*. Melbourne: Thomas C. Lothian.

Myers, Walter Dean. 1997. *Harlem*. New York: Scholastic.

Nye, Naomi Shihab, comp. 1992. *This Same Sky*. New York: Four Winds Press.

———. 1998. *The Space Between Our Footsteps: Poems and Paintings from the Middle East and North Africa*. New York: Simon & Schuster.

Peacock, Molly, Elise Paschen, and Neil Neches. 1996. *Poetry in Motion: 100 Poems from the Subways and Buses*. New York: W. W. Norton.

Randall, Dudley, ed. 1971. *The Black Poets*. New York: Bantam.

Rylant, Cynthia. 1994. *Something Permanent*. San Diego: Harcourt Brace Jovanovich.

UNICEF. 1993. *I Dream of Peace: Images of War by Children of Former Yugoslavia*. Preface by Maurice Sendak. New York: HarperCollins.

Volavkova, Hana, ed. 1993 [1964]. *I Never Saw Another Butterfly*. New York: Schocken Books.

Wong, Janet S. 1994. *Good Luck Gold and Other Poems*. New York: McElderry Books.

———. 1996. *A Suitcase of Seaweed and Other Poems*. New York: McElderry Books.

Wood, Nancy. 1993. *Spirit Walker*. New York: Delacorte Press.

Spanish/English

Alexander, Frances. 1997. *Mother Goose on the Rio Grande*. Lincolnwood, IL: Passport Books.

Carlson, Lori M., ed. 1994. *Cool Salsa: Bilingual Poems on Growing Up Hispanic in the United States*. New York: Henry Holt.

Dabcovich, Lydia. 1992. *The Keys to My Kingdom: A Poem in Three Languages*. New York: Lothrop, Lee & Shepard.

Griego, Margot C., Betsy L. Bucks, Sharon S. Gilbert, and Laurel H. Kimball, comp. and trans. 1981. *Tortillitas Para Mama*. New York: Holt, Rinehart & Winston.

Medina, Jane. 1999. *My Name Is Jorge on Both Sides of the River*. Honesdale, PA: Wordsong/Boyds Mills Press.

Merwin, W. S., trans. 1995. *Pieces of Shadows: Selected Poems of Jaime Sabines*. New York: Marsilio Publishers.

The Day of the Hunter

Edward M. Holmes

Everyone in his home town somewhere east of the Penobscot River knew that, in or out of season, Lyle Hanscom and deer hunting were inseparable. Yet for years no one had been able to garner enough evidence to convict him. Once several casual spectators, stopping along the highway to watch three deer at the other side of a wide field, not only heard the shot that felled one of the animals, but saw a man run from a spruce grove and drag the game back into the woods. No one could quite recognize the man in the strange, drooping overcoat he was wearing, nor was anyone able to track him with success. Still, the town's rumor mill, talk of someone's cooperative dump truck—which circled the town for an hour or two with a dead deer lying in the back—and public confidence in Lyle Hanscom's unparalleled gall unofficially pinned the deed on him.

Small wonder, then, that the nearest game warden kept a sharp watch, as often as he could, on Hanscom. The time came when the officer felt he had something on his man. Somehow word had leaked to him that Lyle had sneaked home with fresh-killed meat. When the warden drove up to Hanscom's, he could see the suspect watching him from one of the front windows. Hanscom met the law at the door and admitted him without a search warrant.

"I'd like to have a look around, if you don't mind, Lyle."

"Don't mind a bit, Joey. Look all you want," Hanscom said. "There's just one thing I want to ask of you."

"Ayeah?"

"My mother in there in the bedchamber is sick. She's had a heart attack."

"Is that so? I'm sorry to hear that."

"Well, you can understand I don't want nothing done that would upset her. You can see that, can't you, Joey?"

"I got to look in that room, same as any other, Lyle."

"Oh, I know that. I just ask that you don't upset her none. Might bring on another attack."

"I'll be careful," Joey said, and began making his search of the kitchen, the three small rooms, and the attic. He apologized to Mrs. Hanscom for intruding upon her, looked under the bed, and would have searched the closets if he could have found any. Back in the kitchen, Lyle sat in a rocking chair, smoking his pipe. "Guess I'll have to take a look in the cellar," the warden said.

"No, I guess you won't neither," Lyle said.

"How's that?"

"I let you in here nice as could be, Joey, and give you a chance to look around. You know as well as I do, I didn't have to. I even let you look in the room where my mother was laying sick, but I draw the line at the cellar. I don't want no game wardens nor nobody else poking around in no cellar of mine."

"You know I don't have to go above two miles," Joey said, "to get me a warrant."

"Then you'll just have to do it that way," Lyle said. "Call it a freak notion if you want, but I ain't giving no man permission to snoop in my cellar."

So Joey did it that way. When he came back, he presented Lyle with the warrant, and Lyle read it, every word, as slow as he could. "All right, warden, I see I'll have to let you look in the cellar if you're bound and determined to do it. You may have a mite of trouble, though: so far as I know, this house is built on cedar posts. I ain't crawled underneath lately looking for no cellar, but of course you might find one."

It was built on cedar posts, too, about a foot off the ground, and that was the end of that, except, of course, that Lyle Hanscom's mother has given him notice, if he ever puts a fresh-killed deer in bed with her again, heart attack or no heart attack, she will turn him over to the warden herself.

APPENDIX H
Forms

H.1 Things We Can Read From, A–Z

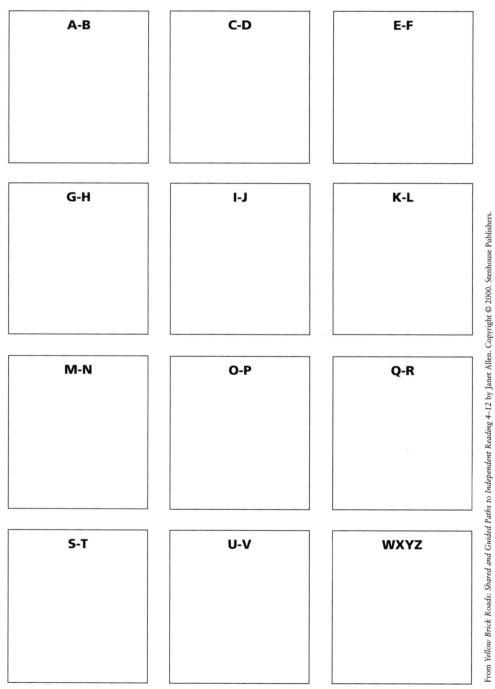

A-B	C-D	E-F
G-H	I-J	K-L
M-N	O-P	Q-R
S-T	U-V	WXYZ

H.2 Independent Reading Log

Date	Title, author	Pages I read from __ to __	**Response guides:** I'm wondering… I remember… I'm thinking that… I feel sorry for… I connected to… Can you believe… When I read __ I… I was reminded of… Wow!

H.3 Writing to Learn

Source:	**Source:**	**Source:**
Facts:	**Facts:**	**Facts:**
Response:	**Response:**	**Response:**
	Connection:	**Connection:**
	I wonder:	**Now that I know:**
	I want to know:	**I'm interested in knowing…**

H.4 B-K-W-L-Q (Adapted from Ogle 1986)

Build background	What do I know?	What do I want to know?	What did I learn?	What new questions do I have?

H.5 Fleshing Out a Character

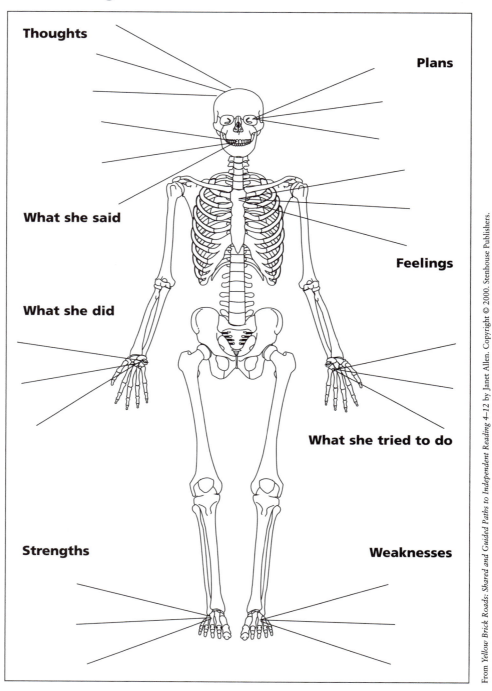

Thoughts

Plans

What she said

Feelings

What she did

What she tried to do

Strengths

Weaknesses

H.6 Looking at Our Options

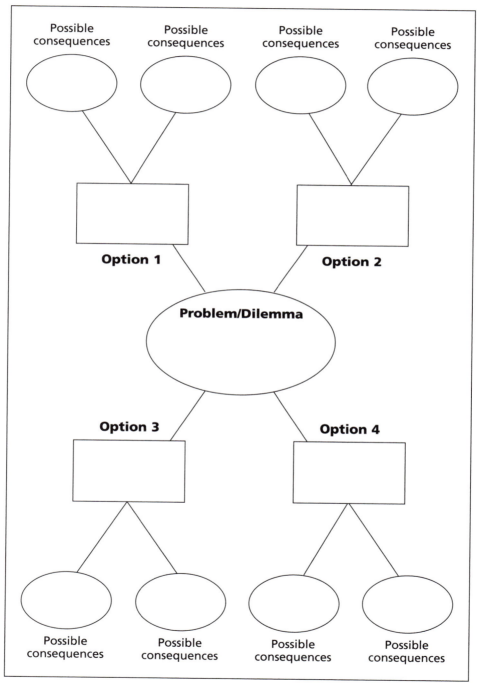

H.7　Multiple Sources, Multiple Perspectives

Sources	Factual information	Reading between the lines information	Questions

H.8 Compare and Contrast

Title	
Setting	
Time period	
Conflicts	
Resolution	
Development of main character	
Challenges	

H.9 Book Pass

Title	Author	Comment

H.10 Ideas for Writing

Date	Read-aloud	Conversation	Writing idea

H.11 Word Questioning

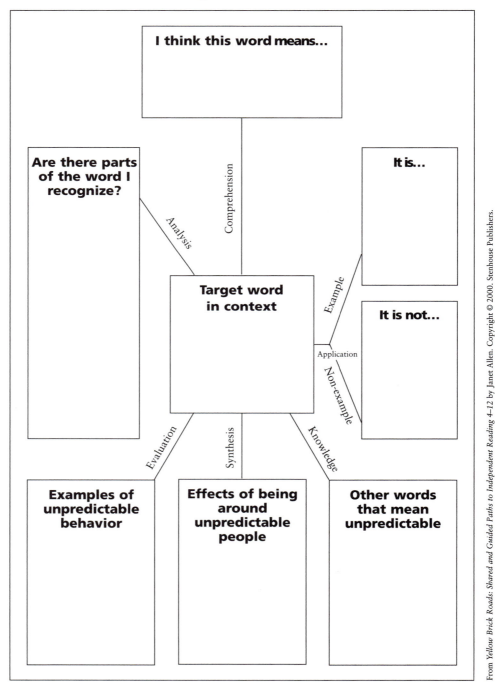

H.12 Language Collection

Words/images that make me smile or laugh

Smells, sights, sounds that bring tears to my eyes

Words/phrases that paint a picture

Words that make noise

Forbidden words

Action words

H.13 Language Choices

Instead of saying...	I could say...

H.14 Language Register

Everyday voice	Formal language

H.15 Concept Attainment

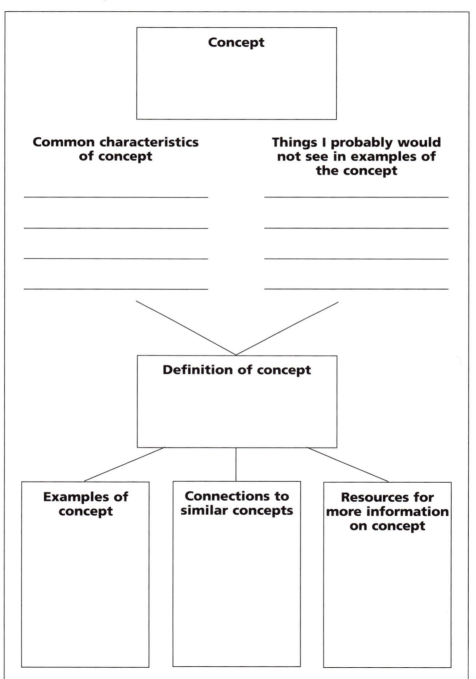

H.16 Fall Survey, Reading/Writing

From *Yellow Brick Roads: Shared and Guided Paths to Independent Reading 4–12* by Janet Allen. Copyright © 2000. Stenhouse Publishers.

Name _____

1. Has anyone ever talked with you individually about the following:
   a: your writing   no   yes
   b: a book you've read   no   yes
   c: your journal   no   yes
   d: your goals/future plans   no   yes
   e: your classes   no   yes
   f: you as a person   no   yes

2. What are your favorite classes in school?

3. What are your least favoriate classes?

4. What do you think are the most important qualities for a teacher to have?

5. What books have you read in the past few years?

6. What is your favorite book?

   What makes this book special?

   Do you have a favorite author? If so, what makes this person a good author?

7. What have you disliked about previous reading/English classes?

   What could have made the class better?

8. What have you enjoyed about previous English classes?

9. How important do you consider reading to be in your life?
   not very   important   extremely
   important   important

10. How important do you consider writing to be in your life?
    not very   important   extremely
    important   important

11. How would you rate yourself as a reader?
    below average   average   above average

12. How would you rate yourself as a writer?
    below average   average   above average

13. Do you consider yourself (a) a better reader than writer (b) a better writer than reader (c) equally good in both reading and writing.

14. Who do you know that is a good reader?

15. What do you think has made this person a good reader?

continued on next page

H.16 Fall Survey, Reading/Writing (continued)

16. What does this person do that makes you think he/she is a good reader?

17. Which of these remarks comes closest to the way you feel about reading?
    a: "I hate reading."
    b: "Reading is something you do if someone makes you, but I don't enjoy it."
    c: "Reading is OK. Sometimes I pick things up to read."
    d: "I like to read but have a hard time with it."
    e: "I really enjoy reading and often read when I have free time."

18. Please check all that you like to read.
    ____ plays   ____ newspapers
    ____ young adult novels   ____ magazines
    ____ bestsellers   ____ westerns
    ____ nonfiction   ____ romances
    ____ fiction   ____ historical fiction
    ____ poetry   ____ biographies

19. Which of the following have you written in the past six months?
    a: a letter to a friend   f: a poem
    b: a business letter   g: a short story
    c: a request for something   h: an essay
    d: a personal journal or diary   i: lyrics for a song
    e: an academic journal

20. What do you think I could do to help you become a better reader?

21. What could you do to become a better reader?

22. What could I do to help you become a better writer?

23. What could you do to become a better writer?

24. What is your favorite movie and what did you particularly like about this movie?

25. What magazines do you like to read?

26. What are your favorite television shows?

Classroom Activities—Please check those that you enjoy.
    ____ reading silently   ____ working in a small group
    ____ reading   ____ working alone
    ____ having someone read to you   ____ completing worksheets, workbooks
    ____ writing in journals   ____ doing vocabulary, dictionary work
    ____ watching movies   ____ class discussions
    ____ listening to cassettes (stories,   ____ writing
        poetry)   ____ publishing your writing (classroom
    ____ working as a whole class   magazine, etc.)

H.17 Sentence Completions

Please respond to the following sentence completions by writing the first honest, coherent thought that completes the sentence for you.

1. Today I feel _____

2. When I have to read, I _____

3. I get angry when _____

4. To be grown up _____

5. My idea of a good time _____

6. I wish my parents knew _____

7. School is _____

8. I can't understand why _____

9. I feel bad when _____

10. I wish teachers _____

11. I wish my mother _____

12. Going to college _____

13. To me, books _____

14. People think I _____

15. I like to read about _____

16. On weekends, I _____

17. I don't know how _____

18. To me, homework _____

19. I hope I'll never _____

20. I wish people wouldn't _____

21. When I finish high school _____

22. I'm afraid _____

23. Comic books _____

24. When I take my report card home _____

25. I am at my best when _____

H.18 Sentence Completions

Please respond to the following sentence completions by writing the first honest, coherent thought that completes the sentence for you.

1. When someone assigns a book for me to read, I _____
   _____

2. When I'm asked to write in a journal, I _____
   _____

3. When I think of school, I think of _____ ,
   _____ , _____ and _____
   _____

4. If someone asked me if I were a good reader, my response would be _____
   _____

5. When I am asked to write on a topic I choose, the process I use to decide what to
   write about is _____
   _____
   _____

6. The way I choose a book to read for independent reading is _____
   _____

7. If I were asked to summarize my past reading experiences, I would say _____
   _____

8. The things I think I do well as a reader are _____
   _____

9. The biggest problem for me when I try to read is _____
   _____

10. The hardest type of reading for me is _____
   _____

11. Given my future plans, I feel that reading and writing _____
   _____

12. Some believe that writing is a gift; others believe that everyone can be a good
   writer. In my opinion, _____
   _____

13. I think that what would make me a better reader is _____
   _____
   _____

From *Yellow Brick Roads: Shared and Guided Paths to Independent Reading 4–12* by Janet Allen. Copyright © 2000. Stenhouse Publishers.

H.19 Observational Checklist: Independent and Commitment to Learning

Yes	No	Observable behaviors
____	____	Monitors own behavior
____	____	Shows leadership capacity
____	____	Helps others
____	____	Works well independently
____	____	Doesn't give in to peer/group pressure
____	____	Maintains focus
____	____	Asks for help after independent attempts
____	____	Shows high level of concentration
____	____	Evaluates own work for completion or work needed
____	____	Articulate in group/class discussion
____	____	Does additional work (home, study, pursues research)
____	____	Makes good decisions about next steps
____	____	Tries to understand *and* complete work
____	____	Chooses challenging material and tasks
____	____	Daydreams frequently
____	____	Easily distracted (auditory, visual, tactile)
____	____	Reacts negatively with structure or challenging tasks
____	____	Needs reminders or task
____	____	Shows pattern of tardiness or absenteeism
____	____	Often submits incomplete or "sloppy" work
____	____	Interferes with others in small or whole group
____	____	Needs frequent praise or questions to stay committed
____	____	Misses directions or needs individual directions
____	____	Fools around during group learning
____	____	Takes role of class clown
____	____	Interferes with others' learning
____	____	Has trouble with organization (materials, time, goals)
____	____	Doesn't work well with others (difficult, aggressive)
____	____	Uses work of others rather than own
____	____	Rushes through assignments
____	____	Makes poor choices
____	____	Needs structure (time, limited choices, brief tasks)

Assessment notes:

H.20 Observational Checklist: Group Learning (Nonfiction)

Yes	No	**Strategic reading behaviors: text supports**
___	___	Used table of contents or index to narrow search
___	___	Previewed reading using titles, headings, captions, art
___	___	Predicted using some of the following features: title, pictures, tables, diagrams, first and last sentences, headings, captions, key words, chapter summaries, or prereading prompts
___	___	Checked for advanced information/organizers
___	___	Used glossary, key words, parentheticals as support

Yes	No	**Strategic reading behaviors: active reading**
___	___	Reread when appropriate (difficult text, clarifying)
___	___	Evaluated and revised predictions
___	___	Used skimming to summarize and clarify
___	___	Prepared for reading by having necessary resources (Post-its, highlighters, dictionary, altas, graphic organizers)
___	___	Made appropriate decisions related to skipping sections
___	___	Used resources in appropriate ways (knowledgeable others, other texts)
___	___	Adjusted reading rates for text difficulty or purpose
___	___	Used questioning to monitor, summarize, and clarify

Yes	No	**Strategic reading behaviors: demonstration of learning**
___	___	Able to summarize
___	___	Shows learning by formulating personal questions
___	___	Responds to reading with opinions, agreement/disagreement
___	___	Creates mind maps to solidify reading connections
___	___	Takes notes in ways that support discussions and connections
___	___	Shows ability to distinguish between central and peripheral information
___	___	Discriminates fact from opinion
___	___	Annotates when appropriate for information retrieval

H.21 End-of-Week Check-in

Things I accomplished this week	I learned	I still need help with...	I'd like to spend more time learning about...

H.22 Assessment: Continuous Learning

I tried to…	But I had difficulties…	I discovered that…	So then I decided to…

H.23 Monitoring Our Reading Process

	What confuses you? What words do you focus on?	What predictions do you make about topics/events?	What rethinking do you do?
Title			
First paragraph			
Continued reading			
End			

H.24 Directed Study: Conference/Self-Evaluation

Name _____ Date _____

Please evaluate your commitment to the class in the following categories. The scale is 1–5; 1 = lowest, 5 = highest.

Regular attendance	1	2	3	4	5
Promptness to class	1	2	3	4	5
Begin work immediately	1	2	3	4	5
Stay on task; working for the full class period	1	2	3	4	5
Choosing reading material that is challenging/interesting	1	2	3	4	5
Not disrupting others' work	1	2	3	4	5
Helping others when necessary	1	2	3	4	5
Taking responsibility for own learning	1	2	3	4	5
Making thoughtful, well-written responses to books read	1	2	3	4	5
Completing outside work on regular basis	1	2	3	4	5

Based on the above self-evaluation and on the work you have completed for this class, what do you think you deserve for a grade? _____

Why do you deserve this grade?

_____

_____

_____

_____

The purpose of this class is to help you become or continue to be active readers and writers. Are you improving in these areas?   yes   no

If yes, what is helping you?

_____

_____

If not, why not?

_____

_____

What could you be doing during this next quarter to help you improve?

_____

_____

_____

_____

Rate your commitment to learning: 1   2   3   4   5

Literature References

Adoff, Arnold, ed. 1994 [1974]. *My Black Me: A Beginning Book of Black Poetry*. New York: Dutton Children's Books.

Aliki. 1987 [1979]. *The Two of Them*. New York: Morrow.

Allen, Roger E. 1995. *Winnie-the-Pooh on Problem Solving*. New York: Dutton.

Anderson, Laurie Halse. 1999. *Speak*. New York: Farrar, Straus, Giroux.

Angelou, Maya. 1993 [1969]. *I Know Why the Caged Bird Sings*. New York: Bantam.

———. 1997. *Poems*. New York: Bantam.

Arnold, Nick. 1997a. *Fatal Forces*. New York: Scholastic.

———. 1997b. *Nasty Nature*. New York: Scholastic.

———. 1998. *Disgusting Digestion*. New York: Scholastic.

Arundel, Honor. 1970. *The Longest Weekend*. New York: T. Nelson.

Avi. 1991. *Nothing but the Truth*. New York: Orchard Books.

Barry, David. 1994. *The Rajah's Rice: A Mathematical Folktale from India*. New York: Scientific American Books for Young Readers.

Baum, L. Frank. 1998 [1900]. *The Wonderful Wizard of Oz*. New York: Quality Paperback Book Club.

Bissel, Charles Ben. 1983. *Letters I Never Wrote, Conversations I Never Had*. New York: Macmillan.

Bitton-Jackson, Livia. 1998. "Hey Jew Girl, Jew Girl." In *I Have Lived 1,000 Years: Growing Up in the Holocaust*. New York: Scholastic.

Blackwood, Gary. 1992. "Ethan Unbound." In *Short Circuits*, ed. Donald R. Gallo. New York: Dell.

Blume, Judy, ed. 1997. *Places I Never Meant to Be*. New York: Simon & Schuster.

Brecher, Erwin. 1994. *Lateral Logic Puzzles*. New York: Sterling.

Byars, Betsy. 1970. *The Summer of the Swans*. New York: Viking Penguin.

Canfield, Jack, Mark Victor Hansen, and Kimberly Kirberger. 1997. *Chicken Soup for the Teenage Soul*. Deerfield Beach, FL: Health Communications.

Carle, Eric. 1994 [1970]. *The Very Hungry Caterpillar*. New York: Philomel.

Carle, Eric, and Bill Martin, Jr. 1996 [1983]. *Brown Bear, Brown Bear, What Do You See?* New York: Henry Holt.

Carson, Jo. 1991. *stories i ain't told nobody yet*. New York: Theatre Communications Group.

Carter, Forrest. 1986 [1976]. *The Education of Little Tree*. Albuquerque: University of New Mexico Press.

Charlip, Remy. 1993 [1964]. *Fortunately*. New York: Aladdin.

Cheripko, Jan. 1996. *Imitate the Tiger*. Honesdale, PA: Boyds Mills Press.

Cisneros, Sandra. 1991. *The House on Mango Street*. New York: Vintage.

Clark, Andrew. 1997. *Stand and Deliver*. New York: Doubleday.

Cleary, Beverly. 1983. *Dear Mr. Henshaw*. New York: Morrow.

Cobb, Vicki, and Kathy Darling. 1983. *Bet You Can!* New York: Avon.

Coman, Carolyn. 1995. *What Jamie Saw*. Arden, NC: Front Street.

Conrad, Pam. 1989. *My Daniel*. New York: HarperCollins.

Conroy, Pat. 1994 [1972]. *The Water Is Wide*. New York: Bantam.

Cooney, Caroline. 1990. *The Face on the Milk Carton*. New York: Bantam.

Cormier, Robert. 1991. *I Have Words to Spend: Reflections of a Small-Town Editor*. New York: Delacorte Press.

Craig, Eleanor. 1994. *The Moon Is Broken*. New York: Signet.

Crutcher, Chris. 1993. *Staying Fat for Sarah Byrnes*. New York: Greenwillow.

———. 1995. *Ironman*. New York: Greenwillow.

Cullum, Albert. 1971. *The Geranium on the Window Sill Just Died, But Teacher You Went Right On*. New York: Harlin Quist.

Curtis, Christopher Paul. 1995. *The Watsons Go to Birmingham—1963*. New York: Delacorte Press.

———. 1999. *Bud, Not Buddy*. New York: Delacorte Press.

Cusick, Richie Tankersley. 1990. *Teacher's Pet*. New York: Scholastic.

Dahl, Roald. 1983. *Revolting Rhymes*. New York: Bantam Skylark.

———. 1984. *Boy: Tales of Childhood*. New York: Viking Penguin.

———. 1986. *Going Solo*. New York: Penguin.

Deary, Terry. 1994. *The Rotten Romans*. Horrible History Series. New York: Scholastic.

Dillard, Annie. 1989. *The Writing Life*. New York: Harper & Row.

Dispezio, Michael A. 1997. *Great Critical Thinking Puzzles*. New York: Sterling.

Draper, Sharon. 1997. *Buttered Bones*. Cleveland: Sharon M. Draper.

Duane, Diane. 1984. "Midnight Snack." In *Sixteen*, ed. Donald R. Gallo. New York: Dell.

Duncan, Lois. 1966. *Ransom*. New York: Doubleday.

———. 1973. *I Know What You Did Last Summer*. Boston: Little, Brown.

———. 1978. *Killing Mr. Griffin*. Boston: Little, Brown.

Echols, Mike. 1999. *I Know My First Name Is Steven*. New York: Kensington Publishing.

Ehrlich, Amy, ed. 1996. *When I Was Your Age: Original Stories About Growing Up*. Cambridge, MA: Candlewick Press.

Ewing, Lynne. 1996. *Drive-By*. New York: HarperCollins.

Fenner, Carol. 1998. *The King of Dragons*. New York: McElderry Books.

Fischel, Emma. 1993. *Murder Unlimited*. Whodunnits Series. Tulsa, OK: EDC Publishing.

Fleischman, Paul. 1988. *Joyful Noise: Poems for Two Voices*. New York: Harper & Row.

———. 1998. *Whirligig*. New York: Henry Holt.

Fletcher, Ralph. 1994. "Justin and Frank" and "Owl Pellets." In *I Am Wings: Poems About Love*. New York: Bradbury Press.

Fritz, Jean. 1982. *Homesick: My Own Story*. New York: Dell.

Fulghum, Robert. 1988. *All I Really Need to Know I Learned in Kindergarten*. New York: Villard Books.

Gallo, Donald R., ed. 1984. *Sixteen: Short Stories by Outstanding Writers for Young Adults*. New York: Dell.

———. 1999. *Time Capsule*. New York: Delacorte Press.

Ganeri, Anita. 1999. *Odious Ocean*. Horrible Geography Series. New York: Scholastic.

Gardiner, John R. 1980. *Stone Fox*. New York: Harper Trophy.

Giovanni, Nikki. 1988. *Sacred Cows and Other Edibles*. New York: Morrow.

Golding, William. 1954. *Lord of the Flies*. New York: Perigee Books.

Gordon, A. C. 1972. *Solv-a-Crime*. New York: Scholastic.

———. 1978. *More Solv-a-Crime*. New York: Scholastic.

Graves, Donald. 1996. *Baseball, Snakes, and Summer Squash: Poems About Growing Up*. Honesdale, PA: Boyds Mills Press.

Greenfield, Eloise. 1991. *Night on Neighborhood Street*. New York: Bantam Doubleday Dell.

Gwynne, Fred. 1988. *A Little Pigeon Toad*. New York: Simon & Schuster.

Hakim, Joy. 1995. *All the People 1945–1998*. A History of US. Book 10. New York: Oxford University Press.

Hamilton, Jane. 1994. *A Map of the World*. New York: Bantam Doubleday Dell.

Hammond, D., T. Lester, and J. Scales. 1983. *More Plexers: A Collection of Word Puzzles*. Palo Alto, CA: Seymour Publications.

Harden, Mike. 1989. "O, Romeo, O, Like, Wow." *Columbus Dispatch*, November 8.

Harrison, David L., and Betsy Lewin. 1994. *The Boy Who Counted Stars*. Honesdale, PA: Boyds Mills Press.

Hayden, Torey. 1981. *Somebody Else's Kids*. Toronto: Academic Press Canada.

————. 1988. *Just Another Kid*. New York: Putnam.

Head, Ann. 1967. *Mr. and Mrs. Bo Jo Jones*. New York: New American Library.

Heller, Ruth. 1988. *Kites Sail High: A Book About Verbs*. New York: Putnam.

Hemingway, Ernest. 1999 [1952]. *The Old Man and the Sea*. New York: Scribner.

Hesse, Karen. 1997. *Out of the Dust*. New York: Scholastic.

Hilton, James. 1983 [1934]. *Goodbye, Mr. Chips*. New York: Bantam.

Hinojosa, Maria. 1995. *Crews: Gang Members Talk to Maria Hinojosa*. San Diego: Harcourt Brace Jovanovich.

Hinton, S. E. 1967. *The Outsiders*. New York: Dell.

————. 1975. *Rumblefish*. New York: Dell.

————. 1979. *Tex*. New York: Dell.

Hobbs, Will. 1998. *The Maze*. New York: Avon.

Holbrook, Sara. 1996a. *The Dog Ate My Homework*. Honesdale, PA: Boyds Mills Press.

————. 1996b. *I Never Said I Wasn't Difficult*. Honesdale, PA: Boyds Mills Press.

————. 1998. *Chicks Up Front*. Cleveland: Cleveland State University.

Holmes, Edward M. 1976. "The Day of the Hunter." In *Maine Speaks: An Anthology of Maine Literature*. Brunswick, ME: Maine Writers and Publishers Alliance.

The Home University Bookshelf. 1945. New York: University Society.

Hopkins, Lee Bennett. 1995. *Been to Yesterdays: Poems of a Life*. Honesdale, PA: Boyds Mills Press.

Houghton Mifflin Social Studies, Level 6. 1991. Boston: Houghton Mifflin.

Hughes, Langston. 1995 [1958]. "Thank You M'am." In *Jump Up and Say! A Collection of Black Storytelling*, ed. Linda Goss and Clay Goss. New York: Simon & Schuster.

Hunt, Irene. 1976. *The Lottery Rose*. New York: Scribner.

Hyman, Dick. 1976. *Crazy Laws*. Brattleboro, VT: Stephen Greene Press.

Janeczko, Paul. 1993. *Stardust Hotel: Poems*. New York: Orchard Books.

Jennings, Paul. 1996. "A Mouthful." In *Uncovered! Weird, Weird Stories*. New York: Viking Penguin.

Jonas, Ann. 1983. *Round Trip*. New York: Greenwillow.

Jordan, Michael. 1994. *I Can't Accept Not Trying*. New York: HarperCollins.

Juster, Norton. 1989 [1961]. *The Phantom Tollbooth*. New York: Random House.

Keller, Charles, comp. 1991. *Take Me to Your Liter: Science and Math Jokes*. New York: Bantam Doubleday Dell.

Kerr, M. E. 1997. "I've Got Gloria." In *No Easy Answers: Short Stories About Teenagers Making Tough Choices*, ed. Donald R. Gallo. New York: Delacorte Press.

King, Stephen. Dark Tower Series. New York: New American Library. Includes *The Gunslinger* (1982), *The Drawing of the Three* (1987), *The Wastelands* (1991).

———. 1983. *Pet Semetary*. New York: Doubleday.

Klass, David. 1995. *Danger Zone*. New York: Scholastic.

Korman, Gordon. 1998. *The Sixth Grade Nickname Game*. New York: Hyperion.

Korman, Gordon, and Bernice Korman. 1992. *The D- Poems of Jeremy Bloom*. New York: Scholastic.

Krupinski, Eve, and Dana Weikel. 1986. *Death from Child Abuse . . . and No One Heard*. Winter Park, FL: Currier Davis Publishing.

Lasky, Kathryn. 1994. *Memoirs of a Bookbat*. San Diego: Harcourt Brace Jovanovich.

Lederer, Richard. 1987. *Anguished English*. Charleston, SC: Wyrick.

Lee, Joanna. 1978. *Mary Jane Harper Cried Last Night*. New York: New American Library.

Lee, Spike. 1998. *Four Little Girls*. New York: HBO Home Video.

Lewis, C. S. 1955. *The Magician's Nephew*. New York: Macmillan.

Logue, Mary. 1995. *An Eyeful of Mysteries: 52 Illustrated Mysteries*. Roseville, MN: MindWare.

———. 1997. *Bella's Mystery Deck: 52 Illustrated Mystery Cards*. Roseville, MN: MindWare.

"The Long Wait for Justice." 1998. In *Read: Dreams and Voices* (12), February 19. Stamford, CT: Weekly Reader Corporation.

Lowry, Lois. 1993. *The Giver*. Boston: Houghton Mifflin.

Macaulay, David. 1979. *Motel of the Mysteries*. Boston: Houghton Mifflin.

———. 1998. *The New Way Things Work*. New York: Scholastic.

MacCracken, Mary. 1976. *Lovey: A Very Special Child*. New York: New American Library.

MacLachlan, Patricia. 1994. *All the Places to Love*. New York: HarperCollins.

Many, Paul. 1997. *These Are the Rules*. New York: Knopf.

Marquis, Don. 1970 [1927]. *archy and mehitabel*. New York: Anchor.

Marsden, John. 1993. *Tomorrow, When the War Began*. New York: Bantam Doubleday Dell.

———. 1995 [1989]. *So Much to Tell You*. New York: Fawcett.

———. 1997. *Prayer for the Twenty-First Century*. Melbourne, Australia: Thomas C. Lothian.

Mazer, Harry. 1998. *The Wild Kid*. New York: Simon & Schuster.

McCutchen, Bragdon. 1981. *History of a Free People*. New York: Macmillan.

McLerran, Alice. 1990. *Roxaboxen*. New York: Lothrop, Lee & Shepard.

Medearis, Angela Shelf. 1995. *Skin Deep and Other Teenage Reflections*. New York: Macmillan Books for Young Readers.

Medina, Jane. 1999. *My Name Is Jorge on Both Sides of the River: Poems in English and Spanish*. Honesdale, PA: Wordsong/Boyds Mills Press.

Meyer, Carolyn. 1989. *Wild Rover*. New York: Macmillan.

Miller, Arthur. 1953. *The Crucible*. New York: Viking.

———. 1949. *Death of a Salesman*. New York: Viking.

Mitsui, James Masao. 1986. "Destination: Tule Lake Relocation Center, May 20, 1942" and "Holding Center, Tanforan Race Track, Spring 1942." In *After the Long Train*. Marina Del Ray, FL: Bieler Press.

Moss, Steve, ed. 1998. *The World's Shortest Stories*. Philadelphia: Running Press.

Neufeld, John. 1995. *Almost a Hero*. New York: Atheneum.

O'Dell, Scott. 1960. *Island of the Blue Dolphins*. New York: Dell.

Ogden, Maurice. 1959. "The Hangman." Garden Grove, CA.

Park, Frances, and Ginger Park. 1998. *My Freedom Trip: A Child's Escape from North Korea*. Honesdale, PA: Boyds Mills Press.

Paterson, Katherine. 1996. *Jip, His Story*. New York: Penguin Putnam.

Paulos, Martha, ed. 1994. *Insectasides*. New York: Viking Penguin.

Paulsen, Gary. 1986. *Sentries*. New York: Bradbury Press.

———. 1987. *Hatchet*. New York: Bradbury Press.

———. 1988. *The Island*. New York: Orchard Books.

———. 1989. *The Winter Room*. New York: Orchard Books.

———. 1994. *The Car*. San Diego: Harcourt Brace Jovanovich.

Peck, Richard. 1984. "Priscilla and the Wimps." In *Sixteen*, ed. Donald R. Gallo. New York: Bantam Doubleday Dell.

Peck, Robert Newton. 1972. *A Day No Pigs Would Die*. New York: Dell.

———. 1989. *Arly*. New York: Walker.

Philbrick, Rodman. 1993. *Freak the Mighty*. New York: Scholastic.

Piper, Watty. 1998 [1930]. *The Little Engine That Could*, illus. Richard Bernal. New York: Dutton.

Platt, Richard. 1992. *Stephen Biesty's Incredible Cross Sections*. New York: Knopf.

Prather, Hugh. 1990 [1970]. *Notes to Myself: My Struggle to Become a Person*. New York: Bantam.

Quinlan, Susan E. 1995. *The Case of the Mummified Pigs and Other Mysteries in Nature*. Honesdale, PA: Boyds Mills Press.

Randall, Dudley, ed. 1971. *The Black Poets*. New York: Bantam.

Raskin, Ellen. 1978. *The Westing Game*. New York: Avon.

Rawls, Wilson. 1961. *Where the Red Fern Grows*. New York: Doubleday.

Robbins, Tom. 1984. *Jitterbug Perfume*. New York: Bantam.

Rylant, Cynthia. 1982. *When I Was Young in the Mountains*. New York: Dutton.

———. 1985. *The Relatives Came*. New York: Bradbury Press.

Sachar, Louis. 1998. *Holes*. New York: Farrar, Straus, Giroux.

Salinger, J. D. 1951. *Catcher in the Rye*. Boston: Little, Brown.

Salisbury, Graham. 1992. *Blue Skin of the Sea*. New York: Dell.

Schwartz, Alvin. 1988. *Gold & Silver, Silver & Gold*. New York: Farrar, Straus, Giroux.

———. 1992 [1976]. *Kickle Snifters and Other Fearsome Critters*. New York: HarperCollins.

Scieszka, Jon. 1989. *The True Story of the Three Little Pigs!* New York: Viking.

———. 1991. *The Not-So-Jolly Roger*. Time Warp Trio Series. New York: Viking Penguin.

———. 1996. *Tut, Tut*. Time Warp Trio Series. New York: Viking Penguin.

Scoppettone, Sandra. 1976. *The Late Great Me*. New York: Putnam.

Shannon, George. 1985. *Stories to Solve: Folktales from Around the World*. New York: Greenwillow.

Shapard, Robert, and James Thomas, ed. 1986. *Sudden Fiction: American Short-Short Stories*. Salt Lake City: G. M. Smith.

Simmons, Steven J. 1997. *Alice and Greta: A Tale of Two Witches*. Watertown, MA: Charlesbridge.

Skinner, David. 1995. *The Wrecker*. New York: Simon & Schuster.

Sloane, Paul. 1991. *Lateral Thinking Puzzlers*. New York: Sterling.

———. 1994. *Test Your Lateral Thinking IQ*. New York: Sterling.

Sloane, Paul, and Des MacHale. 1997. *Perplexing Lateral Thinking Puzzles*. New York: Sterling.

Soto, Gary. 1990 [1971]. *A Summer Life*. New York: Dell.

Sparks, Beatrice, ed. 1971. *Go Ask Alice*. New York: Avon.

———. 1994. *It Happened to Nancy*. New York: Avon.

———. 1996 [1979]. *Jay's Journal*. New York: Pocket Books.

Spaulding, Nancy. 1994. *Heath Earth Science*. Boston: Houghton Mifflin.

Speare, Elizabeth George. 1983. *The Sign of the Beaver*. Boston: Houghton Mifflin.

Spinelli, Jerry. 1984. *Who Put That Hair in My Toothbrush?* Boston: Little, Brown.

———. 1997. *Wringer*. New York: HarperCollins.

Stahl, James, and Jo-Ann Langseth, eds. 1994. *White Knuckles: Thrillers and Other Stories by American Teen Writers*. East Greenwich, RI: Merlyn's Pen.

Steiger, Sherry Hansen, and Brad Steiger. 1995. *Mysteries of Animal Intelligence*. New York: Tor.

Steinbeck, John. 1937. *Of Mice and Men*. New York: Viking.

Stevenson, Robert Louis. 1980 [1886]. *Kidnapped*. Mahwah, NJ: Watermill Press.

Stine, R. L. 1990. *The Boyfriend*. New York: Scholastic.

Strasser, Todd. 1987. "On the Bridge." In *Visions*, ed. Donald R. Gallo. New York: Dell.

Strickland, Michael, comp. 1993. *Poems That Sing to You*. Honesdale, PA: Boyds Mills Press.

Swarthout, Glendon. 1970. *Bless the Beasts and Children*. New York: Doubleday.

Teaching Tolerance. 1992. *A Time for Justice: America's Civil Rights Movement*. Montgomery, AL: Southern Poverty Law Center.

———. 1995. *The Shadow of Hate*. Montgomery, AL: Southern Poverty Law Center.

Testa, Maria. 1995. *Dancing Pink Flamingos*. Minneapolis: Lerner.

Thomas, Ruth. 1989. *The Runaways*. New York: Lippincott.

Townsend, Sue. 1982. *The Secret Diary of Adrian Mole, Aged 13¾*. New York: Avon.

Treat, Lawrence. 1991. *Crime and Puzzlement: My Cousin Phoebe*. New York: Henry Holt.

Tsuchiya, Yukio. 1988 [1951]. *Faithful Elephants: A True Story of Animals, People, and War*. Boston: Houghton Mifflin.

Viorst, Judith. 1972. *Alexander and the Terrible, Horrible, No Good, Very Bad Day*. New York: Macmillan.

———. 1973. *How Did I Get to Be 40 and Other Atrocities*. New York: Simon & Schuster.

Voigt, Cynthia. 1985. *The Runner*. New York: Atheneum.

Volavkova, Hana, ed. 1993 [1964]. *I Never Saw Another Butterfly*. New York: Schocken Books.

Voorhees, Don. 1995. *Why Does Popcorn Pop?* Secaucus, NJ: Carol Publishing Group.

Walker, Alice. 1988. *To Hell with Dying*. San Diego: Harcourt Brace Jovanovich.

White, Bailey. 1993. *Mama Makes Up Her Mind*. Reading, MA: Addison-Wesley.

White, E. B. 1999 [1952]. *Charlotte's Web*. New York: HarperTrophy.

White, Robb. 1972. *Deathwatch*. New York: Doubleday.

White, Ruth. 1995. *Belle Prater's Boy*. New York: Farrar, Straus, Giroux.

Whole Story Series. New York: Penguin Putnam. Includes *Little Women* (1997), *The Jungle Book* (1996), *The Call of the Wild* (1996), *Frankenstein* (1998), *Heidi* (1996), *Tom Sawyer* (1996), *Around the World in Eighty Days* (1996).

Williams, Tennessee. 1972 [1945]. *The Glass Menagerie*. New York: Signet.

Professional References

Allen, Janet. 1995. *It's Never too Late: Leading Adolescents to Lifelong Literacy*. Portsmouth, NH: Heinemann.

————. 1999. *Words, Words, Words: Teaching Vocabulary in Grades 4–12*. Portland, ME: Stenhouse.

Allen, Janet, and Kyle Gonzalez. 1998. *There's Room for Me Here: Literacy Workshop in the Middle School*. Portland, ME: Stenhouse.

Allen, Roach Van, and C. Allen. 1966. *Language Experiences in Reading: Teacher's Resource Book*. Chicago: Encyclopedia Britannica Press.

Allington, Richard L., and Patricia M. Cunningham. 1996. *Schools That Work: Where All Children Read and Write*. New York: HarperCollins.

Alvermann, Donna. 1987. "Developing Lifetime Readers." In *Research Within Reach Secondary School Reading: A Research Guided Response to Concerns of Reading Educators*, ed. Donna Alvermann, David W. Moore, and Mark W. Conley. Newark, DE: International Reading Association.

Anderson, Richard C., Elfrieda Hiebert, et al. 1985. *Becoming a Nation of Readers: The Report of the Commission on Reading*. Washington, DC: National Institute of Education.

Atwell, Nancie. 1987. *In the Middle: Writing, Reading and Learning with Adolescents*. Portsmouth, NH: Heinemann-Boynton/Cook.

————. 1998. *In the Middle: New Understandings About Writing, Reading, and Learning*. 2d ed. Portsmouth, NH: Heinemann-Boynton/Cook.

Baker, Scott, Deborah C. Simmons, and Edward Kameenui. 1995. *Vocabulary Acquisition: Curricular and Instructional Implications for Diverse Learners*. Technical Report No. 13. Eugene: University of Oregon, National Center to Improve the Tools for Educators.

Bauermeister, Erica, Jesse Larsen, and Holly Smith. 1994. *500 Great Books by Women: A Reader's Guide*. New York: Penguin.

Bauermeister, Erica, and Holly Smith. 1997. *Let's Hear It for the Girls: 375 Great Books for Readers 2–14*. New York: Penguin.

Bodard, Joni. 1980. *Booktalk! Booktalking and School Visiting for Young Adult Audiences*. New York: H. W. Wilson.

Bransford, J. D., R. Sherwood, and Ted Hasselbring. 1988. "Effects of the Video Revolution on Cognitive Development: Some Initial Thoughts. In *Constructivism in a Computer Age*, ed. G. Foreman and P. Pafall. Hillsdale, NJ: Erlbaum.

Brendtro, Larry K., Martin Brokenleg, and Steve Van Bockern. 1992. *Reclaiming Youth at Risk: Our Hope for the Future*. Bloomington, IN: National Educational Service.

Bridges, Lois. 1995. *Assessment: Continuous Learning*. Portland, ME: Stenhouse.

Bridges and Borders: Diversity in America. 1994. By the editors of *Time* Magazine. New York: Warner Books.

Brooks, Jacqueline Grennon, and Martin G. Brooks. 1993. *In Search of Understanding: The Case for Constructivist Classrooms*. Alexandria, VA: Association for Supervision and Curriculum Development.

Bruchac, Joseph. 1998. Personal communication.

Butson, Ann Marie Radaskiewicz. 1989. "Inside the Classroom." *Newsweek*, June 6.

Caine, Renate, and Geoffrey Caine. 1994. *Making Connections: Teaching and the Human Brain*. Menlo Park, CA: Addison-Wesley.

Calkins, Lucy McCormick. 1994. *The Art of Teaching Writing*. New ed. Portsmouth, NH: Heinemann.

Cambourne, Brian. 1988. *The Whole Story: Natural Learning and the Acquisition of Literacy in the Classroom*. Auckland, NZ: Ashton Scholastic.

Carlsen, G. Robert. 1980. *Books and the Teenage Reader*. 2d rev. ed. New York: Harper & Row.

Carter, Candy, and Zora M. Rashkis, eds. 1980. *Ideas for Teaching English in the Junior High and Middle School*. Urbana, IL: National Council of Teachers of English.

Chambers, Aidan. 1996. *Tell Me: Children, Reading, and Talk*. Portland, ME: Stenhouse.

Chandler, Kelly, and the Mapleton Teacher-Research Group. 1999. *Spelling Inquiry: How One Elementary School Caught the Mnemonic Plague*. Portland, ME: Stenhouse.

Children's Book Council. 1992. *Kids' Favorite Books: Children's Choices 1989–1991*. Newark, DE: International Reading Association.

Clay, Marie M. 1974. "Involving Teachers in Classroom Research." In *Teachers and Research: Language Learning in the Classroom*, ed. G. S. Pinnell and M. L. Matlin. Newark, DE: International Reading Association.

Codell, Esme Raji. 1999. *Educating Esme: Diary of a Teacher's First Year.* Chapel Hill, NC: Algonquin Books.

Davey, B. 1986. "Using Textbook Activity Guides to Help Students Learn from Textbooks." *Journal of Reading* 29: 489–494.

Davies, Robertson. 1990. *A Voice from the Attic: Essays on the Art of Reading.* Rev. ed. New York: Penguin.

Day, Frances Ann. 1997. *Latina and Latino Voices in Literature for Children and Teenagers.* Portsmouth, NH: Heinemann.

Day, Richard R., and Julian Bamford. 1998. *Extensive Reading in the Second Language Classroom.* New York: Cambridge University Press.

Duckworth, Eleanor. 1996. *"The Having of Wonderful Ideas" and Other Essays on Teaching and Learning.* New York: Teachers College Press.

———. 1997. *Teacher to Teacher: Learning from Each Other.* New York: Teachers College Press.

Eisner, Elliot W. 1991. *The Enlightened Eye.* New York: Macmillan.

Elley, Warwick B. 1992. *How in the World Do Students Read? IEA Study of Reading Literacy.* The Hague: International Association for the Evaluation of Educational Achievement.

Fletcher, Ralph. 1993. *What a Writer Needs.* Portsmouth, NH: Heinemann.

Fletcher, Ralph, and JoAnn Portalupi. 1998. *Craft Lessons: Teaching Writing K–8.* Portland, ME: Stenhouse.

Fountas, Irene C., and Gay S. Pinnell. 1996. *Guided Reading: Good First Teaching for All Children.* Portsmouth, NH: Heinemann.

Freebody, P., and A. Luke. 1990. "Literacy Programs: Debates and Demand in Cultural Context." *Prospect* 5 (3): 7–16.

Freeman, Evelyn, and Diane Goetz Person, eds. 1992. *Using Nonfiction Trade Books in the Elementary Classroom: From Ants to Zeppelins.* Urbana, IL: National Council of Teachers of English.

Fry, E. 1977. "Fry's Readability Graph." *Journal of Reading* 21 (3): 249.

Goodlad, John I. 1984. *A Place Called School: Prospects for the Future.* New York: McGraw Hill.

Goodman, Kenneth. 1986. *What's Whole in Whole Language?* Portsmouth, NH: Heinemann.

Goodman, Yetta, Wendy Hood, and Kenneth Goodman, eds. 1991. *Organizing for Whole Language.* Portsmouth, NH: Heinemann.

Graves, Donald. 1983. *Writing: Teachers and Children at Work.* Portsmouth, NH: Heinemann.

———. 1991. *Build a Literate Classroom: The Reading/Writing Teacher's Companion.* Portsmouth, NH: Heinemann.

Halliday, M.A.K. 1973. *Explorations in the Functions of Language.* London: Edward Arnold.

Harvey, Stephanie, and Anne Goudvis. 2000. *Strategies That Work: Teaching Comprehension to Enhance Understanding*. Portland, ME: Stenhouse.

Huck, Charlotte. 1986. "The Power of Children's Literature: To Know the Place for the First Time." *The Best of Bulletin*, Spring.

Jobe, Ron, and Mary Dayton-Sakari. 1999. *Reluctant Readers: Connecting Students and Books for Successful Reading Experiences*. Markham, Ontario, Canada: Pembroke.

Kaywell, Joan. 1993. *Adolescents at Risk: A Guide to Fiction and Nonfiction for Young Adults, Parents, and Professionals*. Westport, CT: Greenwood Press.

Keene, Ellin Oliver, and Susan Zimmermann. 1997. *Mosaic of Thought: Teaching Comprehension in a Reader's Workshop*. Portsmouth, NH: Heinemann.

Kirby, Dan, Tom Liner, and Ruth Vinz. 1988. *Inside Out: Developmental Strategies for Teaching Writing*. 2d ed. Portsmouth, NH: Heinemann-Boynton/Cook.

Kohl, Herbert. 1994. *"I Won't Learn from You" And Other Thoughts on Creative Maladjustment*. New York: New Press.

Kohn, Alfie. 1993a. "Choices for Children: Why and How to Let Students Decide." *Phi Delta Kappan* 75 (1): 8–16, 18–21.

———. 1993b. *Punished by Rewards: The Trouble with Gold Stars, Incentive Plans, A's, Praise, and Other Bribes*. Boston: Houghton Mifflin.

Lamott, Anne. 1994. *Bird by Bird: Some Instructions on Writing and Life*. New York: Pantheon.

Langer, Judith A. 1995. *Envisioning Literature: Literary Understanding and Literature Instruction*. New York: Teachers College Press.

Lavoie, Richard D. 1996. *Understanding Learning Disabilities: How Difficult Can This Be? The F.A.T. City Workshop*. Washington, DC: PBS Video.

Levy, Steven. 1996. *Starting from Scratch: One Classroom Builds Its Own Curriculum*. Portsmouth, NH: Heinemann.

MacBride, Bill. 1997. *Entertaining and Elephant: A Novel About Learning and Letting Go*. New York: Pearl Street Press.

Macrorie, Ken. 1988. *The I-Search Paper: Revised Edition of Searching Writing*. Portsmouth, NH: Heinemann-Boynton/Cook.

Meek, Margaret. 1982. *Learning to Read*. Portsmouth, NH: Heinemann.

Meltzer, Milton. 1994. *Nonfiction for the Classroom: Milton Meltzer on Writing, History, and Social Responsibility*. New York: Teachers College Press.

Mohr, Carolyn, Dorothy Nixon, and Shirley Vickers. 1991. *Books That Heal: A Whole Language Approach*. Englewood, CO: Teacher Ideas Press.

Mooney, Margaret. 1990. *Reading To, With, and By Children*. Katonah, NY: Richard C. Owen.

————. 1991. *Developing Life-Long Readers.* Wellington, NZ: Learning
Media, Ministry of Education.

Moore, David, Thomas W. Bean, Deanna Birdyshaw, and James A. Rycik.
1999. *Adolescent Literacy: A Position Statement.* Newark, DE:
International Reading Association.

Nehring, James. 1989. *"Why Do We Gotta Do This Stuff, Mr. Nehring?"* New
York: Fawcett Columbine.

————. 1992. *The Schools We Have, the Schools We Want.* San Francisco:
Jossey-Bass.

Neill, A. S. 1960. *Summerhill.* New York: Hart Publishing.

Neilsen, Lorri. 1994. *A Stone in My Shoe: Teaching Literacy in Times of
Change.* Winnipeg, Canada: Peguis Publications.

Newkirk, Thomas, ed. 1992. *Workshop 4: The Teacher as Researcher.*
Portsmouth, NH: Heinemann.

Newman, F. M. 1988. "Can Depth Replace Coverage in the High School
Curriculum?" *Phi Delta Kappan* 69: 345–348.

Odean, Kathleen. 1997. *Great Books for Girls: More Than 600 Books to
Inspire Today's Girls and Tomorrow's Women.* New York: Ballantine.

————. 1998. *Great Books for Boys: More Than 600 Books for Boys 2–14.*
New York: Ballantine.

Ogle, D. M. 1986. "K-W-L: a Teaching Model That Develops Active Reading
of Expository Text." *Reading Teacher* 39: 564–570.

Ohanian, Susan. 1994. *Who's in Charge? A Teacher Speaks Her Mind.*
Portsmouth, NH: Heinemann-Boynton/Cook.

Peck, Richard. 1992. "Nobody But a Reader Ever Became a Writer." In
Author's Insights: Turning Teenagers into Readers and Writers, ed. Donald
Gallo. Portsmouth, NH: Heinemann-Boynton/Cook.

Pennac, Daniel. 1999. *Better Than Life.* Portland, ME: Stenhouse.

Phelan, Patricia, ed. 1996. *High Interest–Easy Reading: An Annotated Booklist
for Middle School and Senior High School.* 7th ed. Urbana, IL: National
Council of Teachers of English.

Postman, Neil. 1979. *Teaching as a Conserving Activity.* New York: Dell.

Postman, Neil, and Charles Weingartner. 1969. *Teaching as a Subversive
Activity.* New York: Dell.

Power, Brenda M., and Kelly Chandler. 1998. *Well-Chosen Words: Narrative
Assessments and Report Card Comments.* Portland, ME: Stenhouse.

Rief, Linda. 1992. *Seeking Diversity: Language Arts with Adolescents.*
Portsmouth, NH: Heinemann.

Romano, Tom. 1987. *Clearing the Way.* Portsmouth, NH: Heinemann.

Routman, Regie. 1994. *Invitations: Changing as Teachers and Learners K–12.*
Portsmouth, NH: Heinemann.

Seligman, M.E.P. 1975. *Helplessness: On Depression, Development and Death*. San Francisco: Freeman.

Smith, Frank. 1988a. *Joining the Literacy Club*. Portsmouth, NH: Heinemann.

———. 1988b. *Understanding Reading*. 4th ed. Hillsdale, NJ: Lawrence Erlbaum Associates.

Smith, J.W.A., and W. B. Elley. 1994. *Learning to Read in New Zealand*. Katonah, NY: Richard C. Owen.

Snow, Catherine E., M. Burns, and Peg Griffin, eds. 1998. *Preventing Reading Difficulties in Young Children*. Washington, DC: National Academy Press.

Spaulding, Nancy E., and Samuel N. Namowitz. 1994. *Heath Earth Science*. Lexington, MA: D. C. Heath.

Tierney, Robert J., and Timothy Shanahan. 1991. "Research on the Reading-Writing Relationship: Interactions, Transactions, and Outcomes." In *Handbook of Reading Research*, Vol. 2, ed. Barr, Kamil, Mosenthal, and Pearson. White Plains, NY: Longman.

Trelease, Jim. 1985. *The Read-Aloud Handbook*. New York: Penguin.

Tunnell, Michael, and Richard Ammon. 1993. *The Story of Ourselves: Teaching History Through Children's Literature*. Portsmouth, NH: Heinemann.

"U.S. Schools: They Face a Crisis." 1950. *Life* 29 (16): 11.

Valencia, Sheila W., Elfrieda H. Hiebert, and Peter P. Afflerbach. 1994. *Authentic Reading Assessment: Practices and Possibilities*. Newark, DE: International Reading Association.

Wells, Gordon. 1986. *The Meaning Makers: Children Learning Language and Using Language to Learn*. Portsmouth, NH: Heinemann.

Wheldall, Kevin, and Judy Entwistle. 1988. "Back in the USSR: The Effect of Teacher Modelling of Silent Reading on Pupils' Reading Behaviour in the Primary School Classroom." *Educational Psychology* 8: 1–2.

Wurth, Shirley, ed. 1992. *Books for You: A Booklist for Senior High Students*. 11th ed. Urbana, IL: National Council of Teachers of English.

Zemelman, Steven, Harvey Daniels, and Arthur Hyde. 1998. *Best Practice: New Standards for Teaching and Learning in America's Schools*. 2d ed. Portsmouth, NH: Heinemann.

Index

academic failure, reading success and, 38–39
academic journals
    code breaking and, 152
    for "I Don't Know How" readers, 35
    Language Collection section, 152, 187
    language experience activity (LEA) and, 24
    for personal responses to literature, 27
    reading portfolios and, 225
    Spelling section, 152
    test-taking and, 215
    Things I Know How to Do section, 35, 152
    Things I'm Learning How to Do section, 35, 152
    Things We Do Together section, 152
    writing resource logs, 180
active learning. *See also* learning
    conditions for, 9–13
    shared responsibility for, 201
active listening, 49–50
active reading
    guided reading and, 89
    reluctant readers and, 34
Adoff, Arnold, 153
Adventures of Tom Sawyer (Whole Story Series), 177
Afflerbach, Peter P., 224

Alexander and the Terrible, Horrible, No Good, Very Bad Day (Viorst), 193
Alice and Greta (Simmons), 43–44
Aliki, 182
Allen, Janet, 40
Allen, Roach Van, 24
Allen, Roger, 228
Allington, Richard L., 98
All I Really Need to Know I Learned in Kindergarten (Fulghum), 182, 183
All the People 1945–1998 (Hakim), 177
All the Places to Love (MacLachlan), 182
Almost a Hero (Neufeld), 195
alphabetic awareness, 155–156
alphabet picture books, 145
Alvermann, Donna, 112
American Teen Writer Series, 96
Anderson, Laurie Halse, 56, 71, 153
Anderson, Richard C., 45
anecdotal records
    about independent reading, 110
    assessment through, 208–212
Angelou, Maya, 49, 130, 132, 153, 172, 182
Anguished English (Lederer), 153
apathy, 160

approximation, as condition for learning, 27–30
archy and mehitabel (Marquis), 48
Are You Being Served?, 234
Arly (Peck), 106
Arnold, Nick, 46
Around the World in Eighty Days (Whole Story Series), 177
artifacts
    for read-alouds, 52
    for shared reading, 74
Arundel, Honor, 172
assertive readers, 113
assessment, 199–228
    anecdotal records, 208–212
    characteristics of fluent readers, 208
    checklists, 208–212
    collaborative learning explorations, 220–222
    evaluation and, 200, 225–226
    exit slips for, 201
    fairness in, 225–226
    feedback provided by, 199
    formal tests, 212–220
    goals and, 199
    grading and, 225–226
    independent reading and, 101–102
    independent study, 222–224
    individualized tests, 217–220

interviews for, 206–208
inventories for, 206–208
observations, 208–212
performance tasks, 220–224
progress notes, 208–212
purpose of, 200–201
reading portfolios, 224–225
reflective teaching and,
    227–228
sentence completion for,
    204–205
student understanding of,
    228
surveys, 202–204
types of, 201–225
whole-group, 201
of writing samples, 202
*Assessment: Continuous
    Learning* (Bridges), 212
Assessment: Continuous
    Learning form, 288
"At the End of the Rainbow,"
    183–184
Atwell, Nancie, 107, 108
audio books. *See* books on
    tape
authentic experiences, inde-
    pendent reading and,
    98–99
*Authentic Reading
    Assessment: Practice and
    Possibilities* (Valencia,
    Hiebert, and Afflerbach),
    224
author baskets, 121
Avi, 100, 160, 172, 222

background knowledge
    activating, 129–132
    content area reading and,
        128–132
    learning and, 190
bad language, 188–189
Bailey, Ann, 75–76, 107, 158
Baker, Scott, 184, 190
"Ballad of Birmingham"
    (Randall), 48, 134–136
Bamford, Julian, 47, 127
"Band-Aids and Five Dollar
    Bills" (Draper), 160

Barry, David, 46
*Baseball, Snakes, and Summer
    Squash* (Graves), 182
Baum, L. Frank, 1, 229
Becoming a Nation of Readers
    (Anderson), 45
bed-to-bed stories, 182
Been to Yesterdays (Hopkins),
    182
behavior
    of fluent readers, 141
    modeling reading behaviors,
        112–113
    monitoring reading behav-
        iors, 112
    during read-alouds, 51–52
    of struggling readers, 32
Bella's Mystery Deck (Logue),
    50
Belle Prater's Boy (White),
    155, 197
Bensinger, Tara, 137
*Best Practice: New Standards
    for Teaching and
    Learning in America's
    Schools* (Zemelman,
    Daniels, and Hyde), 101
Better Than Life (Pennac),
    100
*Bird by Bird: Some
    Instructions on Writing
    and Life* (Lamott), 178
Bissel, Charles Ben, 21
Bitton-Jackson, Livia, 89
B-K-W-L-Q graphic organizer,
    132, 136–137, 269
Black Poets, The (Randall),
    48, 134
blame, assigning, 22
*Bless the Beasts and the
    Children* (Swartout), 40
block classes, 17
Blue Skin of the Sea
    (Salisbury), 196
Blume, Judy, 160
Bodard, Joni, 103
Bone, Becky, 106
"bookbats," 31
book choice
    book pass for, 103–106

book talks for, 103
computer logs of, 107
demonstrating, 104
diversity of, 106
for guided reading, 92–93,
    95–97
helping students with,
    102–107
inappropriate, 40–41
by lifelong readers, 19
for literature circles, 106
one-line signed reviews for,
    107
random, 156
for read alouds, 49
for shared reading, 67–74,
    68–74
student responsibility for,
    17–19
supporting, 121
text supports and, 156
waiting lists and, 107
book interviews, 156
bookmarks, 110–111
book pass, 103–106
    graphic organizer, 176, 274
    World War II texts, 174, 176
book reviews, 107
books
    access to, 99
    buying, 71
    collecting for classroom
        library, 102–103
    controversial, 160
    criticism of, 173–177
    emotional responses to, 173
    finding comfort in, 172–173
    judgments about, 50
    personal response to, 26–30,
        93, 160, 172–173
    physical characteristics of,
        49
    recording, for shared read-
        ing, 62–63
    for reluctant readers,
        171–172
    sampling, 103–106
    teacher notes about, 71–74
books on tape
    available books, 249–251

for independent reading, 108
for in-school suspension
(ISS) programs, 109
keeping track of, 109
for shared reading, 62–63
booktalks, 103
Boy (Dahl), 182
Boyfriend, The (Stine), 29
Boy Who Counted Stars, The
(Harrison), 154
Brecher, Erwin, 50
Brendtro, Larry, 149
Bridges, Lois, 212
*Bridges and Borders: Diversity
in America*, 134, 237
Brokenleg, Martin, 149
Brooks, Jacqueline Grennon,
144
Brooks, Martin G., 144
Brown Bear, Brown Bear
(Carle), 173
Bruchac, Joseph, 45
Bud, Not Buddy (Curtis), 72
Butson, Ann Marie
Radaskiewicz, 193
Buttered Bones (Draper), 153,
160
Byars, Betsy, 172

Caine, Geoffrey, 34
Caine, Renate, 34
Call of the Wild, The (Whole
Story Series), 177
Cambourne, Brian, 14, 20, 22,
27–28, 30
Car, The (Paulsen), 23
Carle, Eric, 173
"Carole," 137
Carson, Jo, 153
Carter, Candy, 103
Carter, Forrest, 182
*Case of the Mummified Pigs,
The* (Quinlan), 35
Castaway, 218
Catcher in the Rye (Salinger),
26–27
challenging texts
content area, 128
shared reading of, 76–78
textbook reading, 128, 139

Chambers, Aidan, 94, 144, 166
change, in instruction methods
implementing, 5
need for, 2–3
characters
Fleshing Out a Character
graphic organizer,
161–162
Knowing a Character charts,
84
opinions about, 50
Charlip, Remy, 193
Charlotte's Web (White), 43
checklists, assessment through,
208–212
Cheripko, Jan, 182
Chicken Soup for the Soul, 96
Chicks Up Front (Holbrook),
77, 182
choice. *See also* book choice
organizing for, 114–126
reflections on, 121–126
resources for, 121
supporting, 115, 118–121
teacher-directed activities vs.,
114
value of, 114–115
"Choices for Children"
(Kohn), 101
choices for learning
motivation and, 19
by students, 4, 17–19
by teachers, 4
whole-group, 18–19
choices for reading. *See* book
choice
Cinderella literary projects,
221, 222
Cisneros, Sandra, 153, 182
Clark, Andrew, 164, 174
Clark, Lana, 74
class discussions, 180
class expectations, 14–15
classical music, 178
classic literature, 40–41, 171
classroom libraries
building, 102–103
choice and, 115
using, 103–107
value of, 107

classroom speakers, 61
class schedule
extended block, 116
single-period class, 117
transitions, 178
class sets, 121
Clay, Marie, 31
Cleary, Beverly, 35
Cliffs Notes, 76
code breaking
defined, 152
oral and print connections,
153–156
by reluctant readers, 152–160
requirements for, 152
Codell, Esme Raji, 5
collaborative literature explorations, 220–222
collaborative research,
119–121
Columbus Dispatch, 52
Coman, Carolyn, 195
comfort, finding in books,
172–173
Commentary, 42
Compare and Contrast organizer, 174, 175, 273
comparisons
Compare and Contrast, 174,
175, 273
to other works of literature,
49
comprehension. *See also*
meaning making
checking for, during read-
alouds, 57
shared reading and, 61,
63–64
teacher questioning about, 81
computer logs, for book
choices, 107
Concept Attainment graphic
organizer, 197, 280
conferences
Directed Study:
Conference/Self-
Evaluation, 290
independent reading and,
112
writing, 194

connection response questions, 94

Conrad, Pam, 182

Conroy, Pat, 222

consequences graphic organizer, 164–165

constructivist teaching, 144–145

content area reading
assessment of, 211–212
background knowledge and, 128–132
challenges of, 128, 139
owning and transferring learning, 144–248
postreading support, 144–148
prereading support, 128–132
readability and, 141–144
read-alouds, 46
reading management, 138–144
structures supporting, 132–137
textbook reading, 128, 138–144, 139, 176–177, 211–212
text structure and, 138–141

content area writing
mathematics, 145–146
scientific method, 147–148

content literacy, 127–148

Continuous Learning graphic organizer, 212

controversial books, 160

Cooney, Caroline, 106, 172

cooperative lesson planning, 231–232

Corey, Lee, 141, 143

Cormier, Robert, 182

counseling, 165

Craft Lessons (Fletcher and Portalupi), 179, 194

Craig, Eleanor, 23

Crazy Laws (Hyman), 35

Crews: Gang Members Talk to Maria Hinojosa (Hinojosa), 35

Crime and Puzzlement (Treat), 50

critical response questions, 94

critical thinking puzzles, 50, 239

criticism of books, 173–177

Crucible, The (Miller), 172

Crutcher, Chris, 95, 108–109

Cullum, Albert, 189

Cunningham, Patricia M., 98

curriculum planning, 37. *See also* lesson planning

Curtis, Christopher Paul, 72

Cusick, Richie Tankersly, 172

Dahl, Roald, 153, 182, 221–222

Dancing Pink Flamingos (Testa), 196

Daniels, Harvey, 101

Dark Towers series (King), 62

Davey, B., 139, 141

Davies, Robertson, 47

Day, Richard R., 47, 127

Day No Pigs Would Die, A (Peck), 24, 182, 217

"Day of the Hunter, The" (Holmes), 82–87, 95, 263–264

Dayton-Sakari, Mary, 32

Dear Mr. Henshaw (Cleary), 35

"Death by Algebra" (Anderson), 56

Death from Child Abuse . . . and No One Heard (Krupinski and Weikel), 172

Death of a Salesman (Miller), 40–41

Deathwatch (White), 69

decoding, 61

demonstrations, 22–27
of language, 24–26
of learning, student work as, 26–27
of literacy, 22–24
by students, 26–27
by teachers, 22–26

"Destination: Tule Lake, Relocation Center, May 20, 1942" (Mitsui), 168

details, in writing, 181

Developing a Set for Literacy, 170–171

Developing Life-Long Readers (Mooney), 170

dialogue, in read-alouds, 54–55

Dillard, Annie, 182

Directed Study: Conferences/Self-Evaluation, 290

Disgusting Digestion (Arnold), 46

Dispezio, Michael A., 50

diversity in reading, 9–30

Dog Ate My Homework, The (Holbrook), 56

D- Poems of Jeremy Bloom, The (Korman and Korman), 153, 187

Draper, Sharon, 153, 160

Drive-By (Ewing), 33

Duane, Diane, 123

Duckworth, Eleanor, 3, 9, 148

Duncan, Lois, 106, 154, 172, 187

Echols, Mike, 191

editing, 194

Educating Esme: Diary of a Teacher's First Year (Codell), 5

educational programs, 231

Education of Little Tree, The (Carter), 182

Ehrlich, Amy, 182

Eisner, Elliot, 228

Elephant Tree, The (Luger), 218

emergent readers, 170

Emerson, Ralph Waldo, 22, 137

emotional responses, 173. *See also* personal response to literature

End-of-Week Check-In, 213, 287

engagement
importance of, 30
reluctant readers and, 34

English as a Second Language (ESL), 22

Entwistle, Judy, 112

environments for reading, 9–30

  active learning and, 9–13

  approximation, use, and response, 27–30

  conditions inviting learning, 13–30

  demonstrations, 22–27

  expectation, 14–17

  immersion, 20–22

  responsibility, 17–19

  risk taking and, 28–29

essays, patterned writing in, 193–194

"Ethan Unbound," 222

evaluation, 200. *See also* assessment

Ewing, Lynne, 33

examinations. *See also* tests

  on independent reading, 217–220

  writing prompts for independent reading on, 106–107

exit slips, 201

expectations, 14–17

extended block literacy schedule, 116

extended writer's craft lessons, 194–198

Extensive Reading in the Second Language Classroom (Day and Bamford), 47, 127

Eyeful of Mysteries, An (Logue), 50

Face on the Milk Carton, The (Cooney), 106, 172

failure

  academic, 38–39

  control of, 4

FAIR: Fairness & Accuracy in Reporting, 96

fairy tales, 221–222

Faithful Elephants (Tsuchiya), 46

Fall Survey, Reading/Writing form, 281–282

F.A.T. City: Frustration, Anxiety and Tension— What It Feels Like to Be Learning Disabled (Lavoie), 226

Fenner, Carol, 73

fiction

  effective leads in, 195–198

  personal response to, 160

  for reluctant readers, 171–172

figurative language, 155

five-paragraph essays, 193

fix-up strategies, 34

Fleischman, Paul, 35, 153

Fleshing Out a Character graphic organizer, 161–162, 270

Fletcher, Ralph, 131, 153, 160, 179, 182, 194

fluency

  creating, 63

  decoding and, 61

  shared reading and, 61–62, 63–68

fluent readers

  characteristics of, 63, 208

  monitoring behaviors of, 141

  questioning by, 34

  read alouds and, 47

focus, in read-alouds, 52

forms, 265–290. *See also* graphic organizers

  Assessment: Continuous Learning, 288

  B-K-W-L-Q, 269

  Book Pass, 176, 274

  Compare and Contrast, 174, 175, 273

  Concept Attainment, 197, 280

  Continuous Learning, 212

  Directed Study: Conference/Self- Evaluation, 290

  End-of-Week Check-In, 213, 287

Fall Survey, Reading and Writing, 281–282

  Fleshing Out a Character, 161–162, 270

  Guiding Readers Through Text, 73–74

  Ideas for Writing, 180, 275

  Independent Reading Log, 267

  Language Choices, 189, 278

  Language Collection, 185, 187–188, 277

  Language Register, 189–190, 279

  Looking at Our Options, 164–165, 271

  Monitoring Our Reading Process, 212, 214, 289

  Multiple Sources, Multiple Perspectives, 169, 272

  Observation Checklists, 209–211, 285–286

  Peeling the Layers, 162, 163

  Reading and Writing from the Inside Out, 198

  Sentence Completions, 204–205, 283–284

  Status-of-the-Class, 110, 111

  Things We Can Read From, A-Z, 266

  Word Questioning, 186, 276

  Writing to Learn, 268

Fortunately (Charlip), 193

"Fortunately (NOT)", 193

Fountas, Irene C., 80

Four Little Girls, 136–137

Frankenstein (Whole Story Series), 177

Freak the Mighty (Philbrick), 96, 162

Freebody, P., 151

Frick, Barbara, 21

Fritz, Jean, 129, 182

Fry readability graphs, 142–144

Fulghum, Robert, 182, 183

futility, sense of, 39

Gallo, Donald R., 72

Gardiner, John R., 33

genre boxes, 121
"Georgie," 191–192
Geranium on the Window Sill Just Died, but Teacher You Went Right On, The (Cullum), 189
Giard, Mary, 18, 19, 49–50, 178
Gibson, Gail, 6
Giovanni, Nikki, 182
GIRFT (get it right the first time), 28
Giver, The (Lowry), 106
Glass Menagerie, The (Williams), 171
global expectations, 14–15
goals
  in education, 199
  establishing, 16
  grading and, 17
  of guided reading, 80
  for lifelong readers, 15
  for literacy, 170–171
  for shared reading, 118
Go Ask Alice (Sparks), 212
Going Solo (Dahl), 182
Golding, William, 62
Gonzalez, Kyle, 5, 109, 151, 152, 201
Goodbye, Mr. Chips (Hilton), 171
Goodlad, John, 98
Gordon, A. C., 50
Goudvis, Anne, 231
grade-level reading scores, 141–142
grading, 200
  fairness in, 225–226
  goals and, 17
grammar Web sites, 246–247
graphic organizers. *See also* forms
  for making predictions, 162–163
  for meaning making, 161–165
  for problem-solving, 162–165
Graves, Donald, 57, 181–184, 182

Greenfield, Eloise, 153
groups
  for guided reading, 92
  whole-group assessment, 201
  whole-group learning, 18–19
  whole-group shared reading, 59–60
growing up poetry collections, 258–259
guided reading, 80–97
  active reading during, 89
  cutting into text strips, 83
  finding texts for, 92–93, 95–97
  finding time for, 92
  goals of, 80
  grouping students for, 92
  guiding readers through text *vs.*, 81–82
  lessons, 82–88, 92–93, 95
  postreading processing, 88
  predictions in, 82–83, 87, 88
  purposes of, 81, 95
  questioning in, 88–89, 93–94
  shared reading *vs.*, 80–81, 89
  student role, 88–89
  teacher role, 89–92, 101
  time for, 92
  value of, 80
Guided Reading: Good First Teaching for All Children (Fountas and Pinnell), 80
guided writing, 194–198
guiding readers through text, 81–82
  forms, 73–74

Hakim, Joy, 176
Halliday, M.A.K., 189
hamburger paragraph essays, 193
Hamilton, Jane, 196
Hammond, D., 50
"Hangman, The" (Ogden), 95
Harden, Mike, 52
Harrison, David, 153–154
Harvey, Stephanie, 231

Hatchet (Paulsen), 33, 35, 106, 172, 218
Having of Wonderful Ideas, The (Duckworth), 148
Hawthorne, Nathaniel, 39
Hayden, Torey, 222
Head, Ann, 40
Heath Earth Science (Spaulding), 157
Heidi (Whole Story Series), 177
"Hells' Bells," 218–219
helplessness
  learned, 4, 39
  reading success and, 39
Hemingway, Ernest, 180
Hesse, Karen, 74, 153
Hewitt Trussville Middle School, Alabama, 137
"Hey Jew Girl, Jew Girl" (Bitton-Jackson), 89, 91
Hiebert, Elfrieda H., 224
Hilton, James, 171
Hinojosa, Maria, 35
Hinton, S. E., 33, 217, 218
History of a Free People (McCutchen), 134
History of US, A series (Hakim), 176–177
Hobbs, Will, 69
Hoffman, Alice, 39
Holbrook, Sara, 56, 77, 153, 182, 235
"Holding Center, Tanforan Race Track, Spring 1942" (Mitsui), 168
Holes (Sachar), 33, 69, 162
Holmes, Edward M., 82, 263
Holt, John, 230
Homesick (Fritz), 129, 182
Home University Bookshelf: Famous Stories and Verses, 43
hope, sense of, 39
Hopkins, Lee Bennett, 182
Horrible History/ Geography/Science series (Scholastic), 96
House on Mango Street, The (Cisneros), 153, 182

How Did I Get to Be 40 and Other Atrocities (Viorst), 24

How Difficult Can This Be? The F.A.T. City Workshop (Lavoie), 60–61

Huck, Charlotte, 79

Hughes, Langston, 89

humor poetry collections, 256–257

Hunt, Irene, 12–13, 28, 165, 172, 181, 191

Hyde, Arthur, 101

Hyman, Dick, 35

I Am Wings (Fletcher), 153, 160, 182

I Can't Accept Not Trying (Jordan), 182

"I Can't" readers, 32–33

Ideas for Teaching English in the Junior High and Middle School (Carter and Rashkis), 103

Ideas for Writing form, 180, 275

"I Don't Care" readers, 36–37

"I Don't Know How" readers, 33–35

"I'd Rather" readers, 35–36

I Have Words to Spend (Cormier), 182

I Know My First Name Is Steven (Echols), 191, 192

I Know What You Did Last Summer (Duncan), 106, 172

I Know Why the Caged Bird Sings (Angelou), 49, 182

ILE. *See* independent literacy explorations (ILE)

illustrated classics poetry collections, 257–258

images, helping students create, 158

Imitate the Tiger (Cheripko), 182

immersion, as condition for learning, 20–22

Immokalee High School (Immokalee, Florida), 22, 212

independent learning
encouraging, 18
student interest in, 177
value of, 123

independent literacy explorations (ILE), 17
assessment during, 119
intervention during, 112
introducing, 118–119
observation during, 209
possibilities for, 120
providing options for, 119–121
research during, 119–121
scheduling, 116–117

independent reading, 98–113
books on tape for, 108–109
building into curriculum, 99
choice and, 115–116
classroom libraries and, 102–107
control and, 100–101
facilitating, 101–109
issues, 108
modeling, 112–113
record keeping for, 109–111
rereading during, 99
scheduling, 116–118
shared reading and, 62–63
as sustained silent reading, 111–112
teacher role in, 101
test question on, 217–220
value of, 98–100, 113
writing prompts for, 106–107

Independent Reading Log form, 267

independent social studies exploration (ISSE), 123

independent study, 122–124, 222–224
grading, 226

I Never Said I Wasn't Difficult (Holbrook), 153

I Never Saw Another Butterfly (Volavkova), 187

inference, as meaning making, 160–165

inferential level, 75

informational texts
encouraging sustained reading with, 35–36
readability of, 141–144
text structure of, 138–141

in-school suspension (ISS) programs
audio books for, 109
language collection in, 188–189

In Search of Understanding: The Case for Constructivist Classrooms (Brooks and Brooks), 144

Insectasides (Paulos), 187–188

"Inside the Classroom" (Butson), 193

interest
demonstrating through read alouds, 22–24
in independent learning, 177
lack of, 99, 109, 160
reading success and, 38–39

International Association for the Evaluation of Educational Achievement, 99

International Reading Association, 232
Commission on Adolescent Literacy, 234

interviews
for assessment, 206–208
book, 156

In the Middle (Atwell), 107

inventories, for assessment, 206–208

"Invisible" (Medina), 151

Ironman (Crutcher), 108–109

I-Search, 123–124

Island, The (Paulsen), 217–218

Island of the Blue Dolphins (O'Dell), 106

It Happened to Nancy (Sparks), 160

It's Never Too Late (Allen), 40

"I've Got Gloria" (Kerr), 158
"I Won't Learn from You"
    (Kohl), 14, 17–18, 37

Janeczko, Paul, 153
Jay's Journal (Sparks), 100,
    123, 160, 218
Jennings, Paul, 64, 66, 67
Jessup, Harper, 31
Jip, His Story (Paterson),
    44–45, 75
Jitterbug Perfume (Robbins),
    199
Jobe, Ron, 32
Jordan, Michael, 182
Journal of Reading, 139
Joynt, Julie, 145
Jungle Book, The (Whole
    Story Series), 177
Juster, Norton, 96, 153, 231
"Justin and Frank" (Fletcher),
    160

Kaiser, Lynnette, 161–162,
    174
Kameenui, Edward, 184, 190
Kerr, M. E., 158
Kidnapped (Stevenson), 160
kid-watching, 112
Killing Mr. Griffin (Duncan),
    172, 187
King, Stephen, 62
King of the Dragons, The
    (Fenner), 73
Knowing a Character charts,
    84
Kohl, Herbert, 14, 17, 37
Kohn, Alfie, 101, 114
Korman, Bernice, 153, 187
Korman, Gordon, 55, 153,
    172, 187
Krupinski, Eve, 172
K-W-L (Know, What to Know,
    Learned), 132

Lamott, Anne, 178
Lang, Holly, 222
Langer, Judith A., 170
language
    bad, collecting, 188–189

code breaking and, 152
demonstrations of, 24–26
immersion in, 20–22
literal *vs.* figurative, 155
local, 155
oral, 153–156
statements about, 49
variation in, 189–190
Language Choices chart, 189,
    278
language collection, 185–190
    in-school suspension (ISS)
        programs, 188–189
    in shared reading, 186–188
Language Collection graphic
    organizer, 187–188, 277
Language Collection section,
    academic journals, 152,
    187
language experience activities
    (LEA), 24–26, 179
language patterns
    anticipating, 154–155
    fill-in-the-blanks activities,
        154–155
    predictable, reinforcing,
        153–154
language register, 189–190
Language Register chart,
    189–190, 279
Lasky, Kathryn, 31
"Last Spin, The," 174
Late Great Me, The
    (Scoppettone), 209
Lateral Logic Puzzles
    (Brecher), 50
lateral thinking books, 50, 239
Lateral Thinking Puzzlers
    (Sloan), 50
Lavoie, Richard, 60–61, 226
LEA. *See* language experience
    activities (LEA)
leads
    class definition of, 197
    effective, 195–198
    evaluating, 197–198
    models of, 195–197
learned helplessness, 4, 39
learning
    active, 9–13, 201

assessment of, 199
background knowledge and,
    190
conditions inviting, 13–30
demonstrations of, 26–27
as mimetic activity, 144
read alouds and, 47–48
resistance to, 14
shared responsibility for, 37
student responsibility for,
    18–19
support for, 9
learning to read
    read alouds and, 47–48
    shared reading and, 62
Learning to Read (Meek), 19
Lederer, Richard, 153
Lee, Joanna, 112
Lee, Spike, 136
legends, 222
Leighton, Sandra, 6
lesson planning
    assessment and, 201
    cooperative, 231–232
    creative, 231
    Web sites, 242–243
Lester, T., 50
letter people, 33
*Letters I Never Wrote,
    Conversations I Never
    Had* (Bissel), 21
Levy, Steven, 123
lifelong readers
    defined, 15
    expectations and, 14–15
    independent reading and, 112
    reading choices by, 19
life stories writing assignment,
    181–184
literacy
    demonstrations of, 22–24
    goals, 170–171
    principles supporting,
        234–235
Literacy Workshop, 201
literal language, 155
literal level, 75, 81
literary elements, 158–160
literature
    anthologies, 96, 255–256

comparisons, 49
poetry collections, 255–256
as source of writer's craft lessons, 194
Web sites, 245
literature circles, 106
Little Engine That Could, The (Piper), 43
Little Women (Whole Story Series), 177
local language, 155
logs
  computer, for book choice, 107
  Independent Reading, 267
  writing resource, 180
Logue, Mary, 50
Long Beach Prep Academy, California, 45, 89, 107
Longest Weekend, The (Arundel), 172
"Long Wait for Justice," 92
Looking at Our Options graphic organizer, 164–165, 271
Lord of the Flies (Golding), 62
Lottery Rose, The (Hunt), 12–13, 28–29, 165, 172, 181, 191
Lovey (MacCracken), 12, 171, 172
Lowry, Lois, 106
Luka (Vega), 191
Luke, A., 151

Macaulay, David, 35
MacCracken, Mary, 12, 171, 172, 222
MacHale, Des, 50
MacLachlan, Patricia, 182
magazine articles
  for guided reading, 96
  independent reading and, 111–112
Magner, Heather, 45
Maine Educational Assessment (MEA), 213–215
Maine Speaks, 82

Making Connections (Caine and Caine), 34
Mama Makes Up Her Mind (White), 182
Mann, Horace, 149
Many, Paul, 196
Map of the World, A (Hamilton), 196
Marquis, Don, 48
Marsden, John, 153, 196
Mary Jane Harper Cried Last Night (Lee), 112–113
mathematics
  literature supporting, 239–240
  poetry collections, 258
  student-written text, 145–146
Maze, The (Hobbs), 69
Mazer, Harry, 33
McLeran, Alice, 153
McTeague, Frank, 166
Meaning Makers, The (Wells), 58
meaning making, 160–170. *See also* comprehension
  factors affecting, 47
  graphic organizers for, 161–165
  guided reading and, 81
  personal response and, 160
  by reluctant readers, 160–170
  teacher responsibility for, 231
  through inference, 160–165
  through questioning, 165–170
Medearis, Angela, 153
media, variety in, 24
media center, 102
media literacy Web sites, 243–244
Medina, Jane, 151
Meek, Margaret, 19
Meltzer, Milton, 128
Memoirs of a Bookbat (Lasky), 31
memories, writing about, 181–184

mental models, 46–47
Merlyn's Pen, 237
metacognitive level, 75
metacognitive response questions, 94
Meyer, Carolyn, 196
micro-story collections, 96
midbook tests, 215
"Midnight Snack" (Duane), 123
Miller, Arthur, 40, 172
MindWare, 237
modeling
  leads, 195–197
  life stories writing assignment, 181–184
  mental, 46–47
  reading behaviors, 112–113
  strategic reading, 74–76
monitoring
  behaviors of fluent readers, 141
  Monitoring Our Reading Process, 212, 214, 289
  reading, reluctant readers and, 34
  reading behaviors, 112
Monitoring Our Reading Process graphic organizer, 212, 214, 289
Mooney, Margaret, 42, 45, 48, 81, 88, 101, 170
Moon Is Broken, The (Craig), 23
Moran, John, 6
More Solv-a-Crime (Gordon), 50
"Most Dangerous Game, The" (Connell), 83
Motel of Mysteries (Macaulay), 35
"Motivate," 19
motivation
  opinions about, 50
  problems, 31–32
  reading success and, 38–39
  self-motivation, 31
  student choice and, 19
"Mouthful, A" (Jennings), 64–66

Mr. and Mrs. Bo Jo Jones (Head), 40
multiple-choice questions, 215
Multiple Sources, Multiple Perspectives graphic organizer, 169, 272
music
    as classroom transition signal, 178
    poetry collections, 258
My Black Me (Adoff), 153
My Daniel (Conrad), 182
My Freedom Trip: A Child's Escape from North Korea (Park and Park), 46
My Name Is Jorge on Both Sides of the River (Medina), 151
mysteries, 50
Mysteries of Animal Intelligence (Steiger and Steiger), 35

"Naked" (Holbrook), 77–78
National Council of Teachers of English, 232
Nehring, James, 124, 232
Neill, A. S., 17
Neilson, Lorri, 235
Neufeld, John, 195
Newkirk, Thomas, 227
Newman, F. M., 129
newspaper articles
    for guided reading, 96
    independent reading and, 111–112
Newsweek, 193
New Way Things Work, The (Macaulay), 35
Night on Neighborhood Street (Greenfield), 153
"No Losers, No Weepers" (Angelou), 130, 172
nonfiction, 121
    encouraging sustained reading with, 35
    personal response to, 160
    for reluctant readers, 171–172
nonword responses, 49

notebooks, 71–74
Notes to Myself (Prather), 24
Nothing but the Truth (Avi), 100, 160, 172, 222
not-learning, 14, 37
novels
    for read alouds, 49
    for shared reading, 49, 71–73
    teacher notes about, 71–73

Oak Ridge High School, Orlando, 141
observation
    assessment through, 208–212
    kid-watching, 112
Observational Checklist form, 209–211, 285–286
O'Dell, Scott, 106
Of Mice and Men (Steinbeck), 153, 171, 172, 215
Ogden, Maurice, 95
Ohanian, Susan, 9, 12
Old Man and the Sea, The (Hemingway), 180
online bookstores, 71
"On the Bridge" (Straser), 187
open-ended questions, 215
oral language
    pleasure of, 153
    print connections, 153–156
Orange County literacy project, 5
"O Romeo, O, Like Wow" (Harden), 52–54, 60–61
Out of the Dust (Hesse), 74, 153
Outsiders, The (Hinton), 33

Park, Frances, 46
Park, Ginger, 46
Paterson, Katherine, 44, 75, 160
patterned writing, 190–194
    essays, 193–194
    picture books, 193
    song lyrics, 191–193
Paulos, Martha, 187

Paulsen, Gary, 21, 23, 33, 35, 48, 106, 172, 182, 187, 217–218, 218
Peck, Richard, 95, 158–159, 187, 198
Peck, Robert Newton, 24, 106, 182
Peeling the Layers graphic organizer, 162, 163
Penguin Putnam, 177
Pennac, Daniel, 100
performance tasks, assessment through, 220–224
Perplexing Lateral Thinking Puzzles (Sloan and MacHale), 50
Perry, Jill, 145
personal connections, in content area reading, 140–141
personal history writing assignment, 181–184
personal response to literature
    apathetic, 160
    comfort and support, 172–173
    generating, 26–27
    meaning making through, 160
    questions, 93, 160
    risk-taking and, 28–30
    tape recorded, 29–30
    written, 28–29
Phantom Tollbooth (Juster), 96, 153, 231
Philbrick, Rodman, 96, 162
picture books, patterned writing in, 192
Pike, Christopher, 106, 143
Pinnell, Gay Su, 80
Piper, Connie, 6
Piper, Watty, 43
Place Called School, A (Goodlad), 98
Places I Never meant to Be: Original Stories by Censored Writers (Blume), 160
Platt, Richard, 35
Play Production class, 26

plays, student-written, 26
plotline, 50
Poems (Angelou), 153
Poems That Sing to You
    (Strickland), 153
poetry
    collections, 255–262
    for guided reading, 92, 96
    patterned, 191–194
    for questions game, 166–169
    as response to literature, 218
    for shared reading, 73
    song lyrics, 191–193
Portalupi, JoAnn, 179, 194
portfolios, assessment
    through, 224
Postman, Neil, 7, 231
postreading support, 144–148
Prather, Hugh, 24
*Prayer for the Twenty-First
    Century* (Marsden), 153
predictions
    graphic organizers for,
        162–163
    in guided reading, 82–83,
        87, 88
prepared questions, 16
prereading, 128–132
"Priscilla and the Wimps"
    (Peck), 95, 158–159, 187
problem-solving
    choosing the right problem,
        228
    examining options for,
        162–165
product-oriented questions, 81
progress notes, assessment
    through, 208–212
projects, assessment through,
    220–224
punctuation, 194
Punished by Rewards (Kohl),
    37, 114
puzzle books, 50

questions
    for assessment, 205–206
    background knowledge and,
        169–170
    complex, 94

connection response, 94
critical response, 94
determining comprehension
    with, 81
on formal tests, 215–220
for guided reading, 88–89,
    93–94
individualized, 217–220
learning to ask, 165–170
meaning making through,
    165–170
metacognitive response, 94
multiple-choice, 215
open-ended, 215
personal response, 93
as personal response, 160
prepared, *vs.* self-question-
    ing, 16
product-oriented, 81
reluctant readers and, 34
scaffolding, 166
structures supporting,
    132–137
student responsibility for
    finding answers to, 18
by students, 121–123
surface-features-of-text
    response, 94
for teachers, 235
questions game, 166–169
Quinlan, Susan E., 35

*Rajah' Rice, The: A
    Mathematical Folktale
    from India* (Barry), 46
Randall, Dudley, 48, 134
Ransom (Duncan), 154–155,
    172
Rashkis, Zora M., 103
Raskin, Ellen, 35
Rawls, Wilson, 69
readability, 141–144
Read-Aloud Handbook, The
    (Trelease), 47
read alouds
    active listening responses,
        49–50
    checking for understanding
        in, 57
    content area, 46

daily, 47–48
demonstrating interest
    through, 22–24
dialogue in, 54–55
environment for, 51–52
finding text for, 52–56
ideas expressed in, 180
learning to read and, 47–48
length of, 117
mental models and, 46–47
as non-teaching, 49
preparing students for, 51–52
reading to learn and, 47–48
as risk-free time, 45–46, 57
student roles in, 49–50
teacher preparation for, 51
teacher role in, 101
value of, 43–57
young children and, 43–44
"Reader's Bill of Rights," 100
Reader's Digest, 52
readers' theater, 145
reading. *See also* content area
    reading; environments for
    reading; guided reading;
    independent reading;
    shared reading; textbook
    reading
active, 34, 89
changing habits, 99
demonstrating interest in,
    22–24
disinterest in, 99, 109, 160
interest in, 38–39
modeling behaviors, 112–113
monitoring behaviors, 112
obstacles to enjoyment, 15
obstacles to success, 31–32,
    37–42, 232–233
principles supporting suc-
    cess, 234–235
recording books for, 62–63
redefining success, 42
reluctant reader types,
    32–37
self-motivated readers, 31
time for, 71
writing improvement and,
    117
written responses to, 28–29

Reading and Writing From the Inside Out, 198
reading between the lines, 84, 88, 160–165
reading choices. *See* book choice
reading diversity, 20
reading interviews, 206–208
reading management, 138–144
  readability and, 141–144
  text structure and, 138–141
reading mood, 104
reading portfolios, 224–225
reading preferences
  independent reading and, 112
  student survey of, 69
reading prompts, 179
Reading Road to Writing, 130
Reading To, With, and By Children (Mooney), 81
reading to learn
  read alouds and, 47–48
  shared reading and, 62
Read magazine, 92, 96, 119, 137, 237–238
Reclaiming Youth at Risk (Brendtro, Brokenleg, and Van Brokern), 149
Recorded Books, Inc., 63, 237–238, 249
recordkeeping, for independent reading, 109–111
reference books, 121
reflection, 212
reflective teaching, 227–228
Relatives Came, The (Rylant), 182
reluctant readers, 149–177.
  See also struggling readers
  attitudes of, 149–150
  books for, 171–172
  books on tape for, 109
  challenges of, 149–151
  as code breakers, 152–160
  communicating learning by, 34
  "I Can't" readers, 32–33
  "I Don't Care" readers, 36–37

"I Don't Know How" readers, 33–35
"I'd Rather" readers, 35–36
  as independent readers, 177
  interventions for, 151–177
  as meaning makers, 160–170
  monitoring by, 34
  negative experiences of, 150
  questioning by, 34
  supported time with text for, 170–171
  as text critics, 173–177
  as text users, 170–173
  types of, 31–37
Reluctant Readers (Jobe and Dayton-Sakari), 32
repeated reading, of shared reading, 67, 78
rereading, during independent reading, 99
research
  collaborative literature explorations, 220–222
  during independent literacy exploration, 119–121
  independent social studies exploration (ISSE), 123
  independent study, 122–124, 222–224, 226
  I-Search, 123–124
  resources, 39–41
responsibility for learning
  as condition for learning, 17–19
  shared, 37, 201
revision, 25–26
Revolting Rhymes (Dahl), 153, 221–222
Rief, Linda, 108
risk taking
  environments valuing, 28–29
  immersion in language and, 21–22
  read alouds and, 45–46, 57
rites of passage poetry collections, 258–259
Robbins, Tim, 199
Roberts, Nancy, 59
Robertson, Carole, 137

Romeo and Juliet, 52–54, 141
Roosevelt Middle School, San Diego, 46
round-robin reading
  problems with, 15–16
  reading enjoyment and, 15–16
  shared reading vs., 60–62
Routman, Regie, 43
Roxaboxen (McLerran), 153
RPMs (recall, predict, move on), 68, 138
rubrics, 228
Rumblefish (Hinton), 217
Runaways, The (Thomas), 196
Runner, The (Voigt), 123
Rylant, Cynthia, 182

Sachar, Louis, 33, 69, 162
Sacred Cows and Other Edibles (Giovanni), 182
Salinger, J. D., 26
Salisbury, Graham, 196
scaffolding
  components of, 179
  content area reading and, 128
  in shared writing, 179
Scales, J., 50
school-related poetry collections, 259–260
Schools We Have, the Schools We Want, The (Nehring), 232
science
  literature supporting, 240
  poetry collections, 260–261
  student-written text on scientific method, 147–148
science fiction/fantasy, 35
Scieszka, Jon, 35, 46
Scope, 119
Scoppettone, Sandra, 209
scoring guides, 228
Secrete Diary of Adrian Mole, Aged 13 3/4, The (Townsend), 182
Seeking Diversity (Rief), 108
self-evaluation, 226

self-motivation, 31
self-reflection, 212
sentence completion
  for assessment, 204–205
  forms, 283–284
  on tests, 215
sentence length, 142
sentence starters, 215
Sentries (Paulsen), 182
shared reading, 58–79, 179
  defined, 58
  fluency and, 61–62, 63–68
  goals for, 118
  guided reading *vs.*, 80–81,
    89
  independent reading and,
    62–63
  language collection in,
    185–186
  overcoming text challenges
    with, 76–78
  pacing of, 67–68
  purposes of, 60
  repeated, 67
  round-robin reading *vs.*,
    60–62
  scheduling, 116–118
  strategies and, 74–76
  teacher role in, 101
  texts for, 66–67, 68–74
  value of, 59, 79
  whole-group, 59–60
  word study in, 186–187
shared responsibility for learning, 37, 201
shared writing, 179–194
  creating word banks,
    184–190
  patterned, 190–194
  providing examples of effec-
    tive writing, 180–184
  scheduling, 116–118
short-answer questions,
  205–206
short stories, 96
  collections, 252–254
  encouraging sustained read-
    ing with, 35
  readers' theater presentation
    of, 145

for shared reading, 69
"show me" portfolios, 224
"show me" prompts,
  224–225
Sign of the Beaver (Speare),
  220
Simmons, Deborah C., 184,
  190
Simmons, Steven, 43
single-period class literacy
  schedule, 117
*Sixth Grade Nickname Game,
  The* (Korman), 55
skimming, 139–140
*Skin Deep and Other Teenage
  Reflections* (Medearis),
  153
Skinner, David, 196
Sloane, Paul, 50
Smith, Frank, 129
Smith, Glenna, 6
social issues poetry collections,
  261
social studies
  literature supporting, 241
  poetry collections, 261
Solv-a-Crime (Gordon), 50
So Much to Tell You
  (Marsden), 218
song lyrics, 191–193
Soto, Gary, 182
sounding out, 33
Spanish/English poetry collec-
  tions, 262
Sparks, Beatrice, 100, 123,
  160, 212
Speak (Anderson), 56, 71–72,
  153
Speare, Elizabeth George, 220
spelling
  collaborative approach to,
    232
  helping students with, 194
  Web sites, 247–248
*Spelling Inquiry: How One
  Elementary School
  Caught the Mnemonic
  Plague* (Chandler), 232
Spelling section, academic
  journals, 152

Spinelli, Jerry, 69, 96, 106,
  153, 182, 186
St. Cloud High School, 222
Stand and Deliver (Clark),
  164, 174
standardized testing
  state tests, 193–194, 199
  strategies for, 42
Stardust Hotel (Janeczko),
  153
Starting from Scratch: One
  Classroom Builds Its Own
  Curriculum (Levy), 123
state-mandated tests
  inadequacy of, 199
  of writing, 193–194
status-of-the-class forms, 110,
  111
Staying Fat for Sarah Brynes
  (Crutcher), 95
Steiger, Brad, 35
Steiger, Sherry Hansen, 35
Steinbeck, John, 153, 171,
  172
Stephen Biesty's Incredible
  Cross Sections (Platt), 35
"Steven," 192–192
Stevenson, Kelly, 212
Stevenson, Robert Louis, 160
Stine, R. L., 106, 108
Stone Fox (Gardiner), 33, 217
Stonewall Jackson Middle
  School, Orlando, Florida,
  161–162
stories i ain't told nobody yet
  (Carson), 153
storyboards, 158–159
Story of the Lonely X, The,
  146
Strasser, Todd, 187
strategic reading, 74–76
strategies
  fix-up, 34
  guidelines for lessons, 75
  for standardized tests, 42
  teaching, 2–3, 5, 7–8
strategies banner, 152
Strategies That Work (Harvey
  and Goudvis), 231
Strickland, Michael, 153

struggling readers. *See also*
    reluctant readers
  behavioral indicators, 32
  books on tape for, 109
  fix-up strategies and, 34
  guided reading and, 89
  read alouds and, 47
student academic journals. *See*
    academic journals
students
  behavior during read-alouds,
    51–52
  demonstrations of learning
    by, 26–27
  guided reading role, 88–89
  surveys of, 202–204
student-written text
  alphabet picture books, 145
  mathematics, 145–146
  scientific method, 147–148
study guides
  for *Death of a Salesman*,
    40
  reading enjoyment and, 16
substitute teachers, 19
Summer Life, A (Soto), 182
Summer of the Swans, The
    (Byars), 172
"Sunday School Bombing,
    The," 135
surface-features-of-text
    response questions, 94
surveys
  for assessment, 202–204
  on impediments to reading
    success, 232–233
  of student reading prefer-
    ences, 69
survival theme books, 106
sustained silent reading
  benefits of, 112
  encouraging, 35–36
  independent reading as,
    111–112
  value of, 116
Swartout, Glendon, 40
synonyms, 186

TAG (textbook activity guide),
    139–141

"Take the Old Man Home,"
    180–181
tall tales, 222
tangled readers, 31, 149–177.
    See also reluctant readers;
    struggling readers
teacher-directed activities,
    114
teachers, 229–235
  effective, characteristics of,
    6–7
  guided reading role, 89–92
  modeling reading behaviors
    by, 112–113
  questions for, 235
  read-aloud preparation, 51
  reading success and,
    234–235
  recording notes about
    books, 71–74
  resources of, 229–235
Teacher's Pet (Cusick), 106,
    172
Teacher to Teacher
    (Duckworth), 3
*Teaching as a Subversive
    Activity* (Postman and
    Weingartner), 7, 231
teaching journals, 110, 160
teaching strategies
  change needed in, 2–3, 5
  effective, 7–8
Teaching Tolerance, 96,
    237–238
technology literacy Web sites,
    243–244
TeenInk (The 21st Century),
    96, 237–238
*Tell Me: Children, Reading,
    and Talk* (Chambers), 94,
    166
Testa, Maria, 196
tests. *See also* examinations
  formal, 212–220
  grades, 226
  individualized, 217–220
  multiple-choice questions on,
    215
  open-ended questions on,
    215

state-mandated, 193–194,
    199
  strategies, 42
Test Your Lateral Thinking IQ
    (Sloan), 50
text asides, 152
textbook activity guide (TAG),
    139–141
textbook reading
  assessment of, 211–212
  challenges of, 128, 139
  readability, 141–144
  skimming, 139–140
  social studies, 176–177
  supplementing, 128
  text structure and, 138–141
text conventions, 152
text criticism, 173–177
text language, 152
text patterns, 152
text sets, 121, 175
text strips, for guided reading,
    83
text structure, 138–141
text subtleties, 152
text supports, 140
  code breaking and, 152
  learning to use, 156–160
text-to-self connections, 118,
    140–141, 170
text-to-text connections, 118,
    170, 215
text-to-world connections,
    118, 170
text using
  creating eager readers with,
    171–172
  finding comfort in books,
    172–173
  by reluctant readers,
    170–173
  supported time with text,
    170–171
"Thank You, M'am"
    (Hughes), 89, 90
There's Room for Me Here
    (Allen and Gonzalez), 5,
    109, 151
These Are the Rules (Many),
    196

Things I Know How to Do section, in academic journals, 35, 152

Things I'm Learning How to Do section, in academic journals, 35, 152

Things We Can Read From, A-Z form, 266

Things We Do Together section, in academic journals, 152

Thomas, Ruth, 196

"three before me" rule, 18

Time Capsule (Gallo), 72–73

Time Machine: The American History Magazine for Kids, 96, 237–238

Time magazine, 134

Time Warp Trio (Scieszka), 35

Titusville High School, 145

To Hell with Dying (Walker), 182

Tomorrow, When the War Began (Marsden), 196

Townsend, Sue, 182

trade books, 141–144

Treasure Island (Whole Story Series), 177

Treat, Lawrence, 50

Trelease, Jim, 47

"Trouble with My House, The" (Harrison), 154

True Story of the Three Little Pigs, The (Scieszka), 46

Tsuchiya, Yukio, 46

"Tuning" (Paulsen), 21, 48

tuning points, 13–14

Two of Them, The (Aliki), 182

Uncovered! Weird, Weird Stories (Jennings), 64–66, 67

unique words, mimicking, 50

Valencia, Sheila W., 224

Van Bockern, Steve, 149

Vega, Suzanne, 191, 192

Very Hungry Caterpillar, The (Carle), 173

Viorst, Judith, 24, 193

vocabulary, 2
building with word banks, 184–190
readability and, 142, 143
Web sites, 247–248

"Vocabulary" (Korman and Korman), 187

Voice from the Attic, A (Davies), 47

Voigt, Cynthia, 123

Voorhees, Don, 35

Walker, Alice, 182

Water Is Wide, The (Conroy), 222

Watsons Go to Birmingham— 1963 (Curtis), 72, 132, 134, 137

Web sites, 232, 242–248
children's and adolescent literature, 245
grammar and writing, 246–247
lesson plans, 242–243
media and technology literacy, 243–244
spelling and vocabulary, 247–248

Weikel, Dana, 172

Weingartner, Charles, 7, 231

Welch, Lew, 97

Wells, Gordon, 58

Westing Game, The (Raskin), 35

What Jamie Saw (Coman), 195

Wheldall, Kevin, 112

When I Was Young in the Mountains (Rylant), 182

When I Was Your Age (Ehrlich), 182

Where the Red Fern Grows (Rawls), 69

Whirligig, The (Fleischman), 35

White, Bailey, 182

White, E. B., 43

White, Robb, 69

White, Ruth, 155, 197

whole-group learning, 18–19

whole-group shared reading, 59–60

Whole Story, The (Cambourne), 14

Whole Story series (Penguin Putnam), 177

Who Put That Hair in My Toothbrush? (Spinelli), 96, 153, 182, 186

Who's in Charge? (Ohanian), 9, 12

Why Does Popcorn Pop? (Voorhees), 35

"Why Do We Gotta Do This Stuff, Mr. Nehring?" (Nehring), 124

Wild Kid, The (Mazer), 33

Wild Rover (Meyer), 196

Williams, Tennessee, 171

"Winners" (Holbrook), 56

Winnie-the-Pooh on Problem Solving (Allen), 228

Winter Room, The (Paulsen), 21, 48, 187

Wizard of Oz, The, 1–3, 4

Wonderful Wizard of Oz, The (Baum), 1, 229

word banks, 184–190

Word Questioning graphic organizer, 186, 276

words
length of, 142
unique, mimicking, 50

Words, Words, Words (Allen), 184–185

Workshop 4: The Teacher as Researcher (Newkirk), 227

World War II texts, 174, 176

Wrecker, The (Skinner), 196

Wringer (Spinelli), 69, 106

writing, 178–198
assessment of samples, 202
back-to-basics in, 194–195
details in, 181
editing *vs.,* 194–198
effective examples of, 180–190
extended writer's craft lessons, 194–198

guided, 194–198
ideas expressed in, 180
importance of, 178
improving through reading,
   117
life stories writing assignment, 181–184
patterned, 190–194
as response to literature, 218
scaffolding, 179

shared, 179–194
song lyrics, 191–193
variety in styles, 24
Web sites, 246–247
writing conferences, 194
Writing Life, The (Dillard),
   182
writing prompts, 179
  generic, 215, 217
  student-developed, 180

writing resource logs, 180
Writing to Learn graphic
   organizer, 132–134, 137,
   268
writing workshop
  organization of, 178
  scheduling, 116–117, 118

Zemelman, Steven, 101